A Nation of Immigrants Reconsidered

STUDIES OF WORLD MIGRATIONS

Madeline Hsu and Marcelo Borges, editors

A list of books in the series appears at the end of the book.

A Nation of Immigrants Reconsidered

US Society in an Age of Restriction, 1924–1965

Edited by
MADDALENA MARINARI
MADELINE Y. HSU
MARÍA CRISTINA GARCÍA

© 2019 by the Board of Trustees
of the University of Illinois
All rights reserved
1 2 3 4 5 C P 5 4 3 2 1
∞ This book is printed on acid-free paper.

Library of Congress Cataloging-in-Publication Data
Names: Marinari, Maddalena, editor. | Hsu, Madeline Yuan-yin,
    editor. | Garcia, Maria Cristina, 1960– editor.
Title: A nation of immigrants reconsidered : US society in an age of
    restriction, 1924–1965 / edited by Maddalena Marinari, Madeline
    Y. Hsu, Maria Cristina Garcia.
Description: [Urbana] : University of Illinois, [2019] | Series: Studies
    of world migrations | Includes bibliographical references and
    index.
Identifiers: LCCN 2018027423| ISBN 9780252042218 (cloth : alk.
    paper) | ISBN 9780252083969 (pbk. : alk. paper)
Subjects: LCSH: United States—Emigration and immigration—
    History—20th century. | United States—Emigration and
    immigration—Government policy. | Immigrants—United
    States—History—20th century.
Classification: LCC JV6455 .N37 2019 | DDC 305.9/06912097309041--
    dc23 LC record available at https://lccn.loc.gov/2018027423

Ebook ISBN: 978-0-252- 05095-4

Contents

Acknowledgments   vii

Introduction   1

PART I. POLICY AND LAW

1 Beyond Borders: Remote Control and the Continuing Legacy
of Racism in Immigration Legislation   25

  Elliott Young

2 Gatekeeping in the Tropics: US Immigration Policy
and the Cuban Connection   45

  Kathleen López

3 Contested Terrain: Debating Refugee Admissions
in the Cold War   65

  Laura Madokoro

4 The Geopolitical Origins of the 1965 Immigration Act   83

  David FitzGerald and David Cook-Martín

PART II. LABOR

5 Hunting for Sailors: Restaurant Raids and Conscription
of Laborers during World War II   107

  Heather Lee

6 The State Management of Guest Workers: The Decline
of the Bracero Program, the Rise of Temporary Worker Visas   123

  Ronald L. Mize

7 Setting the Stage to Bring in the "Highly Skilled":
Project Paperclip and the Recruitment of German Specialists
after World War II   144

  Monique Laney

8 Japanese Agricultural Labor Program: Temporary Worker
Immigration, US-Japan Cultural Diplomacy, and Ethnic
Community Making among Japanese Americans   161

  Eiichiro Azuma

PART III. "WHO IS A CITIZEN? WHO BELONGS?"

9 The Undertow of Reforming Immigration   191

  Ruth Ellen Wasem

10 Foreign, Dark, Young, Citizen: Puerto Rican Youth
and the Forging of an American Identity, 1930–70   213

  Lorrin Thomas

11 Japanese War Brides and the Normalization of Family Unification
after World War II   231

  Arissa H. Oh

12 Love as Mirror and Pathway: The Undocumented Emotive
Configuration of Mexican Immigration   255

  Ana Elizabeth Rosas

  Afterword: The Black Presence in US Immigration History   273

  Violet Showers Johnson

  Contributors   285

  Index   291

Acknowledgments

The editors wish to thank a number of people who played a critical role in the development of this anthology. We are grateful to our fourteen contributors (in alphabetical order): Eiichiro Azuma, David Cook-Martín, David FitzGerald, Monique Laney, Heather Lee, Kathleen López, Laura Madokoro, Ronald Mize, Arissa Oh, Ana Elizabeth Rosas, Violet Showers Johnson, Lorrin Thomas, Ruth Ellen Wasem, Elliott Young. Your scholarship inspires us, and we could not imagine this anthology without your participation. Thank you for your support and enthusiasm for this project and for your many helpful suggestions.

During the initial stages of planning this project, the editors agreed that it would be beneficial for the contributing authors to meet as a group and discuss how their scholarship elucidated the key themes of the anthology. We also hoped that bringing the authors together would foster an intellectual community across scholars working in different disciplines and contribute to a more nuanced understanding of the different approaches to the study of migration. We organized a workshop in March 2016 at the University of Texas at Austin, hosted by the Department of History and its affiliated Institute for Historical Studies (IHS), which accomplished these goals. Our conversations helped each of us gain a better understanding of the 1924–1965 period and clarified the multiple ways in which policies shaped immigration flows during these misunderstood yet formative years. For their generosity and vision, we thank History Department Chair Jacqueline Jones as well as Dean Randy Diehl of the College of Liberal Arts. Our project also received significant funding from Dean Angela Evans and Professor Edwin Dorn of the LBJ School of viii • *Acknowledgments*

Public Affairs, Director Pauline Strong of the Humanities Institute and the Sterling Clark Holloway Centennial Lectureship in the Liberal Arts, Director Charles Hale of the LLILAS Benson Latin American Studies Institute and Collections, Director John Morán González of the Center for Mexican American Studies, Chair Nicole Guidotti-Hernández of the Department of Mexican American and Latino Studies, Director Huaiyin Li of the Center for East Asian Studies, IHS Director Seth Garfield, and Director Sharmila Rudrappa and Assistant Director Sona Shah of the Center for Asian American Studies. Jacquelin Llado processed accounting transactions and Christina Villareal served as our note taker for all proceedings.

During that long weekend, three of our contributors, Ana Elizabeth Rosas, David FitzGerald, and Ruth Wasem (as well as Kelly Lytle Hernandez), generously participated in a well-received public roundtable, "Controlling the Border? Labor, Lives, and Policy." We owe particular thanks to program coordinator Courtney Meador for her grace, good cheer, and resourcefulness in arranging the logistics of our workshop and public roundtable as well as our travel and accommodations.

We are grateful to Gaynel Kline and Gary Voerman for offering us their lovely Seattle home as a retreat where we could write the introduction of the anthology and begin the first round of edits. Sherman Cochran and Bryan Messerly later read the introduction and offered us helpful comments that made it more accessible to a non-specialist audience. We are also grateful to the anonymous reviewers for their careful reading of the chapters and their thoughtful suggestions.

We had the exceptional good fortune to work with James Engelhardt at the University of Illinois Press, who could not have been a more supportive and helpful editor. We are excited that the book is published as part of UIP's Studies of World Migration series, and we are grateful to Marcelo Borges, Madeline Hsu's series co-editor, for his suggestions. We are grateful to Alison Syring, the assistant acquisitions editor, for her suggestions, and to the production and marketing team for publishing this anthology in a timely fashion.

We also want to thank our family and friends for their love and support in all our professional endeavors. Last but not least, we are grateful that we had an opportunity to work together on this project. From the beginning, we believed in the contribution that this project could make, especially during today's highly politicized debates on immigration, but it was wonderful to discover how well we worked together. Our collaborative efforts have showcased how fruitful and meaningful can be the outcomes of fostering intellectual communities and speaking across disciplines and regional specializations toward attaining a broader and better understanding of the difficult world we share.

A Nation of Immigrants Reconsidered

Introduction

In October 1945, German scientist Wernher von Braun arrived in the United States to begin work for the US Army. His development of the German V-2 rocket made him one of the most sought-after scientists of the postwar period. In order to facilitate his arrival, government authorities expunged records of his memberships in the Nazi Party and the German elite paramilitary organization known as the SS. They also expedited his immigration and security clearance so he could develop ballistic missiles for the United States and, eventually, design the NASA rockets that transported the first satellites and men into space. By 1955, he was an American citizen.

Three years after von Braun came to the United States, Sachiko Pfeiffer, a Japanese national, immigrated as the war bride of an American military veteran. Though most Asians were barred by law from immigrating to the United States at this time, Pfeiffer and her white husband were able to settle in Illinois, one of the few states where interracial marriage was possible. Sachiko's path to integration took longer than von Braun's for she would not even qualify for citizenship until the 1952 McCarran-Walter Act permitted Japanese immigrants to naturalize. Though sympathetically portrayed in a *Life* magazine article in 1955 by novelist James Michener, it took until the birth of her first son for Sachiko to overcome the reservations of Frank's family and her neighbors.

Unskilled workers faced new barriers in the 1950s too. Following in the footsteps of many other Mexicans, Lorenzo Macías left his family and friends to find higher-paying employment in Los Angeles, California. Lured by the robust postwar

2 · *Introduction*

economy, he was one of the thousands of Mexican migrants who arrived without authorization to work in agricultural fields, factories, loading docks, construction sites, and service industries. As an undocumented worker, Macías labored long hours in very difficult conditions, hoping to avoid deportation; he tried to save enough money to buy an apartment and marry Judith, his fiancée. Despite his many sacrifices, the young couple was unable to survive the distance and the separation, a loss Macías would mourn decades later.

The experiences of Wernher von Braun, Sachiko Pfeiffer, and Lorenzo Macías, discussed by three of the contributors to this anthology, exemplify some of the major shifts in immigration policies and priorities that emerged in the United States between 1924 and 1965. These stories show that policies were far from fixed.[1] Von Braun's expedited immigration reveals, in dramatic fashion, the federal government's expanding interest in the recruitment of highly skilled workers in service of American economic and technical competitiveness. Pfeiffer's immigration story illustrates how the government's commitment to family reunification allowed many to bypass the race-based restrictions. In contrast, Macías's story demonstrates that even those who lacked skills and family connections could still find ways to enter and remain in the United States, even though a lack of authorized status marginalized them in certain sectors of the US economy and imposed severe constraints on their personal lives.

Readers may find these accounts surprising. The period 1924 to 1965 has often been portrayed as an unremarkable interlude between two great eras of mass migration to the United States: 1880–1924, when more than twenty million people entered the country, and the post-1965 period, which has witnessed the arrival of more than fifty-nine million people. This periodization has oversimplified a complicated history and obscured histories that do not fit into neat chronological categories. It has also incorrectly suggested that the draconian system in place successfully brought immigration to a halt and fully "Americanized" immigrants already in the United States. To this day, critics of open immigration point to this period as a time when immigration policy successfully stemmed the tide of unwanted immigrants.[2]

Building on recent trends in research, the authors in this anthology challenge the traditional periodization in US immigration history and explain how and why the years from 1924 to 1965 constitute a formative—not a static—period.[3] Immigration to the United States did decrease in the wake of the 1924 Johnson-Reed Act, but it did not stagnate. Instead, it changed form, composition, aspiration, and legal expression. The years 1924–1965 solidified trends that had first emerged at the end of the nineteenth century and laid the foundations for many of the developments attributed to the 1965 Hart-Celler Immigration Act, such as removing discriminations based on race and national origins, prioritizing family reunification and skilled labor as selection criteria, and establishing permanent provisions for the admission of refugees. This anthology brings together leading scholars of migration, ethnicity, race, and labor in a broadly comparative reconsideration of how immigration policy became a site for reimagining the attributes of citizenship, realigning labor priorities, and reconfiguring international relations.

The chapters demonstrate that the 1965 Hart-Celler Immigration Act was not a dramatic departure from the status quo but rather the product of longstanding political struggles and debates of the preceding four decades. The discriminatory national-origins quotas attracted criticism as soon as they became policy in 1924, but the deeply contested nature of the congressional legislative process made reforms difficult and slow to enact. Instead, legislators took advantage of the gaps, exceptions, and loopholes in the national-origins system to shape the American workforce and society toward particular ends. A broadening range of considerations determined who received immigration visas to come to the United States, among them family relationships, educational and employment credentials, investment capacities, foreign-policy priorities, and humanitarian concerns. Concurrently, as Mae Ngai so authoritatively discusses, this era also witnessed the expansion of legal and enforcement bureaucracies targeting "impossible subject" categories of workers defined as temporary and thus deemed ineligible for citizenship and its protections from deportation.[4] Thus, changing conceptions of race relations, parameters for citizenship, and America's role in the world, as well as new demands for specialized labor, produced a number of policy shifts between 1924 and 1965 that made both the positive and negative aspects of the 1965 Hart-Celler Immigration Act possible. The debates and struggles of the period critically reshaped American society in ways that reverberate to this day.

The contributors to this volume also make a persuasive case for recognizing the intersection between foreign policy and immigration. Immigration policy, traditionally viewed as a domestic matter, served as a tool for the advancement of geopolitical interests abroad after 1924. If immigration was central to nation-building in the nineteenth century, it became critical to state-building in the twentieth, the so-called American Century.[5] The national-origins quotas deeply offended US allies in Asia, whose support was increasingly critical during the Cold War. Congress muted international criticism by enacting immigration policies that emphasized economic rather than racial criteria for admission. Congress also became increasingly responsive to a broader array of domestic actors, namely ethnic and religious groups, who adopted the language of US Cold War priorities to lobby for a more humane immigration reform. These developments facilitated shifts in the sources and patterns of migration flows.

In addition, the chapters in this collection highlight the ideological and strategic transformations in policy and society through the four cataclysmic decades that

4 • *Introduction*

witnessed the Depression of the 1930s, the Second World War, the decolonization campaigns around the world, the global human rights movement, and the emerging Cold War. In comparing the trajectories of various immigrant, ethnic, and racial groups, this anthology illustrates how powerfully immigration laws enact and maintain inequalities and socioeconomic hierarchies that affect the various immigrant groups differently. More important, the authors reclaim the period from 1924 to 1965 as a critical watershed in US history—a period that profoundly reshaped ideas about American identity and the types of immigrants that should be prioritized for admission to the United States.

A Nation of Immigrants Explained

During the second half of the nineteenth century, immigration flows to the United States shifted and came increasingly from Asia, southern and eastern Europe, and Mexico.[6] Americans of northern and western European ancestry regarded immigrants from these areas of the world as nonwhite, biologically and culturally inferior, and unassimilable. These perceptions stemmed from the United States' first decades as a nation, when race, national origins, and religion emerged as key markers of eligibility for citizenship. Drawing on the 1790 Nationality Act, which restricted citizenship by naturalization to "free white persons," Congress produced the legal category of "aliens ineligible for citizenship," which remained in place until 1952, when Congress abolished racial restrictions on citizenship altogether.[7] These ideas about race, citizenship, and belonging had a long-term impact on the country's immigration policy and on American perceptions of new immigrants.

Drawing on these well-established ideas about citizenship, Congress took action to protect the Anglo-Saxon heritage of the nation and enacted the first federal immigration controls beginning in the 1870s.[8] Chinese were the first targets of these restrictions because many Americans saw them as the quintessential "other." Following passage of the 1882 Chinese Exclusion Act, established leaders of northern and western European descent turned their attention to other groups. They mobilized and passed legislation that limited the legal entry and citizenship rights of other newcomers, especially those from southern and eastern Europe. While some of the new restrictions relied on race and national origins to determine admissibility, other restrictions were more qualitative in nature. By the beginning of the twentieth century, immigration laws categorized potential immigrants by socioeconomic class, literacy, criminality, political beliefs, diplomatic standing, physical and mental health, and sexuality. Immigration authorities often used the "likely to become a public charge" clause (LPC) to turn away the poor and unmarried or unaccompanied women. Alongside the expanding array of legislation, the federal government developed institutions to enforce the laws, including the creation in 1891 of the Immigration Bureau. First located in the Treasury Department, the bureau transferred to the Department of Commerce and Labor (1903–1913) and the Department of Labor (1913–1933), revealing the different areas of government concerned with immigration restriction over time.[9] The government also opened immigrant inspection stations on Castle Garden (1855), Ellis Island (1892), and Angel Island (1910). Beginning in 1904, the Immigration Service's special force, the "Mounted Guards," patrolled the US-Mexico border to stop unauthorized Chinese immigration.

Many of these developments reflected the influence of eugenics, a pseudoscience popular during the era, which encouraged controlled breeding to ensure the reproduction of desirable traits such as intelligence, thrift, and industriousness in the interest of creating a healthy and productive population. Legislators in the United States used eugenics to offer scientific justification for the harsh and often violent action to repress persons and behaviors considered disruptive to American progress. Its principles permeated educational, health, and carceral policies across the country. Immigration policy emerged as a critical arena to put such beliefs into practice.

In drafting new immigration policies, legislators regularly consulted eugenicists of national prominence, such as Harvard-educated Prescott Hall of the Immigration Restriction League and Harry H. Laughlin, superintendent of the Eugenics Record Office. The 1907 Immigration Act, for example, imposed a head tax on every "alien" entering the country and gave authorities great latitude to bar the entrance of "idiots, imbeciles, feeble-minded persons, epileptics, insane persons . . . paupers; persons likely to become a public charge; professional beggars; persons afflicted with tuberculosis or with a loathsome or dangerous contagious disease" and any others found to be "mentally or physically defective" and unable to earn a living.[10] The 1917 Immigration Act imposed a literacy test and outlawed the immigration of "inferior peoples" from the "Asiatic barred zone," a vast territory that extended from the Middle East to East Asia, excluding only the US territory of the Philippines. The newly barred joined Chinese immigrants, who had been excluded since 1882, and Japanese immigrants, whose migration was controlled by the 1907–1908 Gentlemen's Agreement. None of these laws reduced overall immigration numbers, however, because most immigrants were European. Immigration numbers did not begin to fall until the 1921 Emergency Quota Act, which imposed the first numerical limits on European immigration. Individual country quotas were limited to 3 percent of the total number of foreign-born persons from each European country recorded in the 1910 United States Census. Three years later, the 1924 Johnson-Reed Immigration Act further reduced European immigration through a cap of 165,000 per year on immigration from the Eastern Hemisphere and by instituting a system of national-origins quotas calculated at 2 percent of the

6 · *Introduction*

total number of foreign-born persons recorded in the 1890 census, before eastern and southern European immigration reached its peak. Through this "scientific" approach, Congress set Germany's quota at almost twenty-six thousand while limiting Armenia and Albania to tiny quotas of one hundred each.

Like many of the immigration laws that followed it, the Johnson-Reed Act revealed the tensions and contradictions between the calls for restriction and the demands for family reunification and certain types of highly valued labor. The law expanded the ban against Asians to exclude almost all "aliens ineligible for citizenship," but it also exempted from exclusion specified categories of highly skilled immigrants, domestic servants, and the wives or unmarried minor children of US citizens. Laborers from Latin America and the Caribbean, who were exempt from the quota system, subsequently compensated for the lost European and Asian labor—a manpower which was still desperately needed in the factories, mines, and agricultural fields of the continually growing nation. Even so, Congress created the Border Patrol to police the southern border with Mexico to prevent the migration of potential undesirables who might become public charges.[11] This tension between nativist desires to control the composition of US society and the reality of labor priorities virtually guaranteed that the 1924 Immigration Act would not halt immigration to the United States despite the rhetoric and promises of nativists.

Other contradictions emerged in the 1930s. Although Congress had severely restricted immigration from southern and eastern Europe, legislators allowed tens of thousands of Europeans unlawfully in the United States to adjust their legal status so they could remain in the country. Asian immigrants, on the other hand, faced an almost complete ban, except for Filipinos, who, as American nationals from a US territory, migrated freely until 1934, when the Tydings-McDuffie Act put the Philippines on the path toward independence so that their immigration could be restricted.[12] Western Hemisphere countries may have been exempt from quotas, but this did not protect their nationals from discrimination. During the 1930s, the federal government, working with state and local authorities and the Mexican consulates in the southwest, repatriated hundreds of thousands of workers of Mexican origin and their families, including some US-born citizens.[13]

Throughout the 1930s, the Immigration and Naturalization Service, now located in the Department of Justice, also regulated immigration flows through a system of "remote control," a process identified by political scientist Aristide Zolberg, that relied on consulates and embassies abroad to cut back on the number of visas to the United States.[14] This system became particularly effective at curtailing immigration before it even reached US shores and helped to ensure that the annual cap remained unfilled for the entire decade. This system of remote control also accounted for the great ethical failures of the 1930s. Though facing one of the greatest humanitarian crises of the twentieth century, the United States routinely denied entry to

Jewish refugees fleeing Hitler's Third Reich unless they were persons of extraordinary accomplishment like Albert Einstein, Edward Teller, and Hans Bethe. Even when national quota slots remained available, consular and immigration officials refused to grant visas to refugees on the grounds that they might inadvertently allow spies and saboteurs to enter the country. At home, nationalist and anti-Semitic congressmen blocked a vote on the Wagner-Rogers bill that would have allowed twenty thousand Jewish refugee children to enter the United States. In response to these developments, Jews and others fleeing from Europe settled in Palestine and other countries or found ways to circumvent US immigration law. Some exploited a loophole that entailed settling somewhere in the Americas and then immigrating as citizens of those countries. Because of its geographic proximity, Cuba was particularly popular as a destination for this purpose.[15] Others simply entered the United States without authorization and later adjusted their status. Despite the unfilled quotas, the number of immigrants increased as the 1930s came to an end, especially as immigrants took advantage of the family reunion provisions of the existing immigration system to enter the United States. In the 1940s and 1950s, this strategy became even more popular.[16]

World War II forced US policymakers to modify immigration policies to manage demands for different kinds of labor on the home front as well as to honor allies critical to the war effort. From 1939 to 1965, Congress passed legislation on an ad hoc basis that allowed certain groups of immigrants to sidestep restrictionist barriers. The 1943 Magnuson Act, for example, repealed Chinese exclusion in acknowledgement of the United States' chief ally in the Pacific. Although the act only assigned Chinese immigrants a token immigration quota of 105, it granted them the right to naturalize, a critical first step toward the complete elimination of racial barriers on citizenship in 1952. Congress also bowed to pressure from southwestern growers and authorized the Bracero Program to bring temporary farm workers from Mexico beginning in 1942.[17] This set a precedent for the postwar temporary-worker programs discussed in this anthology that brought farm laborers from the Caribbean, Mexico, and Japan. Factory owners, chambers of commerce, business coalitions, agricultural organizations, and employment agencies in the United States also intensified earlier efforts to recruit Puerto Rican workers. As US citizens from an American territory, Puerto Ricans could travel unhindered to the United States to provide critically needed labor.

With the onset of the Cold War in the 1940s and 1950s, advocates of immigration reform mobilized and pushed Congress to abolish the discriminatory national origins quota system in the interest of international goodwill and positive foreign relations, economic competitiveness, and racial equality. Many critics of immigration restriction argued that these changes would prevent the Soviet Union from using the racist US immigration policy for propaganda. Congress continued to

8 · *Introduction*

respond on an ad hoc basis. Recognizing the need to honor wartime obligations, legislators lifted the bars to Indian and Filipino migration and granted nationals of these countries the right to naturalize. Congress also passed the War Brides Act of 1945, the Fiancées and Fiancés Act of 1946, the Displaced Persons Act of 1948 (renewed in 1950), and the Refugee Relief Act of 1953 to facilitate the entrance of thousands of immigrants who would have been inadmissible before the war. Many of these policies were token gestures, however, rather than a true commitment to substantive change. Once again, Congress kept numbers small, set narrow limits on who was eligible, and imposed deadlines for entry. India and the Philippines, for example, received token quotas of one hundred. The displaced persons (DPs) admitted to the United States counted against the yearly quotas assigned to their countries of origin, thus creating decades-long backlogs for their countrymen trying to secure visas. The DP acts also overwhelmingly favored European refugees and, within Europe, privileged the admission of Protestant and Catholic over Jewish refugees. Because it served American Cold War interests, Congress also helped to bring former Nazi scientists like Wernher von Braun to the United States to prevent them from using their expertise to help the Soviet Union. In all of these cases, the restrictionists in Congress grudgingly agreed to these reforms because of their limited or temporary nature but feared the legislative changes would provide "side doors" for entry and portend long-term trends that would undermine the national origins system and American society's racial status quo.[18]

Under pressure for an overhaul of the entire immigration policy, restrictionists in Congress, led by Senator Patrick McCarran (D-NV), grew alarmed and tried to wrestle the reform process away from their more liberal colleagues. The McCarran-Walter Act of 1952, enacted over President Truman's veto, perfectly incarnated the politicized atmosphere of the early Cold War period.[19] Responding to fears of communist infiltration and subversion, the act retained the national-origins quota system, introduced more screening measures to bar those who were ideologically suspect, and incorporated harsher provisions for the exclusion and deportation of undesirables. At the same time, the act increased overall immigration slightly (from 153,714 to 154,657), ended racial restrictions on citizenship, and extended immigration quotas, albeit small ones, to all nations.[20]

Despite its nods to egalitarianism, the act still reserved more than 80 percent of visas for western and northern Europeans. Asians gained citizenship rights and the right to immigrate, but they remained the only group tracked by race rather than nationality or place of birth, with overall numbers capped at two thousand. A Cuban of Chinese ancestry, for example, was counted against China's national quota. As nations around the world decolonized and won their independence, each newly established nation received an immigration quota. Such gestures of respect weighed against the practical reality that certain immigrants to the United

States faced greater obstacles. No longer did Caribbean islands under British rule fall under the generous British quota. Instead, the McCarran-Walter Act created a small token quota for West Indian Blacks out of concern that the new immigrants would alter American society's racial status quo.

Its contradictions notwithstanding, the 1952 McCarran-Walter Act, along with other immigration and refugee acts passed in the 1950s, profoundly reshaped immigration flows to the United States and paved the way for the legislative changes that allowed a more diverse American society after 1965. These developments, like many of those that followed passage of the 1965 immigration act, were unintentional. The sponsors and supporters of the 1952 immigration act had hoped that the law would continue to stifle immigration, especially from Asia. However, prioritizing family reunification and skills—50 percent of visas went to persons with higher education, technical training, or some other specialized knowledge or exceptional ability, and their family members—created possibilities for circumventing the law. Many prospective immigrants from Asian countries, though bound by tiny quotas, immigrated at higher levels than their prescribed numbers by entering the country as highly skilled migrants or international students, applying for permanent status with the help of their employers, and then sponsoring their families.[21] By the mid-1960s, this immigration flow of highly skilled individuals produced what some in the countries of origin called a "brain drain," with Taiwan, India, and South Korea the most affected. International adoptions, which became popular as an emergency measure to evacuate the mixed-race children of American GIs during the Korean War, also became a regular form of non-quota immigration until 1961, when it became categorized as a form of family reunification.[22]

Refugee policy in the 1950s provided another "side door" entry to the United States. From 1948 to 1965, the US government responded to several political and humanitarian emergencies around the world, including the Hungarian Revolution and the Suez crisis of 1956, the Cuban Revolution of 1959, and the Hong Kong crisis of 1962. Displaced persons, refugees, and "escapees" numbering 430,000 entered the United States during the period 1948–1956 under various congressional acts.[23] Sidestepping Congress, the executive branch also drew on the then little-known "parole" authority granted in the McCarran-Walter Act to admit people of humanitarian interest outside of the numerical quotas. In such cases, special legislation (the so-called "adjustment acts") then allowed these "parolees" to become legal permanent residents.[24] The majority of refugees, displaced persons, "escapees," and "parolees" admitted before 1965 came from communist countries, in line with the geopolitical interests of the day, and this remained true for the rest of the Cold War. These admissions operated in ways unanticipated by the sponsors of the 1952 McCarran-Walter Act by providing legal means to increase admissions for groups with few regular options to immigrate. As with family reunification provisions,

10 • *Introduction*

immigration liberalizers continued chipping away at the national origin system's restrictionist agendas and increasing the categories of persons with legitimate grounds to immigrate into the United States.

These slight expansions of permanent immigration based on family reunification, the recruitment of skilled labor, and foreign-policy interests ran parallel to the exploitation and marginalization of workers from Mexico. In 1951, as a concession to agricultural interests, the US government negotiated a new bilateral agreement with Mexico to bring in hundreds of thousands of the temporary farm workers called "Braceros"—a program that lasted until 1964. Thousands more crossed the border, sometimes without authorization, in search of economic opportunities in the United States, hoping one day to return to their country with their hard-earned savings, as their countrymen had done for generations. Unauthorized entry was fairly easy during the postwar period since vast stretches of the US-Mexico border remained poorly patrolled and immigration authorities often turned a blind eye when demands for workers were high. Regional growers, hungry for cheap labor, sent representatives to border towns to recruit workers who had recently crossed.[25] Although many Mexican workers did not enter the United States with the idea of permanent settlement, policymakers became concerned by the "uncontrolled immigration" of Mexicans. This led federal authorities to enact "Operation Wetback" in 1954, which resulted in the forced removal of an estimated 250,000 "illegal" Mexican workers (some sources place the number at closer to one million).[26] Ironically, as the US government brought in thousands of braceros to meet the needs of American growers, it was expelling thousands of the braceros' countrymen.

In 1965, after four decades of protracted struggles, Congress finally abolished the racist national-origins quota system. Immigration reform, which had been a priority for President John F. Kennedy, became a reality under his successor, President Lyndon Baines Johnson, who leveraged his electoral mandate to include it in the sweeping civil rights legislative package along with the 1964 Civil Rights Act and the 1965 Voting Rights Act. Although he had been a latecomer to the cause of immigration reform, Johnson signed the Hart-Celler Immigration Act on October 3, 1965, during a ceremony held at the base of the Statue of Liberty. His speech acknowledged that the national-origins system, in place since the 1920s, had been "un-American." It had violated the basic principle of American democracy: "the principle that values and rewards each man on the basis of his merit as a man."[27]

The 1965 Hart-Celler Immigration Act replaced the national-origins quotas with a system of hemispheric caps. The law set an annual limit of 170,000 visas for immigrants from the Eastern Hemisphere, with no country allowed more than twenty thousand visas. To appease supporters of the national origins quota system, the act imposed for the first time a numeric cap on immigrants from the Western

Hemisphere, which was set at 120,000. While the skills and training of applicants were important considerations in the issuing of visas, the law reserved three-fourths of admissions for the relatives of US citizens and permanent residents at the insistence of leading conservative politicians such as Rep. Michael Feighan (D-OH), who sought to maintain the nation's predominantly European stock. (In 1965, whites of European descent made up 84 percent of the US population). The act also exempted the immediate relatives—spouses, minor children, and parents—of US citizens and permanent residents, which meant that the number of immigrants who entered each year was always much larger than the annual cap. In 1976, Congress amended the 1965 law further to impose a twenty-thousand-per-country limit on the Western Hemisphere as well as the Eastern Hemisphere; and in 1978 it abandoned the hemispheric caps altogether in favor of a global immigrant ceiling of 290,000 a year.

The law also included a small numerical allotment for refugees, recognizing a continuing humanitarian and international obligation to assist displaced peoples. The law defined refugees as those persecuted on account of race, religion, or political opinion; those uprooted by natural calamity; those fleeing from communist or communist-dominated countries; or those fleeing from the Middle East.[28] Fifteen years later, Congress amended the definition of "refugee" once again in the 1980 Refugee Act, adopting the United Nations' definition.[29]

Hart-Celler has been called the immigration act that "inadvertently" changed the demographics of the United States and created the "illegal immigration problem."[30] If the architects of the bill imagined these possibilities, they never said so publicly. Senator Edward Kennedy (D-MA), one of the bill's most vocal supporters, stated: "The bill will not flood our cities with immigrants. It will not upset the ethnic mix of our society. It will not relax the standards of admission. It will not cause American workers to lose their jobs."[31] Likewise, President Johnson assured Americans that Hart-Celler did not signal revolutionary change: "It does not affect the lives of millions," he said. "It will not reshape the structure of our daily lives, or really add importantly to either our wealth or our power."[32]

Despite attempts to maintain the predominantly European ancestry of the US population, European migration to the United States fell in the final decades of the twentieth century. The rapid postwar recovery of Western European nations, greatly facilitated by the financial assistance the US Marshall Plan provided, meant that citizens of these countries no longer felt compelled to emigrate, while totalitarian governments in poorer nations in eastern and central Europe blocked aspiring migrants from leaving altogether. Meanwhile, the demands to emigrate increased in Latin America, Asia, and Africa. Improvements in healthcare and education created highly mobile populations who sought better wages in industrialized nations,

12 • *Introduction*

while others crossed international borders because of war, revolution, economic displacement, or environmental disasters.

In 1920, 13.2 percent of the US population was foreign-born; by 1965, that number had dropped to just under 5 percent and over three-quarters of the foreign-born had come from Europe and Canada.[33] Yet, as this anthology demonstrates, this lower percentage obscures many trends that emerged from 1924 to 1965, including the recruitment of highly specialized labor, the rise of temporary labor migration, the migration of US citizens from Puerto Rico who do not appear in immigration statistics, and the arrival of international students from Asia who later remained in the United States and sent for their family members. Five decades later, a significant demographic change had occurred in large part because of these trends: half of all immigrants were from Latin America and the Caribbean, and 27 percent were from Asia.[34] The bearers of the so-called "green cards"—the residency visas—also steadily rose from 297,000 in 1965 to an average of one million each year since around 2005.[35] As a result, by 2014, 13.2 percent of the US population were once again foreign-born (forty-two million).[36] Mexico, India, the Philippines, China, Vietnam, El Salvador, Cuba, South Korea, the Dominican Republic, and Guatemala, accounted for nearly 60 percent of the immigrant population.[37]

The Hart-Celler Immigration Act also produced a rise in undocumented immigration, especially from the Americas. Prior to 1965, immigrants from Mexico and other parts of Latin America and the Caribbean circulated to and from the United States comparatively freely because of the lack of numerical quotas on most of the Americas. It was common for Mexican and other Latin American/Caribbean workers to spend part of their working lives in the United States and then return to their homelands with the wages they had saved. Once Hart-Celler imposed caps on the Western Hemisphere, however, these long-established migratory patterns suddenly—and officially—became "unauthorized" and were subjected to escalating levels of surveillance and restriction. The cap of twenty thousand on each country (raised to 26,500 in 1990) meant that many of the workers who had traveled unhindered across the border for work were now "illegal," and they had limited avenues for lawful entry. The imposition of uniform quotas for each nation—presented by restrictionists as an egalitarian remedy to the discriminatory national-origins quotas—created new and severe forms of inequality. National Visa Center bulletins showed that in some countries the waiting period for a green card was a decade or longer.[38] This prompted many either to cross the US-Canada or US-Mexico border without authorization, or to come in with tourist, student, or other temporary visas and then remain in the United States past the expiration of their visas. The twenty-first century's crisis of undocumented immigrants is rooted in these legal changes that tried to alter longstanding practices of mobility.

Thematic Overview

We, the co-editors, are excited to introduce readers to this small but illustrative sample of the rich historical scholarship that is changing our understanding of immigration and US society during 1924 to 1965, a formative period in US history. Collectively, the contributors to this anthology draw on a wide range of sources, topics, methodologies, and histories to demonstrate that, even when political actors sought to block entry to the United States, the American population replenished itself through immigration. The chapters also demonstrate that immigration policy, though regarded as domestic policy, is also foreign policy. Immigration policy may originate in a desire to protect national sovereignty, safeguard economic interests, and shape US society, but it is often crafted with an eye to international relations and relies on international collaboration to be enforced.

The anthology is divided into three sections, each with its own introduction to the main themes explored in the chapters. The first section, "Policy and Law," with contributions from Elliott Young, Kathleen López, Laura Madokoro, and David FitzGerald and David Cook-Martín, focuses on the intersections of immigration policy and foreign policy. Even though restrictionists embraced isolationism in the interest of national sovereignty, immigration policy from 1924 to 1965 showed how much immigration law remained intertwined with international interests and US foreign policy. In order for the United States to consolidate its regime of immigration restriction, it had to rely on the collaboration of sending and transit countries, especially when it came to creating systems of remote control. This interdependency highlighted the reach but also the limitations of US influence. Once the role of the United States changed in the geopolitical order that emerged after the end of World War II, foreign policy considerations and international developments profoundly shaped immigration and refugee policy in the 1950s and 1960s. This shift allowed supporters of immigration reform to connect their domestic agenda to broader foreign policy priorities, but, in the face of xenophobia and nativism, their efforts yielded contradictory results. As the next two sections of the anthology show, these international dimensions had profound domestic repercussions for Americans' ideas about labor, citizenship, and identity.

The second section, "Labor," with contributions from Heather Lee, Ronald Mize, Monique Laney, and Eiichiro Azuma, explores changing labor markets and the emerging legal distinctions between skilled and unskilled workers. During this period, immigration policies became more explicitly linked to advancing economic agendas. Policymakers began to privilege the migration and settlement of workers with education, credentials, and specializations in fields they viewed as enhancing the nation's drive to lead the world in technical and scientific innovation. Concurrently, while demands for unskilled labor remained high, especially among

14 · *Introduction*

agricultural growers in the Southwest, temporary labor programs restricted their protections and access to citizenship. Though often pawns in the United States' agenda to become a world leader, immigrants still found ways to use US immigration policy to further their own advancement.

The third section, "Who is a Citizen? Who Belongs?" with chapters from Ruth Ellen Wasem, Lorrin Thomas, Arissa Oh, and Ana Elizabeth Rosas, examines understandings of citizenship and belonging during this formative period. Those who secured admission to the United States during the 1924–1965 period—or traveled from a US territory, as in the case of the Puerto Ricans and Filipinos—encountered a suspicious American population that needed their labor, and occasionally facilitated their entrance, but viewed them as potential economic, cultural, and political threats to the nation. Adaptation to "American" cultural norms did not guarantee acceptance or political rights and legal protections, especially if immigrants were racial minorities or lacked permanent immigrant status. Those who arrived without authorization found themselves in an especially precarious position, marked as perpetual outsiders unless they found ways to normalize their legal status. The chapters in this section discuss the various ways newcomers claimed an American identity or carved a place for themselves in US society through their labor and/or political and civic engagement. Contrary to traditional immigration narratives, immigrants did not always shed their previous identification with the homeland. An American identity—and any claim to citizenship—was crafted in relation to two (or more) countries. This was especially true for those who, for reasons of work and family, traveled back and forth between countries.

The contributors to this volume address only some of the transformations that occurred from 1924 to 1965. In an effort to encourage further exploration, the anthology ends with an afterword by Violet Showers Johnson, who discusses migrations from Africa and the West Indies during this era and the dearth of scholarship on these flows for the period. She directs our attention to populations usually not associated with immigration before 1965 and, in so doing, underscores not only the remaking of racial categories and migration flows but also raises important questions about why some histories receive scholarly attention while others are obscured. Although immigration from Africa remained low for most of the period covered in this anthology, immigration reforms had a transformative effect on the composition of the African diaspora in the United States. African migrants created thriving communities in the United States or returned home to become involved in nation-building. The stories she weaves through her afterword demonstrate the centrality of the African experience in US immigration history even before 1924, illustrate the striking similarities with the experiences of migrants from other parts of the world discussed in this volume, and integrate more fully these neglected migration flows into traditional histories of immigration.

We hope that these chapters will challenge readers to reconsider some of the widely held but misguided interpretations of the immigrant experience that circulate in school curriculums, journalism, and popular culture. The familiar trope describing the United States as a "nation of immigrants" is as true in the twenty-first century as it was in the nineteenth and twentieth. Political and civic engagement requires us to be familiar with this history and reality.

Notes

1. In *Coming to America*, for example, Roger Daniels writes that although "immigration never ceased," the national-origins system, the Great Depression, and World War II "brought an entire era of American immigration to an end." See Roger Daniels, *Coming to America: A History of Immigration and Ethnicity in American Life* (New York: Perennial, 1991), 287. In the first edition of *Natives and Strangers*, the authors wrote that immigration restriction in the 1920s "cut the flow of unskilled labor to America, but the nation's economy no longer needed so many unskilled workers for its mines and mills." They also argued that the 1965 Immigration Act "led to a major transformation in the national origins of immigrants to the United States" because of the "growing ethnic tolerance in American society." See Leonard Dinnerstein, Roger L. Nichols, and David M. Reimers, *Natives and Strangers: Ethnic Groups and the Building of America* (New York: Oxford University Press, 1979), 246–47. Reed Ueda noted that while the overall number of immigrants decreased during this period, their numbers "were still quite substantial." In reference to the 1965 act, Ueda writes that the "liberalization of immigration policy (following the 1965 Act) . . . did not produce geographic balance in immigration sources; instead, it reversed the former imbalance in which Europe predominated over other regions" See Ueda, *Postwar Immigrant America: A Social History* (Boston: Bedford/St. Martin's, 1992), 31–32 and 58. Mae Ngai writes that as a result of immigration reform in 1965, "patterns of migration to the United States changed tremendously in the last decades of the twentieth century." See Ngai, *Impossible Subjects: Illegal Aliens and the Making of Modern America* (Princeton, N.J.: Princeton University Press, 2004), 227. In reference to the impact of the changes in immigration after 1965, David Reimers titled one of his books *Still the Golden Door: The Third World Comes to America* (New York: Columbia University Press, 1992). Other books that have focused on the passage of the 1965 immigration act as a new beginning of mass migration include Deward Clayton Brown, *Globalization and America since 1945* (Lanham, Md.: Rowman and Littlefield, 2003); Gabriel J. Chin and Rose Cuison Villazor, eds., *The Immigration and Nationality Act: Legislating a New America* (Cambridge: Cambridge University Press, 2015); Tom A. Gjelten, *Nation of Nations: A Great American Immigration Story* (New York: Simon and Schuster, 2015); and Margaret Sands Orchowski, *The Law that Changed the Face of America: The Immigration and Nationality Act of 1965* (Lanham, Md.: Rowman and Littlefield, 2015).

2. See, for example: Center for Immigration Studies, "The Legacy of the 1965 Immigration Act," September 1, 1995, https://cis.org/Report/Legacy-1965-Immigration-Act; David North, "The 'Most Favored Nation' Approach in America's Immigration

16 · *Introduction*

Policy," November 25, 2014, https://cis.org/Most-Favored-Nation-Approach-Americas
-Immigration-Policy; and Otis L. Graham, Jr., "Tracing Liberal Woes to '65 Immigration Act," December 28, 1995, https://cis.org/Tracing-Liberal-Woes-65-Immigration
-Act. The 1924 law also continues to influence current policymakers. See, for example
Ben Mathis Lilley, "Jeff Sessions Once Said Restrictions on Jewish and Italian Immigration Were 'Good for America,'" *Slate*, September 5, 2017, http://www.slate.com/blogs/
the_slatest/2017/09/05/jeff_sessions_praise_of_1924_eugenics_immigration_law_
remains_insane.html.

3. In addition to the publications of the authors in this volume, Marilyn Halter, Marilynn Johnson, Katheryn Viens, and Conrad Wright's 2014 anthology and Nancy Foner and George Fredrickson's edited collection identified some of the continuities and discontinuities in the pre- and post-1965 experience. See *What's New about the "New" Immigration? Traditions and Transformations in the United States Since 1965* (New York: Palgrave Macmillan, 2014) and *Not Just Black and White: Historical and Contemporary Perspectives on Immigration, Race, and Ethnicity in the United States* (New York: Russell Sage Foundation, 2004). See also Charlotte Brooks, *Alien Neighbors, Foreign Friends: Asian Americans, Housing, and the Transformation of Urban California* (Chicago: University of Chicago Press, 2009); Kitty Calavita, *Inside the State: The Bracero Program, Immigration, and the INS* (New Orleans: Quid Pro, 2010); Lori Flores, *Grounds for Dreaming: Mexican Americans, Mexican Immigrants, and the California Farmworker Movement* (New Haven, Conn.: Yale University Press, 2016); Libby Garland, *After They Closed the Gates: Jewish Illegal Immigration to the United States, 1921–1965* (Chicago: University of Chicago Press, 2014); Cindy I-Fen Cheng, *Citizens of Asian America: Democracy and Race During the Cold War* (New York: New York University Press, 2014); S. Deborah Kang, *The INS on the Line: Making Immigration Law on the U.S.-Mexico Border, 1917–1954* (New York: Oxford University Press, 2017); Scott Kurashige, *The Shifting Grounds of Race: Black and Japanese Americans in the Making of Multiethnic Los Angeles* (Princeton, N.J.: Princeton University Press, 2010); Mireya Loza, *Defiant Braceros: How Migrants Workers Fought for Racial, Sexual, and Political Freedom* (Durham: University of North Carolina Press, 2016); Cindy Hahamovitch, *No Man's Land: Jamaican Guestworkers in America and the Global History of Deportable Labor* (Princeton, N.J.: Princeton University Press, 2011); Kelly Lytle Hernandez, *Migra! A History of the U.S. Border Patrol* (Oakland: University of California Press, 2010); Natalia Molina, *How Race is Made in America: Immigration, Citizenship, and the Historical Power of Racial Scripts* (Oakland : University of California Press, 2014); Deirdre Moloney, *National Insecurities: Immigrants and U.S. Deportation Policy Since 1882* (Chapel Hill: University of North Carolina Press, 2012); Ellen Wu, *The Color of Success: Asian Americans and the Origins of the Model Minority* (Princeton, N.J.: Princeton University Press, 2015); Allyson Varzally, *Making a Non-White America: Californians Coloring Outside Ethnic Lines, 1925–1955* (Berkeley: University of California Press, 2008).

4. Ngai, *Impossible Subjects*.

5. The United States' emergence as a global economic and military power led many social scientists, historians, and even literary critics to refer to the twentieth century as the "American Century." See, for example, Walter LaFeber, Richard Polenberg, and Nancy Woloch, *The American Century: A History of the United States Since 1941*, 6th ed. (Armonk,

N.Y.: Sharpe, 2008); Alfred E. Eckes and Thomas W Zeiler, *Globalization and the American Century* (Cambridge: Cambridge University Press, 2003); Joseph S. Nye, *Is the American Century Over?* (Cambridge: Polity, 2015); Jeremi Suri, *Henry Kissinger and the American Century* (Cambridge, Mass.: Belknap/Harvard University Press, 2007).

6. Over half of what became US territory belonged to France, Spain, and Mexico until the first decades of the nineteenth century. The 1819 Adams-Onís Treaty, the Texas Revolution of 1836, and the Mexican War of 1846–48 led to the acquisition of these territories and extended the United States to the Pacific coast.

7. Early immigration laws included the Alien and Sedition Acts and an 1803 act banning importation of "any negro, mulatto, or other person of colour" (Act of Feb. 28, 1803, ch. 10, 2 Stat. 205), but these were not systematically enforced.

8. The United States was not unique in these efforts. See David C. Atkinson, *The Burden of White Supremacy: Containing Asian Labor Migration in the British Empire and the United States* (Chapel Hill: University of North Carolina Press, 2017); see also Marilyn Lake and Henry Reynolds, *Drawing the Global Colour Line: White Men's Countries and the International Challenge of Racial Equality* (Cambridge: Cambridge University Press, 2008), on global efforts to curb the circulation of immigrants of color; Adam McKeown, *Melancholy Order: Asian Migration and the Globalization of Borders* (New York: Columbia University Press, 2008), on how practices of border control arose from attempts to control Asian migration around the Pacific; and Erika Lee, *The Making of Asian America: A History* (New York: Simon and Schuster, 2015), on the hemispheric exclusion of Chinese immigrants. For efforts to regulate immigration at the local level prior to federal efforts, see Hidetaka Hirota, *Expelling the Poor: Atlantic Seaboard States and the Nineteenth-Century Origins of American Immigration Policy* (New York: Oxford University Press, 2017), and Beth Lew-Williams, "Before Restriction Became Exclusion: America's Experiment in Diplomatic Immigration Control," *Pacific Historical Review* 83, no. 1 (February 2014): 24–56.

9. Today these functions are lodged in the Department of Homeland Security, revealing the growing importance of national defense in goals for immigration controls.

10. "Immigration Act [1907]," http://www.historycentral.com/documents/immigrationact.html.

11. The Land Appropriate Act of 1924 established the Border Patrol as part of the Immigration Bureau in the Department of Labor. On the use of the "LPC Clause" to control Mexican immigration at a time when it was exempt from the national-origins quota system, see Moloney, *National Insecurities*, ch. 2.

12. For a discussion of the rights of Filipinos and Puerto Ricans from the "unincorporated territories," see Christina Duffy Burnett and Burke Marshall, *Foreign in a Domestic Sense: Puerto Rico, American Expansion, and the Constitution* (Durham, N.C.: Duke University Press, 2001); Charles R. Venator-Santiago, *Puerto Rico and the Origins of U.S. Global Empire: The Disembodied Shade* (Milton Park, Abingdon, Oxon: Routledge, 2015); and Allan Punzalan Isaac, *American Tropics: Articulating Filipino America* (Minneapolis: University of Minnesota Press, 2006).

13. Francisco Balderrama and Raymond Rodríguez estimate that as many as two million Mexican-origin people were deported in the 1930s and 1940s, and as many as 60 percent

18 · *Introduction*

were US citizens. See Francisco E. Balderrama and Raymond Rodriguez, *Decade of Betrayal: Mexican Repatriation in the 1930s*, rev. ed. (Albuquerque: University of New Mexico Press, 2006).

14. Aristide Zolberg, "The Archaeology of Remote Control," in Andreas, Fahrmeir, Olivier Faron, and Patrick Weil, *Migration Control in the North Atlantic World: The Evolution of State Practices in Europe and the United States from the French Revolution to the Inter-War Period* (New York: Berghahn, 2003), 195–222. See also Daniels, *Guarding the Golden Door*, ch. 3, and Tichenor, *Dividing Lines*, ch. 6.

15. Robert M. Levine, *Tropical Diaspora: The Jewish Experience in Cuba* (Gainesville: University Press of Florida, 1993). On Jewish refugees' efforts to enter the United States, see also Garland, *After They Closed the Gates*.

16. Daniels, *Guarding the Golden Door*, ch. 3, and Tichenor, *Dividing Lines*, ch. 6.

17. For a discussion of the history and chronology of the Bracero Program, see Rosas's and Mize's chapters in this anthology.

18. Madeline Hsu, *The Good Immigrants: How the Yellow Peril Became the Model Minority* (Princeton, N.J.: Princeton University Press, 2015), 5. See also Zolberg, *A Nation by Design*, 20.

19. Truman opposed the national-origin quotas retained in the legislation because they perpetuated racism and discrimination. He subsequently appointed a commission to review the nation's immigration policy. The commission's report recommended that national-origin quotas be replaced by a system that privileged family reunification, labor skills, and refugees. See President's Commission on Immigration and Naturalization, *Whom Shall We Welcome?* (Washington, DC: US GPO, 1953), https://archive.org/details/whomweshallwelco00unit.

20. The McCarran-Walter legislation based the annual number of immigrant visas on the 1920 census and set the level at one-sixth of 1 percent of the 1920 population of the United States. On the passage of the McCarran-Walter Act, see Maddalena Marinari, "Divided and Conquered: Immigration Reform Advocates and the Passage of the 1952 Immigration and Nationality Act," *Journal of American Ethnic History* 35, no. 3 (Spring 2016): 9–40.

21. Hsu, *Good Immigrants*.

22. See Arissa Oh, *To Save the Children of Korea: The Cold War Origins of International Adoption* (Palo Alto, Calif.: Stanford University Press, 2015); Eleana Kim, *Adopted Territory: Transnational Korean Adoptees and the Politics of Belonging* (Durham, N.C.: Duke University Press, 2010); and SooJin Pate, *From Orphan to Adoptee: U.S. Empire and Genealogies of Korean Adoption* (Minneapolis: University of Minnesota Press, 2014).

23. The Displaced Persons Act authorized the admission of two hundred thousand European refugees, and the 1953 Refugee Relief Act authorized an additional 214,000 over the next three years. The US Escapee Program, authorized under the Mutual Security Act of 1951, brought in an additional fourteen thousand "escapees" from the Communist bloc countries. See "Mutual Security Act 101 (a)(1) MSA 1951 Escapee Program," https://www.cia.gov/library/readingroom/docs/CIA-RDP80R01731R003300330002-2.pdf.

24. Parole status did not offer a path to citizenship, and parole status could be revoked at any time. The best-known of the adjustment acts is the Cuban Adjustment Act of 1966,

which allowed the Cuban parolees to adjust their status and remain permanently in the United States. See María Cristina García, *Havana USA: Cuban Exiles and Cuban Americans in South Florida, 1959–1994* (Berkeley: University of California Press, 1996).

25. Two excellent discussions of the role of the US Border Patrol along the border with Mexico are Lytle Hernandez, *Migra!* and Patrick W. Ettinger, *Imaginary Lines: Border Enforcement and the Origins of Undocumented Immigration, 1882–1930* (Austin: University of Texas Press, 2009).

26. Juan Ramon García, *Operation Wetback: The Mass Deportation of Mexican Undocumented Workers in 1954* (Westport, Conn.: Greenwood, 1980); Avi Astor, "Unauthorized Immigration, Securitization and the Making of Operation Wetback," *Latino Studies* 7, no. 1 (2009): 5–29; Kelly Lytle Hernández, "The Crimes and Consequences of Illegal Immigration: A Cross-Border Examination of Operation Wetback, 1943 to 1954," *Western Historical Quarterly* 37, no. 4 (Winter 2006), 421–44; and Thomas C. Langham, "Federal Regulation of Border Labor: Operation Wetback and the Wetback Bills," *Journal of Borderlands Studies* 7, no. 1 (1992): 81–91.

27. "President Lyndon B. Johnson's Remarks at the Signing of the Immigration Bill, Liberty Island, New York, October 3, 1965," http://www.lbjlib.utexas.edu/johnson/archives .hom/speeches.hom/651003.asp.

28. The numerical allotment for refugees was set at 6 percent of overall admissions. The Middle East was defined as the territory between and including Libya on the west, Turkey on the north, Pakistan on the east, and Saudi Arabia and Ethiopia on the south. See the text of the "1965 Immigration and Nationality Act" at http://library.uwb.edu/ static/USimmigration/1965_immigration_and_nationality_act.html.

29. The 1980 Refugee Act defined a refugee as "any person who is outside any country of such person's nationality or, in the case of a person having no nationality, is outside any country in which such person last habitually resided, and who is unable or unwilling to return to, or is unable and unwilling to avail himself or herself of the protection of that country because of persecution or a well-founded fear of persecution on account of race, religion, nationality, membership of a particular social group or political opinion. "United Nations Convention and Protocol Relating to the Status of Refugees," http://www.unhcr .org/en-us/protection/basic/3b66c2aa10/convention-protocol-relating-status-refugees .html.

30. See, for example, Tom Gjelten, "The Immigration Act that Inadvertently Changed America," *The Atlantic*, October 2, 2015. http://www.theatlantic.com/politics/ archive/2015/10/immigration-act-1965/408409.

31. "Edward Kennedy," http://www.u-s-history.com/pages/h2015.html.

32. "President Lyndon B. Johnson's Remarks at the Signing of the Immigration Bill, Liberty Island, New York, October 3, 1965," http://www.lbjlib.utexas.edu/johnson/archives .hom/speeches.hom/651003.asp.

33. US Census Bureau, "Table 1: Nativity of the Population and Place of Birth of the Native Population: 1850 to 1990," https://www.census.gov/population/www/ documentation/twps0029/tab01.html.

34. Andrew Kohut, "Fifty Years Later, Americans Give Thumbs-Up to Immigration that Changed the Nation," *Pew Research Center*, February 2, 2015, http://www.pewresearch

20 · *Introduction*

.org/fact-tank/2015/02/04/50-years-later-americans-give-thumbs-up-to-immigration-law-that-changed-the-nation.

35. Muzaffar Chishti, Faye Hipsman, and Isabel Ball, "Fifty Years On, the 1965 Immigration and Nationality Act Continues to Shape the Nation," *Migration Policy Institute*, October 15, 2015.

36. Pew Research Center, "Statistical Portrait of the Foreign-Born Population of the United States, 2014," http://www.pewhispanic.org/2016/04/19/2014-statistical-information-on-immigrants-in-united-states. Pew Research Center, "U.S. Foreign-Born Population Trends," ch. 5 of "Modern Immigration Wave Brings 59 Million to U.S., Driving Population Change and Growth through 2065," September 28, 2015, http://www.pewhispanic.org/2015/09/28/chapter-5-u-s-foreign-born-population-trends.

37. Migration Policy Institute, "Largest US Immigrant Groups over Time, 1960-Present," http://www.migrationpolicy.org/programs/data-hub/charts/largest-immigrant-groups-over-time.

38. "Annual Report of Immigrant Visa Applicants in the Family-Sponsored and Employment-Based Preferences Registered at the National Visa Center as of November 1, 2016." https://travel.state.gov/content/dam/visas/Statistics/Immigrant-Statistics/WaitingListItem.pdf. See also Jacquellena Carrero, "The Immigration Line: Who's on It and for How Long?" April 11, 2013, http://nbclatino.com/2013/04/11/the-immigration-line-whos-on-it-and-for-how-long.

PART I

Policy and Law

The chapters in the first section of the book focus on the intersections between immigration policy and US international history. In the late nineteenth and early twentieth centuries, US legislators, in response to the largest global migration in world history, wrested immigration policy away from state powers and centralized immigration control, but they also placed parts of immigration enforcement in the hands of consular offices, shipping companies, and authorities in sending countries. From the very beginning then, immigration policy, usually presented as an instrument of domestic policy, was profoundly intertwined with US foreign policy and international developments.

Challenging the traditional periodization of immigration control, Elliott Young traces the long history of remote control practices—such as medical inspections, visas, and passports—and their long-term repercussions for sending and receiving nations from the late nineteenth century to the present. Young also shows how remote control affected all immigrants, even those from the Americas who were exempted from the harsher provisions of the 1924 Immigration Act. For example, while American growers and other businesses actively recruited Mexican labor, immigration officials still found ways to curtail their entry because Mexicans did not conform to policymakers' notions of ideal workers and citizens.

Expanding on Young's argument that the success of restrictive US immigration policy depended heavily on international cooperation, Kathleen

López explores the impact of US immigration restriction on the Caribbean. She powerfully shows how a major unintended consequence of the new quota system in the United States was the diversion of migrants to countries with less restrictive immigration policies in the Caribbean and Latin America. Immigrants from eastern Europe, for example, traveled in large numbers to Cuba, where some strategically tried to acquire Cuban citizenship and later migrate to the United States as non-quota immigrants. Others paid smugglers to transport them across the short stretch of ocean that separated Cuba from the United States. In response to these developments, the federal government encouraged steamship companies to collaborate in the policing of the high seas to capture smugglers and their human contraband. The United States also pressured countries to adopt more restrictive immigration policies to keep "undesirables" out of the hemisphere. Developing countries like Cuba acquiesced because immigration gatekeeping was a symbol of modernism and created leverage with the United States, its major economic market.

Although the commitment to immigration restriction remained strong throughout the entire period covered in this anthology, the outbreak of World War II and the geopolitical order that emerged with the onset of the Cold War forced legislators to reconsider and amend, at least superficially, the country's immigration policy. These changing foreign policy priorities provided an opening for supporters of immigration to push for a more humane immigration system. Laura Madokoro examines how the refugee crises of the 1940s and 1950s presented Americans with a moral dilemma. In response to hundreds of thousands of people uprooted by war and revolution around the world, many Americans argued that their country, as the new world leader, had a humanitarian obligation to assist refugees and other displaced persons. Sensing an opening, religious and secular humanitarians emphasized the benefits of refugee admissions for the US economy and international relations, but they faced resistance from restrictionists in Congress who fought hard to maintain the status quo. The tension between those who supported an international vision of immigration policy and those who argued that immigration was the purview of domestic policy produced mixed policy results. Pro-refugee legislators succeeded in pushing for piecemeal legislation that allowed several hundred thousand refugees (mostly European) to relocate to the United States. They also succeeded in carving out a small refugee quota in the 1965 Immigration and Nationality Act, but it would not be until 1980 that Congress passed more comprehensive refugee legislation.

By looking at the international debates about immigration restriction, David Cook-Martín and David FitzGerald challenge yet another assumption about the reasons behind the passage of the 1965 Immigration and Nationality Act. While the authors do not deny that the language of Cold War civil rights contributed to the push for immigration reform in 1965, they argue that critical geopolitical developments in the Western Hemisphere influenced the 1965 Immigration and Nationality Act just as deeply. By focusing on the elimination of restrictive immigration laws in Latin American countries, they demonstrate that the passage of the 1965 act was part of larger regional efforts to reduce racialized laws. The authors' discussion of the influence of Latin American countries in debates over immigration policy in the United States underscores the need for a more nuanced understanding of the relationship between the United States and its neighbors. They also provide a fresh perspective on the role that foreign policy played in the passage of the act as much of the existing scholarship focuses on the role that US interests in Asia and Africa played during the debates over immigration reform.

CHAPTER 1

Beyond Borders

Remote Control and the Continuing Legacy of Racism in Immigration Legislation

ELLIOTT YOUNG

> Don't you see that the man who comes here selects us,
> And that is what causes our worry and fuss:
> Our selection of aliens should begin over sea.
> And not when they enter this land of the free.
>
> —Terence Powderly, Grand Master of Knights of Labor and
> Commissioner General of Immigration (1892–1902)

> It is much easier to refuse a visa than to deny admittance to the suspected person after he has arrived at a port of entry of the United States.
>
> —Secretary of State Robert Lansing to President Woodrow Wilson,
> August 20, 1919

Controlling immigration to the United States became effective in the 1920s only when the government learned how to stop migrants before they left their home countries, but the US government tried to develop a system of remote control long before that. Immigration authorities created a system of medical inspections, visas, and passports that turned consular offices and shipping companies into frontlines for immigration enforcement. By the 1920s, these extraterritorial boundaries became the most significant obstacle to entry, more daunting for immigrants than the inspection checkpoints at US ports of entry. These overseas inspections could prevent migrants from departing their home countries and thus control immigration flows far more effectively. That the United States secured this international cooperation reflected its growing influence around the world. These practices were not solely a symbol of US imperial reach, however, but of an expanding global system of border security and migration control. Concerns over national security and the regulation of borders pushed countries to enforce migration laws by what political scientist Aristide Zolberg calls "remote control."[1]

Remote control refers to the practices and mechanisms to enforce immigration policy beyond the nation's borders as well as the efforts to outsource enforcement to private companies. Reliance on private companies has expanded and contracted since the late nineteenth century, but the overall trend has been toward greater direct government control over immigration enforcement. While pushing private companies to enforce immigration laws may be read as a sign of state power, it also reflects the inability of the state to enforce its own regulations. As Adam McKeown shows in *Melancholy Order*, the US government's efforts to gain control over the visa and documentation process in China, where it first became a regular practice in the mid-nineteenth century, were continuously undermined by Chinese officials and private entrepreneurs.[2] The aim of extraterritorial migration control was to be able to track migrants and to distinguish between citizens, legal residents, and inadmissible aliens before they even boarded ships or trains. Passports and other letters of introduction have a longer history, but until there was a centralized state bureaucracy to standardize these documents, they were not useful for tracking and regulating mobility.[3] Remote control through medical inspections and certificates of residency for Chinese were thus the primary mechanisms to regulate movement before the standardization of the passport during World War I. By the time of the 1924 Johnson-Reed Act, remote-control practices had become institutionalized through consulates that were responsible for sorting and selecting immigrants based on national quotas.

Historians of migration who still see the world through national lenses focus on what happens once migrants reach a port of entry. A transnational perspective that allows us to see the entire migratory circuit reveals that exclusion occurs more often before migrants leave their home countries or in third-countries surrounding the intended destination. The extraterritorial enforcement of immigration restrictions emerged in the nineteenth century as a way for countries to keep undesirable migrants from their shores. From World War I through the 1920s, this system of remote control solidified through the internationalization and regimentation of a regime of passports and visas that has now become standard practice around globe. Although the United States was at the forefront in establishing a robust immigration bureaucracy in the late nineteenth century, it was by no means the only country to erect immigration restrictions. The cooperation of countries in controlling the movement of people was a new way of recognizing the sanctity of national boundaries and national sovereignty. While the United States coaxed other countries to comply with its restrictions, those countries often resisted US demands or had their own reasons for implementing restrictionist policies. The global system of migration restriction put in place in the 1920s emerged out of these earlier efforts. The pre- and post-1920s era of migration restriction are inextricably linked and the two periods cannot and should not be seen as distinct phases in US immigration policy history.

Enlisting private transport companies to enforce migration restrictions was central to the emerging new order. From the nineteenth century through the 1920s, the relationship between private transport companies and governments waxed and waned. Although the early outsourcing of inspections in the 1860s and 1870s reflected the inability of government inspectors to get the job done, by the 1920s, the US immigration bureaucracy was robust enough to conduct its own inspections and demand compliance by private companies. The regularization of travel documents and the professionalization of the Foreign Service in the 1920s helped the United States government to gain control over what previously had been a fairly chaotic system of inspections and haphazard travel permissions. It is not a coincidence that the national-origins quota acts emerged in the 1920s. Without a vigorous remote-control bureaucracy in place, it would have been impossible to sort through millions of immigrants before they arrived on US shores.

Migration and borderlands scholars have explored exclusions at the borderline, but they have paid short shrift to the bureaucratic mechanisms of extraterritorial immigration control.[4] The large number of migration books with "fence" or "gate" in the title suggests an emphasis on the physical boundary line.[5] While such a focus on gates and borders makes intuitive sense, it has obscured the much more important web of global barriers before migrants even set foot on a particular country's soil. Aristide Zolberg, Adam McKeown, Elizabeth Sinn, Amy Fairchild, and others have highlighted overseas consulates and medical inspections as a site of migration control.[6] It is ultimately these extraterritorial measures that created enforceable borders around the nation and helped to form the global order we know today. The nation-state might imagine itself as a coherent territory demarcated by clear borderlines, but it is actually a web of global economic and political relationships. The more powerful the nation, the more potent are its global tentacles.

The accretion of restrictive immigration legislation in the late nineteenth and early twentieth centuries culminated in the national-origins quotas in the early 1920s. By this point, what had largely been a domestic system of border inspections had become a massive bureaucracy for sifting immigrants in consular offices around the globe. In this era, if an immigrant made it to US shores, they were almost always guaranteed entry. Undocumented entry of migrants from around the globe across land borders with Canada and Mexico continued in spite of restrictionist laws, but the 1924 act managed to make the country whiter by privileging legal entry of northern and western Europeans. The Hart-Celler Act in 1965 ended national-origins quotas and established hemispheric quotas, but rather than an opening,

28 • ELLIOTT YOUNG

these new quotas represented a slamming shut of the door on Mexicans and Canadians who composed the vast majority of immigrants from the Americas. In 1976, national quotas were reintroduced with a maximum of twenty thousand for each country. The drastic reduction of legal immigration from Mexico—from an annual two hundred thousand braceros and thirty-five thousand regular admissions for permanent residency during the 1960s to just twenty thousand—created a new surge in unauthorized entrants.[7] Border enforcement grew throughout the late twentieth century as gaining a visa from particular countries, especially Mexico, became increasingly difficult. The Hart-Celler Act and the 1976 reform created a false appearance of equality by providing each country with the same quota, but given the historically high levels of immigration from particular countries, formal equality created greater de facto restrictions for countries like Mexico. Discrimination continued under a different guise.

Early Remote Control, 1880s–1920

The 1924 nation-based quota restrictions were the culmination of forty years of experimentation with various forms of ethnic and class-based exclusion. The 1880–1920 period is crucial to understanding how the mechanisms for managing migration developed. Historians have tended to focus on debarment or deportation, looking at Ellis Island and Angel Island and the US-Mexico border as the principle sites of exclusion, but blocking migrants before they were even able to leave international ports was numerically much more significant. Historian Deidre Maloney calculates that deportations averaged just 1 to 3 percent of the total number of immigrants admitted in any given year during the twentieth century. Throughout the twentieth century, removals or "debarment" before a migrant had officially entered the country far outpaced deportations.[8] However, accounting for both deportations and removals still hides an important element in the selection process—that is, prospective migrants denied visas by consuls or prevented from traveling by steamship lines for medical or other reasons. These rejections do not show up in the Bureau of Immigration data. Historian Amy Fairchild calculates that the rejection rate in overseas consulates averaged 5 percent between 1926 and 1930, which she notes was 400 percent greater than the average number of rejections at US ports from 1891 to 1930.[9] Evidence from the US consulate in Hong Kong suggests that it preemptively rejected half of all prospective migrants at the beginning of the twentieth century. Although precise numbers are hard to come by for every port of embarkation, it is clear that far more migrants were rejected abroad than in the United States.

Early efforts at remote control were largely ineffective because government officials were not that zealous in enforcing migratory restrictions. Since the mid-nineteenth century when Europeans began to transport large numbers of Asian contract laborers to plantations around the world, consuls acted as labor recruiters and regulators. These dual functions often caused a conflict of interest. After 1862, for example, US consuls in Hong Kong were charged with assuring that all Chinese departing on US ships were leaving voluntarily, but, beginning in 1875, they also became responsible for enforcing the provisions of the Page Act that banned the immigration of prostitutes and Asian contract laborers. After the passage of the 1882 Chinese Exclusion Act, consular officials in Hong Kong were responsible for issuing the Section 6 certificates that exempted students, merchants and diplomats from restriction. When David Bailey became US Consul in Hong Kong in 1871, he criticized his predecessors' efforts to prevent American involvement in the coolie trade as a "complete farce." Eight years later Bailey was accused by his successor of being more interested in collecting fees than enforcing the regulations.[10] Remote control was not very effective when consular officers took little interest or had a financial stake in the trade they were supposed to be regulating.

Although the US consuls were ineffective or disinterested in the 1860s and 1870s, by the 1890s, the Immigration Bureau relied on them because they ostensibly had the local knowledge to be able to detect fraud better than immigration officers at US ports. Consul Rounsevelle Wildman in Hong Kong, for example, charged that some of the bureau's telltale signs to distinguish coolies from merchants made no sense in China. He explained that he checked applicants for the "marks of the coolie," namely calluses on the shoulder and shabby clothes, to detect fraud. In 1898, Consul Wildman proudly noted that he rejected more than half of visa applicants based on his investigations.[11] If Wildman's statement can be believed, getting past the consul in Hong Kong was roughly twice as hard as getting by immigration inspections at US ports, which averaged a 28 percent rejection rate for Chinese.[12] Recriminations between US consuls and the Chinese government over lax regulations of visas finally led to complex procedures in 1896 that required an applicant for emigration to pass through investigations by a local superintendent of customs and then a local viceroy in China before proceeding to a US consul for a visa.[13] In her study of Hong Kong as a hub of Pacific migration, Elizabeth Sinn shows how the British had similar problems enforcing their anti-coolie trade measures until they enlisted the Chinese board of directors of the Tung Wah Hospital in the early 1870s to root out corruption.[14] The reliance of the British on Chinese merchants to help curb trafficking abuses suggests that they needed local help to enforce their own regulations. Between the 1870s and late 1890s, British and US enforcement of migration controls in China became more effective through the cooperation of the Chinese government and local merchants. Remote control was most effective when foreign governments, local merchants, and transport companies were all working together to enforce migration restrictions. After 1924, it was not only Chinese laborers, those likely to become public charges (in other words, the poor), and those with contagious diseases who had to be screened; every immigrant was vetted. The 1924 restrictions shifted the regulatory bureaucracy into overdrive as millions of prospective immigrants had to be sifted and sorted in consular offices around the globe.

Beyond consular evaluations, the most important method of controlling migration and the first line of defense against unwanted immigrants was the US Public Health Service's (PHS) overseas inspections. Medical examiners from the United States were stationed in ports in Japan and China as well as in Canada, Cuba, Western Europe, and Russia; their job was to prevent potential immigrants with diseases from boarding vessels headed to the United States. After the federal Quarantine Law of 1893 and a series of agreements with officials in Naples, Italy, and then China and Japan in 1903, PHS officers began inspecting prospective emigrants in foreign ports. Although the US officials did not technically have the power to prevent departure from these ports, they passed lists of diseased immigrants to the steamship companies, who usually rejected them. It was in the interest of the steamship companies to take the PHS officers' recommendations because the company could be fined $100 for each returned migrant.[15] The 1903 Immigration Act solidified this practice, requiring medical examinations abroad before prospective migrants embarked on their journey. For example, in 1914, even though Wong Hand had a certificate of residency dating to 1894 and passed an inspection by a US public health office in Hong Kong, he still underwent thirty-one medical inspections by the ship's surgeon on the Pacific Mail steamer *Siberia* while en route to San Francisco (see figures 1 and 2). Without this certificate Wong would have been placed in quarantine upon arrival in San Francisco.[16] In 1914 the Surgeon General announced that in Boston authorities noted a marked decrease in the number of immigrants with communicable diseases despite an increase in immigration. He attributed this decrease to the "more careful examination made at the foreign ports of embarkation in order to avoid fines and deportations."[17] Medical inspection abroad was working. After 1924, although there were fixed quantitative quotas for each country (except for the Western Hemisphere and the so-called Asiatic Barred Zone), the qualitative diagnoses of contagious diseases continued to be a major barrier for certain ethnic groups. Although medical diagnoses were supposed to be based in objective science, medical inspectors had racist notions of which bodies would be prone to carry particular diseases.

Medical inspections, like the entire immigration process, were based on racist preferences for white Europeans. PHS officers rejected Asians at much higher rates than they did Europeans, reaching a rejection rate as high as 65 percent in China and Japan compared with only 4 to 6 percent in Naples, Italy.[18] The overall rejection rate at US ports from 1908 to 1932 for non-Chinese was only 3 percent, compared

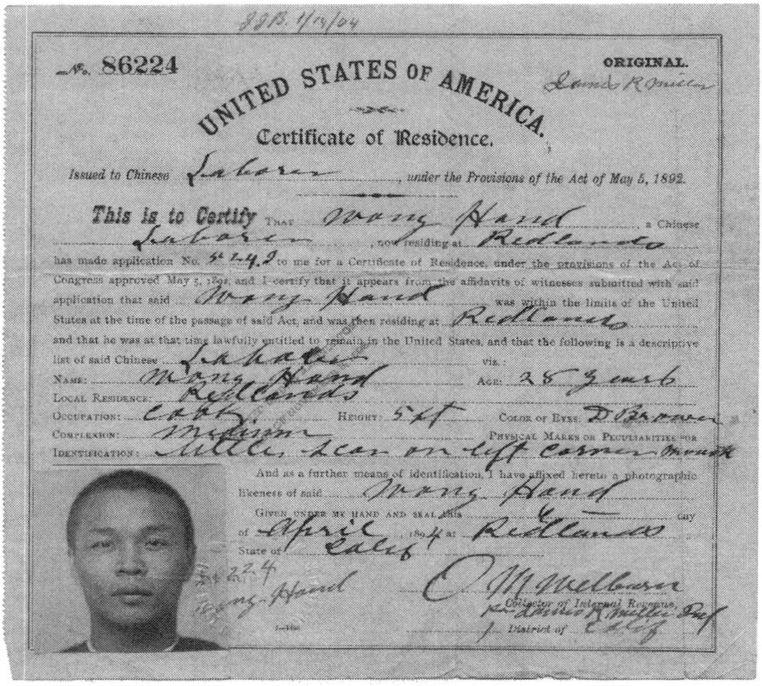
No. 86224 ORIGINAL.

UNITED STATES OF AMERICA.

Certificate of Residence.

Issued to Chinese Laborer, under the Provisions of the Act of May 5, 1892.

This is to Certify That Wong Hand, a Chinese Laborer, now residing at Redlands has made application No. 4242 to me for a Certificate of Residence, under the provisions of the Act of Congress approved May 5, 1892, and I certify that it appears from the affidavits of witnesses submitted with said application that said Wong Hand was within the limits of the United States at the time of the passage of said Act, and was then residing at Redlands and that he was at that time lawfully entitled to remain in the United States, and that the following is a descriptive list of said Chinese Laborer viz.:

Name: Wong Hand Age: 28 years

Local Residence: Redlands

Occupation: Cook Height: 5 ft Color of Eyes: D. Brown

Complexion: Medium Physical Marks or Peculiarities for Identification: Little scar on left corner mouth

And as a further means of identification, I have affixed hereto a photographic likeness of said Wong Hand.

Given under my hand and seal this 6 day of April 1894 at Redlands State of Calif.

O. M. Welburn, Collector of Internal Revenue, per Lewis R Miller Dep, District of Calif.

Figure 1. Wong Hand's certificate of residence showing that he was a resident of Redlands at the time the 1892 Act, requiring Chinese to carry such identification, was passed. Courtesy of the Asian American Studies Collections, Ethnic Studies Library, University of California, Berkeley.

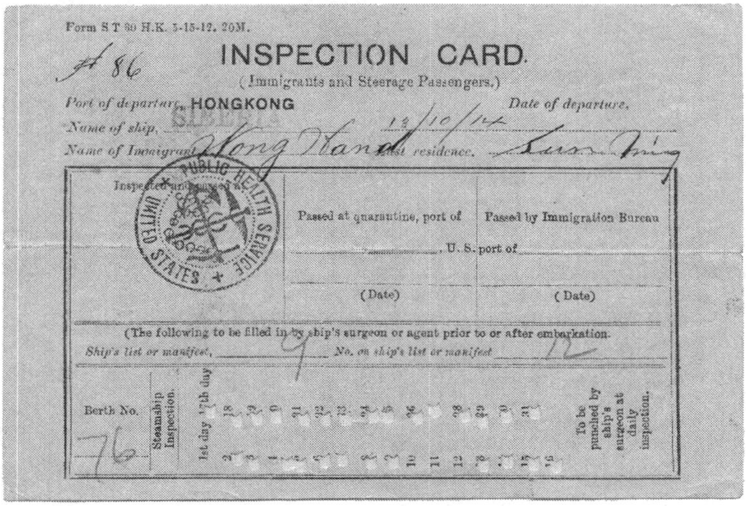
Form S T 30 H.K. 5-15-12. 20M.

#86

INSPECTION CARD.

(Immigrants and Steerage Passengers.)

Port of departure, HONGKONG Date of departure,

Name of ship, SIBERIA 13/10/14

Name of Immigrant Wong Hand Last residence, Sun Ning

Inspected and passed at

Passed at quarantine, port of , U.S. (Date)

Passed by Immigration Bureau port of (Date)

(The following to be filled in by ship's surgeon or agent prior to or after embarkation.

Ship's list or manifest, 9 No. on ship's list or manifest 12

Berth No. 76 Steamship Inspection. 1st day 17th day

To be punched by ship's surgeon at daily inspection.

Figure 2. Wong Hand's 1914 inspection card indicating that he passed thirty-one medical exams on the voyage from Hong Kong to San Francisco. Courtesy of the Asian American Studies Collections, Ethnic Studies Library, University of California, Berkeley.

with 28 percent for the Chinese.[19] Europeans mainly entered through Ellis Island (1892), where only 1 percent were rejected, compared with 18 percent rejection rate at Angel Island, where most Chinese and Japanese arrived.[20] The disproportionate rejection of Asians versus Europeans reflects the racism of consular officials and immigration inspectors as well as the racism embedded in immigration laws. Thus, while all consular rejections were greater than those at ports of entry, this differential was even greater for Asians. The point is that if you could manage to make it to U.S soil and were not Asian, you had a fairly good chance of getting through the gate because the main selection process had already taken place in a foreign country. The supposed objectivity of medical exclusions that were perfected in the 1910s and 1920s foreshadowed the apparently nonracialized objective criteria for admission after 1965. In both cases, the outcomes disproportionately targeted nonwhite immigrants.

In the nineteenth century the bureaucracy for medically inspecting and certifying prospective migrants and determining their eligibility for entry lacked standardization and coherence. The government relied on shipping companies to enforce regulations, making them financially and even criminally liable for bringing in undesirable or unlawful immigrants. As early as the 1837 revision of the alien passenger law, shipping companies were required to post $1,000 bonds for "lunatic, idiot, maimed, aged or infirm" immigrants and to pay a $2 tax to help the state's efforts to maintain paupers.[21] The 1882 Immigration Act levied a fifty-cent tax on all alien passengers for the maintenance and support of the regulatory system, and required shipping companies to assume the transportation costs for any immigrant not permitted to land.[22] The 1891 Immigration Act also levied a fine of up to $1,000 and up to a year in prison for smuggling illegal passengers. For all passengers who were found to have arrived unlawfully, with or without the shipping companies' knowledge, the shipper was fined $300 per immigrant.[23] The 1907 Immigration Act also saddled these companies with the cost of return as well as half of the total deportation costs if immigrants became public charges due to preexisting conditions within three years of their arrival.[24] By making the shipping companies financially responsible in these ways, the government shifted liability for deportations to private companies. The 1907 Act therefore culminated what had been a slowly evolving shifting of responsibility to private companies for determining eligibility for entry to the United States by assessing the legitimacy of entry documents, performing medical exams, and screening for the long list of excludable categories.[25] However, unlike in the 1870s in Hong Kong when the United States relied on steamship companies to enforce migratory regulations because the immigration bureaucracy was undeveloped, by the twentieth century, the US Immigration Bureau outsourced its inspections from a position of relative strength.

This power struggle between the state and private shipping companies played out in Europe in the first decade of the twentieth century as consular officers increasingly exercised their muscle. Fiorello La Guardia, who would later become mayor of New York City, was at the center of that struggle as a young consular agent in Fiume, Hungary (now Rijeka, Croatia). La Guardia arrived in Fiume in 1903 just as a steamship line began offering transportation to New York. Although he was required to certify the health of all passengers and that the ship was free from contagious diseases, there were no specific instructions on how to carry out such inspections. La Guardia decided to hire local physicians to conduct medical exams, a move which ran afoul of the steamship line's managers, who counted on less rigorous exams. La Guardia retaliated by refusing to issue his certificates of health, a decision that would have resulted in stiff fines once the ship arrived in New York. In the end, the steamship company was forced to accept La Guardia's inspections and to pay for them.[26] La Guardia's ad hoc diplomacy in Fiume shows not only how the US government was able to extend its legal reach to foreign ports, but also how it made private companies partners in the execution of US immigration policies in the early twentieth century.

Facing the same kinds of pressures at the beginning of the twentieth century, German steamship lines erected elaborate inspection stations in port cities, and the Prussian railways inspected emigrants before they even arrived at the coast.[27] In a 1902 investigation of the Hamburg inspection facilities, a US official concluded, "It is entirely clear, although the numbers rejected in America may be small, that this is entirely due to the elaborate precautions which are taken before the emigrants start to prevent the possibility of their rejection."[28] The US Immigration Commission of 1907 discovered that the pre-inspection procedures established by the French, Swiss, Hungarians, and Germans were more effective in preventing unauthorized migrants from boarding ships than were US public health inspectors stationed throughout Europe. Their effectiveness can be attributed to their increased financial interest in not shipping diseased migrants. Once European shippers took responsibility for pre-inspections, they could also more easily be held responsible for returning rejected migrants. Given the effectiveness of private companies in enforcing US immigration laws, the US government preferred outsourcing preemptive inspections and therefore recalled US public health officers from Japan, Hong Kong, and the Russian port of Libau in 1909.[29] However, the privatization of the inspection process required a state strong enough to ensure that the private corporations would take seriously the tasks they were assigned. Privatization, in this instance, was a reflection of growing state power.

The overlapping jurisdiction of private companies and state officials led to disagreements in some cases, especially when steamship companies enforced regulations even more strictly than consular officials. In determining which passengers required medical screening, steamship companies first had to determine whether potential passengers were US citizens or aliens. The transport companies accepted only two forms of proof of citizenship, a passport or court documents indicating citizenship.[30] However, before World War I, passports were not in general use, and therefore many US citizens traveled without such documentation. It wasn't until 1914 that the State Department announced that all US citizens "should" have a passport when traveling abroad. A year later President Wilson issued an executive order indicating that passports were a necessity for those traveling to Europe.[31] In 1908 the US consul in Hong Kong, Amos Waldir, complained about the rigidity of steamship companies that resulted in weeks' delay for a Chinese family with US citizenship who were unable to board a ship because their infant child was placed on the "alien list" and then diagnosed with a trace of trachoma. The consul believed that the family would have been able to prove their citizenship and that of their child to immigration authorities in a US port, but the strict rules in Hong Kong made such verification impossible. Recognizing these difficulties, the consul asked that US authorities affirm his power to make an initial determination of US citizenship. Denying the right to prove their citizenship in a US court was, the consul protested, an "unworthy limitation of American citizenship."[32]

In another case, a US-born citizen of Chinese descent was abandoned by her husband in China when he ran off with a second wife. The husband took the passport that listed his wife and their fourteen-year-old daughter as US citizens, both born in the United States. In spite of having the husband's court papers and other proof of citizenship, they were not able to return to Seattle because the steamship company would not accept their documents. The consul was outraged that this "poor woman" and her daughter, "a cultured product of American school and church," would be denied their rights as American citizens to return to their country of birth, or even be given the opportunity in Seattle to prove their citizenship status.[33] The consul's emphasis on the family's Americanization indicated how important cultural assimilation was to claim the benefits of US citizenship. The case also shows the kinds of tensions that emerged between private companies and state officials before the regularization of passports and visas.

These cases reported by the consul in Hong Kong highlighted the immense power that had been placed in the hands of often young and inexperienced medical doctors and low-level steamship employees stationed in foreign ports. The consul was incredulous: "I cannot believe the humane men at the seat of government realize what suffering is caused, what rankling sense of injustice is kindled among the Chinese by gradual growth of the trachoma test, . . . [in which] an inflammation of the inner eyelid is the heart of the momentous Chinese immigration question." At the end of his lengthy letter, he called for further investigation of trachoma to consider "not merely the physiological but the humane and political factors that enter in."[34] However, this was not merely a question of physiology versus politics. The physiological diagnosis of the disease itself was a political question, one that had a different answer in Hong Kong, Vancouver, and San Francisco and depended on which doctor one consulted in each of those places. The steamship companies often enforced US restrictions with more zeal than US officers because the companies were responsible for returning inadmissible aliens. For the steamship companies, it was an economic more than a humanitarian question.

It was not only the steamship companies, however, that were motivated by economic consideration. The Bureau of Immigration proved adept at relaxing medical standards when employers demanded more labor. When Chinese were prevented from returning to the Philippines, then an American territory, because of their high rates of trachoma, the bureau simply encouraged a "more lenient criteria to diagnose trachoma."[35] The need for Chinese labor in the Philippines trumped the fear that migrants would bring in contagious diseases. It is telling that such lenient criteria were never recommended for passengers bound for the United States. The constant disputes between transport companies, immigration officers, medical inspectors, and consuls encouraged the development of an ostensibly more objective quota system with clearer lines of authority for determining entry eligibility. The 1924 Immigration Act did not eliminate the discretion of border guards, but the onus for determining immigrant admissibility shifted to consuls and a bureaucratic visa requirement.

Consolidating Remote Control: The First World War to the 1920s

A more robust system of inspection developed as a result of fears of enemy infiltration during World War I. On July 26, 1917, a joint order by the US Departments of State and Labor established for the first time a visa requirement for entry to the United States. The next year, the Passport Control Act established executive authority over the entry and exit to the United States by both citizens and foreigners. As Secretary of State Robert Lansing advised President Wilson in 1919, "It is much easier to refuse a visa than to deny admittance to the suspected person after he has arrived at a port of entry of the United States."[36] The result of the new passport, visa, and consular inspection requirements meant that the overwhelming majority of immigrants who arrived in the United States would be admitted based on the documents they carried rather than a bodily inspection.

In 1924, the same year Congress passed the Johnson-Reed Act, the Rogers Act created the Foreign Service, professionalizing consular posts, establishing a merit-based system for employment, and giving consular officials the task of conducting immigrant inspections. The professionalization of the Foreign Service gave the government more control over its consular officials. It also helped to create more uniform standards to assess citizenship and avoid the kind of conflicts that had emerged earlier in Hong Kong. By 1925, the PHS inspection line at Ellis Island was ended and instead immigrants were given cursory examinations aboard ships to ensure they had proper visas and clean bills of health.[37] By 1930, only 5 percent of immigrants arriving in New York were sent to Ellis Island, usually because they were suspected of becoming public charges. The new system of screening immigrants before their arrival was working more efficiently and effectively than ever before. In the first four years of enforcement of the 1924 quota restrictions, only .02 percent of those immigrants arriving with visas were rejected.[38] In 1927 the Immigration Service's Second Assistant Secretary W. W. Husband wrote to the surgeon general, exclaiming that the inspection of immigrants abroad has "proven successful beyond any of our fondest dreams."[39] Although transport companies were still responsible for returning rejected aliens, determining eligibility for entry was increasingly the domain of an expanded US immigration and foreign service bureaucracy.

The ability to control migration into and out of its territory was not only the mark of a modern nation, but it also reflected their global influence in garnering the cooperation of other countries. As historian Donna Gabaccia shows in her book *Foreign Relations*, migration control was not simply a "domestic matter."[40] Although the United States attempted to pressure other countries to help enforce its restrictive immigration policies, those countries often resisted or passed restrictive legislation for their own domestic reasons. Military interventions gave the United States more leverage over these other countries' migration policies, but they also had the unintended consequence of creating new migratory streams. In US-occupied Cuba, for example, the US military replicated the Chinese Exclusion Act on the island in 1902 by decree, inhibiting Chinese migration to Cuba (see chapter 2 in this volume). In contrast, the US takeover of the Philippines turned Filipinos into US nationals, which facilitated their migration to the United States by exempting them from the restrictions placed on all other Asians. The 1934 Tydings-McDuffie Act, which paved the way for Philippine independence in 1946, changed the Filipinos' status for the purpose of immigration and gave them an annual quota of fifty.[41]

Canada, Cuba, and Mexico represent three different levels of cooperation with the United States regarding Chinese exclusion. Cuba was the most compliant, replicating the US ban on Chinese labor in 1902. Canada cooperated with the American law early on and eventually imposed its own Chinese labor exclusion in 1923. Mexico resisted these policies the most, at least in the late nineteenth century; but by the 1920s Mexico instituted its own form of nationalist immigration restrictions. Although there were varying degrees of willingness to accede to US wishes, by the 1920s the United States garnered hemispheric cooperation to keep Asians out. It would be a mistake, however, only to credit US hegemony with the development of neighboring countries' immigration policies. Xenophobic movements in Canada, Mexico, and Cuba pressured governments to restrict Asian migration, but in spite of this racial antipathy, business interests often succeeded in keeping the doors open, at least partially and temporarily. In Cuba, for example, plantation owners, many of whom were US citizens, succeeded in securing Chinese workers in 1917 to work in the sugar cane fields.[42] The lack of control over the immigration policies of neighboring countries made it difficult for the United States to prevent clandestine entry. After 1924 these clandestine entries through the so-called back doors became a greater concern as thousands of excluded southern and eastern Europeans began using Cuba, Mexico, and Canada as springboards for illegal entry to the United States.

Asian migrants seeking to avoid the draconian American medical inspections took advantage of laxer policies in neighboring countries to gain access to the United States. The different enforcement of medical exclusion in Canada provides a good example. According to Special Immigration Inspector Braun, US medical examiners in Hong Kong rejected 10 to 60 percent of Chinese and Japanese immigrants, whereas Canadian lines rejected a far lower percentage, and they even allowed ill passengers to sail. The result of this discrepancy led many Chinese and Japanese to seek passage on Canadian ships. Braun worried that the lack of vigilance by the Canadian shipping authorities in Hong Kong might allow diseased passengers traveling in steerage to infect healthy passengers.[43] Furthermore, Canadian officials handled the arrival of sick passengers differently than American authorities. Migrants who were found to have a disease upon arrival in a US port were immediately deported, "there being no redress and no opportunity to be treated or cured." Passengers with diseases arriving at Canadian ports, however, were given medical treatment until cured, at which point, Braun stated, the immigrant was "'railroaded past the Department medical examiner' and enter[ed] the United States to become a menace to its citizens."[44] Even though the Canadian government allowed US medical examiners to inspect immigrants bound for the United States, this was not sufficient, according to Braun, because the Canadian medical examiner inspected and treated immigrants before the American examiner had a chance to determine their admissibility.[45] The differential treatment in neighboring countries often limited the effectiveness of remote-control procedures.

The medical exams themselves were also subject to interpretation, leading to vastly different rates of rejections in Hong Kong, United States, and Canadian ports. The US consul in Hong Kong provided data on trachoma rejections on six British and American ships that had recently sailed to show how much easier it was for Chinese to enter Canada than the United States. Consul Waldir reported that migrants who entered through Vancouver and were tested for trachoma were rejected at a rate of less than 3 percent, whereas 30 percent of passengers heading to San Francisco were rejected in Hong Kong before they could even depart.[46] Given these odds, it is not hard to understand why Chinese or Japanese preferred traveling through Canada rather than directly to a US port. Furthermore, the 30

38 · ELLIOTT YOUNG

percent rejection rate in Hong Kong was almost double the rejection rate at Angel Island, making it twice as difficult a barrier to overcome in the exclusion apparatus.[47] By the early twentieth century, therefore, most Asians were excluded from the United States while still in Asia. Remote control was not ancillary to immigration restriction; it was the main mechanism for exclusion.

Centralizing and Extending Remote Control, 1924–1965

Remote control mechanisms had been slowly developing since the 1880s, and they accelerated during the First World War, but the 1924 Johnson-Reed Act represented the solidification of these practices as the primary means of immigration control. By the 1920s, inspections and visa denials became the principal mechanism for exclusion, but after 1924 this process became institutionalized, and the Department of State officially assumed the role of gatekeeper. The 1921 Quota Act created chaos. Immigrants were counted as they arrived at ports of entry, which encouraged steamship operators to race to port to land their passengers before quota limits had been reached. In the debate over the 1924 Johnson-Reed Act, members of Congress argued that the system of enforcing quota at ports was unwieldy and brought "hardships." Instead, Congress enacted a new system for "enforcement of the numerical limitation not by counting immigrants upon their arrival, but by counting 'immigration certificates' issuable at American consulates overseas."[48] Furthermore, the 1924 immigration act gave consular officials the power to deny visas that was almost absolute. The Secretary of State or the Attorney General could overturn a consular officer decision, but the decision could not be appealed by an applicant or reviewed by the courts.[49] Consular officers had more unchecked power than any other US official, including the president, whose decisions were ultimately reviewable by the Supreme Court.

The remote-control system that emerged in the 1924–1965 period used immigration regulations to further US objectives. During World War II, for example, the United States pressured thirteen Latin American countries to arrest 4,085 Germans, 2,264 Japanese, and 288 Italians who were suspected of being "enemy aliens."[50] Some of the supposed "enemy aliens" were naturalized citizens of the Latin American countries where they resided and were suspects simply because of their ancestry. There are even cases of German and Italian Jews who had escaped concentration camps being interned in alien enemy camps in Panama and the United States.[51] With the collaboration of these Latin American countries, principally Peru and Panama, thousands of civilians were rounded up and shipped to detention camps in Texas, New York, and other locations around the country. These preemptive detentions were part of a secret plan to exchange US prisoners of war for Japanese, Germans, and Italians. The internees were not technically prisoners of war, but they were held in detention centers run by the Immigration and Naturalization Service after being declared "illegal aliens." Even though they were forcibly taken from Latin America and had their passports seized, the US authorities declared their entry unauthorized. During and after the war many were repatriated to Japan and Europe.[52] This most extreme form of remote control in which the US government apprehended foreign citizens in other countries, incarcerated them in US camps, and then deported them as part of a prisoner exchange program shows the extent to which the United States used civilian detention and deportation as a tool of war. Remote control that began as an effort to police the borders of the nation had become by the mid-twentieth century a projection of US military might around the globe.

A Century of Remote Control

The mechanisms of remote control that were established in the early twentieth century and reinforced during the 1924–1965 period have only grown stronger in the ensuing century. In recent years, the United States has detained and tortured enemy aliens beyond the territorial limits of the nation. Since 2001 the Central Intelligence Agency's "extraordinary rendition" program and Guantanamo Bay's prison camp in Cuba demonstrate how the United States extends its military strength through remote control.[53] By 2016, US immigration officers were posted in fifteen locations in six foreign countries (Canada, Ireland, the United Arab Emirates, Bermuda, Aruba, and the Bahamas) to prescreen passengers headed to the United States. These preclearance procedures covered more than 15 percent of travelers to the United States; the government wants to expand the program by 2024 to cover 33 percent of inbound passengers.[54]

The 1965 Hart-Celler Act ended discriminatory national-origins quotas, but discriminatory visa-issuing practices continued, although more hidden from the public eye. In an immigration bureaucracy obsessed with data collection, the fact that there are no easily accessible data that reveal the rejection rate for immigrant visas by country points to one of the ways discrimination remains invisible. In 2013, consular officials initially rejected more than half of the immigrant visa applications (close to 290,000 out of a total of 473,000 applications that were approved). In most of those cases, applicants rectified the causes for denial and their visas were eventually approved, leaving about 95,000 rejections for the year. The final rejection rate was therefore about 17 percent.[55] In that same year, 204,000 aliens arriving at land, sea, and air ports of entry were deemed inadmissible.[56] Thus almost a third of immigrant exclusions occurred in consular offices and not at the borders. The rejection rates for nonimmigrant tourist and business visas in 2015 show a huge variation by country, with some countries having no rejections

(Andorra and Lichtenstein) and others having 85 percent of applications rejected (Federated States of Micronesia).[57] Although there are many factors that may be considered in approving a tourist visa, these wildly different outcomes suggest that visitors from some countries are more welcome in the United States than others. And these data do not even account for those who visit from countries in the Visa Waiver Program for whom no visa is even required, including Austria, France, Germany, and Switzerland. People entering under the Visa Waiver Program composed nineteen million or 40 percent of overseas visitors in 2013.[58]

Today, consulates continue to be the frontlines of immigration control, issuing more than 530,000 immigrant visas along with almost eleven million nonimmigrant visas in 2015.[59] Under Trump, visa denials appear to have increased, but the nonreviewability by courts of individual visa decisions is not a new development.[60] In 2015 the Supreme Court reaffirmed in *Kerry v. Din* the absolute right of consular officers to deny visas, even to a spouse of an American citizen, without needing to provide evidence to back up their reasoning. As Supreme Court Justice Antonin Scalia put it bluntly, "There is no due process to her [the spouse] under the Constitution."[61] Although the new visa quotas may have eliminated the overtly racist national-origins quotas from the 1920s, the visa process continues discrimination through a series of decisions by consular officials that are not subject to appeal or judicial review and that are at the heart of a system of remote control that the United States has built over a century.

Another way in which the equal treatment of countries for visa slots results in disproportionate restriction on particular countries can be seen by analyzing immigrant visa wait lists generated by applicants at consular posts. The family-sponsored visa quota for 2016 was 226,000, and 140,000 for employer-sponsored visas, but each country is limited to fewer than 26,000 visas per year. For Mexico, with over 1.3 million people on the wait list, it would take fifty-two years to clear the backlog, assuming no new applicants registered. The top fifteen countries with the largest waitlists are all in Latin America and Asia.[62] Given the impossibility of garnering a visa in a reasonable amount of time, millions of Mexicans and others were forced to enter illegally or overstay their visas. And many of them end up incarcerated and deported. These developments build on a long history of remote control and discrimination that the US government created at the end of the nineteenth century and consolidated during the 1924–1965 period.

Remote-control efforts at consular posts around the world erect formidable walls to legal entry, walls that are much higher for Mexico than, say, for England. When remote-control efforts fail to keep unwanted migrants out, immigration authorities deploy a punitive detention and deportation system that targets black and brown men. Although on the face of it our immigration quotas stopped favoring white northern Europeans in 1965, we can see the same Johnson-Reed Act de facto discrimination occurring today in terms of immigration enforcement. In recent years, just four countries accounted for more than 90 percent of detentions and removals: Mexico, Guatemala, Honduras, and El Salvador.[63] The 1965 immigration act did not end racist immigration restrictions; it merely shifted them onto the terrain of visa application lines and immigration enforcement practices. President Donald Trump's proposal, when he was the Republican presidential nominee, to ban all Muslim immigrants and his insinuation that Mexican immigrants are "rapists" and criminals suggests that outright racist immigration legislation is a real political possibility in our day. Although district courts on both coasts have declared Trump's blanket ban on six Muslim-majority countries unconstitutional, a narrower ban has passed Supreme Court muster.[64] The faces of the half a million immigrants in detention graphically demonstrate that racism continues in the Hart-Celler era. These incarcerated migrants are the ones who slipped through in spite of remote control. What we do not see are the millions of other potential migrants who remain trapped in their countries or in refugee camps around the world because of the effectiveness of remote control. If we could see these people, the racism of our immigration system would become crystal clear.

Notes

1. Aristide R. Zolberg, *A Nation by Design: Immigration Policy in the Fashioning of America* (New York: Harvard University Press, 2006), 9.

2. Adam McKeown, *Melancholy Order: Asian Migration and the Globalization of Borders* (New York: Columbia University Press, 2008), ch. 8.

3. There is a rich literature on the history of the passport that describes this simultaneous development of a global order and national migration control. See, particularly, John Torpey, *The Invention of the Passport: Surveillance, Citizenship and the State* (Cambridge: Cambridge University Press, 2000); see also Craig Robertson, *The Passport in America: The History of a Document* (New York: Oxford University Press, 2010).

4. Two great volumes on US-Mexico and US-Canadian borderlands history that do not deal with extraterritorial enforcement of borders are: Samuel Truett and Elliott Young, eds. *Continental Crossroads: Remapping the U.S.-Mexico Borderlands History* (Durham, N.C.: Duke University Press, 2004), and Benjamin H. Johnson and Andrew R Graybill, eds. *Bridging National Borders: Transnational and Comparative Histories* (Durham, N.C.: Duke University Press, 2010). For a history of Chinese exclusion in Canada, see Lisa Rose Mar, *Brokering Belonging: Chinese in Canada's Exclusion Era, 1885–1945* (Oxford: Oxford University Press, 2010). For a history of Chinese exclusion in Mexico, see Roberto Chao Romero, *The Chinese in Mexico, 1882–1940* (Tucson: University of Arizona Press, 2010). Two excellent histories of US immigration restrictions that focus on the US borders over global barriers are Mae Ngai, *Impossible Subjects: Illegal Aliens and the Making of Modern America* (Princeton, N.J.: Princeton University Press, 2004) and Erika Lee, *At America's Gates: Chinese Immigration during the Exclusion Era, 1882–1943* (Chapel Hill: University of North Carolina Press, 2003).

42 · ELLIOTT YOUNG

5. Libby Garland, *After They Closed the Gates: Jewish Illegal Immigration to the United States, 1921–1965* (Chicago: University of Chicago, 2014); Lee, *At America's Gates*; Claire Fox, *The Fence and the River: Culture and Politics of the U.S.-Mexico Border* (Minneapolis: University of Minnesota Press, 1999); Andrew Gyory, *Closing the Gate: Race, Politics, and the Chinese Exclusion Act* (Chapel Hill: University of North Carolina Press, 1998).

6. McKeown, *Melancholy Order*; Elizabeth Sinn, *Pacific Crossing: California Gold, Chinese Migration and the Making of Hong Kong* (Hong Kong: Hong Kong University Press, 2013); and Zolberg, *A Nation by Design*.

7. Ngai, *Impossible Subjects*, 261.

8. Deirde M. Maloney, *National Insecurities: Immigrants and U.S. Deportation Policy Since 1882* (Chapel Hill: University of North Carolina Press, 2012), 8–9.

9. Amy L. Fairchild, *Science at the Borders: Immigrant Medical Inspection and the Shaping of the Modern Industrial Labor Force* (Baltimore, Md.: Johns Hopkins University Press, 2003), 261.

10. Sinn, *Pacific Crossing*, 241–43.

11. McKeown, *Melancholy Order*, 218, 224–28.

12. Lee, *At America's Gates*, 141.

13. McKeown, *Melancholy Order*, 226–27.

14. Sinn, *Pacific Crossing*, 243–48.

15. Fairchild, *Science at the Borders*, 58.

16. Zolberg, *A Nation by Design*, 229.

17. Rupert Blue, *Annual Report of the Surgeon General of the Public Health Service for 1914* (Washington, DC: GPO, 1915), 203.

18. Fairchild, *Science at the Borders*, 59.

19. Lee, *At America's Gates*, 141. The rejection rate for South Asians reached over 54 percent between 1911 and 1915. Erika Lee and Judy Yung, *Angel Island: Immigrant Gateway to America* (Oxford: Oxford University Press, 2010), 158.

20. Roger Daniels, *Guarding the Golden Door: American Immigration Policy and Immigrants since 1882*, 1st ed. (New York: Hill and Wang, 2004), 25.

21. Kunal M. Parker, "State, Citizenship, and Territory: The Legal Construction of Immigrants in Antebellum Massachusetts," *Law and History Review* 19, no. 3 (2001): 610.

22. US Congress, "1882 Immigration Act, 47th Congress Sess. I, Chap. 376 Stat. 214," (Washington, DC: GPO, 1882), 214–15.

23. US Congress, "1891 Immigration Act, 51st Congress, Sess. II Chap. 551; 26 Stat. 1084," (Washington, DC: GPO, 1891), 1084–85.

24. Daniels, *Guarding the Golden Door*, 43–45; Bureau of Immigration and Naturalization, Department of Commerce and Labor, *Immigration Laws and Regulations of 1907* (Washington, DC: GPO, 1910); US House, "An Act to Regulate Immigration," ed. 1st Session 47th Congress (Washington, DC: GPO, 1882), 214–215; US House, "An Act to Regulate Immigration."

25. Department of Commerce and Labor, *Immigration Laws and Regulations of 1907*, 5.

26. Fairchild, *Science at the Borders*, 60–61.

27. Ibid., 61.

28. McKeown, *Melancholy Order*, 112–13.

29. Ibid., 113.

30. Amos P. Waldir, American Consulate-General, Hong Kong, to Asst. Sec. of State, July 24, 1908, NARA, RG 85, entry 9, 51881/85, box 275, p. 1–2.

31. Torpey, *Invention of the Passport*, 117–18. Robertson, *Passport in America*, 186.

32. Waldir to Asst. Sec of State, July 24, 1908, 3–4.

33. Ibid., 8–9.

34. Ibid., 9–10.

35. E. Carleton Baker, Vice Consul, Amoy, to W. W. Rockhill, American Minister, Peking, April 30, 1908, NARA, RG 85, entry 9, 51881/85, box 275.

36. Robert Lansing, Secretary of State, to President Woodrow Wilson, August 20, 1919, in Woodrow Wilson, "Continuance of the Passport-Control System," (Washington, DC: Government Printing House, 1919), 3–4.

37. Fairchild, *Science at the Borders*, 258, 272.

38. Robertson, *Passport in America*, 187, 205.

39. Fairchild, *Science at the Borders*, 258.

40. Donna R. Gabaccia, *Foreign Relations: American Immigration in Global Perspective* (Princeton, N.J.: Princeton University Press, 2012), 50, 13.

41. Ngai, *Impossible Subjects*, 101.

42. Young, *Alien Nation*, ch. 6.

43. Digest and Comment upon Report of Immigrant Inspector Marcus Braun, October 9, 1907, NARA, RG 85, entry 9, 51630/44F, box 115, p. 29.

44. Ibid.

45. Ibid., 17.

46. Trachoma, an infection of the eye that can cause blindness if not treated, was found primarily in poor communities with an inadequate water supply. The statistics that Consul Waldir lists yields an average rejection rate of 27 percent for six ships sailing May–July 1908, with some ships rejecting as many as 43 percent and others as few as 15 percent. Waldir to Asst. Sec of State, July 24, 1908, 6–7.

47. Daniels, *Guarding the Golden Door*, 25. Fairchild, *Science at the Borders*, 59–60.

48. House Report No. 350 accompanying H.R. 7995, 68th Congress, as cited in Abba P. Schwartz, "The Role of the State Department in the Administration and Enforcement of the New Immigration Law," *Annals of the American Academy of Political and Social Science* 367 (1966): 96.

49. Ibid., 98.

50. Jan Jarboe Russell, *The Train to Crystal City: FDR's Secret Prisoner Exchange Program and America's Only Family Internment Camp during World War II* (New York: Scribners, 2015), xix.

51. Russell W. Estlack, *Shattered Lives, Shattered Dreams: The Disrupted Lives of Families in America's Internment Camps* (Springville, Utah: Bonneville, 2011), 83, 162. Memorandum, British Legation, Panama City, February 10, 1942, National Archives Record Administration (NARA), RG 389, A1466J, box 13, Paolo Ottolenghi, 2–3.

52. C. Harvey Gardiner, *Pawns in a Triangle of Hate: The Peruvian Japanese and the United States* (Seattle: University of Washington Press, 1981), ch. 8.

53. Monica Hakimi, "The Council of Europe Addresses CIA Rendition and Detention Program," *American Journal of International Law* 101, no. 2 (2007); A. Naomi Paik, *Rightlessness: Testimony and Redress in U.S. Prison Camps since WWII* (Chapel Hill: University of North Carolina Press, 2016).

54. US Customs and Border Protection, "Preclearance Expansion: FY2016 Guidance for Prospective Applicants," https://www.cbp.gov/sites/default/files/assets/documents/2016-May/FY16_Preclearance_Guidance_Feb2016_05%2016%2016_final_0.pdf.

55. This rejection rate was calculated by combining two different data sets. The USCIS data lists all immigrant visas issued by foreign posts, and the Department of State's Visa Office indicates the total number of applications that were rejected and the rejections that were overcome. US Department of State, "Table 1: Immigrant and Nonimmigrant Visas Issued at Foreign Service Posts Fiscal Years 2011–2015," https://travel.state.gov/content/dam/visas/Statistics/AnnualReports/FY2015AnnualReport/FY15AnnualReport-TableI.pdf; see also US Department of State, "Report of the Visa Office 2013," (2013).

56. Office of Immigration Statistics, "Immigration Enforcement Actions: 2013," Department of Homeland Security, 2014, table 3.

57. US Department of State, "Adjusted Refusal Rate—B-Visas Only by Nationality, Fiscal Year 2015," https://travel.state.gov/content/dam/visas/Statistics/Non-Immigrant-Statistics/RefusalRates/FY15.pdf. The "adjusted" refusal rates undercount actual rejections because only the final determination within a calendar year is counted. A person may be rejected twice and gain admission on a third application, but these data will only count the final determination.

58. Lisa Seghetti, "Border Security: Immigration Inspections at Ports of Entry" (Congressional Research Service, 2015), 9.

59. State, "Table 1: Immigrant and Nonimmigrant Visas Issued at Foreign Service Posts Fiscal Years 2011–2015."

60. Dara Lind, "The Art of Denial," *Vox*, March 31, 2017, https://www.vox.com/policy-and-politics/2017/3/31/14985324/visa-denial-why-trump-change-vetting.

61. *Kerry v. Din* 576, US 15 (2015).

62. These quotas exclude immediate family members. United States Department of State, "Annual Report of Immigrant Visa Applicants in the Family-Sponsored and Employment-Based preferences Registered at the National Visa Center as of November 1, 2015," https://travel.state.gov/content/dam/visas/Statistics/Immigrant-Statistics/WaitingList/WaitingListItem_2017.pdf

63. Security, "2015 Yearbook of Immigration Statistics," table 34.

64. Michael D. Shear and Adam Liptak, "Supreme Court Takes Up Travel Ban, and Allows Parts to Go Ahead," *New York Times*, June 26, 2017, https://www.nytimes.com/2017/06/26/us/politics/supreme-court-trump-travel-ban-case.html?_r=0.

CHAPTER 2

Gatekeeping in the Tropics

US Immigration Policy and the Cuban Connection

KATHLEEN LÓPEZ

Twenty-five years ago, when the ship *Golden Venture* ran aground off the Rocka-way peninsula of Queens, New York, nearly three hundred smuggled Chinese migrants jumped into the frigid waters and attempted to reach shore. The incident, coupled with haunting media images of malnourished bodies, led to a government crackdown on illegal immigration and change in asylum procedures. Within a short time, however, smugglers developed alternate routes by small boats from Caribbean islands or by airplane using fraudulent documentation. More recently, US officials expressed concern that Chinese contract workers who come to the Caribbean for construction projects may find their way north through these ports, in addition to the more well-traveled Mexico route.[1] A long view of US immigration policy and law, however, reveals that the circum-Caribbean has long provided alternate gateways for international migrants seeking to enter to the United States.

From 1882, when Chinese laborers were banned from entering the United States, to 1924 and beyond, when the gates further closed on all Asians as well as southern and eastern Europeans, potential immigrants from these restricted groups diverted their paths elsewhere in the hemisphere. A cornerstone of US policy therefore focused on preventing other hemispheric nations with seemingly more porous boundaries, such as Canada, Mexico, and Cuba, from serving as "back doors" through which nonwhite and politically and culturally undesirable migrants could gain entry.

46 · KATHLEEN LÓPEZ

The use of neighboring countries as stepping stones to the United States—an unintended consequence of the immigration restrictions—shaped policies and practices well beyond US borders.[2] US gatekeeping strategies in the hemisphere entailed influencing immigration policy and policing its land borders shared with Canada and Mexico. Additionally, US officials confronted a web of bustling ports, jagged, unguarded coastlines, and sparsely inhabited islands that formed a murky, porous boundary surrounding its "American lake" to the south. By the early twentieth century, Latin American and Caribbean nations generally agreed to support the immigration laws of the United States, in part motivated by a desire to uphold their own sovereignty by retaining their northern neighbor as ally and business partner.[3] Immigration officials' experiences with widespread smuggling by land and sea contributed to the beginnings of a more general shift in policy, one that eventually became embodied in the preferences for certain occupational categories and the leveling of the quota system in the 1965 immigration act.

This chapter examines US domestic immigration policy and the movement of people to, within, and from the Caribbean region as a dynamic, intertwined process. The island of Cuba, ninety miles from the Florida Keys, has played a unique role in US immigration law and policy, due to geographical proximity, business and cultural ties, and shifting geopolitics. In particular, Chinese and Eastern European Jewish migrations to Cuba in the early twentieth century can be used to examine US attempts to control the policy of other hemispheric nations as well as the limits of its power to enforce effective gatekeeping.

Tropical Gatekeeping in the "American Lake"

Beginning with the Louisiana Purchase of 1803 and the Monroe Doctrine of 1823, which declared the closing of the Western Hemisphere to further colonization by European powers, the young American republic positioned itself to dictate hemispheric policy, albeit without military muscle behind its claims. However, defeat of Spain in 1898 secured the US position, resulting in the occupation of Cuba and the annexation of Puerto Rico, the Philippines, and Guam. In 1904 what became known as the "Roosevelt Corollary" to the Monroe Doctrine enabled the United States to assume the role of international police power in Latin America and the Caribbean to ensure repayment of European debt and political stability, thus protecting North American economic and strategic interests. For the next three decades, the United States intervened in Cuba, Haiti, the Dominican Republic, Mexico, Nicaragua, and Panama, taking control of the canal in 1904. The greater Caribbean became known as an "American lake" marked by economic investment, political and cultural influence, and military interventions during the first few decades of the twentieth century.

Protection of these interests and support from the region became key factors in debates on whom to accept as immigrants. In the months before the passage of the Immigration Act of 1924, when a bill that would extend immigration quotas to Latin American and Caribbean nations was under consideration, hemispheric neighbors of the United States let their disapproval be known. Such a measure, wrote the Salvadorian representative, appeared to depart from the premise that "the relations of the United States with its sister republics are above all inspired by the strong ties of interest which are born of neighborhood."[4] Cuban Ambassador Cosme de la Torriente wrote to the US Secretary of State declaring that restrictions on Cuba "might affect the commercial relations of the two countries and would greatly hamper the coming to the United States of thousands of Cuban citizens who are not immigrants."[5] The landmark Immigration Act of 1924 limited the annual number of immigrants of any nationality to 2 percent of its total population recorded in the 1890 census. The selection of 1890 as a base year effectively reduced the share of quotas for southern and eastern Europeans while maintaining preference for settlement of northern and western Europeans. In the interest of diplomacy and US business goals, the act exempted independent republics in the Western Hemisphere from the immigration quota system. This benefit extended to the Caribbean islands of Cuba, the Dominican Republic, and Haiti, while the colonial British West Indies remained under the generous quotas established for Britain.

The circum-Caribbean region, as an early site of globalization, colonization, enslavement, and migration of peoples from Europe, Africa, and Asia, is well suited to a case study on the reverberation of law and policy across borders and cultures. Since the demise of African slavery over the span of the nineteenth century, the plantation system and export economies of recently independent republics and European colonial possessions attracted migrants, both from within the Caribbean and beyond. From 1870 to 1930 large numbers of West Indian men and women left home in search of better opportunities and resources. Most Caribbean migrants moved within the region—according to the needs of US labor interests as well as their own social networks—from Barbados to the Panama Canal Zone, from Haiti and Jamaica to Cuba, and from Puerto Rico to the Dominican Republic and distant Hawai'i. Circulating alongside the working-class descendants of enslaved Africans in the region were Chinese, Japanese, Indians, Spanish, Canary Islanders, Italians, Germans, and others, forming "an ethnic mosaic of peoples and languages stretching from the eastern Caribbean into northern South America, a pattern created by cumulative, planter-sponsored in-migrations of people from throughout the world."[6] Interwoven among them were groups restricted by law from entering the United States. As migrants from Asia and Europe circulated in the Americas, so did discourses of dangerous or subversive aliens approaching US shores.

Extending Chinese Exclusion in Cuba

Even before formal exclusion from the United States, Chinese were migrating to and settling throughout Latin America and the Caribbean. From 1847 to 1874, planters and industrialists in the Spanish colony of Cuba and recently independent Peru recruited about 250,000 Chinese indentured laborers, known as "coolies," for work primarily in the sugar industry. The system of indentured labor received international attention for its abuses and ended by the 1880s. Havana's Barrio Chino and smaller towns across the island became important nodes for laborers, artisans, and peddlers, as well as transnational Chinese merchants from California and Mexico. By the early twentieth century, the Chinese population had become largely urban and commercial, with small businesses established across the island. In addition to Chinese, Cuba relied on neighboring black West Indians (Haitians and Jamaicans) to fuel the sugar economy. The largest numbers of immigrants, however, came from Spain and the Canary Islands, as Cuba continually attempted to whiten the population.

With the passage of the 1882 Chinese Exclusion Act in the United States, the Chinese had become the first group excluded on purely racial or national terms. The closing of the gates to working-class Chinese diverted potential migrants, from San Francisco south of the border to Mexico and elsewhere in Latin America and the Caribbean. The attempts to prevent Chinese from using the "back doors" of Canada, Mexico, and the Caribbean or other loopholes led to the development of modern bureaucratic and legal immigration and deportation systems.[7]

From 1899 to 1902 the US military government in Cuba laid the foundation for a political system that would support American interests, including its own immigration laws. The Platt Amendment of 1901, a condition for withdrawal of troops, assured the United States the right to intervene in Cuban affairs in order to defend "a government adequate for the protection of life, property, and individual liberty." Cuba had little choice but to comply with US policies. Just five days before the end of the US occupation government, on May 15, 1902, Military Governor Leonard Wood issued Order No. 155 of the Headquarters Division of Cuba. This document applied the immigration laws of the United States to Cuba, and, with modifications, it served as the official basis of Cuba's immigration policy through the first half of the twentieth century. Sections 7 and 8 excluded the Chinese, with the exception of those classified as merchants, students, diplomats, and tourists. Furthermore, the law prohibited the entry of contract laborers from any nation.[8]

Although the origins of anti-Chinese policies in Cuba can be found partly in this US-imposed legislation, it also stemmed from a deeply ingrained ideology among white political and intellectual elites concerning the ideal composition of a progressive and prosperous nation. Cuba looked to other Latin American countries attempting to reconcile their indigenous and African colonial heritage as models for a civilized nation, "whitened" through European immigration. The US-imposed Chinese exclusion policy in Cuba resonated with this vision, one that had been articulated by Creole elites since the early nineteenth century. The Cuban government followed with the passage of a 1906 law that allocated funding for a massive project to settle Canary Islanders and Northern Europeans.

As new immigration restrictions followed during the first few decades of the twentieth century, Chinese diplomats and merchants in Cuba continually pressed for the repeal of the 1902 ban on Chinese entry. To be placed on an equal footing with other foreigners was aligned with a rising nationalism in China and among diasporic communities and furthermore would facilitate the mobility of transnational merchants.[9] In 1909, when a Chinese diplomatic representative petitioned for lifting restrictions on Chinese entry, Cuban Commissioner of Immigration F. E. Menocal responded with a lengthy memorandum discussing economic competition, morality and hygiene, and racial difference. Significantly, he also offered diplomatic justifications for continued restrictions. His arguments demonstrate intimate knowledge of US immigration policy and a desire to use it as a model for Cuba. The Platt Amendment as a condition for independence also compelled Cuba to placate the United States in international and domestic policy. "Cuba," Menocal suggested, "should obtain laws that are, inasmuch as possible, homogenous with the American laws." On a practical level, if Cuban ports were open to Chinese immigration, the United States would surely retaliate against Cuba "every time that the Chinese come to the island as the next stop to the American coast." Menocal recommended an even more rigorous enforcement of the existing anti-Chinese law, acknowledging the high numbers of Chinese who entered falsely as merchants or students.[10]

These exclusionary immigration policies encountered opposition from Cuban and American sugar magnates, who pushed for cheap, imported labor from China and the West Indies (especially Haiti and Jamaica). In August 1917, at the outset of World War I, sugar companies won a major round in Cuban immigration policy debates with the temporary relaxation of the ban on Chinese laborers. American business interests succeeded not only in altering Cuban immigration policy (and, by default, US immigration policy), but also in making a dent in the gatekeeping abilities of the US government. Although Chinese had previously entered Cuba surreptitiously or with false documents, official records indicate that more than seventeen thousand Chinese landed between 1917 and 1924, many attracted by labor opportunities and encouraged by networks of relatives and fellow villagers, but others intending to use the island as a springboard to the United States.[11] Chinese migration to Cuba continued until the 1959 Cuban revolution, its ebb and flow linked more to social networks and economic and political conditions than to effective enforcement of immigration policy.

Jewish Immigrants and "Hotel Cuba"

If anti-Asian legislation in the United States since the nineteenth century diverted Chinese and Japanese migrants south, political and economic conditions in the interwar period propelled large numbers of Europeans to migrate to the Americas. With the new quota restrictions of the 1920s, southern and eastern European migration to Latin America and the Caribbean also increased, among them tens of thousands of Jewish people to Cuba.[12] Beginning in the early twentieth century, Sephardic Jews from Turkey and Syria had come to Cuba for political motivations. Sephardic Jews spoke Ladino, similar to Spanish, which made settlement in Cuba attractive. They became peddlers and small merchants, known for catering to lower social classes and supplying credit for consumer goods. By 1926, an estimated fifteen hundred had settled in Havana with another twenty-five hundred spread throughout Cuba.[13]

Mass Jewish migration to Cuba, however, began with Eastern Europeans fleeing political and religious repression, most after the dislocations of World War I.[14] The choice of Cuba stemmed from the passage of the US Emergency Quota Act of 1921, which drastically reduced the number of entries from each country to 3 percent of its population as recorded by the 1910 census. The act left open a loophole, though, as it permitted a change in legal status for residents of exempt nations in the Western Hemisphere. Jews from Poland, Russia, Lithuania, Romania, and Hungary learned that after residing in Cuba for a year, they could enter the United States under the exemption for Cubans. In December 1921 six migrants made the passage to Cuba, and over the next few months thousands more followed in their footsteps by staying on the island for a year before entering the United States.[15] By the following spring, though, the mandatory period of residence increased to five years.

Eastern European immigrants did not intend to settle in Cuba; rather, they chose the island as a temporary stopover, a stepping stone to US shores necessitated by the passage of new immigration restrictions. Financial assistance from Jewish organizations as well as relatives and friends in the United States encouraged this immigration. However, after a drop in the price of sugar and collapse of the Cuban economy in 1921, charitable organizations began discouraging Jewish immigration to Cuba. Still, seven thousand eastern European Jews made their way to Cuba between 1921 and 1924, taking advantage of the provision for access to the United States.[16]

In June 1923, after the second complete year of the emergency quota act, the US Commissioner of Immigration issued a report on "the growing tendency of inadmissible European aliens to attempt to enter the country surreptitiously, which in turn appears to have led to increased activities on the part of professional smugglers engaged in the business of assisting such aliens to enter over the land and water boundaries."[17] Through this clandestine immigration, the Jewish population in Cuba remained in a constant state of flux; most who had arrived between 1920 and 1923 were no longer in Cuba by 1925. According to data based on the 1,835 immigrants who registered for assistance with the Jewish Committee for Cuba, 85 percent were male, 65 percent were single, and 62 percent were between fifteen and twenty-nine years old in 1925. Of the males, half were unskilled and 20 percent were skilled, while merchants, professionals, students, and farmers made up the rest.[18] Life for the Ashkenazic Jews from eastern Europe was marked by poverty and difficulty adjusting to a different language, culture, and tropical climate. Peddling and working for other Jews in clothing factories, many just got by.[19]

The stiffening of US immigration law in 1924 made this young, transient migration flow more permanent. The 1924 law referred to birthplace rather than residence in an effort to prevent undesirables from legally using other hemispheric nations as a quick springboard to the United States. The US Consul in Cuba estimated fifteen thousand immigrants waiting in Cuba at the time of the publication of 1924 law.[20] Due to the new restriction, thousands of eastern European immigrants ended up staying in Cuba longer than anticipated or permanently; others chose a clandestine route north. In just a short time, the population of Jewish immigrants in Cuba changed drastically. A 1925 report by Harry Viteles estimated five thousand eastern European Jews in Cuba, with four thousand of them coming in 1924 alone. The investigator took note of a decrease in the number of immigrants during the second half of 1924, which he attributed in part to the new US immigration law that no longer made it possible for those remaining for one year in Cuba to enter the United States. He also credited the work of Jewish welfare organizations in the United States and abroad in deterring potential immigrants from coming to Cuba. The Joint Distribution Committee aimed to provide enough aid to alleviate the conditions, but not to make Cuba attractive as a destination for settlement. The 1925 report recommended even more propaganda to prevent further Jewish immigration to Cuba, as "difficulties of adaptation and acclimation are too great to make it desirable to select Cuba as a possible country for colonization for those Jews who cannot remain in Europe and yet cannot be admitted into the US or other countries."[21]

Despite the warnings, eastern European Jews continued to come to Cuba as a back door to its northern neighbor (around four thousand between 1925 and 1935).[22] What had begun as a temporary stay in "Hotel Cuba" turned into a more permanent settlement with the closing of US borders. As the Cuban economy recovered from the sugar crisis, many Eastern European Jews settled into Cuban society, becoming peddlers, craftsmen, and manufacturers of inexpensive shoes and clothing.[23] A 1927 *New York Times* article commented: "Now that they have had to give up all hope of entering the United States, these immigrants are learning Spanish and are preparing to become Cuban citizens. . . . The little Yosels are becoming Josés, the Marushas become Marias, the boys and girls are becoming as completely Cubanized as they would have become Americanized if it were not for the law."

Diplomacy and Policing in the Caribbean after 1924

Like the earlier Chinese exclusion act, the effects of the 1924 immigration act rippled throughout the hemisphere, including the Caribbean islands. After 1924, US hemispheric gatekeeping strategies took two forms. A diplomatic approach attempted to influence immigration policy and practice among exempt Latin American and Caribbean nations, especially nearby Cuba, which continued to serve as a stepping stone to its northern neighbor. A parallel strategy took place not in high-level meetings between US consular officials and their Cuban counterparts but on docks, at sea, and along the coastline of Florida, as immigration officials attempted to capture smugglers and their contraband. While US authorities kept Chinese on their radar, they increasingly demonstrated concern about the entry of "undesirable" and politically radical Europeans.[24]

Attempts by Europeans to enter the United States by way of Gulf Coast shores began with the first quota act of 1921. In 1922 the US Commissioner of Immigration described a new phenomenon of those not subject to "special exclusion legislation" (as the Chinese were) risking a "roundabout, expensive, and somewhat uncertain method of reaching their objective—the United States" and linked it directly with the change in the 1921 quota act. An inspector in Jacksonville reported that in addition to Chinese, there were continual attempts to smuggle Europeans from the West Indies, and especially Cuba, as "a great many aliens during the past 12 months migrated to Cuba on the assumption that when they had lived there one year they would be exempt from the quota act." With the new requirement of a five-year residency period, Europeans were no longer willing to wait.[25] The US Commissioner of Immigration described smuggling between Cuba and the Florida coastline as "having assumed alarming proportions" and sent two officials to each place for a special investigation into the situation. He recommended increased financial resources and cooperation with other government officials to effectively meet the challenges posed by the smuggling machinery: "The forces of the other side are well organized and financed; the Government's should be, else its efforts will be pitiably weak and ineffective."[26]

In 1922 the US Commissioner of Immigration reported thirty thousand Chinese in Cuba, many of whom had entered with the intention of "making their way to near-by inaccessible and unguarded points on the Florida coast and entering surreptitiously." The report painted a dismal portrait of unemployed Chinese in Cuba and of Havana as a hub for "smuggling of aliens of all classes, narcotics, and whisky to points on the Florida coast, and even to points on our coast line more distant, as far north as New York and west as far as New Orleans." Boats in Havana and other harbors were easily available and could carry from twenty to forty or fifty people. "Chinese aliens are willing to pay anywhere from $500 to $1,000 to be smuggled across and into the United States, and aliens of other nationalities from $100 to $200."[27] The well-organized networks extended from south China ports to the Havana harbor and other Cuban towns. Immigration scandals throughout the 1920s involved not only labor recruiters and smugglers but also prominent Chinese transnational merchants and community leaders, as well as representatives of the Cuban and Chinese governments (up until 1924 the Chinese government assumed responsibility for certifying nonlaborers as qualified to immigrate).[28] In addition to the Chinese, the investigators also focused on the new flows of thousands of Europeans through Cuba (some continuing on to Mexico to cross by land).

Almost a year after the passage of the 1924 act, the *New York Times* featured an article on the international industry that had sprung up around the smuggling of substances and migrants, focusing on new problems that had arisen from the quota system. Secretary J. J. Davis of the Department of Labor reported: "They are huddled in the dark holds of smugglers' vessels which ply from the islands of the Caribbean Sea with illicit rum and vile narcotic drugs. They steal across our vast expanse of land border; they come by railroad, automobile and airplane." The report described interlacing smuggling rings coordinated by heads who "manage with one hand the army of runners who round up the aliens in the slum and immigrant districts of Havana, and with the other the transportation facilities, as well as the receiving machinery in the States." The sophisticated industry included sliding fee scales for different categories of passage and of migrants. Women could cross from the Florida Straits as "wives" of officers on freight and passenger ships from Cuba for fees of $450 to $500, which included rail transportation into the US interior. Passage by schooner was the least expensive, for $100 to $180. This kind of transport, in which within a few hours "fast motorboats small enough to operate from out-of-the-way points on the Cuban coast . . . dive into remote landings along the serried coast of Florida," could easily go undetected by US Coast Guard. With ten or twenty migrants per boat, it could be a profitable business, but it carried high risk. Smugglers received the highest fees—from $700 to $1,000—for Chinese "because of the ease with which they can be spotted." If searched, smugglers were known to abandon the migrants in their charge, as in the case where inspectors discovered the body of a Chinese in the furnace.[29]

People seeking to migrate waited for opportunities on the multitude of large steamships circumnavigating Caribbean and American ports. In May 1928 immigration officials discovered stowaways on three ships from the Caribbean in a week. In one instance, inspectors found eight stowaways underneath the engine room floor gratings of the United Fruit Company ship *Manaqui* when it docked on the East River of New York City after stops in ports in Colombia, Panama, and Jamaica. The migrants—four Spaniards, three Syrians, and one Portuguese (all from restricted groups)—had been hidden for twelve days, yet they appeared to be hydrated and well fed. Inspectors routinely searched all ships from these Caribbean ports of South and Central America.[30]

Besides the dark underside of the smuggling business, the May 1925 report detailed the unintended effect of the new immigration policy in overwhelming consular offices abroad. The State Department's "remote control" function in screening potential immigrants *before* their arrival in the United States became more efficient by the 1920s.[31] Still, deciding who could come in under the family provisions clause proved time-consuming and generated long waiting lists. Wives of men who had become citizens and their children under age eighteen were permitted to enter as nonquota immigrants. Deportations were also cumbersome and costly. One investigator estimated the number of migrants smuggled through Cuba alone to be ten thousand annually.

US government officials' assessment of the situation indicated disagreement with the basic premise of exempting hemispheric nations from the quota system, a stance that arose from the increased problems of smuggling and stowaways since the passage of the 1924 act. The labor secretary advocated that New World countries should fall under the quota rule in order to simplify the administration of the law. Both the labor secretary and Commissioner General of Immigration W. W. Husband thought that the occupational needs of the nation should be the paramount criteria for admission, rather than a "first come, first served" policy for granting visas. As he put it, "A shoe string peddler bound for the crowded east side of New York gets a visa if he applies first, even though it means denying a splendid stonecutter the right to emigrate to Vermont, where his work would fill a real need."[32] This kind of preferred status for particular occupational categories and the equalization of the quota system eventually became embodied in the 1965 immigration act.

In the meantime, US officials who were charged with upholding the quota act regarded the new influxes of Europeans as a threat and at a diplomatic level attempted to mold Cuba's immigration policy in order to prevent clandestine entry. In general, Cuban officials demonstrated a willingness to collaborate with their American counterparts in stemming the tide of smuggled immigrants. An examination of diplomatic correspondence, however, reveals Cuba's ability to negotiate agreements that coincided with its own shifting interests and ideology, even while under the constraints of the Platt Amendment.

In the case of the Chinese, after the sugar boom of the early 1920s, Cuba returned to a US-style race-based immigration policy. Since 1902, Chinese diplomats had pressed for a more general ban on contract labor, one that did not single out Chinese and would not affect the coming and going of Chinese transnational merchants. In return, the Chinese government promised to regulate emigration from south China ports. Despite these efforts, in May 1924 Cuba issued its most restrictive anti-Chinese policy to date—a ban on all Chinese except members of the diplomatic service.[33]

However, Cuba was not willing to issue an outright ban on European migrants whose intention may have been to continue to the United States. The Cuban government generally maintained an open-door immigration policy toward non-Chinese through the administration of President Gerardo Machado from 1925 to 1933. While the Cuban government collaborated with US authorities in suppressing contraband immigration and regulating naturalization, it did not cede to all US demands, especially the directive to distinguish between temporary and permanent migrants. Rather, Cuba's longstanding position as an immigrant-receiving nation shifted with the fluctuations in the sugar industry beginning in the mid-1920s, the global economic crisis of the 1930s, and related nativist movements.[34]

An example of Cuba's insistence on upholding its own immigration policies can be found during the extensive negotiations in 1925 for treaties with the United States on consular rights, extradition, and smuggling.[35] In February US Secretary of State Charles Hughes wrote to Enoch Crowder, the ambassador in Cuba, to alert him to the extensive smuggling operations from Cuba of "intoxicating liquors" as well as "narcotics, aliens and goods subject to the payment of customs charges in the United States." He proposed an agreement with Cuba similar to one signed in 1924 by the United States and Canada. The state department wanted Cuban authorities to exercise more stringent surveillance over clearances of vessels and their cargoes.[36]

As Margalit Bejarano notes, US representatives in Havana began to delineate two kinds of immigrants in Cuba: those such as Spanish, Haitians, and Jamaicans attracted by economic pull factors in the sugar industry, and those mostly from eastern Europe and the Middle East who chose Cuba as a temporary destination in order to evade the US quota laws. In March 1925 the American ambassador echoed popular Cuban discourse with his positive view of Spaniards, the largest group of foreigners in Cuba who were thought to assimilate well and contribute to the island's economic and cultural life. Migrants from the second group, however, were viewed as a threat to US immigration policy.[37]

In 1925 a new problem related to the US quota act crossed the radar of Cuban immigration officials. United States authorities had denied entry to five foreigners coming through Mexico (four Italians and one Portuguese) but allowed them to purchase a ticket aboard the *Chalmette* from New Orleans to Cuba. Cuban immigration officials admitted the five, who arrived within the boundaries of Cuban law. Yet the case brought to the surface the critical question of how to proceed should this trend continue and highlights the circular nature of hemispheric migration in the era of exclusion. The Cuban Commissioner of Immigration recommended that the US government not permit such foreigners to embark for Cuba, since they were likely only choosing the island with the intention of re-entering the United States clandestinely. In November the Cuban Secretary of the Treasury submitted a report to the Cuban president recommending that existing Cuban immigration law be revised to address cases of those who had been turned away from the United States.[38]

It took some time for the United States to gain Cuba's help in supporting its immigration law. Negotiations stalled during the administrative transition that brought Cuban President Gerardo Machado to power in May 1925. Throughout the following fall, as the US ambassador was urged to expedite the treaty with Cuba on smuggling, points of difference emerged on issues such as terminology and translation.[39] But in one substantive area Cuba prioritized its own immigration policy toward Europeans. On November 3, 1925, US Ambassador Enoch Crowder wrote to the Secretary of State: "In general I think that the Cuban Government has shown a sincere spirit of good-will in the negotiations, but I am not certain that all of their proposals will be entirely suitable to conditions prevailing in the United States." Crowder emphasized that the first twelve articles of the Cuban draft corresponded to provisions of the American draft. The sticking point was article 5 of the US draft "to the effect that the High Contracting Parties would agree to refuse admission to aliens seeking entry into their territory when there was reason to suspect that such aliens were endeavoring to enter said territory for the purpose of subsequently effecting unlawful entry into the territory of the other High Contracting Party."[40] This point is significant, as it demonstrates Cuba's unwillingness to refuse entry based solely on an individual's intent to enter the United States or to differentiate between temporary as opposed to permanent immigrant status.

In negotiations for a treaty to prevent smuggling, Cuban representatives also insisted on reciprocity with regard to the right to board, inspect, and confiscate goods on Cuban ships—a right that the United States initially was unwilling to grant. A legal adviser to the Cuban government defended Cuba's stance by evoking legendary independence patriot José Martí's words on the nation's need for dignity and respect within the international community. United States officials ultimately conceded to Cuba on key points in a set of treaties signed in 1926. The treaty for the suppression of smuggling signed on March 11, 1926, covered alcohol, drugs, general goods subject to customs tax, as well as illegal aliens.[41] The extended discussions and points of compromise leading to the treaty reveal how smaller Latin American

Gatekeeping in the Tropics • 57

and Caribbean governments successfully negotiated with the United States, even as they remained under the constraints of the northern neighbor's economic and political influence.

Nativist Movements and World War II

In the 1930s, growing nativist and labor movements, global depression, and continued struggles for sovereignty in the face of US domination led to an increase in restrictive immigration measures across Latin America and the Caribbean. Official government discourse in both the United States and Cuba equated immigrants, and eastern Europeans in particular, with political subversion. During the rule of President Gerardo Machado, labor organizations were suppressed, and several immigrants with links to the Cuban Communist Party (founded in 1925)—among them Chinese and Jews—were imprisoned or deported.[42]

Nativist labor legislation went hand in hand with more restrictive immigration policy in Cuba. Given the ties between Cuba and the United States, the *New York Times* reported on a bill under consideration by the Cuban congress in 1931 to curb immigration. The bill proposed unrestricted Spanish and Dominican entry (Spanish-speaking Dominicans were desired as seasonal laborers for the sugar industry). Entries from Haiti, British Jamaica, and French Martinique would be limited to only ten per year, while Germans, Belgians, French, Dutch, English, Italians, Swiss, and Japanese would be capped at two hundred. The Cuban government had recorded 75,593 immigrants by the end of 1930 and emphasized that thousands of all nationalities who had failed to enter the United States were now unemployed on the island.[43]

The tighter immigration restrictions of the 1930s, based on Cuba's social and economic needs, coincided with US interests. The US Consul General in Havana confidentially reported that a $200 deposit requirement for immigrants resulted from his extensive consultation with the Cuban immigration commissioner, in an effort to deter those who upon arrival in Cuba marry US citizens or solicit US visas. Cuban congress debated several proposals for limiting or suspending immigration, including the imposition of quotas and even the suspension of all immigration for two years. Although none of these were enacted, they reflect the mobilization of Cuban society in defense of native workers and previewed the stricter labor and immigration laws after the revolutionary government of 1933. Under the short-lived populist administration in Cuba, the passage of the Nationalization of Labor law in 1933 required 50 percent of all workers in agricultural, industrial, and commercial enterprises to be Cuban-born. Many immigrants responded to the economic depression by returning to Spain, China, and elsewhere. Others applied for citizenship, especially after the 50 percent quota encompassed naturalized citizens in a 1936 adjustment to the labor law. The law also reinforced the occupational role of immigrants such as Chinese and Jews as small entrepreneurs. A 1937 law required immigrants entering Cuba to deposit a bond of $500, and visas would be granted only to immigrant settlers who would contribute in a positive manner to the nation's development.[44]

The Second World War brought shifts in international alignments and adjustments to immigration policies and practices in the hemisphere. Nazi persecution led to another wave of Jewish immigration to Cuba and elsewhere in Latin America, among them wartime refugees and postwar survivors. Oppressed European Jewish populations began to emigrate in large numbers beginning in 1933. They encountered obstacles not only from immigration quotas but also in the form of a literacy test for potential emigrants older than sixteen. Some US consular officials in Havana worked within the bureaucratic machinery to ensure that refugees cleared these hurdles. Niles W. Bond, who served as a consular officer from 1939 to 1940, recalls a woman who was unable to read the standard literacy examination cards in Yiddish or Hebrew supplied by the office. Yet the migrant insisted that she could read. Bond's secretary (an Irish woman who happened to know Yiddish) procured a Yiddish Jewish newspaper from the immigrant neighborhood in Havana. The woman proceeded to read the newspaper (material that was more familiar to her than the Shakespearean and Biblical quotations on the cards), and Bond certified her as being able to read. When a Miami official later declared her illiterate, Bond defended her case so that she could remain in the United States.[45]

Jewish organizations in the United States continued to lobby other countries that could serve as a safe haven. The Joint Distribution Committee in New York formed the Jewish Relief Committee in Havana to aid war refugees. Cuba admitted them on a tourist visa, thus bypassing existing immigration restrictions. The US consulate in Havana made use of visas under the quota allocated to Germans. From 1937 until the end of the war, most Jews entering Cuba came from Germany and Poland. (About seven thousand total from twenty-five countries registered with the Joint Distribution Committee, and another thousand came from the United States as tourists to obtain visas from the US Consul in Havana). During the war, the overwhelming majority of these refugees remigrated to the United States (and a small number to Mexico).[46]

As occurred elsewhere in the region, the visible presence of German Jewish war refugees in Cuba generated anti-Semitism among different sectors of the population. Spanish merchants and other influential groups in Cuba demanded an end to the immigration. At the July 1938 Conference of Evian, Cuba declared that it would assist with the refugees, but only in accordance with existing legislation and while maintaining the national interest. Almost a year after the Evian conference, the shift in Cuba from welcoming haven to gatekeeper of undesirables dramatically played out on the world stage when the ship *St. Louis* was turned away from the port of Havana. It wandered Caribbean waters for several days before departing back to Europe on June 6, 1939, with more than nine hundred passengers. United States and Cuban authorities signaled a message that their respective immigration laws were not to be compromised, even to offer a safe haven. However, with the new presidency of Fulgencio Batista in 1940, the Cuban administration overlooked immigration policy and issued visas to large numbers of European Jews fleeing persecution.[47]

The Path to 1965 and the Primacy of Politics

Over the course of the twentieth century, Latin American and Caribbean nations sought to assert and defend their sovereignty in the shadow of the colossal power to the north. Immigration gatekeeping became one way to define modern national identities, even while acquiescing to US policies. Elliott Young's comment about hemispheric nations in the early twentieth century can aptly be applied to the Americas today: "Politicians, journalists, and intellectuals increasingly began to equate the strength of a nation with its ability to manage its borders against a seemingly ever-changing and always threatening enemy: the illegal alien."[48] In the years surrounding the passage of the US Immigration Act of 1924, government reports were dominated by two groups—Chinese and eastern Europeans—who used Cuba as a back door to US shores. The intricate networks of Chinese in port cities across the Americas demonstrate the historical roots and routes of transnational clandestine border crossing by land and sea since the passage of the 1882 exclusion act. And the unprecedented waves of Europeans to Cuba in the decades after 1924 challenge modern-day politicized assumptions about *illegality* as a recent phenomenon that only involves migrants from Asia, Africa, the Middle East, and Latin America and the Caribbean.[49]

Like the United States, Cuba in the early twentieth century was an immigrant-receiving and gatekeeping nation. Taking cues from its northern neighbor, Cuba generally supported US immigration policies. After all, Cubans did not want to risk losing the benefit of traveling freely to the United States, whether it be for work, school, investment, tourism, or shopping. However, Cuba's acceptance of US directives was neither complete nor unquestioned. The relatively marginal consequence of US policy on halting undesirable immigration to Cuba was further subverted by rampant smuggling operations, ineffective border control, corruption, and organizing within migrant communities.

As David FitzGerald and David Cook-Martín demonstrate in chapter 4 of this volume, debates since 1924 on quota exemptions reveal the shifting geopolitical factors that underlay the eventual passage of the US Immigration and Nationality

Act of 1965. World War II proved to be a turning point in hemispheric immigration history, as US policy met with domestic and international challenges. In the 1930s and 1940s, several Latin American countries ended restrictions on immigration of particular national and racial groups. Cuba, which in 1902 had accepted the US-mandated Chinese exclusion policy, overturned it in 1942. The United States did not repeal it until the following year, in 1943, and, even then, with a quota of only 105. The across-the-board removal of race-based restrictions among Latin America and Caribbean nations began decades before the shift in US policy. Latin American immigrant-receiving countries (such as Argentina, Brazil, Cuba, and Mexico) came to the consensus that gatekeeping policy should be consistent with principles of equality governing modern nations.[50]

In the Cold War context, strategic relations with other nations in the Americas remained paramount. As in 1924, the 1952 McCarran-Walter Act upheld the concept that immigration quotas were incompatible with good-neighbor foreign policy objectives. Debates about quotas for Western Hemisphere nations during the 1950s and 1960s reveal resistance to admission of people from Latin America and the Caribbean into the United States. Liberals argued that the establishment of a uniform global policy would put these nations on an equal footing with others. Sociologists and demographers reported an increase in population in the region, and conservatives warned of US borders being inundated by migrants from the south should the nonquota policy remain. The *New York Times* editorialized that immigrant quotas could serve as a safeguard, noting Britain's recently erected barriers against Caribbean migration as something to emulate. Quotas would also limit the immigration of Asians residing in Latin America and the Caribbean, which by midcentury was substantial.[51]

In the wake of the Cuban Revolution of 1959, the US welcomed the largely white, upper- and middle-class Cubans fleeing communism. Ironically, among these refugees were the same Chinese and Jews (or their Cuban-born children) who had been denied entry to the United States after the 1924 immigration act.[52] Under the Cuban Adjustment Act of 1966, Cubans seeking to enter the United States who reached a port of entry—by any means—and passed an inspection could apply for legal permanent residence. Cubans thereby held special status under US immigration law. Agreements between the United States and Cuba in 1994 and 1995 modified the Cuban Adjustment Act to establish what became known as the "wet-foot, dry-foot" policy, under which Cubans intercepted at sea were returned to the island, but those who reached land were permitted to stay.

Even with the dismantling of the nation-based quota system in 1965, the persistence of migrant routes and practices attests to the limits of law and policy. As they did in the early twentieth century, migrants from around the world continue to use Caribbean port cities as back doors to the United States or Canada. President

Barack Obama's December 17, 2014, announcement on the normalization of relations with Cuba met with euphoric, if cautious, celebration on the island. It also generated a spike in unauthorized Cuban emigration among those who feared a reversal of their preferential immigration status. In fiscal year 2014, 24,278 Cubans entered the United States through ports of entry, followed by 43,159 in fiscal year 2015 (a 78 percent increase) and 56,406 in fiscal year 2016 (a 31 percent increase). As they had in the past, Cuban migrants attempted to reach US borders by sea—many on makeshift rafts—or by land in a roundabout way through Central America and Mexico. Others flew to Ecuador, which permitted Cuban entry without a visa. As Central American nations attempt to halt this flow, however, some Cubans became stranded.[53] On January 12, 2017, during the last days of his administration, President Obama announced the end of the "wet foot, dry foot" policy as part of a continued path toward normalization of US-Cuba relations. While the long-term effects of this reversal remain to be seen, it immediately resulted in the returning of Cuban nationals from hemispheric countries and a reduction in the number of Cubans attempting the risky journey to US shores.[54]

Such shifts in migration patterns—whether stemming from the restrictive quota acts almost a century ago, the government crackdown after the 1993 *Golden Venture* incident, or the ongoing changes in US policy toward Cubans—all attest to the interconnections between US law and international migrant practice and the necessity of adopting a hemispheric frame for understanding the reverberations of immigration policy and reform.

Notes

1. Ashley Dunn, "After Crackdown, Smugglers of Chinese Find New Routes," *New York Times*, November 1, 1994; Anthony M. Destefano, "1993 Ship Grounding Affected Immigration Policy," *Newsday*, June 1, 2013, www.newsday.com; Jacqueline Mazza, "Chinese Migration to Latin America and the Caribbean," *The Dialogue*, October 2016, 8; Inter-American Dialogue, www.thedialogue.org.

2. For an in-depth analysis of immigration policies across the Americas, see David Scott FitzGerald and David Cook-Martín, *Culling the Masses: The Democratic Origins of Racist Immigration Policy in the Americas* (Cambridge, Mass.: Harvard University Press, 2014).

3. The decision to accept US policy came when it aligned with Latin American nations' own interests. Elliott Young points out that after 1882, when the United States solicited Mexico's assistance in preventing Chinese from crossing the southern border into US territory, Mexico rejected the treaty on the basis of its own 1857 constitution that upheld the right of immigration, emigration, and transit: "the absolute freedom of movement into, through, and out of the country regardless of race or nationality." In the 1920s and 1930s, however, Chinese exclusion and expulsion resonated with a Mexican revolutionary *mestizo* national identity. Young, *Alien Nation: Chinese Migration in the Americas from the Coolie Era through WWII* (Chapel Hill: University of North Carolina Press, 2014), 99–101.

62 · KATHLEEN LÓPEZ

4. Letter from Héctor David Castro to US Secretary of State, January 4, 1924. US Department of State, *Papers Relating to the Foreign Relations of the United States* [hereafter *FRUS*], 1924 (US GPO, 1924), 1:212.

5. Letter from Cosme de la Torriente to US Secretary of State, January 14, 1924, *FRUS*, 1924, 1:212–13.

6. Bonham C. Richardson, "Caribbean Migrations, 1838–1985," in *The Modern Caribbean*, ed. Franklin W. Knight and Colin A. Palmer (Chapel Hill: University of North Carolina Press, 1989), 208–9; Lara Putnam, *Radical Moves: Caribbean Migrants and the Politics of Race in the Jazz Age* (Chapel Hill: University of North Carolina Press, 2013).

7. Robert Chao Romero, "Transnational Chinese Immigrant Smuggling to the United States via Mexico and Cuba, 1882–1916," *Amerasia Journal* 30, no. 3 (2004): 1–16; Erika Lee, "Orientalisms in the Americas: A Hemispheric Approach to Asian American History," *Journal of Asian American Studies* 8, no. 3 (2005): 235–56; Grace Peña Delgado, *Making the Chinese Mexican: Global Migration, Localism, and Exclusion in the US-Mexico Borderlands* (Stanford, Calif.: Stanford University Press, 2012); Young, *Alien Nation*.

8. Duvon Clough Corbitt, "Immigration in Cuba," *Hispanic American Historical Review* 22, no. 2 (1942): 280–308.

9. For a comparison of efforts by Chinese elites in Cuba, Peru, and Mexico to bolster their status as foreign residents, see Kathleen López, "In Search of Legitimacy: Chinese Immigrants and Latin American Nation Building," in *Immigration and National Identities in Latin America 1850–1950*, ed. Nicola Foote and Michael Goebel (Gainesville: University Press of Florida, 2014), 182–204.

10. Archivo Nacional de Cuba, Secretaría de la Presidencia, leg. 121, exp. 83 (1909–1921).

11. Numerous records from US immigration officials deal with the clandestine entry of Chinese and others in the decades leading up to 1924. See, for example, United States National Archives, RG 85 Records of the Immigration and Naturalization Service, Segregated Chinese Records, box 3, folder 309, entry 135, Chinese Smuggling File, 1914–ca. 1921.

12. For a comprehensive treatment of the effect of the quota restrictions on Jews seeking to come to the United States, see Libby Garland, *After They Closed the Gates: Jewish Illegal Immigration to the United States, 1921–1965* (Chicago: University of Chicago Press, 2014). A small number of American Jews with capital settled in Cuba for commercial opportunities before 1898 (numbering up to 150 by World War I and 300 by the Cuban Revolution of 1959). They generally distanced themselves from the later waves of Jewish immigrants in the 1920s. Sender M. Kaplan, Raúl Moncarz, and Julio Steinberg, "Jewish Emigrants to Cuba: 1898–1960," *International Migration* 28, no. 3 (1990): 295–310.

13. Margalit Bejarano, "The Jewish Community of Cuba: Between Continuity and Extinction," *Jewish Political Studies Review* 3, nos. 1–2 (1991): 115–40, esp. 120.

14. For overviews of the different groups of Jewish migrants to Cuba, see Kaplan, Moncarz, and Steinberg, "Jewish Emigrants to Cuba," and Bejarano, "Jewish Community of Cuba." For an in-depth ethno-history of Jewish immigrants in Cuba, see Robert Levine, *Tropical Diaspora: The Jewish Experience in Cuba* (Gainesville: University Press of Florida, 1993).

15. "Barred Here, Jews Settle Cuba Colony," *New York Times*, February 20, 1927.

16. Harry Viteles, *Report on the Status of the Jewish Immigrants in Cuba* (New York: Joint Distribution Committee, 1925), 5–6.

Gatekeeping in the Tropics • 63

17. Bureau of Immigration. *Annual Report of the Commissioner General of Immigration* (1923), 1.

18. Viteles, *Report on the Status*.

19. Levine, *Tropical Diaspora*.

20. Bejarano, "La inmigración a Cuba y la política migratoria de los EE.UU. (1902–1933)." *Estudios Interdisciplinarios de América Latina y el Caribe* 4, no. 2 (1993).

21. Viteles, *Report on the Status*, 41–46, 5–6.

22. Kaplan, Moncarz, and Steinberg, "Jewish Emigrants to Cuba," 299.

23. Bejarano, "Jewish Community of Cuba," 121–22.

24. FitzGerald and Cook-Martín, *Culling the Masses*, 202–10.

25. A joint resolution extended the quota act to two years from June 30, 1922, and increased to five years the time "to acquire exemption in contiguous and neighboring countries and adjacent islands."

26. Bureau of Immigration, *Annual Report of the Commissioner General of Immigration to the Secretary of Labor* (Washington, DC: GPO, 1922), 15–17. That year, among the 4,366 deportees were 411 Chinese, 214 Hebrew, 373 Southern Italian, 113 Japanese, and 879 Mexican.

27. Bureau of Immigration, *Annual Report* (1922), 15–16.

28. Miriam Herrera Jerez and Mario Castillo Santana, *De la memoria a la vida pública: Identidades, espacios y jerarquías de los chinos en La Habana republicana (1902–1968)* (Havana: Centro de Investigación y Desarrollo de la Cultura Cubana Juan Marinello, 2003).

29. "Immigration Law Evaded by Smugglers of Aliens," *New York Times*, May 17, 1925.

30. "'Land Ho!' Is Mirage for Eight Stowaways," *New York Times*, May 10, 1928.

31. For changes over time in the regulation of immigration from abroad, see Aristide R. Zolberg, *A Nation by Design: Immigration Policy in the Fashioning of America* (Cambridge, Mass.: Harvard University Press, 2006) and Elliott Young's chapter 1 in this volume.

32. "Immigration Law Evaded by Smugglers of Aliens," *New York Times*, May 17, 1925.

33. FitzGerald and Cook-Martín, *Culling the Masses*, 202.

34. Bejarano, "La inmigración a Cuba," 1993.

35. For negotiations between the United States and Cuba on these issues, see *FRUS* 1925, 2:14–31.

36. The US ambassador in Mexico City was directed to conclude a similar treaty with Mexico. By July 1925 Mexico and the United States agreed upon a draft that the Secretary of State considered "more advantageous" than the Canadian treaty. US Secretary of State to Enoch Crowder, February 2, 1925, *FRUS* 1925, 2:16–17.

37. Bejarano, "La inmigración a Cuba," 1993.

38. Archivo Nacional de Cuba, Secretaría de la Presidencia, leg. 115, exp. 106 (1925).

39. Apparently, Cuba stalled the smuggling treaties until the United States considered Cuban wishes regarding the consular treaties as well as a proposal for an agreement on "false indications of Cuban origin" that would restrict usage in the United States of the words "Cuba" "Habana" "Vuelta Abajo" and "any other geographical term of the Republic of Cuba." Enoch Crowder to US Secretary of State, January 15, 1926; Joseph C. Grew to Enoch Crowder, January 29, 1926. *FRUS*, 1926, vol. 2:37.

40. *FRUS*, 1925, 2:29.

41. *FRUS*, 1926, vol. 2:23–27. Similar agreements to prevent alcohol smuggling with Britain, Norway, Denmark, Germany, Sweden, Italy, Panama, and the Netherlands included the clause that the Cuban representatives rejected. Eduardo Sáenz Rovner, *The Cuban Connection: Drug Trafficking, Smuggling, and Gambling in Cuba from the 1920s to the Revolution*, trans. Russ Davidson (Chapel Hill: University of North Carolina Press, 2009), 23.

42. Among them were Fabio Grobart, who became a key figure in Cuba's communist movement when he returned, and José Wong, who ran an underground Chinese communist newspaper and was murdered in jail.

43. "Cuba Plans a Curb on the Influx of Aliens," *New York Times*, July 5, 1931.

44. Bejarano, "La inmigración a Cuba," 1993; Kathleen López, *Chinese Cubans: A Transnational History* (Chapel Hill: University of North Carolina Press, 2013), ch. 7.

45. Charles Stuart Kennedy and Niles W. Bond, *Interview with Niles W. Bond*, 1998, "Manuscript/Mixed Material," retrieved from the Library of Congress, https://www.loc.gov/item/mfdipbib000114.

46. Kaplan, Moncarz, and Steinberg, "Jewish Emigrants to Cuba," 301. Besides offering legal assistance and moral support, the Jewish Joint Distribution Committee administered financial assistance of $20 monthly per couple and $5 for each dependent.

47. Ibid., 302. In neighboring Dominican Republic, dictator Rafael Trujillo tempered US-influenced exclusion of Asians and welcomed Jews during World War II. Jewish and later Japanese settlement coincided with Trujillo's plans for promoting a positive public image while continuing to "whiten" and "Europeanize" the Dominican nation, especially in the wake of the 1937 massacre of Haitians and people of Haitian descent on the border. While Trujillo declared he would admit one hundred thousand Jews, only about seven hundred settled in Sosúa. Allen Wells, *Tropical Zion: General Trujillo, FDR, and the Jews of Sosúa* (Durham, N.C.: Duke University Press, 2009).

48. Young, *Alien Nation*, 131.

49. Libby Garland notes that Jews and other Europeans ultimately became delinked from assumptions about illegal immigration, in part through the political efforts of Jewish American citizens. Garland, *After They Closed the Gates*.

50. FitzGerald and Cook-Martín, *Culling the Masses* and this volume.

51. Mae N. Ngai, *Impossible Subjects: Illegal Aliens and the Making of Modern America* (Princeton, N.J.: Princeton University Press, 2004), 254–58.

52. Levine, *Tropical Diaspora*; Caroline Bettinger-López, *Cuban-Jewish Journeys: Searching for Identity, Home, and History in Miami* (Knoxville: University of Tennessee Press, 2000); López, *Chinese Cubans*, ch. 8.

53. Jens Manuel Krogstad, "Surge in Cuban Immigration to US Continued through 2016," *Pew Research Center* (January 13, 2017), www.pewresearch.org.

54. In a public statement harking back to the Cold War era, on June 17, 2017, President Donald Trump announced the reversal of some of these policy changes; however, embassies remain open and the "wet foot, dry foot" policy has not been reinstated. The longstanding economic embargo remains in effect.

CHAPTER 3

Contested Terrain

Debating Refugee Admissions in the Cold War

LAURA MADOKORO

In January 2016 the *New York Times Magazine* published a feature story by Elizabeth Griswold about the admission of Syrian refugees, or lack thereof, to the United States. Titled "Why Is It So Difficult for Syrian Refugees to Get into the US?" the piece explored the limited commitments made by the Obama administration to refugees from Syria and the labyrinth of screening measures and security obstacles that prospective migrants were encountering. The subtext was that the American response to migrants fleeing the civil war in Syria was atypical and belied the traditional openness of the United States to refugees from around the world. Yet an examination of the history of refugee admissions to the United States during the Cold War suggests instead that the debate about Syrian refugees was, in fact, quite representative of historic discussions around welcoming refugees as potential citizens.

Debates about whether to assist certain groups of refugees—and how best to do so—characterized discussions among US government officials and religious and secular humanitarians in the postwar period, especially prior to the milestone year of 1965. These conversations became increasingly politicized during the tension-seeped days of the early Cold War.[1] Supporters of refugee admissions argued their case by insisting alternatively on reforms to US immigration laws or the provision of financial and social resources to orchestrate the resettlement of refugees across borders. Although religious and secular humanitarians generally framed their arguments in terms of both US responsibility and the potential benefits that refugee admissions portended, there was no consensus among supporters about whether admitting or resettling refugees was in fact the most desirable or effective form of humanitarian assistance.

Differences in opinion among advocates, and evolving notions about what constituted appropriate assistance and what such help signified, influenced the manner in which appeals to officials in Washington were formulated and pursued. This, in turn, shaped the legal landscape in which refugee admissions and reforms to American immigration law were developed prior to 1965. The question of whether assisting migrants through admission opportunities was a viable, and helpful, contribution to humanitarian crises around the world shaped the context in which proponents advanced proposals about refugees throughout the Cold War, particularly those traditionally marginalized in US immigration policy, and ultimately shaped the modest refugee reforms embodied in the 1965 Immigration and Nationality Act.

The 1965 act removed the national quotas that had shaped migrant admissions to the United States since 1924. In signing the act into law, President Lyndon Johnson declared that it "repaired a very deep and painful flaw in the fabric of American justice."[2] Indeed, the 1965 Act has been roundly celebrated for putting an end to race-based discrimination. Recent scholarship, however, has pointed to the limitations of the legislation in dismantling exclusionary structures.[3] This is particularly true of refugee admissions.[4] Until 1965, refugee admissions were developed in an ad hoc manner, and the US government relied heavily on religious groups and NGOs to provide material, social, and spiritual support to new arrivals.[5] The 1965 amendments created a slight opening for refugees as a distinct category of migrants, allowing for the admission of a maximum of 10,200 refugees per year. Preference was given to those with relatives in the United States.[6] The moderate changes expressed in the 1965 Immigration and Nationality Act resulted from the differing, and sometimes conflicting, visions that various religious and secular organizations advanced as their ideas and strategies about how best to assist the world's refugees evolved throughout the Cold War. Exploring how arguments put forward by religious groups and NGOs, including the American Jewish Committee (AJC), the National Lutheran Council, the American Friends Service Committee (AFSC), Aid Refugee Chinese Intellectuals Inc. (ARCI) and the United Presbyterians, changed over the course of two decades, this chapter highlights the many divergent viewpoints on refugee admissions during the Cold War and how these contributed to carving out a small space for refugees in the scope of the much-fêted 1965 Immigration and Nationality Act.

After the Second World War, the United States and other white settler societies experienced a growing conflict between their ongoing repression of indigenous peoples, their restrictive and selective immigration programs, which worked to displace and dispossess indigenous peoples, and an increasingly pervasive global

Contested Terrain · 67

humanitarian agenda around refugees. Built on immigration policies that were at their core exclusionary, rather than inclusionary, white settler societies sought to protect the hierarchy of desirable migrants and settlers established by their immigration programs even as they paid lip service to the evils of race-based discrimination and the merits of humanitarian initiatives, including refugee assistance, admission, and resettlement.[7]

At the core of postwar humanitarian campaigns were the efforts of religious and secular organizations, which built on earlier strategies to assist refugees in order to convince American policymakers and politicians of the merits of the diverse solutions they envisioned for refugees. This work required concerted effort, as Congress had proved to be almost entirely resistant to the idea of admitting refugees to the United States throughout the 1930s and early 1940s. Although Presbyterian and Catholic church groups experienced some success in sponsoring and supporting refugees, admissions were only facilitated on an ad hoc basis. Campaigns to secure the entry of Jewish refugees were generally rebuffed.[8] Renewed and intensified efforts to secure the admission of Jewish refugees from Europe after the Second World War were therefore critical in shaping the postwar humanitarian landscape in the United States.[9] Campaigns by the AJC—established in 1906 in response to religious persecution in Russia—shaped the landscape in which subsequent reforms were undertaken.[10] These campaigns evolved as the AJC grew from an organization with a few select members to a more broad-based organization focused on social justice and human rights issues, including "education and 'prejudice reduction' programs."[11]

In the face of sustained congressional opposition to refugee admissions but with the support of groups such as the AJC, President Truman issued an executive order, remembered as the "Truman Directive," on December 22, 1945. This directive initiated a practice of executive discretion on refugee admissions, a practice that endured for decades. The order designated existing immigration quotas for displaced persons. As a result, almost twenty thousand people, the majority of whom were Jewish, were admitted to the United States between December 1945 and 1947. The AJC and other advocates built on this initial effort and lobbied Congress for further admissions emphasizing the need for emergency legislation that would "alleviate the distress of non-Jews as well as Jews."[12] Although the AJC was preoccupied first and foremost with the plight of Jewish people in Europe, it recognized that to gain any traction with Congress, it needed to build a coalition of supporters among Catholic and Protestant churches.

This mindset led to some progress, but the limited quotas meant there was also considerable interfaith conflict about admissions—most obviously with the passage of the 1948 Displaced Persons Act.[13] The legislation allowed for the admission of two hundred thousand displaced persons or refugees, as defined by the

International Refugee Organization, in its first two years of operation. The legislation was highly restrictive, limiting eligibility to persons who had been in camps in Europe before December 22, 1945.[14] Moreover, the Displaced Persons Act did not substantively increase the total numbers of people admitted to the United States. It was therefore "a way to admit refugees without admitting more people than the ceiling allowed."[15] Two thousand visas were set aside for nonquota refugees, and another three thousand were designated for orphaned children. Relatives were given preference, and any excess admissions per country were mortgaged against future entries. Four hundred thousand displaced persons were ultimately admitted to the United States under this legislation.

Yet even though it was numerically significant, the 1948 Displaced Persons Act was troubling for the manner in which it discriminated against Jewish migrants. The 1948 Act favored "agricultural workers," a category that rendered many Jewish refugees inadmissible. Members of the AJC were dismayed by the restrictive nature of the legislation, calling it a "disaster," while other religious groups were relieved that the needs of groups they favored, such as Baltic refugees, were addressed.[16] The 1948 Act's discriminatory provisions made Jewish activists all the more committed to securing a sustained commitment for refugee admissions. In a letter to President Truman in July 1948, AJC officials declared that the Displaced Persons Act "contains provisions which in their effect, if not in each case by design, impose the most rigorous limitations upon the admission to the United States of Jewish displaced persons. The fact that the bill does not establish religious quotas in no [ways] reduce its discriminatory effects."[17] In calling for a series of ten amendments to "re-write this discriminatory and exclusionist bill into a genuine displaced persons bill," the AJC emphasized that Congress needed to introduce legislation that was "worthy of our great democratic nation and its traditions as a haven for the oppressed."[18]

Appeals to an imagined history of refuge and sanctuary were instrumental in advancing the case for refugee admissions, particularly as the United States sought to position itself as a kinder, gentler nation vis-à-vis the Soviet threat in the emerging Cold War.[19] Amended in 1950 to be more favorable to Jewish refugees, the 1948 Displaced Persons Act was the last piece of legislation that emerged specifically out of the European refugee crisis. From then on, refugee initiatives were bound up explicitly with the politics of the Cold War; the language and strategies of groups invested in securing refugee admissions evolved accordingly.[20]

In contrast to its efforts with regard to the 1948 Displaced Persons Act, the AJC used pointed Cold War rhetoric to advance its agenda around refugee admissions in 1953, the year the Eisenhower administration introduced and passed the Refugee Relief Act. With the Refugee Relief Act, the US government sought to carve out space (and secure propaganda points) for the admission of refugees from communism. The 1953 Refugee Relief Act allowed for 205,000 "non-quota" immigrant visas to be issued until December 31, 1956, and included room for up to three thousand Asian refugees in the Far East as well as two thousand visas specifically for Chinese refugees from the People's Republic of China. With these provisions, the Refugee Relief Act essentially "assimilated" refugee policy "back into the mainstream of immigration politics, where generosity was measured out according to its potential domestic effect."[21]

The Refugee Relief Act was a critical piece of legislation, for it followed on the 1952 McCarran-Walter Act, which had preserved the national-origins quota system almost intact.[22] For the AJC and other Jewish organizations, the refugee legislation represented an opportunity to undo some of the work of the previous year. In a joint memorandum to AJC offices across the country, Sidney Liskofksy and Sol Rabkin, active human-rights campaigners, noted that despite the progress suggested by the Refugee Relief Act, the national origins legislation remained "the chief obstacle to the orderly handling of this emergency immigration program."[23] Rather than dwell on the quota system, however, AJC leaders underscored the importance of adopting "the bill on humanitarian grounds and on the further ground that it will enhance America as well as serve as an example to other countries in a position to receive immigrants."[24] The AJC was not alone in evolving its campaigns on refugee admissions and marrying them to a Cold War paradigm. The National Council of Jewish Women, the Hebrew Sheltering and Immigrant Aid Society, and the United Service for New Americans, in a statement to the US Senate Committee on the Judiciary, explained:

> We recognize that even the admission of 240,000 persons in two years will not fully solve the problem of the refugee, the displaced and the unsettled. However, this action has great significance for the world as a demonstration of the interest and responsibility of the US and as a stimulus to other receiving countries which look to the United States for leadership in the solution of such problems. We believe that it will hearten the displaced and unsettled persons including those who have risked their lives fleeing from Communist terror to seek refuge in the Western democracies.[25]

The three organizations then proceeded to tie immigration reform and the admission of Jewish refugees, especially those who had moved to China during World War II while Shanghai remained an open port, to the principled role they envisioned for the United States as a humanitarian leader internationally. Although they, and the AJC, continued to advocate on behalf of Jewish refugees in particular, the rhetoric of their advocacy campaigns had evolved in a few short years from merit-based claims to assistance tied to the experience of Jewish refugees in World War II, and then to broader appeals for refugee admissions based on the politics of the global

70 · LAURA MADOKORO

Cold War and the role that they believed the United States should be playing in the battle against communism.[26]

The emphasis that religious and secular organizations placed on the United States as a role model with regard to the plight of refugees globally was unique among white settler societies. Elsewhere, such as in Canada, Australia, and New Zealand, advocates spoke about the need to demonstrate a commitment to humanitarianism, but without referencing a global leadership position, as was the case in the United States.[27] As a result, the attention to America's profile internationally meant that the issue of refugee admissions to the United States became profoundly politicized—to the delight of some humanitarian leaders, and the dismay of others.

The conflict over politicized refugee admissions was perhaps most evident in the case of Chinese refugees from the People's Republic of China. Chinese migrants had been excluded from permanent settlement in the United States for decades, and, as in the case of other white settler societies, it took decades more to dismantle the formal structures of exclusion.[28] The 1790 Naturalization Act, for instance, had made it impossible for migrants from Asia to become naturalized; the 1875 Page Act had prohibited the admission of forced laborers and prostitutes before the 1882 Chinese Exclusion Act banned almost all permanent migration from China. The exclusion era formally ended in 1943 with the Magnuson Act, which established an annual quota of 105 Chinese migrants globally. The act was a piece of compromise legislation, reflecting China's allied status during World War II as well as the American government's continued anxiety about admitting subjectively large numbers of Chinese migrants.

Cold War security concerns in particular meant that fear continued to drive migration policy in the United States even after the formal end of the exclusion era. Political turmoil in Asia compounded these anxieties, as did the movement of large numbers of people in the wake of various wartime upheavals, including the decolonization of many parts of Southeast Asia. Massive displacement followed the expansion and defeat of the Japanese empire as well as decolonization conflicts in Malaysia, Indonesia, the Philippines, and Vietnam. The decade-long civil war in China, which culminated in the establishment of the People's Republic of China in 1949, propelled millions of people to seek refuge in Hong Kong and Taiwan.[29] In subsequent years, humanitarians in Hong Kong and the *Guomindang* government in Taiwan worked persistently to secure humanitarian support for Chinese refugees. It was a difficult course, as barriers to entry in the United States and other white settler societies limited the possibility of refugee admissions.

The inclusion of Chinese refugees and other refugees in Asia within the scope of the 1953 Refugee Relief Act was a token nod toward the large and pressing humanitarian situations in the region. Somewhat paradoxically, these limited openings spawned intense debates about the best way to assist refugees in Asia.

The possibility of admitting Chinese refugees gave proponents the opportunity to campaign for their vision of a liberal, democratic, and humanitarian America based on their perception of how best to assist a migrant group previously marginalized in US government policy, and by American society more generally. Still, some humanitarians disapproved of using refugee admissions to cast American society in a particular light, believing that admissions, and resettlement programs in particular, did not effectively address the needs of refugees themselves. The substance of what constituted a humanitarian nation was very much up for debate. As a result, there was open conflict between groups such as the AFSC, which believed in long-term relief projects in Hong Kong (where many Chinese migrants had sought shelter) and ARCI, which sought to exploit the humanitarian situation in the British colony for political gain domestically and internationally.

The AFSC was established in 1917, following the lead of Quakers who had been involved in war-relief efforts in Britain from the early 1800s.[30] The original premise of the organization was to provide conscientious objectors with the opportunity for nonmilitary service in providing aid; the AFSC only worked belatedly on the question of refugee reception in the United States. In 1938 the AFSC established a refugee committee in the wake of *Kristallnacht*. However, an apathetic support base hindered the intended largesse of the organizers' efforts. Staff were engaged with the issue of refugee resettlement, but "rank and file Quakers were uninterested."[31] The organization's focus therefore shifted toward providing welcome programs through "hostels, American seminars, summer camps, college workshops, and other educational projects", which were designed to "Americanize" and assist the few arriving refugees from Europe in order to send a signal to "the large relief agencies [about] the 'Quaker Way' in which refugees should be treated."[32] Throughout their work with refugees, the AFSC sought to maintain a distinct identity and voice on the question of relief work. This led to strained relations with the United Nations Relief and Rehabilitation Administration in postwar Europe, as the AFSC pursued "spiritual reconstruction" in the context of an organization dedicated to "physical relief."[33] For this reason, the AFSC was much more inclined to operate independently in the field of refugee relief, as it did in Asia.

The AFSC was active in China during the civil war; however, after 1951, it shifted its operational base to Hong Kong, joining other Western missionaries and humanitarians who were expelled or barred from entering the People's Republic of China. Determined to continue their work in Asia, many religious and secular organizations relocated their offices to Hong Kong with the idea of waiting out the political turmoil on the Chinese mainland. Once in the British colony, however, the AFSC and others became attuned to the humanitarian need created by the movement of almost a million people in the short period following the establishment of the People's Republic of China. As a result, the AFSC gradually became invested in providing relief services in the colony, focusing its attention on social welfare programs such as community daycares and pursuing critical infrastructure projects, including the construction of roads and paths that facilitated agricultural production among some of the more rural settlements.

Although the bulk of the US government's attention was on refugees in Europe and defectors from the Soviet Union, humanitarian appeals and campaigns for international support to provide for Chinese refugees did reach sympathetic ears in Washington. Working with Western humanitarian organizations in Hong Kong, including the AFSC as well as the World Council of Churches and the Lutheran World Federation, the US government gradually increased the financial and material resources it dedicated to humanitarian aid in the region. In 1954 President Eisenhower introduced the Far East Refugee Program (FERP), born of the United States Escapee Program introduced two years prior to encourage defections from the Soviet Bloc.[34]

The Escapee Program helped qualified individuals who were fleeing from communist rule to resettle to the United States. However, FERP, as it operated in Hong Kong, was focused less on encouraging defections, which required admission and settlement in the United States, and more on relief and rehabilitation projects. These initiatives ranged in scope from medical clinics and programs to an array of food distribution projects.[35] FERP was designed to advance the image of the United States as a humanitarian nation without requiring the government to invest heavily in this work. Instead, the program provided financial support to private US interests who then delivered relief and support to the refugees in question. The ultimate aims of the program, as well as this hands-off approach, were understood by all levels of government involved in the delivery of refugee programs. As Richard Brown, head of the Refugee Migration Unit in Hong Kong noted, "the bulk of support for refugee assistance throughout the world should come from the free will private offerings of the American citizens rather than by through government subsidy."[36] Through FERP, the Refugee and Migration Unit in Hong Kong provided funds to a number of NGOs in the colony and "assisted with the resettlement abroad of over 19,000 refugees and . . . provided direct help in the local integration of over 156,000 refugees."[37] Organizations such as the AFSC were wary of the program's political overtones and were therefore reluctant to accept FERP funds.[38] At the other end of the spectrum, organizations such as ARCI embraced the political nature of refugee admissions to the United States and exploited this opening to push for the resettlement of refugees from Hong Kong to America.

ARCI was established in 1952, the inspiration of Ernest Moy, a Chinese American and avowed anticommunist with close ties to the Republican Party, who dreamed up the idea of an organization to identify and resettle "intellectual refugees" to the United States. The result was ARCI, a small organization with powerful supporters that successfully lobbied for Chinese refugee resettlement to the United States. The organization's focus was explicitly on "intellectuals," defined as anyone who had studied at an American university. This careful scoping tapped into the long history of Chinese students abroad and was practical as well as strategic: "intellectuals" were desirable citizens.[39] Moreover, there was significant propaganda value in having intellectuals resettled to the United States, dovetailing with Moy's beliefs that supporting refugees was a critical element in the battle against communism.

In addition to advancing America's propaganda efforts, ARCI regularly used the idea of saving refugees as a way of garnering financial and political support for its work. For instance, in September 1942, ARCI's chair (the former medical missionary and congressman Walter Judd) wrote, "It is in our power to give opportunity for a new life to many Chinese men and women who have made the greatest sacrifices to remain free. If we stand aside they will be destroyed or absorbed and enslaved. Nothing can be of greater importance to those of us who are concerned with the world-wide struggle to preserve freedom for all mankind."[40] Judd and other ARCI leaders wanted the US government to resettle refugees from Hong Kong for a number of reasons. For one, they firmly believed that it was in the best interest of people who had escaped from communist oppression to be given opportunities in the United States. They also saw refugee resettlement as critical to advancing the battle against communism and shoring up the moral authority of the United States globally. Their ambitions were complicated, however, by the fact that resettling refugees was expensive. As one internal ARCI memorandum observed, the costs involved went beyond the act of resettlement; they emerged the moment that a commitment was made to a family "in order to resettle people they have to be supported, kept alive, their families kept together during the period of weeks, months and sometimes years before actual resettlement is accomplished."[41]

The cost of resettlement and the realities of FERP and existing immigration legislation meant that there was actually very little scope for assisting refugees in Asia through resettlement programs. Indeed, the gulf between rhetoric and practice proved almost insurmountable. Resettlement was limited and strategic, and most of the refugees that ARCI worked with in Hong Kong were ultimately resettled to Taiwan between 1952 and 1969.[42] It was one thing to voice support for refugees in Asia but quite another to actively facilitate the admission of persons long excluded on racial, economic, and political grounds. Still, despite their limited success, ARCI staff insisted that the resettlement of even a few refugees to the United States was evidence of America's benign character and its welcome embrace of people from all parts of the world.[43]

The politics of resettling and admitting refugees during the Cold War simultaneously advanced and undermined US efforts to represent a more humanitarian image of the country. The resettlement and admission of refugees was measured in terms of how they might refract an improved perception of the United States domestically and globally. As policy documents made clear, assistance (financial, material, or via resettlement) would "be undertaken only for refugee groups or individuals where such assistance demonstrably contributes to the advancement of US political, psychological or intelligence objectives."[44] For staff of the AFSC such objectives undermined the humanitarian character of the supposed relief efforts.[45] Staff considered the use of refugee relief for political gain to be the equivalent of "political warfare" that did little to benefit the refugees themselves.[46] In private correspondence, AFSC members observed that because the "large numbers of Chinese" leaving China appeared to symbolize "a condemnation of the Red Regime," the US government had developed an interest in the migrants. The concern was that the people of Hong Kong had become "politically exploitable."[47] Despite such criticisms, and even though AFSC staff in Hong Kong were generally opposed to resettlement initiatives given the political and financial costs and the limited number of people who were assisted, a number of local AFSC chapters in the United States did pursue resettlement opportunities, believing in the merits of welcoming refugees within and giving weight to claims of humanitarian generosity.[48]

As suggested by the split within the AFSC on refugee admissions, the question of how best to provide humanitarian assistance to the world's refugees was one that combined short-term concerns with broader considerations about the implications of ad hoc and inherently politicized admissions. In contrast to the efforts of local chapters, AFSC leaders advocated for long-term admission opportunities rather than piecemeal initiatives. After the Kennedy Administration used its executive authority to parole five thousand refugees to the United States in response to a major influx of migrants from the People's Republic of China to Hong Kong in the spring of 1962, William Channel of the AFSC noted that Hong Kong "is the world's most densely populated city, increasing in numbers every year. The problems of housing, feeding, clothing and caring for the needs of these people are overwhelming ones."[49] Although he commended the parole initiative, he insisted that the United States should "take greater numbers of Chinese immigrants and refugees," arguing that "raising the quota on Chinese immigrants from 105 to more than 5,000 and permitting the admission of up to 50,000 refugees a year—including Chinese refugees—[will] encourage a more liberal policy on the part of other nations."[50]

The tenor of Channel's intervention, which focused on the merits of structural reform for domestic and international purposes, revealed the manner in which the politics of refugee admissions evolved from the immediate postwar period over the course of the Cold War. Advocacy was no longer dominated by groups that focused on refugee admissions solely on the basis of the needs of one ethnic group; rather, refugee policy was understood as an essential crucible upon which the United States could reform its restrictive immigration programs and project an image of benign humanitarianism globally. When efforts emerged in the early 1960s to introduce new immigration legislation, religious and secular organizations intervened to voice their concerns about the ongoing limitations of the national-origins system and the need to embrace refugee admissions as a regular, rather than exceptional, component of America's immigration system.

Organizations that had been involved with refugee settlement work in the United States previously lent credence to the symbolic and utilitarian value of incorporating refugee admissions into US immigration policy more generally.[51] The AJC spoke out on behalf of immigration reform, and other religious groups had their interventions read into the *Congressional Record* as evidence of the moral merits of reform. At the 1963 General Assembly of United Presbyterians, attendees agreed that immigration laws should be revised to "remove restrictive and discriminatory provisions" and to "provide for the admission of refugees in large-enough numbers to alleviate emergency situations which result in refugee communities requiring resettlement."[52] The National Lutheran Council declared its "firm conviction that the existing immigration legislation has severe short-comings, as a result of which neither traditional Christian humanitarianism nor enlightened self-interest are adequately exhibited." The council argued that the United States needed to assume its "proper share of international responsibility for the resettlement of refugees and of other persons urgently in need of the compassionate haven of a new homeland."[53]

Ultimately, the 1965 Immigration and Nationality Act incorporated refugee policy into its framework by creating a new category of quota immigrants, that of individuals from "Communist or Communist-dominated lands."[54] The idea was to create a permanent conduit through which to assist refugees. The initial categorization of refugees as victims from communism, which was later amended to include refugees from natural calamities, reflected the dominant cold war paradigm that had emerged in the postwar period. In rallying support for the bill, the author of the legislation, Congressman Emanuel Celler (NY), noted "special provisions [were] made for emergency situations, thus eliminating the need for emergency legislation which we have been called upon to pass over the years."[55] More generally, Celler emphasized that the "fundamental feature" of the proposed legislation was "the elimination from our laws of the fallacious belief that the place of birth or the racial origin of a human being determines the quality or the level of a man's Intellect, or his moral character or his suitability for assimilation into our Nation and our society."[56] Pointing to the "two Displaced Persons Acts" as "the first loud and public admission of the obsolescence and the unworkability of the national origins formula of the 1924 law," Celler noted that the Refugee Relief Act of 1953 remained "an equally convincing piece of evidence of the bankruptcy of the system [National Origins Act] so very unfortunately incorporated in the statute now in

76 · LAURA MADOKORO

effect [McCarran-Walter Act]."[57] Celler's vision of immigration reform—and one that was shared by many—was that it should be a tool to dismantle exclusionary immigration programs as well as a strategy for advancing a particular version of US humanitarianism.

Despite Celler's aspirations, the 1965 act provided only a modest opening for refugee admissions by setting out a fixed number in the annual quota for this purpose. Critics, including Congressman John Lindsay (NY), believed that the government needed to do more. Lindsay proposed that the 1965 act be amended to dedicate space, time and funds to the issue of resettling refugees—in other words, to actively selecting and relocating refugees across international borders to the United States. This was the kind of work that ARCI had promoted and pursued in Hong Kong. Lindsay proposed that the Secretary of State "be authorized to make grants to public or private agencies in the United States to assist them in resettling within the United States needy hard-core refugees admitted under the Immigration and Nationality Act, including the furnishing of care and rehabilitation services." Lindsay also suggested that an appropriation of $2.5 million be authorized for this purpose.[58] His efforts, however, were in vain.[59] The 1965 Immigration and Nationality Act created a small opening for permanent, ongoing refugee admissions to the United States but fell short of facilitating and encouraging the work of resettling refugees that had animated the efforts of more politicized humanitarian organizations during the Cold War.

Conclusion

Debates over how best to serve the interests of refugees and what qualities constituted a humanitarian nation foreshadowed congressional debates on the 1965 Immigration and Nationality Act.[60] In the early years of the Cold War, secular and religious humanitarians were divided on the best way to approach the question of refugee relief in the context of America's international and domestic concerns. Groups such as the AJC focused initially on the plight of Jewish refugees before expanding their scope to invest in more broad-based alliances and campaigns. In doing so, they began to use rhetoric that positioned the United States as a humanitarian nation. Such rhetoric required substantive action, and the nature of such overtures was the subject of considerable debate among those involved in refugee-relief efforts. The refugee situation in Hong Kong was particularly illustrative of this dynamic as it reflected the paradox of organizations interested in using refugee relief and resettlement for propaganda purposes and those invested in structural humanitarian assistance.

The 1965 Immigration and Nationality Act, and its limited inclusion of refugees as a distinct category of immigrant admissions, reflected the mixed humanitarian advocacy in the previous years and foreshadowed the continued piecemeal approach to refugee admissions in the United States despite efforts to establish a firm structure for admissions. Notwithstanding the opening created by the 1965 Act, the Executive Branch continued to rely on parole authority for substantial admissions, especially for Cuban refugees. Only with the Indochinese refugee crisis of the late 1970s did Congress pursue significant legislative action, resulting in the United States Refugee Act of 1980 that facilitated permanent rather than conditional entries. The legacy of the debates over humanitarian assistance to refugees in the lead-up to 1965 is therefore mixed. This outcome is perhaps not surprising given the diversity of opinions and ideas about whom the American government should assist and how, particularly in the early days of the global Cold War. The 1965 Immigration and Nationality Act reflected the contests that attended relief and humanitarian efforts throughout the Cold War. That these debates continue to the present day, manifested most demonstrably in discussions over the admission and resettlement of refugees from Syria, points to the limited nature of the humanitarianism envisioned and ultimately embraced in Cold War America.

Notes

1. The prevailing consensus is that America's postwar refugee policy was shaped, domestically and internationally, by the geopolitics of the Cold War, which in turn informed the character of the 1965 Immigration and Nationality Act. Indeed, scholars, including Madeline Hsu, Michael G. Davis, and Aristide Zolberg, have identified the treatment of refugees during the Cold War, and refugees from Asia in particular, as a key factor in the 1965 reforms. They argue that encounters between lawmakers, refugee advocates, and the refugees, as well as the Cold War rhetoric that accompanied the movement of refugees to the United States, transformed notions of desirability and created the framework in which future, and more substantive reforms could be argued. See Madeline Hsu, *The Good Immigrants: How the Yellow Peril Became the Model Minority* (Princeton, N.J.: Princeton University Press, 2015); Michael G. Davis, "Impetus for Immigration Reform: Asian Refugees and the Cold War," *Journal of American—East Asian Relations* 7, nos. 3–4 (Fall–Winter 1998): 127–56; Aristide Zolberg. *A Nation by Design: Immigration Policy in the Fashioning of America* (Cambridge, Mass.: Harvard University Press, 2006). This chapter's focus on religious and secular organizations is in keeping with the renewed focus on nongovernmental actors in shaping policy at home and abroad. Historians have begun to shed new light on the work of voluntary agencies in shaping laws, policies, and regulations in the domestic context of the United States as well as the country's international affairs. See Akira Iriye, *Global Community: The Role of International Organizations in the Making of the Contemporary World* (Berkeley: University of California Press, 2004).

2. "President Lyndon B. Johnson's Remarks at the Signing of the Immigration Bill, Liberty Island, New York, October 3, 1965," LBJ Presidential Library, http://www.lbjlibrary .org/lyndon-baines-johnson/timeline/lbj-on-immigration.

3. Jesse Hoffnung-Garskof, "The Immigration Reform Act of 1965" in *The Familiar Made Strange: American Icons and Artifacts after the Transnational Turn*, ed. by Brooke L. Blower and Mark Philip Bradley (Ithaca, N.Y.: Cornell University Press, 2015), 127.

4. Aristide Zolberg, "The Roots of American Refugee Policy," *Social Research* 55, no. 4 (1988): 667. Scholars remain divided on the overall impact of the 1965 Immigration and Nationality Act on American refugee policy. Historian Libby Garland, for instance, suggests that the law "spoke to the ongoing power of the more conservative, restrictionist side of US immigration politics." She notes that the law did "grant a permanent place in US immigration policy to refugees" but that this was a very small place, amounting to only 6 percent of the visas allotted. She notes that the language of the act reinforced the centrality of the Cold War in shaping America's refugee policy, resulting in a kind of "sorting mechanism." *After They Closed the Gates: Jewish Illegal Immigration to the United States, 1921–1965* (Chicago: University of Chicago Press, 2014), 211. Other scholars describe the act as a "halfway measure," in that it made progress on race but took the opposite tack on numerical limits, a description that applies to the refugee-specific clauses as well. Cheryl Shanks, *Immigration and the Politics of American Sovereignty, 1890–1990* (Ann Arbor: University of Michigan Press, 2001), 144. Brian Soucek also notes that although the act provided the "first permanent statutory basis for the admission of refugees . . . the 1965 Act's refugee scheme embraced so many tensions that its permanence was bound to be temporary." "The Last Preference: Refugees and the 1965 Immigration Act," in *The Immigration and Nationality Act of 1965: Legislating a New America*, ed. Gabriel J. Chin and Rose Cuison Villazor (Cambridge: Cambridge University Press, 2015), 183. Soucek underscores in particular the limited geographical reach of the refugee provision, which he sees as a perpetuation of the "national origin discrimination." Such discrimination, he maintains was contrary to the act as a whole and, more pointedly, "did nothing for the thousands of refugees arriving in the United States each month from communist Cuba in the Western Hemisphere." Meanwhile, scholars Gil Loescher and Jon Scanlan emphasize the 1965 Immigration and Nationality Act as a jumping-off point for further advocacy. They observe that during the late 1960s and early 1970s, "churches, human rights organizations, and public interest law firms began to champion the causes of refugees who lacked broad ethnic support, and whose admission into the United States either served no clear foreign policy interest or ran counter to the prevailing cold war ideology." *Calculated Kindness: Refugees and America's Half-Open Door, 1945 to the Present* (New York: Simon and Schuster, 1998), 86.

5. On the critical role churches and NGOs played in resettling and welcoming refugees, see Anastasia Brown and Todd Scribner, "Unfulfilled Promises, Future Possibilities: The Refugee Resettlement System in the United States," *Journal on Migration and Human Security* 2 (2014): 101–20; Todd Scribner, "'Pilgrims of the Night': The American Catholic Church Responds to the Post–World War II Displaced Persons Crisis," *American Catholic Studies* 124, no. 3 (2013): 1–20.

6. "Amending the Immigration and Nationality Act, and for Other Purposes" US Congress, Senate Committee on the Judiciary, Calendar no. 733, Report no. 748, September 15, 1965.

7. Zolberg, "Roots of American Refugee Policy," 668. On the pervasiveness of exclusionary politics, see Marilyn Lake and Henry Reynolds, *Drawing the Global Colour Line: White Men's Countries and the International Challenge of Racial Equality* (Cambridge: Cambridge University Press, 2008).

8. Judith Tydor Baumel-Schwartz, *Unfulfilled Promise: Rescue and Resettlement of Jewish Refugee Children in the United States, 1934–1945* (Juneau, Alaska: Denali, 1990); Saul Friedman, *No Haven for the Oppressed: United States Policy toward Jewish Refugees, 1938–1945* (Detroit, Mich.: Wayne State University Press, 1973).

9. See Genizi Haim, *America's Fair Share: The Admission and Resettlement of Displaced Persons, 1945–1952* (Detroit, Mich.: Wayne State University Press, 1994).

10. Margaret Sands Orchowski, *The Law That Changed the Face of America: The Immigration and Nationality Act of 1965* (New York: Roman and Littlefield, 2015), 42; Garland, *After They Closed the Gates*, 194.

11. See Jerome A. Chanes, "American Jewish Committee" in *Encyclopaedia of Race, Ethnicity, and Society*, ed. Richard T. Schaefer (Thousand Oaks, Calif.: SAGE, 2008), 65–66.

12. Memorandum, Dorothy M. Nathan, Community Service Department, November 29, 1946, AJC Subject Files (RG–347.17.10), box 132, folder–Displaced Persons Act / Legislation, American Jewish Committee Archives, New York.

13. Haim Genzi, "Interfaith Cooperation in America on Behalf of the DP Acts, 1948–1950," *Holocaust and Genocide Studies* 8, no. 1 (1994): 75–93.

14. Haim, *America's Fair Share*, 78.

15. Shanks, *Immigration*, 131.

16. S. Andhil Fineberg, Community Service Department, Memorandum, July 21, 1948, AJC Subject Files (RG–347.17.10), box 132, folder—Displaced Persons Act / Legislation, American Jewish Committee Archives, New York. By contrast, the historian Genzi Haim argues that the act was "a turning point in American immigration policy," as it emphasized "resettlement, rather than immigration." He observers further that "the Act required advance social planning, including assurances for housing and employment." In other words, the government was making a commitment not only to the admission of displaced persons but also to ensuring that they would be successful as new Americans. *America's Fair Share*, 114.

17. Letter to President Truman, July 23, 1948, AJC Subject Files (RG–347.17.10), box 132, Folder—Displaced Persons Act /Legislation, American Jewish Committee Archives, New York.

18. Ibid.

19. For a full discussion of refugees and the emergence of the Cold War in Europe, see Daniel Cohen, *In War's Wake: Europe's Displaced Persons in the Postwar Order* (New York: Oxford University Press, 2012).

20. For an elaboration, see Carl Bon Tempo, *Americans at the Gate: The United States and Refugees during the Cold War* (Princeton, N.J.: Princeton University Press, 2009), 7.

21. Loescher and Scanlan, *Calculated Kindness*, 47.

22. Bon Tempo, *Americans at the Gate*, 41.

80 · LAURA MADOKORO

23. Sidney Liskofsky and Sol Rabkin, August 11, 1953, re: Refugee Relief Act of 1953, Joint Memorandum to CRC Offices, AJC Area Offices, AJC–Subject Files (RG–347.17.10), box 150, folder—Refugee Relief Act, 1953, ADL Regional Offices, AJC Archives, New York.

24. Ibid.

25. "Statement to the Senate Judiciary Committee in connection with Hearings on S.1917 in behalf of the National Council of Jewish Women, the Hebrew Sheltering and Immigrant Aid Society, United Service for New Americans," May 28, 1953, AJC–Subject Files (RG–347.17.10), box 150, folder—Refugee Relief Act, 1953, AJC Archives, New York.

26. Memorandum from Sidney Liskofsky to Irving M. Engel, June 3, 1953, AJC—Subject Files (RG–347.17.10), box 150, folder—Refugee Relief Act, 1953, ADL Regional Offices, AJC Archives, New York. Liskofsky discusses the strategy for enlarging categories to benefit Jewish migrants while at the same time not alienating potential support from Catholic and Protestant allies. In doing so, Liskofsky reflected the AJC's (not surprisingly) enduring preoccupations with assisting Jewish migrants, but his views also reflected the shifting politics around refugee admissions in the Cold War. On tensions between the universalist and particularist camps within the AJC, see Marianne Rachel Sanua, *Let Us Prove Strong: The American Jewish Committee, 1945–2006* (Waltham, Mass.: Brandeis University Press, 2007).

27. On refugee admissions specifically, see Laura Madokoro "'Slotting' Chinese Families and Refugees, 1947–1967," *Canadian Historical Revie*, 93, no. 1 (2012): 25–56.

28. See, for instance, Gwenda Tavan, *The Long, Slow Death of White Australia* (Carlton North, Vic.: Scribe, 2005).

29. There is considerable debate about the size of the refugee population in both Hong Kong and Taiwan after 1949 as a result of the politicized manner in which statistics on population movements were compiled. For an outline of the controversy, see Joshua Fan, *China's Homeless Generation: Voices from the Veterans of the Chinese Civil War, 1940s-1990s* (New York: Routledge, 2011), 5.

30. Rebecca Gill, *Calculating Compassion: Humanity and Relief in War, Britain, 1870–1914* (Cambridge: Cambridge University Press, 2013), 2.

31. Haim, *America's Fair Share*, 11.

32. Ibid., 12.

33. Ibid., 45.

34. On Truman's Cold War politics, see Elizabeth Edwards Spalding, *The First Cold Warrior: Harry Truman, Containment, and the Remaking of Liberal Internationalism* (Lexington: University Press of Kentucky, 2006); Melvyn P. Leffler, *A Preponderance of Power: National Security, The Truman Administration and the Cold War* (Stanford, Calif.: Stanford University Press, 1992).

35. Susan L. Carruthers, "Between Camps: Eastern Bloc 'Escapees' and Cold War Borderlands," *American Quarterly* 57, no. 3 (2005): 913. For a fuller discussion of the program as it operated in Eastern Europe and the Soviet Union, including its important publicity components, see Susan Carruthers, "Chapter Two: Bloc-Busters," in *Cold War Captives: Imprisonment, Escape and Brainwashing* (Berkeley: University of California Press, 2009).

36. Richard Brown to Rep. Magnuson, February 27, 1962, 846G.46/8-460, RG 59, box 2535, Central Decimal File, 1960–63, National Archives Records Administration.

37. File 6: Congressional File: Trips—1961/Hong Kong, box 86, AFSC Archives, Philadelphia.

38. Jack and Janet Shepherd to William Barton et al., September 2, 1958, Letters: London to P, Foreign Service Section, AFSC Archives.

39. On ARCI's work, see Madeline Hsu, "'The Best Type of Chinese': Aid Refugee Chinese Intellectuals and Symbolic Refugee Relief, 1952–1960," in *The Good Immigrants: How the Yellow Peril Became the Model Minority* (Princeton, N.J.: Princeton University Press, 2015), 130–65.

40. Walter Judd to Whitney Shepardson, September 17, 1952, III.A.1. A-B, box 6, file 5 ARCI, Carnegie Corporation of New York, Columbia University Archives.

41. Oram to Emmet, January 3, 1952, file 167.2 China File, ARCI Correspondence / General, 1957–59, ARCI Collection, Hoover Institute Archives, Stanford University.

42. In a 1954 report, ARCI acknowledged "openings in other parts of the world have been few: 45 persons were resettled in various parts of Southeast Asia; 17 in the US and Canada." "A Report to Our Contributors," ABMAC / ARCI Collection, box 69, file "A Report to Our Contributors," Rare Books and Manuscripts Library, Columbia University.

43. Thomas Borstelmann, *The Cold War and the Color Line* (Cambridge, Mass.: Harvard University Press, 2003); Mary L. Dudziak, *Cold War Civil Rights: Race and the Image of American Democracy* (Princeton, N.J.: Princeton University Press, 2000).

44. Memo for John H. Ohly, "Preparation of Escapee Program Congressional Presentation," General—Escapee Program, ARCI, A1 1199, box 4, Record Group 59: General Records of the Department of State, 1763–2002, NARA.

45. For a full discussion of the conflict over US refugee policy in Hong Kong, see Laura Madokoro, *Elusive Refuge: Chinese Migrants in the Cold War* (Cambridge, Mass.: Harvard University Press, 2016).

46. Frank Hunt to Esther Rhoads, June 20, 1958, [Hong Kong, Letters to Japan, 1958], AFSC.

47. Ibid.

48. "Testimony before Senate Subcommittee to Investigate Problems Connected with Refugees and Escapees of the Senate Committee on the Judiciary," Richard Smith, American Friends Service Committee, July 14, 1961, box: AFSC Minutes: 1961, AFSC Archives.

49. United States Senate, *Refugee Problem in Hong Kong and Macao: Hearings Before the United States Senate Committee on the Judiciary, Subcommittee to Investigate Problems Connected with Refugees and Escapees*, 87th Congress, 2nd Session, (1962), 63.

50. Ibid.

51. ARCI, which had been the most vocal advocate on refugee resettlement as a humanitarian solution, had ceased operations in 1959 and did not contribute to the emerging conversation around immigration reform.

52. Senator Neuberger, Statement in the Senate of the United States, July 29, 1964, *Congressional Record.*

82 · LAURA MADOKORO

53. "Text of a resolution adopted by the National Lutheran Council supporting President Johnson's proposal for revision of the immigration law,—Extension of Remarks of Hon. John Brademas of Indiana," February 18, 1965, United States Congress, House of Representatives, *Congressional Record* (1965), A777.

54. Loescher and Scanlan, *Calculated Kindness*, 69.

55. Statement by Emanuel Celler, New York, House of Representatives, June 16, 1964, *Congressional Record—Appendix* (1964), A3268.

56. Ibid.

57. Ibid.

58. "Speech by Congressman Jon V. Lindsay," April 13, 1965, United States Congress, House of Representatives, *Congressional Record—Appendix* (1965), A1836.

59. See discussion of economic contributions in "Immigration and Nationality Act—Conference Report," September 29, 1965. US Congress, Committee of Conference, 89th Congress, 1st Session, Report No.1101, 1. There was no financial commitment to refugee resettlement in the 1965 Act despite the fact that the Committee on the Judiciary (US Senate) believed that the historic practice of admitting refugees to the United States "through the sponsorship of voluntary agencies and private citizens" should continue "so that each refugee will have an opportunity to adjust and develop in this country without fear of abandonment and without the possibility of becoming a public charge." "Amending the Immigration and Nationality Act, and for Other Purposes," US Congress, Senate Committee on the Judiciary, Calendar no. 733, Report no. 748, September 15, 1965, 16.

60. Soucek, "Last Preference," 175.

CHAPTER 4

The Geopolitical Origins of the 1965 Immigration Act

DAVID FITZGERALD AND DAVID COOK-MARTÍN

The Immigration and Nationality Act of 1965 radically shifted US policy and repainted the face of the nation. Until 1965, national-origins quotas encouraged immigration from countries in northwestern Europe, loosely restricted immigration from southern and eastern Europe, and banned most immigration from Asia, Africa, and the colonized Caribbean. The new law replaced the quota system with selection based on family reunification, high skills, and flight from persecution. The European and Canadian share of legal immigrants fell from 60 percent in the 1950s to 22 percent in the 1970s. By contrast, the Asian share of legal immigration rose from 6 percent in the 1950s to 35 percent by the 1980s, and 40 percent in 2013.[1] Much of the demographic diversity in the US population today is a direct result of the 1965 legislation.

Many scholars assert that the US civil rights movement, which sought to end racial segregation and delegitimize racial discrimination in the United States, drove the demise of the national-origins quotas. For example, legal scholar Gabriel Chin (1996) described the 1965 Act as "The Civil Rights Revolution Comes to Immigration Law."[2] The landmark immigration law passed just a year after the Civil Rights Act of 1964 and in the same year as the Voting Rights Act. Undoubtedly, the ending of the national-origins quotas was affected by the US legislative process, ethnic lobbying, and the civil rights movement. We argue, however, that seismic shifts in world politics created openings for reforms such as the 1965 Immigration and Nationality Act that sharply reduced racialized laws in the United States and beyond. Between 1803 and 1930, every independent country in the Americas

DAVID FITZGERALD AND DAVID COOK-MARTÍN

passed laws to explicitly restrict or exclude at least one particular ethnic group. Of the twenty-two countries, twenty discriminated against Chinese, seventeen against Roma (*gitanos* in most of Spanish America and *ciganos* in Brazil), sixteen against blacks/Africans, fourteen against Japanese, and thirteen against Middle Easterners. The demise of these restrictions began in Latin American countries long before the United States changed its policy in 1965, beginning with Uruguay (1936), Chile (1936), Paraguay (1937), Cuba (1942), Mexico (1947), and Argentina (1949). Anglophone countries without major civil rights movements later followed suit in removing their race-based policies—Canada in the 1960s, Australia in 1973, Britain in 1981, and New Zealand in 1986. In light of this broader pattern, the narrow focus on the US civil rights movement to explain changes in US immigration law is insufficient. While the civil rights movement influenced the creation of the 1965 act, the ending of the national-origins quota system was primarily driven by geopolitical factors.[3]

National Origins Quotas

The 1965 act replaced a system of national-origin and race-based quotas. The Emergency Quota Act of 1921 limited the annual number of immigrants from any country to 3 percent of the number of residents from that country living in the United States in the 1910 census.[4] The policy supported "old-stock" immigration from northern and western Europe at prewar levels and led to a decline of "new-stock" immigration from southern and eastern Europe to a fifth of its prewar level.[5]

Congress enacted a new quota scheme in the Immigration Act of 1924 (Johnson-Reed Act).[6] The 1924 act amplified the preference for old-stock European immigrants by rolling back the base year for calculating the quotas from 1910 to 1890. It also established that until 1927, the annual maximum quota for each nationality would be 2 percent of the total population of that nationality as recorded in the 1890 census, with a minimum quota of one hundred. In practice, that meant that the share of the quotas reserved for southern and eastern Europeans fell from 45 percent to 16 percent.[7] The House committee report adopting the 1890 baseline maintained that "the use of the 1890 census is not discriminatory. It is used in an effort to preserve, as nearly as possible, the racial status quo in the United States."[8]

After 1927 the annual quota of 150,000 immigrants was apportioned among countries by the national origin of the US population in 1920, with a minimum quota of one hundred. A Quota Board calculated the size of each national-origin allotment based on how many people of each nationality appeared in the 1790 census, adjusted for later migration. Quotas applied only to the European-origin population and did not include immigrants from the Western Hemisphere and their descendants, aliens ineligible for citizenship and their descendants, descendants

The Geopolitical Origins of the 1965 Immigration Act • 85

of slaves, and descendants of indigenous Americans.[9] Ethnic associations campaigned against the national-origins system and delayed its implementation until 1929.[10]

The 1924 act excluded almost all Asians by stipulating that "no alien ineligible to citizenship shall be admitted to the United States."[11] Its design targeted nationals from Japan, who had not been included in the 1917 Asiatic Barred Zone that applied to most of the rest of Asia. The Philippines and Guam were a temporary exception because of their quasi-colonial status.[12] Yet the exceptional treatment of the nationals from the Philippines ended when the Tydings-McDuffie Act (1934) restricted Filipino entries to fifty a year.[13]

The 1924 quotas did not apply to immigrants if they were born "in the Dominion of Canada, Newfoundland, the Republic of Mexico, the Republic of Cuba, the Republic of Haiti, the Dominican Republic, the Canal Zone, or an independent country of Central or South America."[14] The 1921 Quota Act had exempted residents of the same independent Western Hemisphere countries who had lived there at least one year. This criterion was tightened in 1924 to apply to residents whose birthplace was in the Western Hemisphere. The goal was to prevent Asians from using neighboring countries as a backdoor into the United States. Territories that were not independent, which in practice meant majority-black colonies in the Caribbean, fell under the quotas of their metropoles, primarily Great Britain. The implementation of the 1924 act deliberately restricted the entrance of Caribbean blacks.[15]

Debates about eliminating the Western Hemisphere exemptions reveal many of the geopolitical considerations that would later play a fundamental role in dismantling the quota system altogether in the 1960s. Would immigration policy express nativist and eugenicist views of the nation or political and economic interests in the region? Nativists like Rep. John Box (D-TX) argued that Mexican immigration created "the most insidious and general mixture of white, Indian, and Negro blood strains ever produced in America" and introduced an unsuccessful bill to include Mexico and other Latin American countries in the quota system.[16] Prominent eugenicist Harry Laughlin testified to the House Immigration Committee that immigration from the Western Hemisphere should be restricted to whites.[17] Public health agencies, patriotic societies, and organized labor made similar arguments for restriction. On the other side, railroad, farming, and livestock employers in the Southwest opposed quotas on Mexican immigration because workers from the southern neighbor would *not* assimilate and would return to Mexico when the work was done.[18]

The president and State Department opposed the inclusion of Latin Americans in the quota system for diplomatic reasons.[19] Consular reports warned that governments in the region would view quotas as an unfriendly gesture. Senator David

Reed, co-author of the 1924 act, opposed a Western Hemisphere quota because it would harm the "Pan-American idea." "If we want to hold them to us—and I think we do so as long as we maintain the Monroe Doctrine—we have got to treat them differently from the rest of the world," he told the Senate.[20] Secretary of State Frank Kellogg warned the Senate Immigration Committee in 1928 that Western Hemisphere quotas "would adversely affect the present good relations of the United States with Latin America and Canada" and "would be apt to have an adverse effect upon the prosperity of American business interest in those countries."[21] A congressional majority, however, still demanded restriction of Western Hemisphere immigration. In 1930, Sen. William Harris (D-GA) introduced such a bill that passed the Senate by a vote of 56–11, but the House leadership killed it in the House Rules Committee after President Hoover threatened a veto.[22]

While the domestic coalition of restrictionists could overcome foreign-policy concerns to exclude immigrants from Asia—where the United States had relatively limited ties aside from the Philippines—and restrict immigrants from parts of Europe, from which the United States was disengaging after World War I—it was not strong enough to override US military, commercial, and diplomatic interests in Latin America under the Good Neighbor policy. Under President Franklin Roosevelt's administration, the United States pulled out of Nicaragua and Haiti, revoked the Platt Amendment in Cuba, gave up financial control in the Dominican Republic, and signed an agreement of non-intervention.[23] The US policy of pursuing more amicable relationships with Latin American governments thus linked the maintenance of the Western Hemisphere quota exemption with broad foreign policy and commercial interests.

Foreign Policy Pressures

World War II and Cold War national-security concerns increased pressure on the United States to end the national-origins immigration system. The Allies in World War II and the West during the Cold War risked losing support from Third World countries whose peoples were excluded by openly racist immigration laws. The shift away from ethnic selection in US immigration policy was primarily a response to foreign-policy pressures from the growing number of independent Asian, African, and Latin American countries that sought to delegitimize racism through Pan-American institutions and the United Nations.

In Latin America, a wave of reaction against US military and economic interventions swept the region in the 1930s. Populist policymakers and intellectuals condemned a long history of US occupations and gunboat diplomacy. Throughout the continent, Latin American elites resented the heavy-handedness of US policymakers who treated Latin Americans as inferiors and threatened to include them in the US national-origins quotas for immigrants. Even though Latin American governments themselves discriminated against their own nonwhite populations, taking up the banner of antiracism was seen as a way to pressure the United States to improve the treatment of Latin American migrants, particularly Mexicans in the US Southwest, Cubans in Florida, and Central Americans and Caribbean islanders in the racially segregated Panama Canal Zone. Antiracism thus became a tool of foreign policy for many Latin American countries in their relationship with the United States.

At the Eighth International Conference of American States in Lima (1938), Latin American countries pushed anti-racist resolutions. One resolution recommended to member states "that they coordinate and adopt provisions concerning immigration, wherein no discrimination based on nationality, creed or race shall be made, inasmuch as such discrimination is contrary to the ideal of fraternity, peace and concord which they undertake to uphold without prejudice to each nation's domestic legislation."[24] The United States eventually acquiesced in some pronouncements of racial nondiscrimination, while making sure that such provisions were weak and unenforceable.

World War II

During World War II, by broadcasting how blacks were treated in the United States, Nazi propagandists in Europe criticized the United States for justifying its involvement in the war as a fight for democracy. Gunnar Myrdal, W. E. B. DuBois, and many others also revealed the gap between US claims of waging a war for equality and human rights abroad and practicing segregation at home. Myrdal cautioned that racism was harming the US war effort and would create problems for its geopolitical goals after the war.[25] All of the independent states in the Western Hemisphere eventually joined the Allies, provided resources for the war, and, in the case of Mexico, sent contracted labor to replace US men sent into battle. The war gave Latin American countries leverage to denounce discrimination against Mexicans living in the United States and Central American and Caribbean islanders working in the segregated Panama Canal Zone, where whites enjoyed US citizenship and a high standard of living, while black workers and their children born there were barred from US citizenship.

The discussion to abolish immigration restrictions of named ethnic groups gained prominence on the hemispheric stage for the first time in October 1943 at the First Inter-American Demographic Congress, which was held to discuss anticipated postwar migrations.[26] The congress included delegations from all twenty-two independent countries in the Americas who officially represented their governments and/or attended as prominent demographers. Its resolutions recommended that countries in the hemisphere categorically reject any racially discriminatory policy.

The shift away from racially discriminatory naturalization policies also demonstrates the effects of world politics. The repeal of Chinese exclusion by the United States in 1943 resulted from the interaction between lobbying by domestic interest groups and foreign policy, but the fact that many other countries in the hemisphere ended Chinese exclusion around the same time reflects the primacy of foreign-policy concerns. Japanese radio broadcasts to China, India, and Latin America reminded listeners that "the Chinese are rigidly excluded from attaining American citizenship by naturalization, a right which is accorded to the lowliest immigrant from Europe."[27] A June 24, 1943, editorial in *China Daily*, the organ of the Reorganized National Government puppet regime, charged, "If the American government does not abolish the discriminatory laws against the Chinese, Asian peoples can never be treated equally."[28] In the United States, diplomats were aware of the propaganda problem in Asia and advocated for a change in nationality policy.[29] Madame Chiang Kai-shek, the wife of the nationalist Chinese leader, toured the United States in early 1943 and publicly called for repeal. President Roosevelt supported the repeal, declaring that it would be "important in the cause of winning the war and of establishing a secure peace" and would "silence the distorted Japanese propaganda."[30] Further support came from pro-business lobbies that anticipated postwar advantages of friendlier relations with China, a country of four hundred million consumers, and from even the Congress of Industrial Organizations (CIO).[31]

Southern politicians, the AFL, American Legion, and Veterans of Foreign Wars opposed repeal.[32] Yet foreign-policy considerations prevailed over domestic objections. The 1943 Magnuson Act repealed the Chinese exclusion acts, established an annual quota of 105 for "persons of the Chinese race," and made "Chinese persons or persons of Chinese descent" eligible for naturalization.[33] Racial restrictions further eased in a 1946 act that exempted Chinese wives of US soldiers from the annual quota, as well as a 1947 amendment that allowed all Asians to obtain US citizenship by marriage. A 1950 act allowed immigration outside the quotas of spouses and adult children, regardless of their race.[34] As soon as India and the Philippines entered the final stages of independence, their citizens became eligible for naturalization and symbolic annual quotas of one hundred.[35] The incremental lifting of anti-Asian restrictions in World War II was clearly a response to international high politics.

Global Anti-Racism

World War II sharply accelerated a process of decolonization that led to a host of newly independent countries in Asia and Africa. While countries of immigration could politically afford to ignore the reactions of colonized peoples and weak states

The Geopolitical Origins of the 1965 Immigration Act • 89

prior to World War II, decolonization and the formation of world institutions such as the United Nations gave postcolonial governments significant influence.[36] In the face of opposition from the governments of Anglophone settler countries, many of these new countries joined Latin American republics, as they used the United Nations as a platform to advance nondiscriminatory statements of principle.[37]

The Dumbarton Oaks meetings that designed the basic outlines of the United Nations in 1944 revealed that the "Big Three"—the United States, Britain, and the Soviet Union—strongly opposed mention of human rights as part of the UN charter. Wellington Koo, China's head delegate, forced human rights and equality onto the agenda. Koo proposed that the new international organization uphold "the principle of equality of all states and all races."[38] The Western participants were categorically unwilling to make any such concessions for domestic and empire-building reasons, and they agreed among themselves that they would "completely eliminate all mention of racial equality."[39]

Latin American leaders felt betrayed by their exclusion from Dumbarton Oaks because they had spent a previous decade rallying around US calls for support in the event of extra-hemispheric aggression. They feared a return to unilateral US decision making in the region, US interventionism, and discrimination against Latin American immigrants in the United States. Latin American governments called for an extraordinary meeting to articulate their own postwar policy and to present it as a bloc. In 1945 they held the Inter-American Conference on Problems of War and Peace in Mexico City to present a unified front to make "every effort to prevent racial or religious discrimination."[40]

When the United Nations Conference on International Organization began its meetings in San Francisco in April 1945, China, India, and the countries of Latin America were prepared to resist the self-serving arrangements made at Dumbarton Oaks by the Big Three. Sensing an opportunity to use the race issue to push a wedge between the First and Third Worlds, the Soviet Union reversed its previously strong opposition to provisions of racial equality and antidiscrimination.[41] China, Brazil, Mexico, Panama, Uruguay, Cuba, Venezuela, and the Dominican Republic then supported a proposal to prohibit racial discrimination, in the face of united opposition from Anglophone settler countries and all European countries except for France. John Foster Dulles, the US delegate, opposed human-rights language in the charter, out of concern that it could require a member state to change its immigration policy and that there would be an international investigation of "the Negro question in this country."[42] Under tremendous pressure from other countries, the Big Three conceded changes that resulted in a more central role for human rights in the charter.[43] Article 1 declared that among the purposes of the United Nations was "promoting and encouraging respect for human rights and for fundamental freedoms for all without distinction as to race, sex, language, or religion."

Before agreeing to these provisions, diplomats from the United States and other Western countries ensured that considerations of national sovereignty trumped the rights language, that the rights language itself was passive rather than active, and that there was no mechanism to enforce the rights provisions.[44] Australia, Canada, New Zealand, and the United States continued to try to block antiracist provisions such as the 1948 Universal Declaration of Human Rights. Yet from its first session, the UN became a forum for governments of most Latin American countries, for the Soviet Union and all of the countries in Africa and Asia and to establish international agencies, treaties, and for other institutions that rendered overt racial discrimination illegitimate.[45]

The Anti-Racist Movement Confronts US Policy

Under international pressure, Secretary of State Dean Acheson wrote to President Truman that "our failure to remove racial barriers provides the Kremlin with unlimited political and propaganda capital for use against us in Japan and the entire Far East."[46] Truman moved civil rights reforms to the top of his domestic agenda.[47] His 1947 Presidential Committee on Civil Rights report cited three critical areas where status quo needed to change: harm to US foreign relations, morality, and economic efficiency.[48] The committee's report strongly recommended the elimination of racial prerequisites to naturalization and called the racialized quota system unfair.[49] The report cited Article 55 of the UN Charter, which referred to "universal respect for, and observance of, human rights and fundamental freedoms for all without distinction as to race, sex, language, or religion," as the potential basis of congressional action to achieve those ends. The president's commission thus invoked the very article that the US delegation had tried to squelch in 1945.[50] In the report's conclusion, the commission made a critical observation to explain why US policy was opposed around the world:

> Discrimination against, or mistreatment of, any racial, religious or national group in the United States is not only seen as our internal problem. The dignity of a country, a continent, or even a major portion of the world's population, may be outraged by it. A relatively few individuals here may be identified with millions of people elsewhere, and the way in which they are treated may have world-wide repercussions. We have fewer than half a million American Indians; there are 30 million more in the Western Hemisphere. Our Mexican American and Hispano groups are not large: millions in Central and South America consider them kin. We number our citizens of Oriental descent in the hundreds of thousands; their counterparts overseas are numbered in hundreds of millions. Throughout the Pacific, Latin America, Africa, the Near, Middle, and Far East, the treatment which our Negroes receive is taken as a reflection of our attitudes toward all dark-skinned peoples.[51]

The national-origins quota system did not fall immediately in the face of international pressures. The White House and State Department were more susceptible to foreign policy arguments and international influences than Congress, which remained more inward looking.[52]

The 1952 Immigration and Nationality Act (McCarran-Walter Act) continued the symbolic opening toward Asia by including a new annual quota of two thousand for the "Asia-Pacific Triangle" but maintained the basic outlines of the national-origins quota system. Each country in the triangle received a quota of one hundred. The Asia-Pacific token quotas were racialized in a way that was not the case for other countries in the world. An "immigrant who is attributable by as much as one-half of his ancestry to a people or peoples indigenous to the Asia-Pacific triangle" was charged to the country of ancestry's quota of one hundred, along with immigrants born in that country.[53] In practice, the 1952 act also restricted the immigration of blacks from the British West Indies by introducing a provision that limited each colony to a maximum quota of one hundred, charged against the quota for the metropole—normalizing the practice that had been in effect since 1925.[54] The act continued the quota exemption for independent countries in the Western Hemisphere.[55]

Supporters of national-origins quotas in the 1950s typically defended discrimination on the grounds of cultural assimilability rather than biology.[56] The bill's sponsor, Sen. Patrick McCarran (D-NV), argued that it eliminated racial discrimination when it opened quotas for the Asia-Pacific Triangle. Despite its reservations, the Japanese American Citizens League supported the law as an incremental improvement over the humiliation of absolute exclusion of Japanese and the people of most other Asian countries. The league urged Truman to accept the quotas in return for removing the racial prerequisites to naturalization that had been in place since 1790.[57] Representatives from northeast districts with large black populations and African American organizations opposed the colonial quotas in the Western Hemisphere as a thinly disguised means of trying to limit black immigration from the West Indies.[58]

The strongest opponents to the bill spoke out against the international consequences of maintaining the national-origins quota system. Senator William Benton (D-CT) highlighted the folly of spending billions of dollars and sacrificing one hundred thousand US soldiers for the Korean War while enacting a bill that discriminates against Koreans and other Asians.[59] Truman vetoed the bill, echoing Benton's warnings of its dangerous implications for the Cold War. His veto message called for a new bill that would remove "racial barriers against Asians" and warned that "failure to take this step . . . can only have serious consequences for our relations with the peoples of the Far East."[60] Congress overrode Truman's veto, and the bill became law.

The 1965 Revolution

A decade later, under the 1965 Immigration and Nationality Act, the United States turned away from selecting immigrants by national or racial origin and toward admission based on family reunification, high skills, and humanitarian need. How do we account for this change? A first set of explanations takes an exclusively domestic perspective and views the end of national-origins quotas in 1965 as a response to the civil rights movement, which had pushed through the Civil Rights Act of 1964 and the Voting Rights Act of 1965.[61] A second perspective minimizes the domestic pressures for reform and emphasizes how foreign-policy considerations affected the development of immigration policy. Yet this second position still adopts the "methodological nationalism" of a US perspective, from the inside looking out at the world, rather than analyzing the interactions of an entire system of states. For example, Cheryl Shanks summarizes, "During this period, external events precipitated arguments for change.[62] Domestic events were relevant when they provided additional evidence supporting reformers' conclusions." The foreign-policy perspective falls short of this chapter's historical institutionalist approach, which shows how previous interactions across a broad, global field of politics and policy diffusion shaped the options of policymakers in 1965.

Two months after McCarran-Walter passed in June 1952, Truman created the Commission on Immigration and Naturalization to hold hearings on immigration reform. The commission report, *Whom We Shall Welcome*, laid out recommendations that eventually formed the outline of the 1965 Immigration Act.[63] While the report acknowledged liberal democratic creeds and the scientific rejection of racism, foreign policy concerns dominated its arguments. The commission endorsed the notion that ethnically discriminatory immigration policies impaired US foreign policy by citing the growth of Japanese militarism directed against the United States after the 1924 exclusion of Japanese immigrants and the blows delivered by various communist countries in the propaganda wars.

Support for the national-origins quota system continued to slide through the early 1950s. By 1956, both the Republican and Democratic Party platforms supported an end to the quotas.[64] After the AFL and CIO joined together in 1955; the new organization supported an end to national-origins quotas so long as the total number of immigrants would not increase. Scholars have suggested that the shift from organized labor's historically restrictionist bent resulted from the booming postwar economy, labor's alliance with the civil rights movement, the incorporation of the CIO with its disproportionately high representation of southern and eastern Europeans whose co-ethnics abroad were disadvantaged by the quotas, and labor's commitment to helping the United States achieve its Cold War goals across the globe.[65] AFL-CIO president George Meany saw ending the national-origins quota

The Geopolitical Origins of the 1965 Immigration Act · 93

as the organization's patriotic duty. He declared that "part of our total program to combat world Communism must be a willingness to welcome a reasonable number to our own shores."[66] Organized labor was most eager to limit the immigration of unskilled workers, a position that in part explains why the final 1965 immigration bill focused so heavily on family reunification rather than economic categories.[67]

By the early 1960s, newly independent countries were on the verge of successfully elevating the International Convention on the Elimination of All Forms of Racial Discrimination (ICERD) to the world stage, and US policies were the targets of sustained international criticism. Supporters of ending national-origins protocols echoed the internationalist arguments made against the 1952 immigration bill.[68] For example, Rep. John Lindsay (R-NY) noted the paradox of fighting for South Vietnam while continuing to exclude all but token numbers of Vietnamese:

> [T]his nation has committed itself to the defense of the independence of South Vietnam. Yet the quota for that country of 15 million is exactly 100. Apparently we are willing to risk a major war for the right of the Vietnamese people to live in freedom at the same time as our quota system makes it clear that we do not want very great numbers of them to live with us.[69]

Secretary of State Dean Rusk told a congressional hearing that US immigration policy had serious foreign policy implications. "What other peoples think about us plays an important role in the achievement of our foreign policies," he argued. "More than a dozen foreign ministers have spoken to me in the last year alone, not about the practicalities of immigration from their country to ours, but about the principle which they interpret as discrimination against their particular countries." Rusk emphasized that "even those [countries] who do not use their quotas . . . resent the fact that the quotas are there as a discriminatory measure."[70] In the same vein, Attorney General Nicholas Katzenbach warned that the "national origins system harms the United States in still another way: it creates an image of hypocrisy which can be exploited by those who seek to discredit our professions of democracy."

Cold War concerns eventually filtered down from the executive branch to the broader public. An August 1963 Harris poll found that 78 percent of white Americans reported that race discrimination in the United States harmed its interests abroad.[71] A Gallup poll two years later found broad support for changing the quota system to one that preferred immigrants based on their skills.[72] White ethnics continued to attack the quota system for discriminating against the Italians, Greeks, Portuguese, Poles, and other Europeans waiting in line for oversubscribed quotas.[73] Ethnic Southern European voices became much more influential by 1965 than in previous legislative debates. The 89th Congress (1965–66) was the first in US history to be majority Catholic. Democrats also held a 2-1 advantage over Republicans in both chambers.[74]

94 · DAVID FITZGERALD AND DAVID COOK-MARTÍN

Massey, Durand, and Malone view the 1965 Immigration Act as one of the achievements of the civil rights movement.[75] Some legislators at the time specifically mentioned the connection between US civil rights and the end of the national-origins scheme.[76] Yet the civil rights movement was primarily framed in the old black/white dichotomous way of understanding US race relations, and the 1965 immigration act was not strongly pushed by US blacks, who were fighting for their civil rights within the United States. Asians in the United States voiced their support through Asian American congressional representatives, but without much effect given their very small numbers. United Farm Worker leader César Chávez was more concerned with ending labor-market competition from the bracero temporary worker program, which gave 4.6 million bracero contracts (mostly to Mexican nationals) between 1942 and 1964, than in changing the whole immigration system.[77] Notwithstanding the affinity between civil rights and ending the national-origins system, the 1965 act was fundamentally driven by geopolitics.[78]

The enacted version of the 1965 Immigration and Nationality Act (Hart-Celler Act),[79] resembled legislation proposed by President John F. Kennedy and taken up by President Lyndon Johnson after Kennedy's assassination.[80] Hart-Celler prohibited preferences or discrimination in the issuance of immigrant visas based on "race, sex, nationality, place of birth, or place of residence" except with regard to specified exceptions.[81] More concretely, it eliminated the national-origins quotas and replaced them with an annual quota of 170,000 visas for immigrants from the Eastern Hemisphere. No country from the Eastern Hemisphere was allowed more than twenty thousand visas. Spouses, minor children, and parents of adult US citizens were exempted from the quotas. Within the quotas, 74 percent of the "preference" categories was reserved for other classes of family members, 20 percent for employment-based visas favoring the highly skilled, and 6 percent for refugees. In keeping with the 1957 refugee legislation, refugees were limited to victims of natural calamities and to those fleeing communism or persecution in the Middle East.

The Western Hemisphere had not been included under the numerical ceiling in the original bills proposed by Senator John F. Kennedy (D-MA), Sen. Philip Hart (D-MI), and Rep. Emanuel Celler (D-NY) from the late 1950s to 1965. During the final negotiations of the 1965 bill, conservative Democrats and Republicans introduced an amendment establishing a quota of 120,000 visas for immigrants from the Western Hemisphere that would take effect in 1968 unless Congress passed a provision to the contrary in the interim. The White House opposed the provision based on its historical concern with protecting US diplomatic interests in its self-described backyard. President Johnson's assistant, Jack Valenti, relayed to the president the concern of Secretary of State Dean Rusk that a system of limiting all immigrants, including those from the Western Hemisphere, would "vex and dumbfound our Latin American friends, who will now be sure we are in final retreat from Pan Americanism."[82] The opposition to a Western Hemisphere exemption invoked the principle of nondiscrimination, thus taking the civil rights language of equal treatment and throwing it back at the White House.[83] Almost all of the Republicans joined conservative Democrats in voting against the Western Hemisphere exemption. Accepting limitations on Western Hemisphere immigration was the political price of ending the national-origins quotas in the Eastern Hemisphere.[84] Eliminating the negative discrimination against Asians, Africans, and southern Europeans would relieve a far greater diplomatic problem than would be created by eliminating the positive preferences for the Western Hemisphere.

Intended Consequences?

The 1965 immigration system quickly transformed the ethnic composition of immigration to the United States. The European and Canadian share of legal immigrants fell from 60 percent in the 1950s to 22 percent in the 1970s.[85] In the long run, the end of the national-origins quotas and emphasis on family reunification accelerated Asian migration. The Asian percentage of legal immigrants rose from 6 percent in the 1950s to 35 percent in the 1980s. The arrival of Indochinese refugees in the 1970s, made possible through special refugee programs, led to more Asian migration as former refugees sponsored their family members' immigration through the reunification provisions of Hart-Celler.

Joppke argues that the emphasis on family reunification in 1965 was "meant to minimize the possibility of ethnic change," as there were relatively few nonwhites in the United States who could sponsor family members in 1965. Economist George Borjas, historian David Reimers, and legal scholar Jan Ting make a similar argument.[86] Gabriel Chin convincingly challenges the argument that the authors of the 1965 act did not realize that it would lead to increased Asian immigration. Opponents of the 1965 law, the INS, and major media outlets expected at the time that Asians would benefit.[87] However, there is a consensus among scholars that the scale of new Asian immigration was unexpected.[88]

Conclusion

The 1965 Immigration and Nationality Act marked a profound and highly consequential shift in US policy away from the blatant racial and ethnic selection that had been in place since the early 1800s. As we argue elsewhere, changes in formal laws matter: they shape who is present to legitimately participate in the political process.[89] The 1965 reforms led to a transformation in the sources of migration away from Europe and toward Asia, and consequently to a change in the ethno-racial configuration of politics in the United States. From the standpoint of observers whose perspective has been shaped by some of the very political changes that followed the 1965 act, its compromises and shortcomings may be more salient than its accomplishments. Yet the reforms of 1943 to 1965 are deeply significant. It is difficult to imagine laws enacted today that would explicitly ban labor migration from Asia and deny Asians the possibility of naturalization—both of which were prominent features of previous policy.

Passage of the 1965 Immigration and Nationality Act was a momentous break from 162 years of continuous legal racial exclusion. This century-and-a-half was a period of liberal democratic governance during which slavery and Jim Crow segregation coexisted with racial exclusions in immigration law. Liberal democracy and racial discrimination in the United States were cut from the same cloth. It would take considerable power to change policy and break with this longstanding history. Foreign policy considerations in World War II and through the Cold War gave less powerful countries the leverage to press principles of antidiscrimination in a way that moved the US executive branch and Congress to change immigration law.

Our argument about the decline in blatant racialization of immigration and nationality policy does not imply that the United States has achieved a post-racial state of affairs. Immigration policy in the United States continues to discriminate surreptitiously in its design, through differential enforcement, and by having disparate effects on people of different origins. For instance, caps in the number of family-preference visas issued by the US government are a means to lengthen the line for immigrants from Mexico and the Philippines, and the so-called Diversity Program is the result of a failed effort to bring in more Europeans. To be clear, we are referring to immigration admissions policies at the border, rather than those aimed at assimilation or integration.

In view of the argument made in this chapter, it is especially important to underscore that the politics of an international system of states continue to matter for domestic immigration policy. A significant number of contemporary anti-immigrant policies in the United States, especially those targeting Latin Americans and Latinos, happen on the state level because it is less susceptible to foreign policy concerns and international norms.

The international field of immigration politics and diffusion of policies continue to matter. This conclusion, however, implies no iron law. As we have shown, there are conditions under which domestic policies may trump international policy considerations. In the contemporary context, countries are more likely to consider categorical discrimination when they perceive immigrants as posing a threat to their basic security through domestic terrorism or the spread of disease. Still, the style of such discrimination has rarely been overt in Western liberal democracies after World War II. More often, discrimination has been surreptitious (calculated

The Geopolitical Origins of the 1965 Immigration Act • 97

to disproportionately affect people by origin) or positive (showing preference for people of particular origins because of their putative cultural affinities to a receiving society or the labor they can provide during a temporary stay). Uncovering the logic and practices of these insidious forms of discrimination represent the next frontier and challenge to students of immigration policy.

Notes

1. Philip Wolgin, "Beyond National Origins: The Development of Modern Immigration Policymaking, 1948–1968," PhD diss., University of California, Berkeley, 2011.

2. See also Douglas S. Massey, Jorge Durand, and Nolan J. Malone, *Beyond Smoke and Mirrors: Mexican Immigration in an Era of Free Trade* (New York: Russell Sage Foundation, 2002); Kevin Johnson, *The Huddled Masses Myth: Immigration and Civil Rights* (Philadelphia: Temple University Press, 2004).

3. David Scott FitzGerald and David Cook-Martín, *Culling the Masses: The Democratic Origins of Racist Immigration Policy in the Americas* (Cambridge, Mass.: Harvard University Press, 2014).

4. Emergency Quota Law of 1921, Pub. L. No. 67-5, 42 Stat. 5 (1921).

5. Robert A. Divine, *American Immigration Policy, 1924–1952* (New Haven, Conn.: Yale University Press, 1957), 5–6.

6. The Immigration Act of 1924 (Johnson-Reed Act), Pub. L. No. 69-139, 43 Stat. 153 (1924). A complete list of the quotas in 1921, 1924, 1929, 1952, and 1965 is in US Bureau of the Census, *Statistical Abstract of the United States* (Washington, DC, 1966), 92–93.

7. Daniel J. Tichenor, *Dividing Lines: The Politics of Immigration Control in America* (Princeton, N.J.: Princeton University Press, 2002), 145.

8. Edward P. Hutchinson, *Legislative History of American Immigration Policy, 1798–1965* (Philadelphia: University of Pennsylvania Press, 1981), 484–85.

9. 43 Stat. 153. Sec. 11(d).

10. Ibid.

11. 43 Stat. 153. Sec. 13 (c).

12. Mae M. Ngai, *Impossible Subjects: Illegal Aliens and the Making of Modern America* (Princeton, N.J.: Princeton University Press, 2004), 103; Rick Baldoz, *The Third Asiatic Invasion: Empire and Migration in Filipino America, 1898–1946* (New York: New York University Press, 2011), 157, 181.

13. The Philippine Independence Act (Tydings-McDuffie Act), Pub. L. No. 73-127 (1934)

14. 43 Stat. 153. Sec.4(c). Precedent for favorable treatment of immigrants from neighboring countries had been established at least as early as the Immigration Act of 1907 (34 Stat. 898), which exempted aliens from a $4 head tax if they were citizens of Canada, Newfoundland, Cuba, or Mexico. During the labor shortages of World War I the US government had waived the literacy tests, restriction on contract labor immigration, and head taxes to bring in seventy-five thousand temporary workers from Mexico (Tichenor, *Dividing Lines*, 169).

15. Aristide R. Zolberg, *A Nation by Design: Immigration Policy in the Fashioning of America* (Cambridge, Mass.: Harvard University Press, 2006), 262; Lara Putnam, *Radical Moves: Caribbean Migrants and the Politics of Race in the Jazz Age* (Chapel Hill: University of North Carolina, 2013).

16. 70 Cong. Rec. S2817–2818 (daily ed. Feb. 9, 1928).

17. *Immigration from Latin America, the West Indies, and Canada*. Hearings before the Committee on Immigration and Naturalization, House of Representatives, Sixty-Eighth Congress, Second Session, March 3, 1925, by Robert F. Foerster (Washington, DC: GPO, 1925).

18. Tichenor, *Dividing Lines*, 171.

19. Patrick D. Lukens, *A Quiet Victory for Latino Rights: FDR and the Controversy over "Whiteness"* (Tucson: University of Arizona Press, 2012), 47.

20. 68 Cong. Rec. S6623 (daily ed. Apr. 18, 1924).

21. 71 Cong. Rec. S6925–6926.

22. Michael C. LeMay, *Guarding the Gates: Immigration and National Security* (Westport, Conn.: Praeger, 2006), 13; Hutchinson, *Legislative History*, 214–18, 486.

23. Arthur P. Whitaker, "Latin America and Postwar Organization," *Annals of the American Academy of Political and Social Science* 240 (1945): 109–15.

24. 8th Pan-American Conference, Resolution XLV, 1939, 268.

25. Gunnar Myrdal, *An American Dilemma: The Negro Problem and Modern Democracy* (New Brunswick, N.J.: Transaction, 1944), 1016.

26. *Acta final del Primer Congreso Demografico Interamericano: Celebrado en México, D.F. del 12 al 21 de Octubre de 1943* (México, DF: S. Turanzas del Valle, 1944).

27. K. J. Leong, "Foreign Policy, National Identity, and Citizenship: The Roosevelt White House and the Expediency of Repeal," *Journal of American Ethnic History* 22, no. 4 (2003): 11.

28. Xiaohua Ma, "The Sino-American Alliance during World War II and the Lifting of the Chinese Exclusion Acts," *American Studies International* 63, no. 2 (2000): 45–46.

29. Ibid., 49.

30. Divine, *American Immigration Policy*, 150.

31. Leong, *Foreign Policy*, 7–8.

32. Ibid., 16.

33. An Act to repeal the Chinese Exclusion Acts, to establish quotas, and for other purposes, Pub. L. No. 78-199, 57 Stat. 600 (1943).

34. Chinese War Brides Act, Pub. L. No. 79-713, 60 Stat. 975 (1946); Act of July 22, 1947, 61 Stat. 401 (1947); Act on Alien Spouses and Children, 64 Stat. 464 (1950).

35. Luce-Celler Act of 1946, 60 Stat. 416 (1946).

36. Penny M. Von Eschen, *Race against Empire: Black Americans and Anticolonialism, 1937–1957* (Ithaca, N.Y.: Cornell University Press, 1997), 125.

37. Frank Füredi, *The Silent War: Imperialism and the Changing Perception of Race* (New Brunswick, N.J.: Rutgers University Press, 1998), 14.

38. Paul Gordon Lauren, *The Evolution of International Human Rights: Visions Seen*, 2nd ed. (Philadelphia: University of Pennsylvania Press, 2003), 161.

39. Ibid., 163.

The Geopolitical Origins of the 1965 Immigration Act • 99

40. Ibid., 171.

41. Mary Ann Glendon, "The Forgotten Crucible: The Latin American Influence on the Universal Human Rights Idea," *Harvard Human Rights Journal* 16 (2003): 27–39; Johannes Morsink, *The Universal Declaration of Human Rights: Origins, Drafting and Intent* (Philadelphia: University of Pennsylvania Press, 1999); Paolo Wright-Carozza, "From Conquest to Constitutions: Retrieving a Latin American Tradition of the Idea of Human Rights," *Human Rights Quarterly* 25, no. 2 (2003): 281–313.

42. Thomas Borstelmann, *The Cold War and the Color Line: American Race Relations in the Global Arena* (Cambridge, Mass.: Harvard University Press, 2001), 41; Füredi, *Silent War*, 191; Carol Anderson, *Eyes off the Prize: The United Nations and the African American Struggle for Human Rights, 1944–1955* (Cambridge: Cambridge University Press, 2003), 49.

43. See UN Charter and Articles 1, 13, 55, 62, 68, 76 of the initial draft.

44. Paul Gordon Lauren, *Power and Prejudice: The Politics and Diplomacy of Racial Discrimination* (Boulder, Colo.: Westview, 1996).

45. Borstelmann, *Cold War and Color Line*, 269.

46. Gabriel J. Chin, "The Civil Rights Revolution Comes to Immigration Law: A New Look at the Immigration and Nationality Act of 1965," *North Carolina Law Review* 75 (1996): 288.

47. Azza Salama Layton, *International Politics and Civil Rights Policies in the United States, 1941–1960* (New York: Cambridge University Press, 2000), 4.

48. Mary L. Dudziak, *Cold War Civil Rights: Race and the Image of American Democracy* (Princeton, N.J.: Princeton University Press, 2000).

49. US President's Committee on Civil Rights, *To Secure These Rights: The Report of the President's Committee on Civil Rights*, 1947, 32–33, https://www.trumanlibrary.org/civilrights/srights1.htm.

50. Lauren, *Power and Prejudice*, 167.

51. US President's Committee on Civil Rights, *To Secure These Rights*, 147.

52. John D. Skrentny, *The Minority Rights Revolution* (Cambridge, Mass.: Harvard University Press, 2002), 22.

53. The Immigration and Nationality Act of 1952 (McCarran-Walter Act), Pub. L. No. 82-414, 66 Stat. 163 (1952), Sec. 202b.

54. Lara Putnam, *Radical Moves: Caribbean Migrants and the Politics of Race in the Jazz Age* (Chapel Hill.: The University of North Carolina Press, 2013), 88–89.

55. Ngai, *Impossible Subjects*, 255–57.

56. Divine, *American Immigration Policy*, 180–81.

57. Tichenor, *Dividing Lines*, 191; Zolberg, *Nation by Design*, 315.

58. Divine, *American Immigration Policy*, 156; Desmond S. King, *Making Americans: Immigration, Race, and the Origins of the Diverse Democracy* (Cambridge, Mass.: Harvard University Press, 2000), 237.

59. Chin, *Civil Rights Revolution*, 294–95.

60. Reprinted in US President's Commission on Immigration and Naturalization, "Whom Shall We Welcome," 1953, 283.

61. Douglas S. Massey, Jorge Durand, and Nolan J. Malone, *Beyond Smoke and Mirrors: Mexican Immigration in an Era of Free Trade* (New York: Russell Sage Foundation, 2002), 39–40.

62. Cheryl Shanks, *Immigration and the Politics of American Sovereignty, 1890–1990* (Ann Arbor: University of Michigan Press, 2001), 171.

63. US President's Commission on Immigration and Naturalization, "Whom Shall We Welcome," 122.

64. Bill Ong Hing, *Making and Remaking Asian America through Immigration Policy, 1850–1990* (Stanford, Calif.: Stanford University Press, 1993), 39; Shanks, *Immigration and Politics*, 158.

65. Vernon M. Briggs, *Immigration and American Unionism* (Ithaca, N.Y.: Cornell University Press, 2001), 122; Tichenor, *Dividing Lines*, 180; Keith A. Fitzgerald, *The Face of the Nation: Immigration, the State, and the National Identity* (Stanford, Calif.: Stanford University Press, 1996), 226.

66. Ngai, *Impossible Subjects*, 243, 346.

67. Wolgin, *Beyond National Origins*, 181.

68. Shanks, *Immigration and Politics*, 165.

69. Chin, *Civil Rights Revolution*, 299.

70. "Hearings before Subcommittee No. 1 of the Committee on the Judiciary, House of Representatives, 88th Cong. 2nd Session" (Washington, DC: US GPO, 1964) (statement of Dean Rusk, Secretary of State of the United States), 385–408. See the discussion in Robbie J. Totten, "Security and US Immigration Policy," PhD diss., University of California, Los Angeles, 2012.

71. Dudziak, *Cold War Civil Rights*, 187.

72. Skrentny, *Minority Rights*, 54.

73. Wolgin, *Beyond National Origins*, 42.

74. Matthew Frye Jacobson, *Whiteness of a Different Color: European Immigrants and the Alchemy of Race* (Cambridge, Mass.: Harvard University Press, 1998), 8; Hutchinson, *Legislative History*, 368.

75. Massey, Durand, and Malone, *Beyond Smoke*.

76. Cong. Rec. 21783 (August 25, 1965).

77. David Gutiérrez, *Walls and Mirrors: Mexican Americans, Mexican Immigrants, and the Politics of Ethnicity* (Berkeley: University of California Press, 1995).

78. Skrentny, *Minority Rights*.

79. The Immigration and Nationality Act of 1965 (Hart-Celler Act), Pub. L. No. 89-236, 79 Stat. 911 (1965).

80. Hutchinson, *Legislative History*, 359.

81. 79 Stat. 911, Sec. 202(a)

82. Skrentny, *Minority Rights*, 55.

83. Christian Joppke, *Selecting by Origin: Ethnic Migration in the Liberal State* (Cambridge, Mass.: Harvard University Press, 2005), 59.

84. James G. Gimpel and James R. Edwards, *The Congressional Politics of Immigration Reform* (Boston: Allyn and Bacon, 1999), 103–7; Maddalena Marinari, "'Americans Must

Show Justice in Immigration Policies Too': The Passage of the 1965 Immigration Act," *Journal of Policy History* 26, no. 2 (2014): 219–245.

85. Wolgin, *Beyond National Origins*, 124.

86. Joppke, *Selecting by Origins*, 57; David Reimers, "An Unintended Reform: The 1965 Immigration Act and Third World Immigration to the United States," *Journal of American Ethnic History* 3, no. 1 (1983): 9–28; George J. Borjas, *Friends or Strangers: The Impact of Immigrants on the US Economy* (New York: Basic, 1990); Jan C. Ting, "Other than a Chinaman: How US Immigration Law Resulted from and Still Reflects a Policy of Excluding and Restricting Asian Immigration," *Temple Political and Civil Rights Law Review* 4 (1995): 301–15.

87. Chin, *Civil Rights Revolution*, 314–16.

88. Ibid., 331.

89. FitzGerald and David Cook-Martín, *Culling the Masses*.

PART II

Labor

In this section we explore changing labor markets and growing differentiation between categories of workers as skilled and unskilled. Immigration policies increasingly privileged the migration and settlement of workers with education, credentials, and specializations in fields viewed as enhancing the United States' drive to lead the world in technical and scientific innovation in industry, armaments, and space. Concurrently, while demands for laborers viewed as unskilled remained high, temporary labor programs restricted their protections and access to citizenship, particularly for those from south of the US-Mexico border.

American fears of unfair competition and unfree labor never completely disappeared. However, the demands for educated and trained workers suitable for employment in research, development, and other professional and white-collar sectors steadily grew in influence in the years leading to the passage of the 1965 immigration act. Economic competitiveness in the nineteenth century required stable access to large numbers of inexpensive farm and manufacturing workers, but by the mid-twentieth century, scientific and technological innovation required well-educated and credentialed "knowledge workers" who became critical commodities. Albert Einstein, who immigrated in 1933, can be considered an early example of this kind of high-value immigrant.

After World War II, the US Congress developed a growing array of immigration policies and administrative processes that guaranteed access to a wide range of workers but also produced differential statuses and rights among immigrants based on the kind of labor they performed. These new policies and administrative procedures aligned immigration controls even more closely with the interests of economically motivated constituencies and relied on the collaboration among the US Departments of Labor, Commerce, State, and the immigration bureaucracy.

International competition for the most elite of so-called "skilled" workers, determined on the basis of credentials such as education, training, and acquired expertise in particular fields, resulted in legal accommodations that facilitated their entry and access to permanent residency and citizenship. In contrast, "unskilled" workers were often restricted to temporary visas, which limited their chances for permanent residency, citizenship, and even family unity. These emerging systems of privileging certain categories of workers, while institutionalizing lesser rights and status for others, informed preferences and procedures articulated in the 1965 Immigration Act in ways that have become naturalized in the twenty-first century with programs such as the H-1B visa allotments and greater consideration given to educated and entrepreneurial elites as well as investor categories of immigrants.

Heather Lee's "Hunting for Sailors: Restaurant Raids and the Conscription of Laborers during World War II" showcases an effort by the US Immigration Bureau to discipline unruly workers to serve employer interests. In 1943 the US government acted at the behest of its English ally—a stark case of international cooperation—to retrieve Chinese sailors who had escaped dire conditions on British vessels by jumping ship in New York. Lee's richly detailed account links the imperial legacies of racialized views of Chinese that produced their lower wages and work assignments aboard British ships with the wartime exigencies that justified US intervention on behalf of its ally. It also highlights the networks and communities that enabled the Chinese sailors to find new employment in restaurants and to effectively disappear despite the efforts of two governments seeking to exert immigration controls.

Ronald Mize's "The State Management of Immigrant Labor: The Decline of the Bracero Program, the Rise of Temporary Worker Visas" describes the expanding use of temporary visas that institutionalized the marginalization of "unskilled workers," particularly through the bracero and H-2 programs during the 1950s and early 1960s. After the Bracero Program terminated in 1964, legislators retained "H-2" programs in the 1965 Immigration and Naturalization Act and dramatically expanded them beyond agriculture in the 1986 Immigration Reform and Control Act to include H-2A temporary agricultural workers and H-2B seasonal and unskilled nonagricultural workers.

Legally ineligible for permanent status and eventual citizenship, temporary workers had limited claims on the United States. In many instances, their disposability was accentuated by the proximity of their homelands, such as Mexico and the Bahamas, to the United States which made it easier to expel them once they completed their labor terms.

In "Japanese Agricultural Labor Program: Temporary-Worker Immigration, US-Japan Cultural Diplomacy, and Ethnic Community Making among Japanese Americans," Eiichiro Azuma explores the international, intragovernmental, and intra-ethnic conflicts and compromises that converged to implement a program for the employment of temporary Japanese laborers in California by Nisei farmers between 1956 and 1965. Azuma's chapter demonstrates the remaking of racial criteria as barriers to immigration and the clout of agricultural organizations in lobbying for access to foreign laborers. As Mexican workers grew in militancy and assertiveness after World War II, Nisei citizen farmers sought alternatives in the form of youths from Japan brought on a temporary basis, assuming that Japanese newcomers would be easier to control due not only to their lack of access to legal residency but also because of their shared cultural background. Yet this also meant that Nisei farmers came to construct a new ethnic identity separate from Japanese workers on the basis of citizenship status. These intra-ethnic tensions at times undermined the negotiations between the United States and Japan. Competing priorities on the part of various government agencies representing agriculture, labor, immigration, and foreign relations, as well as lobbying on the part of prospective employer groups, also made negotiations difficult. That this program overcame so many obstacles to run for a decade, and yet has left so few traces on the Japanese American community, historical memory, or scholarship, underscores both the concerted will to develop access to temporary agricultural workers and the determination to see the workers depart when their terms of employment ended.

In contrast, the German and Austrian scientists and engineers featured in Monique Laney's "Setting the Stage to Bring in the 'Highly Skilled'" were readily allowed to shed their former ties to Nazi Germany and become American citizens as bearers of highly valued knowledge and experiences seen as crucial to the US competition against the Soviet Union for technological supremacy in armaments and the space race. Although exceptional at its time, "Project Paperclip" presaged a broader shift in policy toward a system privileging skilled immigrants. At the end of World War II, the allied forces searched for and captured thousands of German and Austrian scientists, engineers, and technicians who specialized in aerodynamics, rocketry, chemical weapons, medicine, and other fields, bringing more than five hundred to the United States under a military operation. While the project initially provided temporary employment, after which the specialists were to return to Europe, Congress soon developed procedures to enable them to become permanent immigrants after protracted negotiations among the Departments of War, Commerce, Labor, and Justice. National security and the intensifying Cold War were the driving rationalizations for these legal accommodations. "Project Paperclip" and other programs that facilitated resettlement by technical and scientific experts reveal the shifting priorities and administrative practices that privileged immigrants with "special skills" that remain in effect today.

CHAPTER 5

Hunting for Sailors

Restaurant Raids and Conscription of Laborers during World War II

HEATHER LEE

On January 9, 1943, five squads of US government agents ripped through New York's Chinese community in the middle of the night. Seventy-four sailors from China had recently abandoned the *Empress of Scotland*, a British naval auxiliary ship, midway through their shipping contracts. To intimidate all Chinese for these men's insubordination, English diplomats called upon the United States government, a wartime ally, for help. Using UK intelligence, fifteen US immigration agents, two translators, and six police detectives stormed places where Chinese mariners commonly gathered. American officials interrogated fifteen hundred Chinese at restaurants, boardinghouses, association headquarters, clubs, poolrooms, and theaters. The raid failed to recover these men. On January 11, the *Empress* navigated the Long Island Sound toward the Atlantic with one returnee and four recruits.[1] British officials claimed success despite the paltry results. The incident, it turned out, gave England pretense to scare Chinese merchant mariners into obedience. An Englishman who helped hunt for sailors from the *Empress* enjoyed "leaving the bewildered inhabitants of Chinatown with a vest-pocket notion of what the original Sack of Rome was like."[2]

British statesmen justified these tactics as wartime expediencies. English ships shuttled the lion's share of fuel, food, ammunition, and machinery for the European front across the Atlantic via New York. These private transporters depended on Chinese sailors, far cheaper than unionized Englishmen, for brute manpower. Approximately ten thousand Chinese nationals worked on English ships during World War II. British liners contracted them in East Asian colonies for the lowest-paid and most strenuous tasks. Chinese seamen appealed for better conditions and, when negotiations collapsed, deserted in protest at the port of New York. Instead of granting parity in contract, England sought support from America for coerced service. Agreeing to an extreme approach, the US War Shipping Administration (WSA) and Immigration and Naturalization Service (INS) designed the Alien Seamen Program with English interests in mind. The program tasked the INS with tracking and finding mariners who sought better employment on US soil. Captured seamen had the option of reshipping with previous employers or deportation to their home countries. Still, Chinese seamen refused British assignments, and Japan's wartime control of the Chinese coast forced the INS to hold Chinese deserters indefinitely. In the words of New York Mayor Fiorello La Guardia, "Internment is paradise to the hell that they have gone through."[3] The Crown, resourceful and desperate, pursued draconian punishments. The British Ministry of War Transportation pushed legislative amendments to US immigration law to deport Chinese to British territories. Under these wartime agreements, England wielded exceptional state power over Chinese nationals within the United States.

England could not will the Chinese into compliance. Chinese sailors benefited from kin networks in New York that helped them disappear and find employment ashore. The earliest Chinese settlers arrived on trading ships in the mid-nineteenth century and parlayed their experiences at sea into viable businesses on land. By the early twentieth century, many mariners-turned-entrepreneurs operated Chinese restaurants or employment brokerages specializing in food service. Former seamen found less-strenuous and better-paying jobs as waiters and cooks. During World War II, when trans-Atlantic assignments risked life and limb and English companies refused adequate compensation, Chinese mariners called upon ex-sailors for assistance. Their supporters built coalitions with local Chinese associations, Chinese diplomats in the United States, the American Civil Liberties Union, and US Seamen's unions for equal benefits to white seamen. The flash point was shore leave, as we shall see. In the ensuing controversy the Ministry of War Transport relented to shore leave to great regret. Many ships lost a third of their kitchen and engine staffs, who preferred working in restaurants and hotels.[4] Captains tightened controls in response, granting a few dozen Chinese leave at a time and refused to issue more until everyone returned. But the damage was done. Once granted, the British could not rescind shore leave without compromising their political position with China and the United States.

During World War II an unexpected game of cat and mouse unfolded in New York's Chinatown. England played cat, Chinese sailors the elusive prey. In an aggressive and fearsome chase, the Crown expanded its reach through the US government, which lent its immigration apparatus to disciplining low-wage Chinese laborers. This history twists the established narrative of US immigration policy, which emphasizes the synergies between national labor and immigration agendas. The struggle of Chinese seamen against English shipping companies on American terra provides a triangulated framing. State power swelled and national borders hardened through the elaboration of immigration law and bureaucracy during the twentieth century. US federal officials used its muscles to serve foreign policy agendas, amending its laws to resolve the labor conflicts of an allied nation at the expense of laborers from another wartime partner. The INS and WSA walked eyes-wide-open into this arrangement despite warnings from legal experts in the Department of Justice against the political, legal, and ethical quandary. The Chinese seamen's response to Anglo-US collaboration was equally global, involving coordinated protests in port cities around the globe. This article emphasizes the contradiction of an authority, predicated on national sovereignty. It served multiple national agendas yet was ineffectual at disciplining a transnational migrant network.

A Wartime Labor Crisis

At the start of armed conflict, British shipping companies took a hardline approach against the Chinese. Captains of English liners expected their Chinese crews would disappear in New York if allowed the opportunity. Taking preventive measures, they detained the Chinese onboard under armed guard, paid wages in British pounds instead of US dollars, and held vital personal documents, like passports and sailor's books. English shipmasters developed these tactics to avoid hefty fines from the Immigration Bureau for runaway sailors. In 1924, US Congressmen raised the penalty from $500 to $1,000 per disappearance, which captains used to justify denying shore leave to the Chinese in New York during World War II. The number of alien sailors detained in US ports skyrocketed, from fewer than one thousand on the eve of war in Europe to more than fourteen thousand three years later. The number of Chinese detainees cannot be disaggregated because the INS lumped together all alien nationals in these figures. Their detentions likely increased disproportionately over this period. In correspondences with US immigration officials, the British insisted on confinement, regardless of how long or under what conditions the Chinese worked at sea. J. F. Delany, INS District Director of Baltimore, worked directly with British diplomats and captains on retention strategies. Delany reported to his superior that English officials blocked all efforts to extend shore leave to the Chinese because of Baltimore's proximity to New York.[5]

Effective in the short term but detrimental to British interests in the long run, these sorts of measures eroded any residual willingness among the Chinese to serve. For years, Chinese seamen agitated for improvements with little success. Captains typically paid the Chinese a fraction of salaries paid to whites for the same duties. In 1939, able-bodied Anglo seamen earned £9.6 per month and Chinese seamen of the same rating earned £2.8 per month. The following year, the gap widened when the Ministry of War Transportation granted £5 war-risk bonuses to white sailors. Outraged Chinese sailors in Liverpool demanded the same benefits. The Ministry of War Transport countered with £2. Street demonstrations continued through early 1941, when Liverpool police started jailing protestors and deporting them to China. With central agitators swept out of the picture, the Chinese ambassador stepped in, reaching an agreement with his British counterpart after long and tense negotiations in April 1942. Shipping companies ignored the concessions, though. Many Chinese sailors never saw war-risk bonuses, back pay, or, in case of death, payment to next of kin.[6] New York attorney Nathan Shapiro helped them sue for compensation and witnessed repeatedly England's blatant disregard of legal commitments. Like his clients, he experienced an utter loss of faith, "[The] British Government has done little or nothing since April, 1942 in its negotiations for an agreement with the Chinese government for the improvement of the status of Chinese seamen."[7]

After more than a month of false promises, April 1942 was a turning point for Chinese mariners circling the globe under the Union Jack. They could not be quieted after a British shipmaster slayed a Chinese seaman. On April 11, 1942, eleven Chinese sailors approached Captain Rowe for leave and back pay. Their vessel, the SS *Silver Ash*, berthed in Brooklyn Pier six weeks earlier. Rowe refused, and the disgruntled sailors turned violent. In the scuffle Rowe shot Lin Young Tsai dead. Two weeks later, a grand jury in New York dismissed charges against Rowe, finding his actions justified in the face of armed rebellion. The Chinese allegedly advanced with weapons to his cabin. Hearing shots, white crewmen arrived on scene to defend Captain Rowe. They overpowered and locked the Chinese below deck until New York police arrived. The Chinese sailors claimed a miscarriage of justice, arguing in a later suit that the court failed to properly take their witness statements. What they saw contradicted the court record, and no one spoke their dialect adequately for them to convey their side. In the end, Rowe served no time, while the ten surviving sailors faced charges of disorderly conduct. Lin's family received no compensation for his death either.[8] The outcome sparked global protests. Chinese sailors grounded ships in the British ports of Jamaica, Sri Lanka, and Mauritius. The colonial office of Kolkata, India dispatched a "strong force of police" to silence two thousand to three thousand Chinese marching in the streets. Chinese crews in New York coordinated their walk out with strikers in New Orleans, encouraging them to preserve in their "united" struggle.[9]

The controversy spiraled out of control, forcing English statesmen to concede on seamen's rights. The Associated Press cabled news of Lin's death on the evening wire; major newspapers across the country ran the story the next day.[10] The rapid publicity brought labor unions and civil rights organizations on the side of the Chinese. Thomas Christensen and Joseph Curran of the National Maritime Union supported the Chinese at an international conference in June, while a Dutch mariner union established a Chinese branch out of solidarity. On June 23, Edward Ross, chairman and general counsel of the American Civil Liberties Union (ACLU), urged Attorney General Francis Biddle to permit shore leave. Sailors typically enjoyed time ashore while their vessels docked for trade and repair, but the British refused the Chinese that privilege. Ross persuaded Biddle to resolve the issue of race-based wage discrimination and mistreatment of a wartime ally with one policy change. He suggested releasing Chinese sailors on bonds secured through local organizations and with the cooperation of foreign diplomats.[11] On the other side of this debate, British shippers argued that the Chinese would disappear on shore leave, but they relented under pressure from high-level diplomats. Consuls General Tsune Chi Yu and Godfrey Haggard ironed out details for a two-month trial on Chinese shore leave. The agreement required Chinese officials to compel crews of China's commitment to England and for mariners to sign reshipping pledges. The plan rested on the dubious assumption that sailors would not allow China to lose face. On August 5, Consuls Yu and Haggard welcomed sixty-two Chinese arriving on a British freighter to New York.[12]

Chinese sailors used these freshly won rights to damage English shipping. British diplomats stipulated that they would retract shore-leave privileges if the Chinese refused to reship. Government officials called this act a "desertion," even though merchant mariners worked as civilians on private shipping missions. The Chinese abandoned their assignments anyway. The United Kingdom lost twice as many sailors after the concession. From September through December 1942, 250 Chinese left sixteen British ships at US ports. Diplomatic historian Meredith Oyen notes that Chinese disappeared en masse, instead of one by one. Because captains relegated them to kitchens and engine rooms, these wholesale departures crippled entire departments and, consequently, grounded ships in port. Vessels traveled in armed convoys across the Atlantic as protection against U-boat attacks. Short-handed ships missed scheduled convoys. Chinese desertions vexed the Atlantic mission, delaying fifty-one Allied ships. The backlog removed five ships temporarily from transoceanic service.[13] Once taken for granted as cheap, subservient laborers, Chinese sailors suddenly wielded outsized power. Oyen writes, "Chinese sailors unexpectedly put the success of the entire supply operation, and by extension the war, in jeopardy." Because so much rested on Chinese willingness, England plied enormous resources to the problem. T. T. Scott directed the British Shipping Mission office in Washington, DC. "The amount of time I and others consume on this problem is amazing," he complained to his superior in London. "I breathe, eat and sleep Chinese."[14]

We Will Not Submit

To evade England's watchful eye, the Chinese counted on friends and family for help disappearing ashore. Since the mid-nineteenth century, Chinese mariners had been jumping ship in New York, establishing a robust community by World War II. Ex-seamen lived separately from other Chinese, forming their own associations and businesses. New York's Chinese population at mid-century was small (fewer than twenty thousand) but fractured along regional lines. Most Chinese came from Taishan, a mountainous county lying southwest of Hong Kong. Sailors typically traced their roots to Dapeng, a peninsula west of the British colony. In the tight urban economy of New York's Chinatown, regional groups helped only their own.[15] According to a British intelligence report, the Tai Pun (Dapeng) Association operated branches in major seaports to help members find temporary employment. Kong Bo, for example, jumped ship in New York early in the war. He vigorously encouraged other Dapengese to follow his example. The British intercepted a letter in which he promised a relative working for Blue Funnel, a Liverpool based transport company, "hundreds of dollars a month." "All you need is [to] come up to Tai Pun Benevolent Association," he instructed, "there will be someone to lead you to my apartment."[16] The British reported that the Dapengese assisted anyone without question. The president of a Tai Pun Association in Hong Kong proudly invoked a family metaphor to describe their devotion: "Because we belong to one Dapeng family. We know each other."[17]

The work that Kong Bo promised was likely at a Chinese restaurant. Twentieth-century Chinese mariners often traded their sailing uniforms for chefs' garb. The restaurant industry expanded rapidly in New York, reaching 18,927 licensed businesses and several thousand informal eateries by 1920. Chinese restaurants occupied a narrow but persistent slice of New York's food industry. According to Fong Wing Kee, a steward in the British merchant marines, ex-sailors secured work for a nominal finder's commission. Taking a don't-ask–don't-tell approach, managers hired the Chinese without learning immigration statuses and shielded them from suspicious INS agents. Hotels and restaurants paid Chinese seamen $32 a week, which was double their earnings at sea. When INS agents went looking for deserters, they searched first in hotel and restaurant kitchens. For this reason, the hunt for *Empress of Scotland* deserters started at Chinese restaurants. District Director of New York W. F. Watkins "commenced a systematic search," using information about native origins to identify three large restaurants in Manhattan and several minor operations in Jersey City.[18]

In the spirit of "one Dapeng family," ex-seamen employed people from their native regions. Ho Ping, for example, was a resourceful and talented cook who started two restaurants within fifteen years of arriving in New York. In 1929 he opened his first restaurant with a distant cousin, who went by Jimmie Ho. Both men came to New York as mariners and learned the restaurant business through kinsmen. Taishanese men dominated New York's food-service industry and would only hire Taishanese. The Hos established restaurants in Brooklyn to stake out a corner of New York as Dapengese territory. Five years after their first restaurant opened, the cousins recruited two new partners for a second eatery.[19] Because they worked with and hired relatives, the Hos' success enriched the Dapengese community and created alternative opportunities for maritime people.

As physical locations, Chinese restaurants doubled as addresses to look up help. Sailors who planned to jump ship carried the business cards of restaurants to sea. Before leaving Liverpool, Chung Wing Kee got You Gee's contact information in Jacksonville, Florida. Chung decided to desert after nearly dying on assignment. Germans torpedoed his ship, and his British shipper granted him only three days' rest. Finding the schedule inhumane, Chung contacted You Gee, who ran a Chinese restaurant in Jacksonville. Chung and four other sailors wanted to reach New York. Agreeing to smuggle them into the country, You Gee met the party at the dock, drove them to a hiding place and arranged train tickets. In another case, Lee Choy and Lee Joe rendezvoused at Tung Kee Restaurant in New York's Chinatown. The restaurant provided a place for the men to plot and carry out escape. Lee Choy arrived on the British steamship *Pyndarius* on March 8, 1942, before the Chinese won shore leave. The captain permitted Lee Choy a few hours to shop in Chinatown under armed guard. Lee Joe was once a sailor and felt obligated to help the Dapengese escape. Lee Choy reached Lee Joe at Lin Fong restaurant, where he cooked; they agreed to meet. Lee Joe arrived with a pocket full of cash to bribe the guard. He offered $500 to let his friend walk free.[20]

Chinese restaurants dotted the eastern seaboard and provided a literal escape route leading to New York. Ho C. Lui organized a path from Jacksonville, Florida, to New York City using restaurants as safe houses. He was a food-service veteran and built an expansive network of industry colleagues along the Atlantic coast. Top Hat Restaurant in Fayetteville, North Carolina, Hing Far Law Restaurant in Washington, DC, and Golden Pheasant Restaurant in Philadelphia were just three locations in a thick address book, places where Ho hid runaway sailors. These businesses served as stopping points in what a US immigration official cheekily called the "underground railway for Chinese." When aspiring deserters arrived in a US seaport, they took shelter at local Chinese restaurants, while Ho arranged the logistics via correspondence. He also helped the Chinese cover their paths. He instructed them in how to avoid detection by shipping companies and advised planting fake intelligence to throw investigators off their trail. Other Chinese designed similar, though simpler, operations.[21]

Discipline and Punish

While the Chinese preferred safer jobs on land, restaurant work did not necessarily appeal to them more than maritime duties. Their chief complaint aimed at racism. British seamen treated them with open contempt, which the Chinese refused to tolerate anymore. After weeks at sea, the racial antagonism threatened to erupt in violence. An English engineer remarked that he "expected to slide down the ladder some night into the engine room with a knife blade between his shoulders." The engineer attempted to explain conditions on the *SS California Standard* to an INS inspector. Twenty-nine of thirty-two Chinese crewmen left the engine room. The desertions made sense to the inspector. He observed Chinese and British sailors brimming with suspicion, anger, and resentment toward one another. From his survey of work relations, he gathered that English officers slept with "guns strapped on or within easy reach." Nathan Shapiro, the New York lawyer, urged a simple solution: he promised that Chinese seamen would return if they were treated like British seamen instead of coolies.[22] To the Chinese the wage differences reflected how little England valued them. The *Chinese Nationalist Daily* and *China Daily News* printed this open letter from a seaman to the Chinese Consul General in New York:

> We left our families behind to serve on Allied ships because we wanted to do our share to gain final victory, but British and Dutch ships distinguish between the white race and the yellow and are prejudiced against us. . . . The object of arrest is apparently to force us to continue working like slave for low wages, with delayed salaries . . . by imprisonment . . . inhuman acts such as these do not differ from Axis dictatorial brutality.[23]

They protested for equal pay as evidence of changed attitudes. British captains agreed with the diagnosis: "It may be that the Chinese had for too long been regarded as a source of cheap labor."[24]

The Chinese were not alone in their opinions. Sailors of all nationalities refused to sail with England because of problems on ship. Historians typically attribute the higher rates of desertion to the U-boat threat. With the United States joining the Allies in 1942, Hitler committed fully to the U-boat strategy, adding to his fleet thirty new submarines each month. Germans sank one million tons of Allied shipping in August and September 1942 alone.[25] While fear of death certainly played a factor, deserters described English shippers as terrible employers. Thomas Christensen of the National Maritime Union surveyed alien seamen held by the INS. The Bureau caught and detained sailors who overstayed their shore leaves on Riker's Island until they accepted new assignments. Christensen interviewed two-thirds of imprisoned sailors in search of causes and solutions to the desertion patterns, none of whom were Chinese. Their responses revealed a systemic problem with

English companies. The interviewees said they would reship with any company but UK lines, with more than half preferring imprisonment. Life on Riker's Island was no vacation either. Christensen observed intolerable conditions. Detainees slept directly on metal bedframes, received no medical treatment for routine and emergency conditions, and suffered malnourishment. Some interviewees lost forty pounds over three months. Many interviewees noted bitterly that German and Italian prisoners, enemy aliens of the state, and convicted criminals lived better than INS detainees. Still, they refused to work for the British.[26]

Consequently, sailors of every nationality left or refused missions from England. English sailors, in fact, held the dubious honor of leading the pack (see table 1). Desertion at US ports peaked in 1942, rising 50 percent over the previous year, from 4,661 to 6,987. Overall desertions fell below six thousand after June 1942, but British shipping continued to suffer. Desertions from England doubled the next year and averaged twenty-three hundred per year until the armistice. Between the German invasion of Poland in September 1939 and German surrender in April 1945, 30 percent of desertions by foreign nationals in the United States left English ships (see figure 1).[27] While British shipping suffered acutely from desertions, Chinese seamen do not deserve all the credit.

Faced with untenable labor unrest, England called upon allies to press mariners into service. Every detainee Christensen interviewed wanted a spot in the US merchant marines. American transporters paid the highest wages among Allied nations. In peacetime, sailors commonly found alternative employment during calls to port, which they colloquially called "floating." The practice allowed seamen to negotiate between shippers for better wages. Arguing that floating harmed wartime shipping, the British orchestrated a pact with other Allied nations called the Alien Seamen Program. Signed in May 1942 by England, the United States, China, and several major shipping nations, the agreement allowed England to preserve its labor practices without losing to other shippers. It limited jobs on US ships to citizens of the United States or its territories and legally bound seamen to their last employer.

Table 1. British and Chinese Desertions in the United States, 1942–1945

	1942	1943	1944	1945	Total
British	1,221	1,205	1,518	1,519	5,463
	17%	21%	26%	27%	23%
Chinese	711	1,786	1,406	1,325	5,228
	10%	31%	24%	24%	22%
Total	6,987	5,683	5,811	5,577	24,058

Source: Calculated from tables "Alien seamen deserted at American seaports, by nationality and flag of vessel and districts," year ended June 30, 1942, 1943, 55854/370R, RG 85, Archive I; *Annual Report of the Immigration and Naturalization Service* (Washington, DC: GPO, 1944; 1945), 99; 7.

Figure 1. Desertions on British Ships by Nationality, 1942–1945

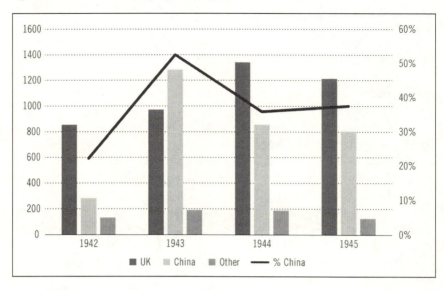

Author-generated data based on yearly desertions on British ships

Year	UK	China	Other	% China
1942	854	281	132	22%
1943	971	1,283	189	53%
1944	1,341	856	187	36%
1945	1,214	804	125	38%

Source: Calculated from tables "Alien seamen deserted at American seaports, by nationality and flag of vessel and districts," year ended June 30, 1942, 1943, 55854/370R, RG 85, Archive 1; *Annual Report of the Immigration and Naturalization Service* (Washington, DC: GPO, 1944; 1945), 99; 7.

The INS agreed to deport insubordinate seamen using an antiquated section of the 1917 Immigration Act, and created a new unit in each district office to handle seamen cases. New York, the highest-traffic port, dedicated ten special agents to inspect the crews of every incoming vessel, register arrivals by name, nationality, birthdate, and rating, and check for missing individuals when ships departed. The US government also footed the bill for finding and imprisoning deserters. In New York, where desertions were highest, Mayor Fiorello La Guardia gave part of county prisons on Riker's Island to the program. English officials placed their bet on the intolerable conditions and threat of deportation to change opinions.[28]

Britain essentially won license to reinstate indentured servitude at sea. Three bodies of laws regulated alien seamen's right of contract in the United States: British maritime statues, international treaties, and US immigration laws. English law defined "floating" as a criminal offense. Sailors signed to British ships faced punishments of hard labor and wage deductions for breaking their contracts. An 1892 treaty with Great Britain obligated US immigration officials to find, arrest, and deport deserters to stand trial before their home authorities. In 1915 the US legislature passed the La Follette Seamen's Act, which rescinded those statues and decriminalized desertion in the United States.[29] Passed during World War I, the act generated concern among congressmen, who worried that sailors would desert, so they incorporated registration and inspection requirements in the 1917 Immigration Act, along with a deportation provision for overstaying shore leave. The Alien Seamen Program resurrected the deportation clause, defining that refusing employment in wartime constituted a violation of US immigration law. The program forced sailors employed by England during World War II to accept British shipping conditions once again, which were utterly dismal.

US and British officials understood the Alien Seaman Program to target the Chinese above other nationalities. Edward J. Shaughnessy, the special assistant to the Commissioner General of Immigration, admitted that England sought cheap labor in the Chinese. "[It] is a well-known fact," he wrote, "that because of the very low rate of wages paid to Chinese seamen, foreign steamship companies would probably be hesitant in discontinuing their employment."[30] Not everyone at the INS agreed with the course of action. Edward J. Ennis moved through the ranks as general counsel at the Justice Department to become director of the Alien Enemy Control Unit. He expressed reservations to the British positions, calling it "bad even for the war effort to use the power of this Government to sustain the substandard conditions on British naval auxiliaries for Chinese seamen by such a new regulation." Agreeing with Ennis, Jack Wasserman produced an elaborate report characterizing US immigration law as the "whipping post for foreign government." Wasserman served on the Board of Immigration Appeals, which made deportation rulings. His time administering the Alien Seamen Program embittered him. He concluded, "It is one thing to cooperate with foreign governments in furtherance of the war effort" but "quite another to cater to foreign self-interest that interferes with our own best interests."[31] For Ennis and Wasserman, carrying out the Alien Seaman Program on England's behalf betrayed China and threatened US postwar politics in East Asia. They stood in the minority.

Still not satisfied, England cut a path through American immigration law to punish Chinese further. By early 1942, Japan controlled China's coast, rendering a major component of the Alien Seamen Program unenforceable in Chinese cases. British diplomats disingenuously cried foul. T. T. Scott directed the British Shipping Mission office in Washington, DC. He complained vociferously to US counterparts, "It is just maddening to think that we must put all this extra work on our fine seamen so that John Chinaman can make his contribution to the war effort by washing dishes or underwear in Chinatown."[32] Scott and other members of the British embassy persuaded the WSA and INS to make Chinese deportations possible. Marshall Dimock, director of the War Shipping Administration, supported changing US immigration laws. Dimock testified before the Senate Committee on Immigration and Naturalization of the favoritism that present circumstances bestowed to the Chinese. "There is no reason in justice or diplomacy" to excuse the Chinese, as "[our] very survival makes it imperative that any and all seamen who desert their post of duty should be deportable."[33] The British wanted all seamen deported to Liverpool, where they would join standing labor pools for reshipment. A US court denied the option, declaring deporting the Chinese to the United Kingdom illegal. The final bill allowed deportation to India for conscription into the Chinese army.[34]

As the bill neared President Roosevelt's desk, Scott giddily wrote his superior officer in London, "We shall have secured the biggest concession over the Chinese problem we could hope for." He dedicated himself to seeing the law fully implemented. Demanding the INS "put ginger into their activities," he asked for a "constant trickle of Chinese deportees." Scott predicted that the Chinese would soon learn to fear England, "Every time a few Chinese are whisked away the news spread around Chinatown and among the other detainees on Ellis Island and the Chinese will begin to think . . . that the Americans [and British] really mean business."[35] The British shipping lines concocted wild theories so US officials would scrutinize the Chinese. Playing on fears of Axis infiltration, a captain for the Anglo-Saxon shipping company alleged that German spies organized Chinese seamen protests. The spies spoke fluent Chinese and socialized with Chinese seamen in New York's Chinatown.[36] The prodding worked. US officials pursued Chinese seamen disproportionately to other nationalities. The INS arrested nearly three thousand Chinese through the Alien Seamen Program, but only two thousand British seamen, the worst offenders to the Allied shipping efforts.[37]

Scott also pursued strategic displays of British power. The INS carried out raids for *Empress of Scotland* deserters on Scott's bidding. Scott chose them because they protested in Liverpool before the *Empress* set sail, which, in his eyes, called for a harsh lesson. Four hundred Chinese had clashed with city police officers in the streets.[38] In New York the protest leaders resumed their demands, calling upon the Chinese to publicly denounce the British. Shipping lines maintained lists of agitators and asked Scott to deport them back to England. They were spreading subversive, anti-British ideas among the local Chinese population. Scott handed over these lists to the INS, insisting their capture would end their Chinese labor problems. On January 5, 1943, the eve of the *Empress*'s departure, INS seamen agents ransacked Chinese residences and businesses. The INS detained roughly fifty-five hundred Chinese over two sweeps.[39] British terror did not end there. The *Empress of Scotland* returned to New York two months later, and Scott prepared for a second raid before it landed. For several days, undercover INS and police agents identified two hundred sites for a "thorough frisk" and gave license to "ransack other spots in the course of the raid." The agents did not capture the deserters, but London was pleased that desertions slowed in New York after this grand display.[40]

Conclusion

What should strike historians of nations and empires is the British effort to carry colonial labor regimes into the nation-state era. Through the wartime seamen policies, the Allies made non-US merchant mariners prisoners of their employers and expanded the ability of nation-states to control laborers beyond their borders. The British, however, used imperial coercion over citizens of another nation. Chinese resisted the British attempt to interpolate them into colonial servitude. In *The Trouble with Empire*, Antoinette Burton flags dissent and disruption as constitutive of empire. Not only was labor agitation and rebellion routine rather than exceptional, the struggle to discipline and govern produced the colonial practices that sustained British power.[41] British officials treated the Chinese as colonial subjects, but the Chinese succeeded at evading British control via extensive Chinese social networks. Meredith Oyen credits the Chinese government with actively defending the rights of Chinese sailors abroad in a role that would have been more effectively filled by international seamen unions, had there been solidarity across racial lines.[42] Its efforts neither brought about parity with white sailors nor halted Chinese desertion, because Chinese officials in the United States and the United Kingdom worked at cross purposes.[43] To be certain, Chinese sailors also lacked confidence in the Chinese government to resolve their conflict with the British. Instead they placed full trust in their kinsmen, who supported their struggle in every way possible. This broad and empathetic network allowed Chinese seamen to engage in sustained and effective protest throughout the war.

The story here, then, is not so much British imperial power in the making, but the ability of transnational communities to check that power. During World War II, when Chinese desertion reached a disturbing milestone, the British worked tirelessly to extend its rule of law into Chinese restaurants of New York with the aid of the US government. In this game of cat and mouse, however, Chinese seafarers were clever prey. They understood their value to the war effort and leveraged the empathy of New York's Chinese community, Chinese statesmen posted in the East Coast, and the wider American public to correct longstanding British mistreatment of Chinese seamen. While they never gained economic parity with Anglo seamen or tempered the racism on British ships, they organized enough momentum to improve work conditions more than all previous efforts. Moreover, their social networks and businesses survived this episode of imperial incursion on land. At the far reaches of empire, Chinese restaurants were only temporarily

120 · HEATHER LEE

under the will of the British Crown. This period of colonial control nevertheless reveals expansive migrant networks that existed to counter the unchecked tyranny of imperial power upon its subjects.

Notes

1. W. F. Watkins to Herman R. Landon, January 9 and 11, 1943; Edward J. Shaughnessy to Earl G. Harrison, January 6, 1943, 56084/639, RG 85, National Archives and Records Administration, Washington, DC (Archives 1).

2. P. C. Devine, Memorandum to M. Borer, March 31, 1943, MT 9/4370, National Archives of the United Kingdom (Archives 1).

3. La Guardia to Cordell Hull, January 18, 1843, folder Chinese Seamen, box 3410, Mayor La Guardia Papers, NYC Municipal Archives (LGA).

4. T. T. Scott to Edward Shaughnessy, February 29, 1944, 55854/370V (Archives 1).

5. J. F. Delaney to Edward J. Shaughnessy, December 31, 1942; January 4, 1943, 56084/639; "Alien seamen arrived and departed," year ended June 30, 1939, 1942, 55854/370R (Archives 1); Anna Pegler-Gordon, "Shanghaied on the Streets of Hoboken: Chinese Exclusion and Maritime Regulation at Ellis Island," *Journal for Maritime Research* 16, no. 2 (2014): 236–37; Meredith Leigh Oyen, "Fighting for Equality: Chinese Seamen in the Battle of the Atlantic, 1939–1945," *Diplomatic History* 38, no. 3 (2014): 532–33; Arnold W. Knauth, "Alien Seamen's Rights and the War," *American Journal of International Law* 37, no. 1 (1943): 77, 79.

6. Tony Lane, *The Merchant Seaman's War* (Manchester, UK: Manchester University Press, 1991), 15, 162–64.

7. Shapiro to Department of Justice, February 15, 1943, 56084/639 (Archives 1).

8. "Raw Deal Handed Chinese Seamen," *The Pilot*, ca. 1943, 56084/639 (Archives 1); Harry Howard, "Chinese Seamen's Flight Shows Exclusion Act Should Be Repealed," reel 213, vol. 2460, Archives of the American Civil Liberties Union, Princeton University (ACLU); Lane, *Merchant Seaman's War*, 167; *People v. Rowe*, 36 NYS 2d 980 (1942).

9. Adolph A. Berle to Fiorello La Guardia, January 21, 1943, folder Chinese Seamen; Minutes, J. Megson, May 4, 1942; Captain J. Milhench to Misters A. Holt & Co., April 4, 1942, CO 323/1818/21 (TNA); J. B., "Extract from Survey No. 45 of Activities of Germans, Italians and Japanese in India for the Week Ending December 26, 1942," January 1, 1943, WO 208/410 (TNA); Lo Hoi to Lam Chap, May 5, 1942, 55854/370F (Archives 1); Nathan Shapiro to Herman Landon, Jan. 8, 1943, 56084/639 (Archives 1).

10. *Atlanta Constitution*; *Baltimore Sun*; *Chicago Tribune*; *Los Angeles Times*; *Washington Post*, April 12, 1942.

11. *New York Tribune*, May 10; June 14, 1942; Ross to Biddle, Jun 23, 1942, 55854/370F (Archives 1).

12. *New York Times*; August 5, 1942; Earl Harrison to District Director of Ellis Island, November 25, 1942, 56084/639 (Archives 1).

13. Calculated from tables "Alien Seamen deserted at American seaports, by nationality and flag of vessel and districts," year ended June 30, 1942, 1943, 55854/370R (Archives 1); Lane, *Seamen's War*, 167; Dimock's Speech to the Senate Committee on Immigration

and Naturalization, April 1, 1943, 55854/370P (Archives I); Oyen, "Fighting for Equality," 526–27.

14. Scott to N. A. Guttery, April 3, 1943, MT 9/4370 (TNA).

15. John Kuo Wei Tchen, *New York before Chinatown: Orientalism and the Shaping of American Culture, 1776–1882* (Baltimore, Md.: Johns Hopkins University Press, 1999), 76–81; Philip A. Kuhn, *Chinese among Others: Emigration in Modern Times* (Lanham, Md.: Rowman and Littlefield, 2008), 107–14, 125–26; Gregor Benton and Edmund Terence Gomez, *The Chinese in Britain, 1800-Present: Economy, Transnationalism, Identity* (Basingstoke: Palgrave Macmillan, 2008), 49–50; Li Minghuan, *"We Need Two Worlds": Chinese Immigrant Associations in a Western Society* (Amsterdam: Amsterdam University Press, 1999), 143–419; US Bureau of the Census, *1950, Population*, vol. 2 (Washington, DC: GPO, 1952), 56.

16. "Former Chinese Seaman Planning for His Relative to Jump Ship in New York," April 1943, 56084/639 (Archives 1).

17. Minghuan, *"We Need Two Worlds,"* 144.

18. Report of Police Commissioner Enright, February 25, 1918, 9, box 81, USFA, Hoover Institution, Stanford University; Interview of Fong Wing Kee, June 22, 1943; Interview of Captain Merser and Officer Riches, May 31, 1943; F. B. A. Rundall to N. A. Guttery, October 16, 1944, MT 9/4370 (TNA); Report of Inspector W. F. Schlaar, December 15, 1915, 53775/149A (Archives 1).

19. Interrogation of Ho Ping by Timothy J. Molloy, December 5, 1939, 172/74 (NARA NY); Report on Ho Sang by Timothy J. Molloy, December 12, 1939; Interrogation of Ho Sang by Timothy J. Molloy, December 12, 1939, 172/75, RG 85, National Archive and Records Administration, New York (NARA NY); W. F. Watkins to Herman R. Landon, January 11, 1943, 56084/639 (Archives 1).

20. Examination of Chung Wing Kee, June 10, 1943, 56151/316, Archives I; Examination of Lee Choy, March 19, 1942; Examination of Lee Joe, March 18, 1942, 173/813, NARA NY.

21. Special Report by Samuel Auerbach, April 23, 1942; Special Report by Louis Wienckowski, April 27, 1943; J. R. Espinosa to Edward J. Shaughnessy, December 15, 1943, 55854/370F (Archives 1).

22. Irving F. Wixon to Edward J. Shaughnessy, January 7, 1943 (Archives 1); Shapiro to O'Laughlin, January 25, 1943, 56084/639 (Archives 1 / TNA).

23. Anonymous, January 27, 1943, *Memorandum: Grievances of Chinese Seamen Now in the United States*, March 31, 1943, MT 9/4370 (TNA).

24. Interview of Captain Merser, June 6, 1943, MT 9/4370 (TNA).

25. Terry Hughes and John Costello, *The Battle of the Atlantic* (New York: Dial, 1977), 9, 224–26.

26. Christensen to La Guardia, October 15, 1942, folder Alien Seamen, box 3375 (LGA).

27. Calculated from tables "Alien Seamen deserted at American seaports, by nationality and flag of vessel and districts," year ended June 30, 1940, 1941, 1942, 1943, 55854/370R (Archives 1); *Annual Report of the Immigration and Naturalization Service* (Washington, DC: GPO, 1944), 99; *Annual Report of the Immigration and Naturalization Service* (Washington, DC: GPO, 1945), 75.

28. *Instruction No. 75: The Alien Seaman Program*, June 29, 1942, 55854/370F (Archives 1); *Circular 44: British and Other Allied Seamen in the United States*, April 9, 1942, 55854/370I,

Archives I; Silvester Pindyck, "The Allied Seamen Program at New York," *INS Monthly Review* 2, no. 1 (July 1944): 3–6. Marshall Dimock to Fiorello H. La Guardia, August 2, 1942; Lemuel B. Schofield to Fiorello H. La Guardia, April 2, 1942, folder Alien Seamen.

29. Conrad Hepworth Dixon, "Seamen and the Law: An Examination of the Impact of Legislation on the British Merchant Seaman's Lot, 1588–1918" (PhD diss., University College London, 1981), 24–25, 207; Knauth, "Alien Seamen's Rights."

30. Edward J. Shaughnessy to Lemuel Schofield, July 8, 1942, 56084/639 (Archives 1).

31. Memorandum by Ennis, March 31, 1943, 55854/370P (Archives 1); Jack Wasserman, "Administration of the Alien Seaman Program," ca. 1944, 55854/370R (Archives 1).

32. Scott to James F. O'Loughlin, April 23, 1943, 55854/370P (Archives 1).

33. Dimock's Speech to the Senate Committee on Immigration and Naturalization, April 1, 1943, 55854/370P (Archives 1).

34. Minutes of Meeting between N. A. Guttery, Dr. Kuo, Mr. Dao, ca. January 1943; 78 Cong. Rec. H89,51 (daily ed. March 23, 1943) (statement of Reps. Schiffler, Marcantonio, and Michener); Lane, *Merchant Seaman's War*, 156, 162–65.

35. Scott to Guttery, March 5, 1943, MT 9/4370 (TNA); "Alien Seamen Deserted from Vessels Arriving in American Seaports, for Year Ended June 30, 1942," September 21, 1942, 55854/370R (Archives 1); "Alien Seamen Deserted from Vessels Arriving in American Seaports, for Year Ended June 30, 1943," September 19, 1932, 55854/370R (Archives 1); T. T. Scott to Marshall Dimock, October 10, 1942; March 5, 1943, MT 9/4370 (TNA).

36. Interview with Captain van de Kooi, May 15, 1943; N. A. Guttery to J. R. Hobhouse, H. W. Rowbottom, and Richard Snedden, March 23, 1943; T. T. Scott to N. A. Guttery, March 5, 1943, MT 9/4370 (TNA).

37. Edward J. Shaughnessy to W. J. Zucker, February 6, 1946, 55854/370Z (Archives 1).

38. A. F. G. Ayling to W. C. Kneale, November 29, 1943; F. J. Hopwood to H. W. Rowbottom, August 30, 1944; T. T. Scott to Marshall Dimock, Mar. 5, 1943, MT 9/4370 (TNA); Lane, *Merchant Seaman's War*, 165–67.

39. W. F. Watkins to Herman Landon, January 9 and 11, 1943; Edward J. Shaughnessy to Earl G. Harrison, January 6, 1943, 56084/639 (Archives 1).

40. W. F. Watkins to Herman Landon, January 11, 1943, 56084/639 (Archives 1); P. C. Devine, Memorandum to M. Borer, March 31, 1943; Note to W. C. Kneale, July 9, 1943, MT 9/4370 (TNA).

41. Antoinette Burton, *The Trouble with Empire: Challenges to Modern British Imperialism* (New York: Oxford University Press, 2015).

42. Oyen, "Fighting for Equality."

43. In negotiations, Chinese foreign minister T. V. Soong sided with the British, supporting deportation to India to punish deserters and requiring consuls in the United States to stand by a weak agreement he made with British on Chinese wages. N. A. Guttery to T. T. Scott, February 9, 1943; July 13, 1943; Minutes of Telephone Conversation between N. A. Guttery to Dr. Kuo, February 12, 1943; T. T. Scott to N. A. Guttery, March 5, 1943, MT 9/4370 (TNA); Viscount Halifax to Foreign Office, July 15, 1943, CAB 122/772 (TNA).

CHAPTER 6

The State Management of Guest Workers

The Decline of the Bracero Program, the Rise of Temporary Worker Visas

RONALD L. MIZE

In 1943, with the United States fully engaged in World War II, the demand for labor, particularly agricultural labor, was most acute. The full range of options were explored—employing Japanese-American internees, prisoners of war, US soldiers, conscientious objectors, women (Women's Land Army), and nonfarm youth (Victory Farm Volunteers).[1] On the East Coast, farm workers from the Bahamas[2] were recruited for their past agricultural experience in Florida, their English-speaking skills, and pliability. As a grower explains why pliability mattered to him in a proposed temporary work contract he submitted to the US Department of Agriculture: "The vast difference between the Bahama Island labor and the domestic, including Puerto Rican, is that the labor transported from the Bahama Islands can be deported and sent home, if it does not work, which cannot be done in the instance of labor from domestic United States or Puerto Rico."[3]

When twentieth-century historians analyze the state's role in managing labor migration, most often the discussion is about the large-scale, US-Mexico Bracero Program, a wartime labor relief measure that began in 1942 but was continued until 1964 at the behest of US agribusiness interests.[4] Less recognized is that in 1952, the US government created a small program for temporary work visas, known as H-2 visas, which allowed agricultural firms on the East Coast to recruit temporary laborers from the Caribbean, particularly the British West Indies. This chapter explains the reasons for the fall of the Bracero Program and the subsequent, concomitant rise of temporary visa "H-2" programs. The program was extended and expanded in the 1965 Immigration and Nationality Act and broadened dramatically beyond agriculture in the 1986 Immigration Reform and Control Act to include H-2A temporary agricultural workers, H-1B specialty occupations, and H-2B seasonal and unskilled nonagricultural workers. Regardless of the persistent political clamoring for another Bracero Program, US immigration policy has consistently maintained temporary work visas over the past seventy-five years to meet the needs of US place-bound industries that in the twenty-first century bring Indian and Chinese software developers to Silicon Valley, Mexican hotel maids to Vail, and Mexican tobacco pickers to North Carolina.

Antecedents of the H-2 Program

The story of migrant labor on the East Coast of the United States begins and ends in the sugarcane fields of Florida. Sugar was originally a slave crop. First cultivated in Asia, the Portuguese and Spanish crowns oversaw the production of sugarcane in Brazil and the West Indies, especially the Caribbean colonial outposts of the Dominican Republic, Cuba, and Puerto Rico. Britain also brought sugar cane to its tropical and subtropical colonies, as well as the slaves to cultivate the crop, and the food became the staple of caloric intake for all classes of British society.[5] Cane labor had been racialized since its colonial origins, from chattel slavery times through the 1990s, with Blacks and Chinese providing most of the labor.

Harvesting sugarcane was—and continues to be—among the dirtiest, most hazardous, and most difficult jobs. Workers used machetes to cut the cane stalk; over time, metal guards for hands, feet and shins were developed to minimize the number of workplace accidents that resulted in contusions and loss of digits and limbs. To facilitate the harvest, growers burned the crops to reduce excess leaves and stalk. In Florida, the controlled burns forced out wildlife (such as rats, cougars, alligators, and venomous snakes) from the fields, endangering workers. Prior to the implementation of safety equipment, the frequent loss of limbs, cuts, burns, and other workplace injuries made sugarcane cultivation one of the most dangerous occupations in the United States. After the abolition of slavery forced growers to enlist paid workers, they depressed wages to the level of debt peonage. The wages, substandard housing, company store arrangements, and other forms of social control were always major sources of contention. These industry practices were called into question during the 1942 season.

Charges were filed by the Department of Justice on November 6, indicting the US Sugar Corporation and four of its supervisors of peonage.[6] Newspaper articles during the season characterized labor relations in Florida's sugar firms in terms of peonage and slavery.[7] A federal warrant was eventually issued for US Sugar's personnel manager and supervisors M. E. Von Mach, Evan Ward McLeod, Neal Williamson, and Oliver H. Sheppard on the charge of peonage. Supervisors at five labor camps were charged with various forms of social control: debt bondage in their piece-rate wage structure; substandard housing conditions; lockdowns on plantations; illegal rules to keep labor captive and tied to labor camps; and binding men to their beds so they could not escape. In response to these investigations, Florida sugar growers shifted from African-American labor to Bahamian labor in 1943, which growers hoped would provide a more passive labor force.

Growers enlisted 4,310 temporary workers from the Bahamas in 1943 to work in the truck crops and fruit crops of eight states initially. This expanded over the next five growing seasons to twenty-five US states. On March 16, 1943, the first contract was signed between the US and British colonial government in the Bahamas, but growers needed more labor, so the US government turned to Jamaica and signed a similar contract on April 2, 1943, resulting in 8,244 laborers distributed across eleven states.[8] In 1944, East Coast agricultural interests also turned to Barbados, primarily for agricultural work in Florida, but about three hundred men also traveled to Delaware and Wisconsin in 1946.

The United Fruit Company (UFC), better known for their banana cultivation in Central America, was given the exclusive subcontract to recruit and process all temporary workers from the Caribbean. As a labor contractor, UFC set up processing centers in the major ports of Nassau, Kingston, and Bridgetown. All potential temporary workers presented themselves to UFC officials to secure work authorization in US agriculture. With significant land holdings in the British West Indies, the company leveraged its influence with the US government to handle the recruitment process. The US government, through the Department of Army, proved it was not up to the task of labor recruitment, and UFC was in the right place with the right track record of recruiting international labor to meet US needs.

The *SS Shanks*, the first of two ships embarking from Kingston to South Florida, transported Jamaican workers at the advent of the 1943 growing season.[9] Equipped to hold a maximum of eighteen hundred passengers, a total of four thousand were crammed onto the boat. Very little oversight by either government led to substandard transport conditions. The ensuing unsanitary conditions, lack of food and water, and military police confiscation of their rum, razors, and bay-rum cologne led to worker protests that were eventually assuaged upon landing on US soil. Intergovernmental correspondence suggests the men were treated better upon arrival, but it is not clear if the US government returned some confiscated goods or repaid workers for lost items, or if men simply found landfall better in comparison to their mistreatment on the ships. Initial government involvement did not allay transportation problems.

The *Shanks* incident was in early May 1943; by early June, another protest arose on the island of Jamaica when the US Army's estimates of the capacity of a transport ship were reduced from three thousand to twenty-seven hundred

Table 1. US Wartime Labor Relief Programs, 1943-1947,[1] by Nation of Origin (Bahamas, Jamaica, Canada)[2]

State	1943			1944			1945			1946			1947		
	B	J	C	B	J	C	B	J	C	B	J	C	B	J	C
Alabama										193					
Arizona								5							
California								2,693							
Colorado								99							
Connecticut		1,000			2,088	97		2,641	119		1,764	69	21	1,764	43
Delaware	105			469	580	17	319	434	17	210	292	9	104	58	3
Florida	260			1,203	1722		4,688	2,141		1,453	139		717	1,530	
Georgia				252									292		
Illinois		638			996		32	643		4	549		5	40	
Indiana		186			334		3	317			217		49		
Iowa		314			429			766							
Kansas								225							
Louisiana											373		21	154	
Maine					642	95		212	106	20	116	60	32	3	26
Maryland	1,785			1,412	585		581	1,297	26	744	424	13	402	149	4
Massachusetts					150	70		362	82	3	222	55	124	14	21
Michigan		747			1,659			604			940		69	133	
Minnesota		357			197		10								
Missouri								143			43			20	
N. Hampshire						80		41	76		164	44		9	31
New Jersey		1,942		12	1,664	72		1,758	89	52	1,508	60	696	239	3
New York	393	1,524			3,005	444		3,072	353	378	2,514	243	851	244	67

State	1943			1944			1945			1946			1947		
	B	J	C	B	J	C	B	J	C	B	J	C	B	J	C
N. Carolina	754			310						772			349		
Ohio		181			1,224			1,217			1,295		216	132	
Pennsylvania		309		90	645	123	2	560	92	298	287	67		347	8
Rhode Island						8			17			7			5
S. Carolina	13														
South Dakota											199				
Tennessee	301			205									157		
Vermont						100			166			113			58
Virginia	699			1,809			206			941			295		
Wisconsin		1,046			1,729		45	1,766		30	1,052		125	23	
U.S.³		12,554			25,246			28,025			21,204			12,600	

1. Numbers are based on one-day figures (a particular day between May and September) and should not be necessarily construed as full-season counts. For instance, Rasmussen (255–56) offers total counts of Jamaicans in 1944 totaling 15,666 Jamaican workers and 17,291 in 1945. These underestimates, compared to the above one-day counts, point to the less-than-perfect accounting of the program.

2. B = Bahamian, J = Jamaican, C = Canadian (Newfoundland)

3. Though not always identified by reception state, Rasmussen notes Barbados sent 909 workers in 1944, none in 1945, 3,087 in 1946, and 2,947 in 1947. "Of these [1946], 75 were employed in Delaware, 2,645 in Florida, and 227 in Wisconsin. . . . [In 1947,] Delaware, 1; Florida, 617; Louisiana, 17; Massachusetts, 2; and New York, 4." U.S. totals include temporary workers from all four nations.

workers. The US Army was charged, under authority of the War Labor Board, to determine maximum capacity for transport ships. Those individuals left at the port, "many of whom had sold much of their personal property and had bought supplies for the trip, demanded compensation. . . . [In response], the American government granted 3 pounds (approximately $12.09) each to 554 of the workers. This was supplemented by an additional grant of 2 pounds each by the Jamaican government and the latter requested reimbursement from the American government."[10] There is no evidence that the United States reimbursed the Jamaican government.

By 1944, some Jamaicans were rounding out their northern contracts by finding winter work in Florida's cane fields. The vast majority of the 17,649 workers were contracted to work in Connecticut, Delaware, Illinois, Indiana, Iowa, Maine, Maryland, Massachusetts, Michigan, Minnesota, New Jersey, New York, Ohio, Pennsylvania, and Wisconsin, but the 1,722 workers tallied in Florida fell well short of labor demands. So, the US Sugar Corporation, the largest and most notorious employer, began to aggressively recruit Jamaicans in the 1945 season; their recruitment program, however, did not entice Jamaicans as anticipated. For example, the first group of 1,523 men traveled on April 1 from Kingston to Port Everglades. But a second shipment carrying only 838 men left on April 11. Even though 1,634 men departed from Kingston on that day, only half were willing to work for US Sugar.[11] When the workers protested the unsatisfactory living conditions and proved troublesome to their employers, the US government allowed Big Sugar to turn to Barbados to recruit workers in 1946. Based on the agreement originally signed between the US and Jamaican governments on July 24, 1944, the US-Barbados agreement was essentially the same, with the exception that a $5 advance given to Jamaican workers upon entry into the United States was not extended to those from Barbados.

One key protection that the Jamaican government secured during the war years, with very little US War Food Administration resistance, was to protect its citizens by barring recruitment to the Deep South. Internal correspondence within the War Food Administration identified a range of concerns, from Jamaicans having different customs and social patterns than African Americans, to the absence of racial segregation and Jim Crow laws in Jamaica, and African American acquiescence to Jim Crow power differentials that officials feared Jamaicans would not tolerate.[12] Conceding that Jim Crow was objectionable to Jamaicans such that they may not serve as ideal (in other words, docile and passive) labor force, the mutual solution was to bar temporary workers south of the Mason-Dixon line.[13] In the first years of the arrangement, Jamaicans were by and large not sent to the Deep South states. Florida was the exception—though, as noted above, treatment of workers in the state was highly objectionable from workers' perspectives.

Canadian workers, primarily from Newfoundland, were recruited to work in the US Northeast beginning in 1942, as the grain harvest relied on workers and machinery freely crossing the border. Yet employing and transporting workers from Newfoundland did not pick up until 1944; such work was most often arranged in the New England and neighboring states. Beyond grain harvesting, Newfoundlanders started picking potatoes in Maine in 1944, and that continued through 1947. The number of Canadian laborers never approached twelve hundred, however: New York was always the largest recipient (444 in 1944, 353 in 1945, 243 in 1946, and 67 in 1947). As soon as the war ended, Newfoundlanders were anxious to return to Canada to make way for returning US veterans. What began as a formalization of a practice decades old, the lending of Canadian labor and machinery over the border was a standard practice of wheat and grain growers, though it never grew in scale to compare to the number of laborers from the Caribbean.

The United States came to Barbados relatively late and sporadically. At the request of the US government, Barbados sent 909 workers in 1944, none in 1945, 3,087 in 1946, and 2,947 in 1947. From 1946 to 1947, most Barbadians in the United States were employed in Florida (3,262), with fewer than one hundred working in Delaware, Louisiana, Massachusetts, New York, and Wisconsin. The focus on Barbados was specifically meeting the demands of US Sugar and to a lesser extent their competitors in Florida. As much as the United States viewed temporary-labor relations as one-sided or at the very least bilateral, both Great Britain and their Caribbean colonies sought more negotiating power. The British West Indies Central Labor Organization (BWICLO) was formed in 1944 to regulate the overseas flow of laborers from British colonial holdings in the Caribbean. A product of finding themselves caught between US and British influence, the coalition was voluntary, with no executive authority; British historian Ashley Jackson contends that it was a product of the Anglo-American Caribbean Commission of 1942 that sought more cooperation among the English-speaking nations and British colonies of the Caribbean, particularly influenced by US interests.[14] Forming the BWICLO was symbolic of the larger British response to coalesce their holdings into a federation. All the pieces were in place when, in 1952, the US Congress reauthorized the Immigration and Nationality Act.

The H-2 Program of 1952

These wartime measures, though clearly small in scale, provided the basis for the enactment of the H-2 temporary visa program in the 1952 McCarran-Walter Immigration and Nationality Act. These measures were continued because growers along the East Coast migrant stream received the type of labor they so desired (pliable, cheap, temporary, and controllable), the colonial governments of the West

Indies had a reliable source of addressing chronic unemployment and underdeveloped economies (labor migration and remittances),[15] and the US government met the demands of agribusiness without relying on undocumented immigrant labor. The full text of 1952 INA Section 101 created what became known as the H-2 program:

> (H) an alien having a residence in a foreign country which he has no intention of abandoning (i) who is of distinguished merit and ability and who is coming temporarily to the United States to perform temporary services of an exceptional nature requiring such merit and ability; or (ii) who is coming temporarily to the United States to perform other temporary services or labor, if unemployed persons capable of performing such service or labor cannot be found in this country; or (iii) who is coming temporarily to the United States as an industrial trainee.[16]

Temporary labor was codified into immigration law if individuals had desired skills or merit in short supply (H-1), were qualified and selected as industrial trainees (H-3), or provided "unskilled" labor when not competing with unemployed US citizens (H-2). In practice, the second article was narrowed to exclusively agricultural labor to accommodate the needs of employers on the East Coast who did not have ready and full access to the Mexican braceros.

The US government facilitated this relationship by creating a temporary-visa contract between the government and grower on a per-worker basis. Growers gained several advantages: contracts could be negotiated in their favor, they could pre-select their workforce, and they could use deportation as a means of control in the fields.[17] Individual work contracts tied the visa holders to a specific employer; protests, work stoppages, or the failure to achieve a certain harvest quota could result in deportation and subsequent blacklisting.

The Rise and Demise of the Bracero Program

As details of the H class visas were hammered out in Congress and officially recorded as law on June 29, 1952, the US Department of Agriculture was putting into practice Public Law 78 that Congress passed on July 12, 1951.[18] The focus of that law was to formalize US-Mexico labor relations in the western half of the United States with another temporary worker program operated on a mass scale to meet the needs of large-scale agribusiness. The Bracero Program facilitated large-scale temporary farm worker recruitment from Mexico, but most operations that utilized the program were west of the Mississippi River (in particular California and Texas by this time). For the few bracero destinations in the southern United States (Arkansas, Georgia, Louisiana, Mississippi, and North Carolina), the Mexican influx was on a much smaller scale (see table 2). Between 1942–1947, 410 braceros

Table 2. US States Employing Braceros, 1952

	Workers Contracted	Workers Recontracted	Workers Employed on 12/31/52
Arkansas	25,658	2,705	500
Georgia	387	209	0
Louisiana	739	83	17
Mississippi	60	0	0
Tennessee	264	142	0
South Region	27,108	3,139	517

"Workers contracted" refers to those newly hired and given a contract, no prior contract being involved. "Workers recontracted" refers to those whose valid but expiring contracts were renewed." Richard Martin Lyon, "The Legal Status of American and Mexican Migratory Farm Labor," PhD diss., Cornell University, 1954, 225.

were employed in North Carolina. Arkansas was an exception, due to its need for a mass temporary labor source as cotton growers in the state prepared to mechanize their operations. No braceros were enumerated in the twenty-two-year history in the states of the Northeast.

From 1942 to 1947, North Carolina growers employed 410 braceros and in effect initiated the first migrant stream from Mexico to the rural South. The author interviewed Don Liberio, a former bracero, who recounted his experiences working in North Carolina in 1947.

> In North Carolina, we were picking green beans. We also picked potatoes. But there were too many men in the fields, and thus not enough work. In potatoes and green beans, we earned forty cents per bushel, or about eight dollars per week, after deductions. After the contract ended, we had to pay transportation home. In North Carolina, we often complained and stopped work because of the rotten food. There was a man, he was protesting and complaining about the food. The next day he was gone, nobody told us what happened to him and we didn't ask. Later we heard that they killed him.[19]

Many stories abounded of braceros who were killed to collect the insurance money or to punish recalcitrant agitators.[20] Quite likely, it was the message itself that mattered, as growers could use fear to keep workers in line with the message that "if you strike, you take your life into your own hands." Don Liberio recalled several contract violations by potato and green bean farmers. He reported that the food served in the camp was occasionally rancid. If the workers united to complain, the quality of food would temporarily improve, only to return to spoiled servings. Yet the program was never designed to meet the needs of growers in the East Coast migrant stream.

The Bracero Program began on August 4, 1942, in Stockton, California, as a result of the US government's response to requests by southwestern agricultural growers for the recruitment of foreign labor. The agreement, negotiated between the federal governments of Mexico and the United States, stated the following general provisions that would come to define the program's twenty-two-year existence.[21] The first provision barred racial discrimination targeted at braceros: "The Mexicans entering the US under provisions of the agreement would not be subjected to discriminatory acts." The second provision guaranteed that US growers would shoulder the costs of migration and temporary settlement: "Workers would be guaranteed transportation, living expenses, and repatriation along the lines established under Article 29 of Mexican labor laws." The third provision concerned the displacement of US workers to guarantee that braceros would not undercut native wages or be used as strikebreakers: "Mexicans entering under the agreement would not be employed either to displace domestic workers or to reduce their wages."[22] Under many of the same agreement guidelines, though utilizing different administrative channels, nine months later the railroad industry secured the importation of Mexican laborers to meet wartime shortages.[23]

The first provision was designed explicitly to ban discrimination against Mexican nationals and served as the key bargaining chip by the Mexican government to promote safeguards of braceros' treatment by Anglo growers. The arrangements of the First Bracero Program, during World War I, were conducted without the input of the Mexican government.[24] As a result, Mexican nationals worked in the United States without protections and, subsequently, workers were subject to a number of discriminatory acts. The protections from discriminatory treatment stemmed from Executive Order 8802, signed by President Franklin D. Roosevelt on June 25, 1941, which stated that, "there shall be no discrimination in the employment of workers in defense industries or government because of race, creed, color, or national origin, and . . . it is the duty of employers and of labor organizations, in furtherance of said policy and of this order, to provide for the full and equitable participation of all workers in defense industries, without discrimination because of race, creed, color, or national origin." In relation to E.O. 8802, the Bracero Program was couched as a government-sponsored program in the larger service of national defense, and it recognized the reality that Mexicans were subject to discrimination, whether on the basis of race, color, and/or national origin.

From 1942 to 1947, no braceros were sent to Texas because of the documented mistreatment of Mexican workers by Texas growers and other citizens. A series of assurances by the Texas state government were secured before growers were allowed to import labor from Mexico. Texas was infamous for the Jim Crow–style segregation and racial violence practices that defined the Postbellum South, and the state was responsible for more lynchings of Mexicans than any other state. Until the 1950s, the Mexican government also blacklisted Colorado, Illinois, Indiana, Michigan, Montana, Minnesota, Wisconsin, and Wyoming for discriminatory practices documented in each of the states. The source of contention was a prevalent practice in the sugar-beet industry that paid Mexican workers considerably less than Anglo workers for the same work. The discriminatory wage structure illustrated a second-class citizenship that Mexican laborers were subjected to throughout the Midwest and Rocky Mountain states. An interview with the tortilla vendor who provided food for braceros in the San Luis Valley of Southern Colorado notes not only the racial discrimination that braceros faced from Anglos but also the complex relations among Anglos, Mexican Americans, and braceros in the Valley.

> SEÑOR PALMAS: There was a certain amount of animosity between the seasonal workers and the Hispanic population here and it's basically just a cultural difference in terms of how they view their Hispanic-ness if you want to put it that way. . . . So those guys are . . . a lot of people here are a bunch of upstarts, blabbermouths, push. . . . They view us as backward, don't even know the language. On and on and on. . . . And of course those people who are Anglo certainly view them as Chicanos and cholos and a little bit of . . . intrinsic fear of an outsider. . . . See what I'm saying? So there's all kinds of degrees there, all kinds of attitudes. There was absolutely no acceptance either from the braceros or the guys that come in. To the Hispanics here they were all wetbacks. Not even braceros. They were just wetbacks.[25]

The provision protected braceros, in theory, from racial discrimination, as Colorado was one blacklisted state due to the sugar-beet industry's discriminatory wage structure (in northeastern Colorado, not the San Luis Valley) but once the ban was lifted, no laws were designed to protect braceros from the discrimination they faced by Mexican Americans who often sought to distinguish themselves from immigrants or what many Anglos saw as all "wetbacks."

The second provision was designed to guarantee workers safe passage to and from the United States as well as decent living conditions while working in the United States. The costs associated with transportation, room, and board would be covered by someone other than the workers if the article was followed to its exact wording. But these costs were subject to negotiation by the Mexican government; as a result, workers had a number of these expenses deducted from their paychecks. Individual work contracts signed by braceros and representatives of both the Mexican and US governments set standards on how much could be deducted for room and board.

Different groups shouldered transportation costs, depending on which time and place the braceros were migrating to and from. Braceros did not pay transportation costs from the recruitment centers in Mexico to the US processing centers and eventual job sites. As Don Francisco noted on his return trips from the US fields: "And from here to there when we went home they paid for our trip to Empalme too. When we were about to leave they bought our ticket so we could go back."[26]

134 · RONALD L. MIZE

But they absorbed the costs associated with getting to the Mexican cities where braceros were recruited, which varied depending on where the recruitment centers were located. Don Andres recalled the best-case scenario when asked if he paid to get from his home to the Mexico recruitment center: "No, because they gave us an official government letter. With that letter we came. There were some that they did charge. But that time they gave us a letter."[27]

Throughout the duration of the program, the US and Mexican governments struggled over where recruitment centers would be located because the United States was responsible for paying the transportation costs. The US government wanted recruitment centers near the US-Mexican border to reduce costs, whereas the Mexican government wanted recruitment centers in the interior of Mexico where the major sending states were located. These struggles had major consequences for the braceros, who had to secure the funds to pay their way to the recruitment centers.

The final provision was designed to reduce competition between domestic and contracted labor, and the United States government played two roles in assuring that competition would not arise. The first role was the determination of the "prevailing wage" in each region of the country. To ensure that braceros were receiving the same wage as domestics, the prevailing wage was determined prior to the harvest season in each locale, and braceros were to receive that wage. The prevailing wage was approved by the Department of Labor, but it was in fact growers who collectively determined the "prevailing wage" they were willing to pay.[28] Braceros often found themselves trying to earn wages at a piece rate (based on how much they could pick by weight) while relegated to the sections and rows of fields where the plants' yields were the lowest. Don Antoñio recalled working in cotton fields where braceros picked from plants that were only knee high, whereas domestic farm workers picked from the taller plants with the best yields.

> **DON ANTOÑIO**: And then they put us in really bad parts sometimes. Parts where it [the cotton] was really small. And those that were from here they put where it was better.
> **INTERVIEWER**: So there still were local people working?
> **DON ANTOÑIO**: Yes, there were local people. Of those that were from here. Of those who got the best job.[29]

It was also the responsibility of the Department of Labor to designate when a certain region had a labor shortage of available domestic workers. Again, growers were the key to this determination because they were responsible for notifying the department when they expected labor shortages to occur. Most often, growers would set a prevailing wage rate so low as to effectively discourage domestics by requiring them to work at wage levels below the cost of living in the United States.

The lack of enforcement by state, federal, and consular agencies often defined the modus operandi of how the Bracero Program was experienced on the ground.

In terms of each provision, the Bracero Program was lived out much differently by the workers than how the program was designed to work on paper. Though intended as a wartime labor-relief measure, the Bracero Program was continually reauthorized until 1964. At a time when the United Farm Workers began to ascend, one of their main targets was the Bracero Program. Ernesto Galarza's *Strangers in Our Fields* (1956) and *Merchants of Labor* (1964) were indictments of how the Bracero Program operated, and the nascent Chicano movement brought Mexican Americans together partially by casting braceros as undesirables and unwelcome competitors in the fields. An advertisement titled "Rotten Deals in Tomatoes: Government Gives Away Our Jobs" in the United Farm Workers trade journal *El Malcriado* employed strong language as to how the growers treated bracero workers:

> The Bracero Program was ENDED by Congress two years ago. . . . The growers pay lousy wages, refuse to sign a contract, and turn local workers away. THEN they scream for braceros. They know they can pay braceros less, since $1 in US money equals $12 in Mexican money. The Bracero Program is just one more weapon which the growers use to beat us down and keep us poor.[30]

The ad goes on to explain that the Teamsters—the competing labor union for farmworkers—supports a temporary-worker program because of its sweetheart deals with growers.

Clearly, the UFW did not consider braceros as "workers"—or at the very least not "our workers"; they are characterized in the ad as simply a weapon in the growers' arsenal. The organized labor divide between Mexican Americans and Mexican immigrants, as Chicano historian David Gutierrez aptly notes, highlights that common ancestry is a tenuous link when labor, border, citizenship, and assimilation pressures are all operating.[31]

Economist Philip Martin identifies other factors that led to the demise of the Bracero Program, claiming it was President Kennedy watching Edward R. Murrow's farmworker expose *Harvest of Shame* that ended the program, while sociologist Kitty Calavita claims the demise was due to bureaucratic battles within the US state that made the program untenable with regard to controlling the illegal immigration problem (basically, the Department of Justice and Immigration and Naturalization Service determined illegal immigration to be a bigger issue than the USDA claim of agricultural labor shortages).[32]

Whereas the Bracero Program expanded dramatically after World War II, the sheer scale of the operations raised concerns by farmworker advocacy organizations, local communities, and small farmers. The United Farm Workers called braceros "scabs," "strike-breakers," and a tool that growers used against

136 · RONALD L. MIZE

Mexican-American farm workers in their struggle for better wages, humane working conditions, and collective-bargaining rights. The mass-deportation campaigns of Operation Wetback in 1954 pointed to the precarious status of braceros and undocumented workers. The exigencies of labor demand could quickly turn to repulsion, repatriation, and deportation when the political winds shifted. The Bracero Program officially ended in 1964, but by no means did that portend an end to temporary-worker programs.

"I Am an H-2 Worker"

The Hart-Celler Act of 1965 was a landmark shift in immigration policy, but all revisions of the INA were in section 201 of the law to end discriminatory national quotas and establish family reunification as the basis for naturalization. The law included the exact provision for temporary visas found in the 1952 Act. Administratively, the H-2 program solidified the relationship between the BWICLO and US Department of Labor to create primarily a sugar plantation labor force, always one step away from slavery and indentured servitude, to serve as the labor safety valve for the East Coast migrant stream. When labor demands increased, the valves were opened to expand the H-2 program; when they decreased, the valve could be shut off. As DeWind, Seidl, and Shenk note, the H-2 program issued more than ten thousand visas per year through the 1960s and 1970s, with the vast majority (about 80 percent) going to the sugarcane firms of Florida.[33] The recruitment process was streamlined to locate men, most often from Jamaica, who were physically able to perform stoop labor, proficient in English and sufficiently intelligent, and possessing the ideal temperament to take orders, observe the law, and avoid behavior that would result in blacklisting. One recruiter described the process:

> We'll run through 800 men a day. . . . Three tables are set up representing three stages of processing. At the first table, we simply look at a man as a physical specimen and try to eliminate those with obvious physical defects. At the second table, we're trying to test intelligence and see if the man can understand English as we speak it by asking simple questions. The third table is where we attempt to find out about the man's work background. We also check our black book to see if a man has been breached (i.e., sent home for violating the contract). . . . The final stage of pre-selection is the check by the Jamaican authorities of police records.[34]

Reports from the BWICLO noted that in the mid-1960s, "West Indian workers struck in protest over low task rates on the average of once a month. . . . Fifteen men were sent home for agitating and inciting others to strike . . . The men returned to work the following day after five men were removed. . . . Since repatriation of one worker who was deemed the ring leader, work has progressed smoothly."[35]

According to Rob Williams of Florida Rural Legal Aid, the wage structure was challenged as early as 1968 and the labor dispute resulted in the deportation of H-2 workers.[36] This created a vicious cycle: growers responded to worker protests with blacklists and deportations, and the Florida Rural Legal Aid filed lawsuits on behalf of H-2 workers to secure the wages promised. It was not until September 11, 1992, that a labor peace accord was struck.[37] US Sugar finally succumbed to all other competitor practices and mechanized one year after the accord; as the H-2A program began to take off, the company—the last holdout to the upfront costs of machinery in the industry that created the program in the first place—was officially out of the business of employing temporary visa workers by 1993.

One way workers were systematically cheated out of wages was the development of a task rate system that took piece rates to a new level of exploitation. The task rate was designed to recognize that not all sugar cane rows are created equal, so a wage system was created to pay by the row, with the price determined on the difficulty of tasks by row. Similar to the low-yield cotton rows that ex-bracero Don Antoñio experienced, many H-2 workers found themselves picking from sugarcane rows with relatively lower yields. Stalks that needed additional clearing, grew unevenly, or posed other complications meant workers were paid a premium in theory—but in reality, it often meant the wages were driven down on the comparatively easiest rows.

Piece rates were employed because they maximized the chances for self-exploitation as workers were led to believe that the harder and faster they worked, the more they would earn. From the company perspective, the ever-shifting piece rate allowed them to maximize profits by securing more labor at lower pay scales. Industry practices often blurred the line between low wages and debt peonage.

The Long-Term Effects of the H-2 Program

The structure of the temporary visas also compounded the issue, particularly the compulsory savings program. The sugar companies deducted transportation, room, and board costs, but a much larger share of deductions comprised the 25 percent the Jamaican government withdrew as part of a compulsory savings program, even though only 23 percent of this deduction was returned to the men in Jamaica. The 2 percent, and often more, was marked for health insurance, but a congressional investigation found the "deduction generated more than $600,000 over and above the costs of the insurance policy covering the workers, and that the policy's benefits were so minimal as to be meaningless in the US healthcare system."[38] Jamaican newspapers also reported how Ministry of Labor officials, charged with serving as the workers' advocates, in their roles as staff of the BWI-CLO, used the compulsory savings to purchase durable goods in Canada and the

United States, only to resell those items and keep both the profits and interest on workers' accounts.

In 1986 the Immigration Reform and Control Act (IRCA) was passed. It not only upheld the temporary visa program but expanded it to several other occupational sectors.[39] Under the new H-2A program, growers could still gain access to a steady stream of temporary labor if they were willing to meet the bureaucratic requirements. The H-2A program was reauthorized through IRCA, and temporary visas were also expanded to include H-1B (specialty occupations) and H-2B (wage-shortage industries) temporary migrants as well. Employers were required to provide free and adequate housing, and code inspectors were quite thorough. As a result, H-2A farm labor camps often offered better housing than any previously available to migrants. Growers also had to adhere to an adverse-effect wage rate and ensure that working conditions did not deter domestic interest.

The H-2A visa is a continuation of the Bracero Program for agribusiness but includes administrative controls, certifications, and oversight written into law. H-1B visas were reserved for specialty occupations, particularly in the computer industry. H-2B visas focused on nonagricultural "wage shortage occupations," including landscaping, hotel cleaning, and seasonal work. For the first time, employers were held accountable for employing undocumented labor, though law enforcement shifted to border defense.

The process has been accelerated and institutionalized by a renewed grower utilization of the H-2A program. Data from 2003 show that agricultural firms in all fifty states employ H-2A labor. In 2002 there were forty-two thousand visas issued, which increased to forty-five thousand in 2003. Tobacco is the largest single crop that employs H-2A workers with tobacco workers constituting 35 percent of all H-2A visas. Tobacco growers are primarily in North Carolina, Kentucky, and Virginia. Mexican workers are the main visa recipients. The Global Workers Justice Alliance estimates 88 percent of H-2A workers are Mexican, according to their analysis of 2006 DOL data (40,283 of 46,432 visa holders) (see table 2).

Based on US Department of Labor data released in FY2014, the H-2A has ballooned to a 116,689-person program utilized by nearly sixty-five hundred US companies in all fifty states. Tobacco cultivators are increasingly relying on H-2A workers, which explains why 12 percent of all workers were contracted in North Carolina. Today, the majority of H-2A workers are employed by the North Carolina Growers Association.[40]

The vast majority of temporary workers come through the H-1B program, which included 946,293 positions certified in FY2014. Social scientist Rafael Alarcón refers to these specialized workers, primarily computer engineers, financial service employees, and scientists, as *cerebreros* (brainers) due to their recruitment for mental labor.[41] A small but significant contingent of Mexican citizens have entered the

United States on H-1B temporary visas, but most are from India, China, and Great Britain. In FY2014, the five largest employers of the H-1B *cerebreros* were Price-waterhouse Coopers, Cognizant Technology Solutions US Corporation, Deloitte Consulting, Wipro Limited, and Tata Consultancy Services.

The H-2B program is the category left for temporary entry as long as an employer demonstrates no native workers are willing to take the jobs at the prevailing wage. Landscaping, hotel cleaning, forestry, and other seasonal occupations, which traditionally rely on undocumented Mexican labor, make up the majority of the 93,649 positions certified. Department of Labor reports identify that in FY2014 the laborer/landscaper position accounted for 37 percent of all H-2B certified occupations. In 2007 the DOL certified 254,615 positions under the H-2B program. The top six employers of those workers included the Brickman Group, hiring 3,020 landscapers and groundskeepers; Vail Corporation, hiring 1,988 sports instructors, housekeepers, and short-order cooks; Trugreen Landcare, hiring 1,731 landscapers and groundskeepers; Marriott International, hiring 1,696 housekeepers, dining room attendants, and kitchen helpers; Eller & Sons Trees, hiring 1,433 forest workers and tree planters; and Agricultural Establishment Landscapes Unlimited, hiring 1,358 landscapers and groundskeepers.[42]

The Vail Corporation was one of the largest employers of temporary visa holders under the H-2B Program. Employers of H-2B visa holders are seeking labor defined as non-specialty, seasonal work when sufficient domestic labor sources cannot be located at comparable wage rates. In 2009, Vail was the third largest employer of H-2B workers hired for housekeeping and short-order cooks. Those top three employers were paying 6,392 visa holders on average $8.16 per hour.[43] By 2010, federal administrative rule changes and stricter enforcement including more frequent audits resulted in Vail no longer employing H-2B workers. The shift has been to employ J-1 visa holders: Vail relies on third parties (online international student exchanges) to facilitate the flow of foreign labor into Vail (followed closely by Aspen, Park City, Winter Park, and Northeast ski resorts). A truism of temporary-worker programs is once the networks are established, there is no such thing as temporary. Permanent settlement, primarily in the bedroom community of Leadville, is where the Mexican undocumented labor force resides to do the unskilled labor in Vail that began as a H-2B temporary visa program.

Conclusion

With the end of the US-Mexico bracero guest-worker program in 1964 and current political appeals in Washington, DC, for a new temporary-worker program, one would think that the United States did not have temporary-worker programs already in place. But since 1965 the US government has continually provided a mechanism for industries, particularly but not only agriculture, to have access to employ temporary immigrant laborers.

With passage of the Immigration and Nationality Act of 1965, one provision extended the Bracero Program with the development of an H-2 temporary visa program. The H-2 (after 1986, the H-2A) program served largely as the safety valve for large-scale agribusiness and its seemingly unending desire for cheap, pliable, temporary labor. The H-2 program was severely underutilized because the other, less bureaucratic option, hiring undocumented immigrants, was never deemed illegal or worthy of sanction until the 1986 Immigration Reform and Control Act (IRCA), which, for the first time in the history of the nation, held employers responsible for knowingly employing undocumented labor.

Long, intractable political debates on immigration at the national level have called for an expansion of temporary-worker programs. The debate is not about whether or not temporary worker programs will be a part of comprehensive immigration reform. Democrats tend to lobby for increasing the number of visas allocated through existing, orderly H-class visa programs. Republicans tend to call for large-scale programs more akin to the Bracero Program with significantly less bureaucratic oversight. Temporary worker programs are certain to be an integral component of US immigration policy well into the future. Yet the plight of farmworkers today is much the same as it was during the H-2 and Bracero Programs.

Notes

1. Oregon State College Extension Service, "Farm Labor News Notes (17)," August 6, 1947, Oregon State University Libraries Special Collections and Archives; Wayne Rasmussen, *A History of the Emergency Farm Labor Supply Program*, 43–7 Ag. Monograph 13 (Washington DC: US Department of Agriculture, Bureau of Agricultural Economics, 1951): 105–50. Eiichiro Azuma explores the effects of these war-era labor arrangements on Japanese immigrants employed by Japanese-American growers in the 1950s in ch. 8 of this volume.

2. Rasmussen, *History,* 233.

3. Rasmussen, *History,* 234.

4. See Rosas (ch. 12 of this volume). In addition, see Deborah Cohen, *Braceros: Migrant Citizens and Transnational Subjects in the Postwar United States and Mexico* (Chapel Hill: University of North Carolina Press, 2011) regarding recent interest in the Bracero Program; see also Gilbert G. Gonzalez, *Guestworkers or Colonized Labor? Mexican Labor Migration to the United States* (New York: Routledge, 2013); Mireya Loza, *Defiant Braceros: How Migrant Workers Fought for Racial, Sexual, and Political Freedom* (Chapel Hill: University of North Carolina Press, 2016); Don Mitchell, *They Saved Our Crops: Labor, Landscape, and the Struggle over Industrial Farming in Bracero-Era California* (Athens: University of Georgia Press, 2012); Ronald L. Mize, *The Invisible Workers of the US-Mexico Bracero Program: Obreros Olvidados* (Lanham, Md.: Lexington, 2016); Ronald L. Mize and Alicia C.S. Swords, *Consuming Mexican Labor:*

From the Bracero Program to NAFTA (Toronto: University of Toronto Press, 2010); Ana Elizabeth Rosas, *Abrazando el Espíritu: Bracero Families Confront the US-Mexico Border* (Berkeley: University of California Press, 2014). The sheer scale of the Bracero Program rationalizes this focus, with more than 4.5 million work contracts signed and braceros working across thirty US states.

5. Sidney Mintz, *Sweetness and Power: The Place of Sugar in Modern History* (New York: Penguin, 1986).

6. Clarence Maurice Mitchell Jr., *The Papers of Clarence Mitchell, Jr., 1942–1943*, ed. Denton L. Watson and Elizabeth Miles Nuxoll (Athens: Ohio University Press, 2005), 32; Daniel E. Bender and Jana K. Lipman, *Making the Empire Work: Labor and United States Imperialism* (New York: NYU Press, 2015), 244; Douglas A. Blackmon, *Slavery by Another Name: The Re-Enslavement of Black Americans from the Civil War to World War II* (New York: Knopf, 2009), 380–81; Cindy Hahamovitch, *No Man's Land: Jamaican Guestworkers in America and the Global History of Deportable Labor* (Princeton, N.J.: Princeton University Press, 2011), 31–32.

7. Newspaper headlines from 1942 read: "Peonage Story Told by Victims: Tell of Mistreatment on Florida Sugar Plantation," "Sugar Firm Officials Indicted on Charges of Enslaving Workers: Florida Sheriff Accused of Using Prisoners on His Farm without Pay," and "Escaped 'Slavery' Farm."

8. Rasmussen, *History*, 249.

9. Account based on ibid., 254.

10. Ibid., 254–55.

11. Ibid., 256.

12. In a May 11, 1943, memorandum from George W. Hill, special assistant to the deputy administrator of the WFA, to Conrad Taeuber, acting chief, Division of Farm Population and Rural Welfare, Bureau of Agricultural Economics, Hill states: "The importation of Negro workers from Jamaica presented certain difficulties. It was recognized that although these Jamaicans were members of the Negro race, their customs and social patterns differ from those of many of the Negroes of the United States and it was further reported that there was little race distinction in Jamaica." Rasmussen, *History*, 258.

13. In a May 17, 1943, memorandum from George W. Hill to Lieutenant Colonel Jay L. Taylor, deputy administrator of the WFA, Hill states: "However, experience with these workers has been that States' Negroes are more amenable to acceptance of the traditional local racial differentials. Summing up all the evidence, I cannot get anyone very enthusiastic over the idea of placing Jamaicans where employers are accustomed to using States' Negroes." Rasmussen, *History*, 258.

14. Ashley Jackson, *The British Empire and the Second World War* (New York: Hambeldon Continuum, 2006), 93.

15. The Caribbean islands that constitute the British West Indies did not secure independence from Great Britain until 1962 (Jamaica), 1966 (Barbados), and 1973 (Bahamas). British Virgin Islands, St. Kitts, Saint Lucia, and the remaining British Caribbean islands and Central American holdings were minimal contributors to this migrant stream.

16. US Congress, Public Law 414 (June 27, 1952), http://library.uwb.edu/static/USimmigration/66%20stat%20163.pdf.

17. See Josh DeWind, Tom Seidl, and Janet Shenk, "Contract Labor in US Agriculture: The West Indian Cane Cutters in Florida," in *Peasants and Proletarians: The Struggles of Third World Workers*, ed. Robin Cohen, Peter C. W. Gutkind, and Phyllis Brazier (New York: Monthly Review Press, 1979), 380–96.

18. US Congress, Public Law 78 (July 12, 1951), http://library.uwb.edu/static/usimmigration/65%20stat%20119.pdf.

19. Don Liberio, "Life Story of Don Liberio," interview by the author, Fresno, California, 1997.

20. See Mize, *Invisible Workers*, 68–73.

21. An initial provision stated, "Mexican contract workers would not engage in US military service." Beyond the focus of this present analysis, it was designed to quell Mexican popular discontent and apprehensions about how earlier uses (during World War I) of Mexican labor were thought to have occurred during what Kiser and Kiser refer to as the First Bracero Program. George C. Kiser and Martha W. Kiser, *Mexican Workers in the United States* (Albuquerque: University of New Mexico Press, 1979). Without government interference, US growers directly recruited laborers from Mexico to meet wartime labor shortages. After World War I, the citizens of Mexico heard rumors that Mexican laborers, brought to the United States to work in the agricultural fields, were forced into military service for the war effort. My research of this contention revealed no evidence of this practice. Both the governments of the United States and Mexico denied that the practice ever occurred. Nevertheless, to quell Mexican popular apprehensiveness and allay fears, the initial article was agreed upon by both governments.

22. Juan Ramon Garcia highlights Bracero Program provisions in *Operation Wetback: The Mass Deportation of Mexican Undocumented Workers in 1954* (Westport, Conn.: Greenwood, 1980), 24.

23. Labor shortages existed, according to Barbara Driscoll, *The Tracks North* (Austin: University of Texas Press, 1999). See also Robert C. Jones, *Mexican War Workers in the US: The Mexican-US Manpower Recruiting Program and Its Operation* (Washington DC: Pan American Union, 1945). Yet the claim of a shortage of domestic labor is a source of contention in the literature. Those who disagree with this prognosis and see braceros as used by growers to undercut domestic wages include Henry Pope Anderson and Ernesto Galarza. See Anderson, *Fields of Bondage* (Berkeley, Calif.: Mimeographed, 1963), and *The Bracero Program in California* (New York: Arno, 1976 [1961]); Galarza, *Strangers in Our Fields* (Washington, DC: United States Section, Joint United States-Mexico Trade Union Committee, 1956), and *Merchants of Labor: The Mexican Bracero History* (Santa Barbara, Calif.: McNally and Loftin, 1964).

24. Kiser and Kiser, *Mexican Workers*.

25. Señor Palmas, interview by author, San Luis Valley, Colorado, 1997.

26. Don Francisco, "Life story of Don Francisco," interview by author, Fresno, California, 1997.

27. Don Andres, "Life story of Don Andres," interview by Sergio Chavez, US-Mexico border, 2005.

28. Galarza, *Merchants*.

29. Don Antoñio, "Life story of Don Antoñio," interview by author, Fresno, CA, 1997.

30. United Farm Workers (UFW), *El Malcriado: Trade Journal of the United Farm Workers* 1 (1996): 18.

31. David Gutierrez, *Walls and Mirrors: Mexican Americans, Mexican Immigrants, and the Politics of Ethnicity* (Berkeley: University of California Press, 1995).

32. Philip Martin, "The Bracero Program: Was It a Failure?" *History News Network* (2006), historynewsnetwork.org/article/27336; Kitty Calavita, *Inside the State: The Bracero Program, Immigration, and the I.N.S.* (NY: Routledge Press, 2010).

33. DeWind, Seidl, and Shenk, "Contract Labor," 386.

34. Ibid., 383.

35. Ibid., 392.

36. Robert Williams, "The H-2A Program," panelist, presented at the National Conference on Migrant and Seasonal Farmworkers, Denver, Colo., May 9–13, 1993.

37. For details of the labor peace accords, see Hahamovitch, *No Man's Land*, 220.

38. David Griffith, *American Guestworkers: Jamaicans and Mexicans in the US Labor Market* (State College: Pennsylvania State University Press, 2007), 70.

39. US Congress, Immigration Reform and Control Act of 1986, http://library.uwb .edu/static/usimmigration/100%20stat%203359.pdf.

40. US Department of Labor, *Office of Foreign Labor Certification 2014 Annual Report* (Washington DC: Employment and Training Administration, Office of Foreign Labor Certification, 2015), 34, https://www.foreignlaborcert.doleta.gov/pdf/OFLC_Annual_Report_ FY2014.pdf.

41. Rafael Alarcón, "Skilled Immigrants and *Cerebreros*: Foreign-Born Engineers and Scientists in the High Technology Industry of Silicon Valley," in *Immigration Research for a New Century: Multidisciplinary Perspectives*, ed. Nancy Foner, Rubén Rumbaut, and Steven J. Gold (New York: Russell Sage Foundation, 2000).

42. US Department of Labor. *The Foreign Labor Certification Report: International Talent Helping Meet Employer Demand* (Washington DC: Employment and Training Administration, Office of Foreign Labor Certification, 2007), https://www.foreignlaborcert.doleta .gov/pdf/FY2007_OFLCPerformanceRpt.pdf.

43. US Department of Labor, *The Foreign Labor Certification Report: 2009 Data, Trends and Highlights across Programs and States* (Washington DC: Employment and Training Administration, Office of Foreign Labor Certification, 2009), http://www.foreignlaborcert .doleta.gov/pdf/2009_Annual_Report.pdf.

CHAPTER 7

Setting the Stage to Bring in the "Highly Skilled"

Project Paperclip and the Recruitment of German Specialists after World War II

MONIQUE LANEY

Electrical engineer Kurt Heinrich Debus and patent attorney Herbert Felix Axster were two of hundreds of German and Austrian scientists, engineers, and technical experts brought to the United States under "Project Overcast" after World War II. The secret military operation, better known under its later name, "Project Paperclip," imported experts in strategic fields such as aerodynamics, rocketry, chemical weapons, and medicine. Unlike most of their colleagues, neither Debus nor Axster were allowed to pursue US citizenship in 1948, as both had been deemed "ardent Nazis." Their situation changed, however, with the 1952 Immigration and Nationality Act (Public Law 414), also known as the McCarran-Walter Act. In a memorandum ordering that Debus's and Axster's applications for authorization of pre-examination be granted, the assistant commissioner of the Inspections and Examinations Division of the Immigration and Naturalization Service explained that their "past membership in organizations which were affiliated with the Nazi party" no longer constituted grounds for inadmissibility. As the central considerations for this decision he offered "that the subjects are engaged in scientific projects deemed essential to the public security" and that they "appear to be otherwise admissible."[1] Their visa applications could finally move forward. While Axster did not take advantage of the new circumstances and instead returned to Germany in 1953, Debus stayed and became a US citizen. In 1962 he became the first director of what would later be known as NASA's Kennedy Space Center at Cape Canaveral, Florida.[2]

Setting the Stage to Bring in the "Highly Skilled" • 145

Scholars and investigative journalists have explored Project Paperclip mainly as a military undertaking, as a story of knowledge and technology transfer, and for its Machiavellian logic.[3] But the program is also important as part of immigration history because it helped set the future agenda, even for current immigration debates and policies.

Paperclip extended favorable treatment to northern Europeans with questionable pasts at the same time that others were severely disadvantaged by the nation's immigration system. The involved government departments went to great lengths to create and then expedite the process that would turn the German and Austrian specialists, who entered the country as enemy aliens, into resident aliens with a path to citizenship. This process occurred when national policies rigorously restricted, and in some cases completely banned, immigrants from non-northern and western European countries.[4] Even the thousands of victims of the Nazi regime who were still suffering in postwar Europe could not immigrate until the implementation of the first Displaced Persons Act in 1948. The decision to offer the scientists and technical professionals a path to citizenship also contrasted with the treatment of agricultural workers from Mexico, who had been brought into the United States since 1942 under the Bracero Program—a guest worker program that offered only temporary visas.

The 1952 McCarran-Walter Act was not designed specifically for Debus and Axster, but its allocation of 50 percent of visas to highly skilled professionals amplified a trend in immigration policy that had its roots in a longer history of preferential treatment of immigrants with desired skills. While immigration laws of the late nineteenth and early twentieth centuries became increasingly restrictive based on an applicant's national origin, they always included exceptions for those who could presumably further the nation's interests. Earlier laws already provided exemptions for teachers, students, and merchants, then for skilled laborers, professionals, actors, ministers, professors, domestic servants, nurses, and agricultural workers.[5] What was new after World War II was an emphasis on professionals with scientific or technical skills.

Immigration historians have only begun to investigate the history of immigrants with special skills.[6] Those concerned with the McCarran-Walter Act have focused primarily on its effect on the contemporary immigration regime as well as efforts leading up to the bill to challenge the national-origins quota system.[7] This chapter brings immigration history, military history, and the histories of science and technology in conversation with each other to explore how Project Paperclip foreshadowed and potentially stimulated the shift in national immigration policies to favor scientists and technical professionals. It lays out the competing interests of various constituencies and how the involved government departments worked out their conflicting agendas. As in most immigration quagmires, many issues were not resolved and linger on as contentious topics until today.[8]

A New Kind of War Reparations

World War II was profoundly affected by new inventions and applications of science and technology. All of the primary participating countries aimed to develop better technologies to gain an advantage over the enemy. At war's end in the European theater, the Allies were therefore not only eager to gain control of Germany's weapons, laboratories, equipment, factories, and documentation, they also wanted to take advantage of those who had developed these technologies. The United States, Britain, France, and the Soviet Union searched for and captured thousands of German and Austrian experts in aerodynamics, radar, rocketry, nuclear technology, chemical weapons, medicine, and other fields, even before the war officially ended. In addition to evidence of a German atomic bomb, the most prominent examples of sought-after technology were Hitler's so-called "wonder" weapons, the jet-powered V-1 cruise missile and the rocket-powered V-2 ballistic missile.[9] Herbert Axster and Kurt Debus were associated with the group that designed the V-2.

The US undertaking was considered a form of "intellectual reparations" — a scientific and technical exploitation program to transfer people, know-how, and matériel from Germany to the United States. For this purpose, American scientists and industry specialists joined military intelligence units in Germany in search for items and people often previously identified. Initially, the utilization of German and Austrian specialists was limited to temporary exploitation to fight Japan in the Pacific arena and aid in postwar military research, after which the military would return them to Europe.[10] The military offered them short-term contracts, and most were brought to New York, where they were separated and sent to different destinations around the country. The specialists were classified as "enemy aliens temporarily in the United States as civilian employees of the War Department."[11] In an effort to keep the project secret and under tight control, the War Department was supposed to segregate the specialists from unauthorized persons, require them to have an escort whenever moving off base, limit their access to classified information, and censor their mail.

It did not take long, however, for circumstances to call for a major shift in the program's goals and thus the treatment of the specialists from Germany. Designed for temporary settlement and exploitation at first, the program would eventually parallel more general immigration policies that encourage permanent settlement and employment. The process of revising the program vividly illustrates the varied priorities of the different government agencies involved.

When the war with Japan ended, denying other countries' access to the specialists' expertise became the main goal. Reports from Germany indicated that French and Russian agents were using attractive offers to entice Germans with desirable skills to work for their respective nations. Many Germans also openly made plans to emigrate to Latin American countries. Stateside, a number of the already captured specialists refused to renew their short-term War Department contracts unless they had a better sense of their long-term futures and knew that their families could join them in the United States. Compounding these concerns, the British government threatened to withhold experts it had captured unless the United States adopted a long-term exploitation policy.[12] Sending the specialists back to Europe seemed to be a bigger security risk than keeping them in the United States permanently. The US government felt pressed to act swiftly and provide more attractive incentives to entice the specialists to move to and then stay in the country.[13]

Meantime, President Truman gave the Executive Order 9604 on August 1945 "to provide for 'prompt, public, free, and general' dissemination of all unclassified 'scientific, industrial, and technical processes, inventions, methods, devices, improvements, and advances' acquired by American missions in Germany," in the hope that this would help the postwar economy by "creating new methods, new products, and greater employment opportunities." The Commerce Department therefore already collected, declassified, and distributed scientific and technical information gathered in Germany to American industry.[14] Unsurprisingly, it was also very interested in taking advantage of the experts from Germany and Austria for American industry.

A newly created Technical Industrial Intelligence Committee in Washington worked with the armed services, private industry, trade associations, and universities to identify people and items for field teams to look for in Germany. Experts joined the field teams as temporary technical consultants to help locate, detain, and interrogate thousands of German scientists and technicians. When the American experts returned, they reported back to their trade, industry, and professional organizations, which used the information to make recommendations for additional investigations and an extension of the wartime program into the postwar period. They also explicitly called for the recruitment of German scientists and technicians, arguing that the British, French, or Russians might get to them first, which would give those countries not only a military but also an industrial advantage.[15]

Secretary of Commerce Henry A. Wallace and the head of the Commerce Department's Office of Declassification and Technical Services, John C. Green, proposed a policy as early as December 1945 for the "transfer of outstanding German scientists to this country for the advancement of our science and industry" in order to fulfill Truman's directive more comprehensively.[16] But bringing the specialists to the United States before they were vetted as eligible to become US citizens meant that the War Department would have to organize the transportation, surveillance, screening, and administration of the specialists, while the Commerce Department reaped the benefits.[17] They agreed instead that the War Department would determine whether specialists whom the Commerce Department had identified were eligible for recruitment for reasons of "national security." As a result, in the early stages only twenty-one Germans entered the United States to work in industry.

Despite not being able to bring in many specialists directly at first, the efforts of the Commerce Department and industry paid off in the long run. The department was still heavily involved in Project Paperclip by arranging the transfer of specialists from military agencies to private industry and universities after they had fulfilled their military obligations. Private companies could interview individual specialists or borrow them for limited times from the various military services, and in some cases they would even request that specific specialists be recruited through Project Paperclip, in order to "borrow" them for their needs. With the passing of the Displaced Persons Acts in 1948 and the resumption of normal consular services in Austria and the American, French, and British zones of Germany, the department finally won approval for a streamlined procedure to acquire specialists in the "national interest."[18]

Turning Enemy Aliens into Immigrants

The change in goals from exploitation to denial provided an almost irrefutable argument for a more permanent and long-term solution. When the project's name was compromised in November 1945, it was changed from Overcast to Paperclip. This was followed almost immediately by a new directive in March 1946, which included the possibility for the specialists to attain citizenship as well as receive long-term contracts, if the administering officials deemed that to be "in the interest of national security."[19] The directive also stipulated that the military could bring a total of 350 German and Austrian scientists, engineers, and technicians to the United States under the project's auspices, that some of the initial security measures would be loosened, and that in coordination with the Commerce Department, civilian industries and laboratories could now also employ the specialists. With these prospects, the specialists' dependents began to join them in the United States within one or two years. In September 1946, another directive raised to one thousand the limit for how many specialists could be brought to the United States.[20]

It was one thing to bring people who had worked for the Nazi war machine to the United States for temporary exploitation, but quite another to put them on a path to citizenship. The War Department had been able to evade close scrutiny of the State and Justice Departments for temporary exploitation, but now it had to convince these entities that the procedures for immigration would ensure that neither war criminals nor so-called "ardent Nazis" could become US citizens. It would take almost two years, several revisions, and multiple compromises in the name

Setting the Stage to Bring in the *"Highly Skilled"* • 149

of "the national interest" before the War, State, and Justice Departments finalized a procedure under which the German and Austrian specialists and their families could become official immigrants. The three departments struggled mainly over what type of information was needed for the pre-examination process and how to evaluate the data. The State Department in particular needed convincing. But since Hitler's regime was defeated and the Cold War conflict with the Soviet Union was becoming more important in international and domestic politics, fears that the Germans might spread Nazi ideology in the United States were waning at the same time that anticommunism was gaining greater momentum. The focus eventually shifted from looking at what the specialists had done in the past under Hitler's regime to what they would do *in* and *for* the United States in the future.

The State Department protested the importation of the specialists on several grounds. One argument was that Project Paperclip would allow them to conduct the kind of research they were prohibited from pursuing in postwar Germany. Another, maybe more important, argument was that it violated inter-American agreements "to reduce Axis 'centers of influence' in the Western Hemisphere." The State Department therefore required thorough investigations of each individual, the nature and extent of which generated significant delays in processing the specialists' applications. The War Department considered this unacceptable, especially since the delays meant that the military had to continue keeping a costly close eye on the specialists, who were growing restless.[21]

It seems ironic that the State Department appeared to be more concerned than the War Department about security issues, but with the Nazi regime destroyed, many areas of government no longer viewed Nazism, but rather the USSR and Communism, as a major threat. The director of the Joint Intelligence Objectives Agency (JIOA) wondered out loud at one point whether the State Department officials were deliberately sabotaging the program by "beating a dead Nazi horse."[22]

The United States had already been privileging Germans with desirable skills when other national interests took precedence. Immediately following the war, it circumvented its own denazification program that was designed to remove Nazis from positions of influence and power. For example, the US Army's agency—Field Information Agency, Technical (FIAT)—that administered the postwar scientific and technical exploitation program in Germany, routinely hired Germans with needed linguistic and technical skills to support its mission, even though they were not eligible based on their denazification records.[23] A more egregious example, perhaps, is that American intelligence agencies began to employ former German intelligence officials, SS officers, police, or non-German collaborators with the Nazis—all potential war criminals—for intelligence gathering against a growing Communist threat.[24] In short, the desire to capture German know-how took precedence over other concerns from the start. In the case of Paperclip, the

150 · MONIQUE LANEY

then-common belief that science and technology was apolitical and value-neutral additionally allowed officials to interpret the specialists' membership in Nazi organizations as motivated by career objectives, not active and enthusiastic ideological support.

The involved parties eventually agreed on immigration directives. As long as the specialists appeared to embrace American democracy and did not promote Nazi ideology, they were considered assets for the nation. The government also considered it imperative for national security and defense that they should not fall into the hands of other nations, and it viewed their immigration to be in the national interest because of the expected long-term benefits for national security and industry.[25] The shift in focus produced revised security reports, which would later lead investigative reporters to question the morality of the entire project. In the context of the emerging Cold War in the late 1940s, however, the circumstances seemed to mandate the compromises.

Implementing the new directives required further modifications to satisfy all involved parties. Before the policy for Project Paperclip changed to include the specialists' potential immigration, the Intelligence Division of the War Department had supplied the Federal Bureau of Investigation (FBI) with photos, fingerprints, and biographical and professional sketches for each of the specialists. This would not suffice to evaluate their suitability for immigration. The dossier now had to also include a denazification record, medical certificate, basic personnel record, questionnaire, monthly statements about the specialist's surveillance, and investigation reports.[26] Both the denazification record and investigation reports were sources of contention among the War, State, and Justice Departments.

The fact that the military brought the scientists, engineers, and technicians to the United States without executing the mandatory denazification procedures, which in Germany were required by the Law for Liberation from National Socialism and Militarism, was one of the major stumbling blocks for speedy processing.[27] To satisfy State and Justice requirements for denazification, the War Department proposed a special procedure: instead of shipping the specialists back to Germany for denazification trials, the specialists would fill out the questionnaire (*Meldebogen/Fragebogen*) required for the denazification process, which would then be forwarded to the US Military Government in Germany and Austria for trials in absentia by a special tribunal created for this purpose.[28] General Lucius D. Clay, head of the Office of Military Government, United States (OMGUS) in Germany, strongly opposed this idea, as it would have resulted in a public display of special procedures for the German specialists already in the United States. He anticipated that this would not only affect German sentiments toward the US occupiers but would also draw unwanted attention to Project Paperclip. In the end, the government departments agreed that, instead of sending the completed forms to Europe,

Setting the Stage to Bring in the "Highly Skilled" • 151

the JIOA would collect them and base further recommendations on them—a very different procedure from those performed in Germany for denazification, where some of the specialists would have been punished with fines, jail terms, employment restrictions, and forfeiture of civic rights.

The other major contention among the US government departments concerned the evaluation of the investigation reports, also referred to as security reports. These had to include the results from surveillance of the specialists in the United States but also reports based on investigations by OMGUS in Europe. In addition, the specialists and their dependents had to submit a typewritten, sworn statement explaining their membership in the NSDAP (Nazi party) and affiliated organizations. Here, they had to describe in detail the degree of their participation and reasons for joining.[29] The investigations in Europe adhered to a lengthy process that frequently created extended delays in the pre-examination of visa applicants. The requirement for local investigations was therefore later limited to applicants whose records "indicate that the specialist was a leader or organizer in the NSDAP or its affiliates or . . . no official records can be found and other sources indicate the possibility of political incrimination."[30] The investigators in Europe used the same criteria that were used for other Germans, however, and found many of the specialists to be "potential security threats" and even "ardent Nazis," which prompted a review of the procedures in the United States.

Since the initial reports from Europe would have had a similarly limiting effect as the State Department's initial requirements, the government changed the policy for how to evaluate the information regarding the specialists' former affiliation with Nazi regime, so that more of the much-desired specialists could receive visas. In September 1946 the State, War, and Navy Departments, as well as President Truman, granted approval for a policy that clarified that while an individual who had been an active member in the Nazi regime could not be brought to the United States, "any honors or positions awarded a specialist by the Nazi Party because of his scientific or technical ability were not to be considered sufficient evidence to disqualify his entry into the United States."[31] This was a major policy shift that suddenly allowed specialists who had previously been classified as ardent Nazis or at a minimum "a potential security threat" to enter the country and eventually apply for citizenship.[32]

The question of how to evaluate the specialists remained a controversial issue, however, and led to another shift in the assessment of the specialists' past behavior. In November 1947 the chief of the Exploitation Branch of the Intelligence Division wrote in protest of security reports that OMGUS had submitted, which would have excluded some of the specialists "based solely on the fact that these specialists have not undergone denazification proceedings and appear to be presumptive class 2 offenders by reason of early membership in the Nazi Party." The chief considered this approach unrealistic and declared that security evaluations should state if a full investigation is not possible and that "where Party membership without rank, activity or Party honors is indicated, a saving clause should be inserted to allow for a change in security evaluation if subject is later denazified or demonstrates his fitness for permanent residence in the United States by his attitude and actions while under supervision for a minimum of six months in the United States."[33] In other words, when in doubt over a specialist's level of involvement with the Nazi regime, the evaluator should assume *less* rather than *more* involvement.

In many cases, information was simply not available because the specialist came from a region of Germany that was now occupied by Soviet forces. Since the information would be missing on the security reports for these specialists, the JIOA director ordered in 1948 that the security report should omit the paragraph that refers to local investigations and renumber the following paragraphs because "the appearance of an incomplete report is undesirable."[34]

One of the War Department inquiries on how to speed up the pre-examination process revealed that, under the direction of J. Edgar Hoover, the FBI was conducting additional extensive investigations of each applicant before recommending approval to the Justice Department. The director of intelligence therefore met with Hoover and convinced him that the investigations of the military services were thorough enough and that the FBI should expedite the approval process in order to "relieve the War Department of its custodial responsibilities."[35]

The government charged the JIOA with the coordination of the finally agreed-upon process. Since many of the specialists were already working on high-priority research-development programs, the potential danger of their capture by an enemy nation if sent back to Europe to obtain visas made that option impractical. Instead, they would undergo a pre-examination procedure in the United States, after which they could obtain a visa at a consulate either in Canada or Mexico, depending on which border was closest. Immigration procedures for individual specialists began only after they had been under observation in the United States for a minimum of six months. In order to begin the process, the secretary of war had to submit a completed dossier for each specialist, certifying that the specialist's entry was "in the national interest, that his permanent residence in this country would aid in furthering national security requirements, and that such entry would not be prejudicial to the interests of the United States." The dossier went to the secretary of state and the attorney general, and if they determined that a visa could be granted, they informed the consul, before whom the specialist was to appear, of the decision. In the meantime, the Justice Department made a final check concerning national security and national interest and informed the Immigration and Naturalization Service of the results.[36]

The government agencies coordinated the procedures for obtaining visas with the respective consuls in Canada and Mexico. In April 1948, the American consul

Setting the Stage to Bring in the "Highly Skilled" • 153

in Niagara Falls, Canada, issued the first visa to a specialist who had arrived under Project Paperclip.[37] The largest cohesive group of specialists who arrived under Paperclip was the team that had developed the V-2 rocket and whose rockets later put the first American satellite into orbit and humans on the Moon. That team was stationed at Ft. Bliss, Texas, and at White Sands, New Mexico, so the army sent the individual members across the Mexican border to obtain their visas. Accompanied by a military escort in civilian clothes, the specialist would appear in front of the consul in Ciudad Juárez with the required documentation. After receiving his visa, the specialist returned to the United States and received resident alien status under US immigration laws. He was no longer in military custody, which meant that his military employers no longer had authority over him. He could now also submit the required forms to initiate the immigration of his dependents.[38]

The program lasted well into the late 1960s under various names, which makes it difficult to determine exactly how many scientists and engineers were eventually brought to the United States under its auspices. The estimated total number in the 1945–1952 period, during which about 90 percent of the German and Austrian specialists were recruited, vary between 518 and 642.[39] According to Clarence Lasby, whose 1971 monograph is still the most reliable comprehensive source (even though he did not have access to many now declassified files), "the Department of Army imported 210 specialists, of whom 29 returned to Europe prior to immigration. . . . The United States Air Force sponsored 260, of whom 36 returned to Germany and 1 re-emigrated to Argentina," and "the Navy selected . . . 111 Paperclip specialists" between 1945 and 1952.[40]

A more comprehensive study for the entire program is still needed, but at least among the rocket team several members experienced delays in the issuance of their visas due to "derogatory background information" and delayed security reports. That said, the army did not send any of them back to Germany due to their early membership in the Nazi Party or for being an "ardent Nazi," even though OMGUS had initially classified several of them as potential threats to the security of the United States.[41] A few left voluntarily, and the army sent one of them back because he had disobeyed orders not to cross the border into Mexico, and another one because he presumably suffered from mental illness. Several others were sent back because their skills were not deemed necessary after all. Most of the remaining members of the rocket team who arrived in the immediate postwar period attained US citizenship by the mid-1950s.

Very few of those who arrived under Project Paperclip were later challenged based on their work for Hitler's regime. The leader of the rocket team, Wernher von Braun, was the best-known recruit under Project Paperclip. His morality was frequently questioned over the years, but he never faced charges in a court of law. Another prominent recruit, Hubertus Strughold, sometimes referred to as "the father of space medicine," came under greater scrutiny for his work under the

154 · MONIQUE LANEY

Nazi regime only after his death in 1986. In 1984 another prominent member of the rocket team, Arthur Rudolph, returned to Germany after signing an affidavit, according to which he "participated . . . in the persecution of unarmed civilians because of their race, religion, national origin, or political opinion" as the production manager for the V-2 rocket.[42]

Project Paperclip and the McCarran-Walter Act

There was evidently good reason to deny Axster and Debus, who were mentioned in the introduction of this chapter, the privilege of pursuing US citizenship. The secretary of war received a letter on April 14, 1947, from the president of the American Jewish Congress, Rabbi Stephen S. Wise, to remind him of the goals of World War II, but primarily to alert him of a dispatch from Berlin published in the *New York Times* on January 4, 1947. It discussed Mr. and Mrs. Axster's activities in Nazi Germany and claimed that, under German denazification laws, Mrs. Axster would be considered a major offender.[43] The army launched a reinvestigation of the Axsters in Europe, and the European Command sent a cable stating: "H. Axster not politically active . . . Ilse Axster—was highly active in Nazi Party, was not a war criminal but was a party member since 1937, an ardent Nazi and fanatical representative of Nazi ideology. Definitely a security threat."[44] These allegations were based on statements from former neighbors who reported on her activities as the head of the local *NS Frauenschaft* (Nazi women's organization) and their observations that she had mistreated foreign laborers who worked on the Axsters' farm during the war.[45] Despite these assessments, agencies within the War Department made several appeals to the State Department and Immigration and Naturalization Service (INS) on their behalf. One of the reasons his employers did not want to see Axster and his wife deported was the fact that he "had access to highly classified information in many fields of guided missile development" and therefore had information that made him "a definite potential security threat to the United States if he [were] deported."[46] Even his wife had presumably "acquired a sufficient technical orientation to be of intelligence value to the Russians or other power" thanks to her mental capabilities and her close association with the project.[47]

Kurt Debus had been considered an "ardent" Nazi because he had applied for membership in the notorious SS (Protection Squadron) in 1940 and had denounced a colleague to Nazi authorities as a traitor in 1942 based on a conversation they had about the causes of the war with Britain.[48] The attorney of the person whom Debus had accused requested that his sentence of two years' imprisonment and payment of court costs be postponed until after the war. Ironically, he argued that the accused was considered an indispensable asset for the German war effort. In 1950 the secretary of the army made a similar argument on Debus's behalf. His letter to the secretary of state in 1950 summarizes the then-prevailing attitude among US government and military officials toward the Nazi pasts of the German and Austrian specialists: "Although he [Debus] was classified as an ardent Nazi by the United States High Commissioner for Germany, surveillance in the United States for a period of four and one-half years has given every evidence that he has embraced democracy and the American way of life. His value to this country, because of his technical qualifications and knowledge of present and future plans in his field, outweighs the consideration of his Nazi activity."[49] Debus was allowed to stay in the country, but he could not apply for citizenship as his colleagues had. This changed with the congressional approval of a new Immigration Act in 1952.

Replacing all prior immigration and naturalization laws, the McCarran-Walter Act signified a remarkable alteration of US policy. It provided 50 percent of visas to immigrants whose services the attorney general determined to be urgently needed because of their higher education, technical training, specialized experience, or exceptional ability, and the belief that they would substantially benefit the national economy and cultural interest or welfare of the United States.[50]

The new law had a profound effect on the status for everyone who was recruited under Project Paperclip. It virtually assured citizenship and freed individuals to seek new opportunities outside of the military on their own accord, while the Joint Chiefs of Staff arranged for civil-service status for those who remained with the military.[51] Since the new legislation did not contain any stipulations that precluded "ardent Nazis" from becoming citizens, it had removed the last restraint, allowing even Axster and Debus to join their colleagues in becoming American citizens.

Conclusion

The agencies involved in Paperclip went to extraordinary lengths to pave a way for former enemies to become US citizens in the name of "national security" for military uses or "national interest" for civilian exploitation, putting them ahead of displaced persons barely surviving in Europe. The government's willingness to circumvent existing laws, take the risk of bringing potential Nazi ideologues and war criminals to the country, and ignore domestic and international criticism while spinning the importation of these specialists as a triumph indicates the value it placed on the expertise of these migrants. It also illustrates that, regardless of politics, individuals who are able to develop and wield certain forms of knowledge benefit from them.

The bargain seemed to pay off. Arguably, many US advancements in science and technology were the direct or indirect result of Project Paperclip. These include NASA's Apollo Program that put humans on the moon and the development of long-range missiles, aerospace medicine, submarine technology, along with numerous other contributions to industry and academia.

By the time most of the German and Austrian specialists and their families who had arrived in the late 1940s became naturalized American citizens in the mid-1950s, the nation had moved on. The emerging Cold War shored up fears of Communism, which quickly outweighed any fears of Nazi infiltration. Changes to the existing immigration laws provided some refuge for displaced persons from Europe, and the war in Korea moved the public focus away from World War II and its aftereffects. Questions about the involvement of some of the specialists in war crimes under the Nazi regime did not become a larger public concern until decades later.

It was the Displaced Persons Act of 1948 that first included conscious labor preferences and job requirements for refugees entering from Europe, but the US government had already demonstrated its intense desire to attract immigrants who could contribute scientific and technological expertise to the nation. The 1952 McCarran-Walter Act further expanded the wartime military logic of Project Paperclip into the civilian realm, marking a significant shift in the admissions program and adding another layer of exclusion to the existing immigration regime that already "contributed," as immigration historian Mae Ngai explained, "to the racialization of immigrant groups around notions of whiteness, permanent foreignness, and illegality."[52] Since then, every successive legal framework governing US immigration has included a quota for the highly skilled, thereby severely disadvantaging those without such skills.

Project Paperclip foreshadowed future immigration debates and policies in multiple ways. It illustrated that "skilled" individuals can accumulate and benefit from knowledge and experience in ways that those considered "unskilled" cannot. Paperclip was the first instance in which the federal government and private industry became involved in the "enticement and persuasion of foreign scientists to work, *through contract*, for the United States" with the prospect of future citizenship. Signaling the important role employers would play in future immigration debates and programs, the stipulations for Project Paperclip reverberate in current H-1B and similar temporary dual-intent work visas, which require sponsorship by an employer for a specific job offer and allow holders to apply for a green card, even though the visa is issued for a temporary stay.[53]

Notes

1. "In Re: Kurt Heinrich Debus and Herbert Felix Axster, From: Assistant Commissioner, Inspections and Examinations Division," February 12, 1953, Foreign Scientist Case Files, 1945–1958, file AXSTER, RG 330, box 5, National Archives, College Park, Md.

2. "Letter from G. W. Crabbe, Colonel, Director USAF, JIOA to James E. Riley, Immigration & Naturalization Service, Chief of Entry and Departure Branch," October 22, 1954, Foreign Scientist Case Files, 1945–1958, file AXSTER, RG 330, box 5, National Archives, College Park, Md.

3. Tom Bower, *The Paperclip Conspiracy: The Battle for the Spoils and Secrets of Nazi Germany* (London: M. Joseph, 1987); John Gimbel, "German Scientists, United States Denazification Policy, and the 'Paperclip Conspiracy,'" *International History Review* 12 (1990): 441–65; Linda Hunt, *Secret Agenda: The United States Government, Nazi Scientists, and Project Paperclip, 1945 to 1990* (New York: St. Martin's, 1991); Annie Jacobsen, *Operation Paperclip: The Secret Intelligence Program to Bring Nazi Scientists to America* (Boston, Mass.: Little, Brown, 2014); Clarence G. Lasby, *Project Paperclip: German Scientists and the Cold War* (New York: Atheneum, 1971); Michael J. Neufeld, "Overcast, Paperclip, Osoaviakhim: Looting and the Transfer of German Military Technology," in *The United States and Germany in the Era of the Cold War, 1945–1990: A Handbook*, ed. Detlef Junker, et al., *Publications of the German Historical Institute* (Cambridge, New York, Washington, DC: Cambridge University Press; German Historical Institute, 2004).

4. Mae M. Ngai, "The Architecture of Race in American Immigration Law: A Reexamination of the Immigration Act of 1924," *Journal of American History* 86, no. 1 (1999): 67–92.

5. Philip Eric Wolgin, "Beyond National Origins: The Development of Modern Immigration Policymaking, 1948–1968," PhD diss., University of California, Berkeley, 2011, 99.

6. Catherine Ceniza Choy, *Empire of Care: Nursing and Migration in Filipino American History*, American Encounters/Global Interactions (Durham, N.C.: Duke University Press, 2003); Fleming, Donald, and Bernard Bailyn. *The Intellectual Migration: Europe and America, 1930–1960* (Cambridge: Belknap / Harvard University Press, 1969); Madeline Yuan-Yin Hsu, *The Good Immigrants: How the Yellow Peril Became the Model Minority*, Politics and Society in Twentieth-Century America (Princeton, N.J.: Princeton University Press, 2015); Mae M. Ngai, *The Lucky Ones: One Family and the Extraordinary Invention of Chinese America* (Boston, Mass.: Houghton Mifflin Harcourt, 2010); Larissa Schütze, *William Dieterle und die deutschsprachige Emigration in Hollywood: Antifaschistische Filmarbeit bei Warner Bros. Pictures, 1930–1940*, Transatlantische Historische Studien (Stuttgart, Ger.: Steiner, 2015).

7. Danielle Battisti, "The American Committee on Italian Migration, Anti-Communism, and Immigration Reform," *Journal of American Ethnic History* 31, no. 2 (2012): 11–40; Marius Albert Dimmitt Sr., "The Enactment of the McCarran-Walter Act of 1952," PhD diss., University of Kansas, 1970; Robert A. Divine, *American Immigration Policy, 1924–1952*, Civil Liberties in American History (New York: Da Capo, 1972); Maddalena Marinari, "Divided and Conquered: Immigration Reform Advocates and the Passage of the 1952 Immigration and Nationality Act," *Journal of American Ethnic History* 35, no. 3 (2016): 9–40; Philip Eric Wolgin, "Beyond National Origins: The Development of Modern Immigration Policymaking, 1948–1968."

158 · MONIQUE LANEY

8. Some of those issues are outlined in my book, from which a few of the ideas presented in this chapter are taken: *German Rocketeers in the Heart of Dixie: Making Sense of the Nazi Past During the Civil Rights Era* (New Haven, Conn.: Yale University Press, 2015).

9. Matthias Judt and Burghard Ciesla, *Technology Transfer out of Germany after 1945*, Studies in the History of Science, Technology and Medicine, vol. 2 (Amsterdam: Harwood Academic, 1996); Neufeld, "Overcast, Paperclip, Osoaviakhim"; John Gimbel, *Science, Technology, and Reparations: Exploitation and Plunder in Postwar Germany* (Stanford, Calif.: Stanford University Press, 1990).

10. Lasby, *Project Paperclip*, 9.

11. "The Paperclip Project: Its Concept, Implementation and Control," no year available, but most likely 1959, Publication "P" Files, 1946–51, RG 319, box 2674, National Archives, College Park, Md., 35.

12. Lasby, *Project Paperclip*, 251.

13. "Memorandum for the Secretariat, State-War-Navy Coordinating Committee: Exploitation of German and Austrian Specialists in Science and Technology in the United States, From: Assistant Secretary of War," August 1, 1946, Army Decimal File, 1941–48, RG 319, box 991, National Archives, College Park, Md., Appendix A: Facts bearing on the problem and discussion.

14. Lasby, *Project Paperclip*, 63, 129.

15. Gimbel, *Science, Technology, and Reparations*, 23, 30.

16. As quoted in ibid., 37.

17. Gimbel, "German Scientists," 454.

18. Lasby, *Project Paperclip*, 53–59 and 235.

19. "Paperclip Project," Publication "P" Files, 1946–51, 5, 74.

20. Lasby, *Project Paperclip*, chapter on "Security and Control."

21. Gimbel, "German Scientists," 449–50.

22. As quoted in ibid., 450.

23. Ibid., 444–47.

24. Richard Breitman, Norman J. W. Goda, Tiffany Naftali, and Robert Wolfe, *US Intelligence and the Nazis* (New York: Cambridge University Press, 2005), 7.

25. "Paperclip Project," Publication "P" Files, 1946–51, 10.

26. Ibid., 46.

27. "HQ European Command: Staff Message Control, Ref. No. WX-83711," August 7, 1947, IRR Impersonal Files, RG 319, box 19, National Archives, College Park, Md.

28. "HQ European Command: Staff Message Control, Ref. No. WX-83711," IRR Impersonal Files, 444–45; Gimbel, "German Scientists," 458.

29. "Memorandum, Subject: Information Required for Immigration of German Scientists, From: Joint Chiefs of Staff, JIOA," April 14, 1947, ACSI, G-2 (Intelligence) Decimal File, 1941–48, RG 319, box 1002, National Archives, College Park, Md.

30. "OMGUS Security Reports for Paperclip Specialists and Dependents, To: Commander in Chief, European Command, From: JIOA," April 14 1948, General Correspondence, 1946–1952, RG 330, box 14, National Archives, College Park, Md.

31. "Paperclip Project," Publication "P" Files, 1946–51, 7.

Setting the Stage to Bring in the "Highly Skilled" • 159

32. Gimbel, "German Scientists," 454.

33. "OMGUS Security Reports on Paperclip Personnel, Exploitation Section, Executive Office, ID," November 28, 1947, ACSI, G-2 (Intelligence) Decimal File 1941–1948, RG 319, box 1005, National Archives, College Park, Md.

34. "OMGUS Security Reports for Paperclip Specialists and Dependents, To: Commander in Chief, European Command, From: JIOA," General Correspondence, 1946–1952.

35. "Paperclip Project," Publication "P" Files, 1946–51, 86; "Memorandum, Subject: Immigration of Paperclip Specialists, From: Director of Intelligence, Department of the Army General Staff, US Army, Washington, DC," May 17, 1948, ACSI, G-2 (Intelligence) Decimal File, 1941–48, RG 319, box 1002, National Archives, College Park, Md.; "Memorandum for Director of Intelligence, Subject: Immigration of German Scientists and Technicians, WDGS, From: JIOA," March 21, 1947, ACSI, G-2 (Intelligence) Decimal File, 1941–48, RG 319, box 1002, National Archives, College Park, Md.

36. "Memorandum for Director of Intelligence," March 21, 1947, 79.

37. Gimbel, "German Scientists," 462.

38. "Paperclip Project" Publication "P" Files, 1946–51, 75, 92–94; "Memorandum to Chief of Administrative and Liaison Group, ID, GSUSA, Subject: Status of Persons Brought to the United States under Paperclip Program, From: JIOA," July 26, 1949, ACSI, G-2 (Intelligence) Decimal File, 1941–48, RG 319, box 1002, National Archives, College Park, Md.

39. Burghard Ciesla, "German High Velocity Aerodynamics and Their Significance for the US Air Force 1945–1952," in *Technology Transfer out of Germany after 1945*, ed. Matthias Judt and Burghard Ciesla, Studies in the History of Science, Technology and Medicine, vol. 2 (Amsterdam: Harwood Academic, 1996); Lasby, *Project Paperclip*.

40. Lasby, *Project Paperclip*, 57, 64, 251.

41. "To: Officer-in-Charge, Ord Res & Dev Div Subo (Rkt), Ft. Bliss, Texas, Subject: Immigration Status of Paperclip Specialists, From: W. J. Durrenberger, War Department," January 16, 1950, Foreign Scientist Case Files, 1945–1958, file AXSTER, RG 330, box 5, National Archives, College Park, Md.; "Memorandum for Executive, ID, GSUSA, Subject: Exploitation of German Scientists, From: JIOA," October 13, 1947, Foreign Scientist Case Files, 1945–1958, file AXSTER, RG 330, box 5, National Archives, College Park, Md; "OMGUS Security Reports on Paperclip Personnel, Exploitation Section, Executive Office, ID," ACSI, G-2 (Intelligence) Decimal File 1941–1948.

42. "Agreement between Arthur Louis Hugo Rudolph and the United States Department of Justice," Department of Justice, Office of Special Investigations, 1983.

43. Delbert Clark, "Nazis Sent to US as Technicians," *New York Times*, January 4, 1947; "Letter from Rabbi S. Wise to Secretary of War, Robert Patterson," April 14, 1947, ACSI, G-2 (Intelligence) Decimal File, 1941–48, RG 319, entry 47B (NM-3), box 1002, National Archives, College Park, Md.

44. "Information upon which to Base an Investigation of Paperclip Activities at Fort Bliss, Texas and White Sands, New Mexico," ACSI, G-2 (Intelligence) Decimal File, 1941–48; "To: Commanding General, Fourth Army, Fort Sam Houston, Texas, From: Intelligence Division, General Staff, United States Army," ACSI, G-2 (Intelligence) Decimal

File, 1941–48. See also: "Subject: The Axster Couple (Formerly Usedom, Pomerania), From: USAF, Captain, Berlin," March 25, 1948, Foreign Scientist Case Files, 1945–1958, file AXSTER, RG 330, box 5, National Archives, College Park, Md.

45. "Subject: The Axster Couple (Formerly Usedom, Pomerania), From: USAF, Captain, Berlin," Foreign Scientist Case Files, 1945–1958, file AXSTER, RG 330, box 5, National Archives, College Park, Md.

46. "Letter to Chief of Ordnance, Subject: Immigration of Paperclip Specialist Herbert Axster, From: James P. Hamill," February 24, 1950, Foreign Scientist Case Files, 1945–1958, file AXSTER, RG 330, box 5, National Archives, College Park, Md.

47. "Letter to Commanding General, Fort Sam Houston, Texas, Subject: Paperclip Personnel Herbert and Ilse Axster, From: Laurin L. Williams, GSC," October 7, 1948, Foreign Scientist Case Files, 1945–1958, file AXSTER, RG 330, box 5, National Archives, College Park, Md.

48. "Geheime Staatspolizei, Staatspolizeistelle Darmstadt," December 18, 1942, Foreign Scientist Case Files, 1945–1958, and "Request from Dr. Jur. Erich Dickow," April 27, 1943, Foreign Scientist Case Files, 1945–1958, file DEBUS, RG 330, box 28, National Archives, College Park, Md.

49. "Letter to the Secretary of State, From: Secretary of the Army," July 3, 1950, Foreign Scientist Case Files, 1945–1958, file DEBUS, RG 330, box 28, National Archives, College Park, Md.

50. 1952 Immigration and Nationality Act (Public Law 414), sec. 203 (a)(1).

51. Lasby, *Project Paperclip*, 265.

52. Ngai, Mae M. "The Architecture of Race in American Immigration Law: A Reexamination of the Immigration Act of 1924," *Journal of American History* 86, no. 1 (1999): 92.

53. Lasby, *Project Paperclip*, 8 (emphasis by Lasby).

CHAPTER 8

Japanese Agricultural Labor Program
Temporary Worker Immigration, US-Japan Cultural Diplomacy,
and Ethnic Community Making among Japanese Americans

EIICHIRO AZUMA

In September 1956 the "Japanese agricultural worker program" (*Nōgyō rōmusha habei jigyō*) was launched with the arrival of nearly four hundred temporary workers (known as *tannō*) from Japan who were sent to rural farm districts in California. Operating across several phases, this scheme brought a total of forty-one hundred Japanese to the Golden State before the program came to an end in October 1966. Unlike other guest farmworker programs, the Japanese labor importation scheme has largely escaped scholarly attention.[1] Nonetheless, the Japanese agricultural worker program is highly noteworthy in its implications for three interrelated themes: ethnic and class politics of second-generation Japanese Americans (*Nisei*), Cold War US diplomacy and Japanese/Japanese American collaborations, and postwar manifestations of Japan's colonial expansionism. The intersections between immigration and labor fostered these developments while advancing the varied interests of diverse historical agents, including Japanese American farmers and community leaders, California's agribusiness elite, government officials, and social elites of the United States and Japan, alongside the young men who came to California as guest workers.

This chapter explains the diverse origins of and varied meanings attached to the immigration of temporary farmworkers from Japan, and particularly middle-class Nisei's attempts to present themselves as assimilated Americans vis-à-vis alien Japanese laborers. To reveal these developments, I employ two interpretive frameworks. First, an inter-imperial framework illuminates colonial collusions between the United States and Japan, albeit under the former's definitive dominance, in

162 · EIICHIRO AZUMA

the Cold War context. Instead of a familiar narrative of US global hegemony and economic imperialism through guest worker importation, this chapter considers how the remnants of Japanese expansionism dovetailed with American Cold War diplomacy by implementing a scheme of supplementary-farm-labor immigration disguised first as "refugee" migration and then as an educational/training program. The second frame of analysis presents an intraracial perspective that elucidates how Japanese Americans deployed the Japanese agricultural worker program to serve the interests of Nisei farmers and community leaders. They gained access to easily controllable alien labor while Nisei also enjoyed the opportunity to publicly distinguish themselves as good ethnic Americans separate from the foreignized co-ethnic others. In combination, these two perspectives reflect the entanglements of varied interests, agendas, and ideas that met and meshed in the Japanese temporary-worker programs of the mid-1950s and the complicated state of postwar US-Japan diplomacy and race relations in California.

Multiple Origins of Japanese Agricultural Labor Immigration

Before World War II, Japanese immigration to the United States was terminated under the 1924 Immigration Act, and not until 1952 did Japan gain a national immigration quota. The McCarran-Walter Act of 1952 provided a token annual quota of 185, but Japanese could already enter from the late 1940s by a few other ways, including hundreds of so-called war brides, and after 1953, with more than twenty-two hundred entering under the Refugee Relief Act.[2]

Another, lesser-known avenue for Japanese immigration opened up by way of an agriculturally oriented education-abroad program for selected rural youths under the joint sponsorship of the California state government and the Association for International Collaboration of Farmers (AICF: Kokusai Nōyūkai). Established in Tokyo, AICF was a brainchild of Shiroshi Nasu and Tadaatsu Ishiguro, Japan's well-known agricultural scientist and influential bureaucrat, respectively, whose careers went back to the prewar years. Hoping to produce the next generation of pro-American grassroots leaders who would "encourage democracy in [post-occupation] Japan," US diplomats cooperated with Nasu and Ishiguro in getting California governor Earl Warren on board for this program.[3] In the summer of 1952 the first contingent of forty-six left for California to experience US agriculture firsthand by engaging in common fieldwork at Japanese American–owned farms. Coupled with later refugee migrations, this "education" abroad initiative provided a precedent for the formal guest-worker program of 1956.

During the 1930s Nasu and Ishiguro had been among the central architects of migration and colonization policies in Japan's key puppet "Manchukuo" in Manchuria. Nasu served as an academic expert for scientific agricultural colonization schemes that Ishiguro was a driving force in implementing as vice minister of agriculture and forestry in the military-dominated bureaucracy of the time.[4] Both had been deeply committed to the cause of Japan's global expansion and conquest of new "frontiers." They looked to the Americas as a model of agricultural settler colonialism and were especially interested in the "success" of Japanese immigrant agriculture in the American West.[5] To Nasu, Ishiguro, and other members of AICF, an agricultural education-abroad program in California represented the possibility of recuperating their original "ideal" in Manchuria—one that was meant for "the development of co-prosperous civilization . . . through the advance of Japanese agricultural techniques."[6] The only difference was that this colonialist ideal would now be practiced under the aegis of Pax Americana, not under the banner of Japanese imperialism. Nasu indeed predicted that after mastering American-style farming methods, young Japanese would again be able to assist agricultural and social "development" in Southeast Asia and Brazil.[7]

In September 1954 Nasu, Ishiguro, and their American supporters sought to expand the AICF program to include not only small numbers of rural "elite" but also ordinary farm youth. Citing the "mutually satisfactory" results of the AICF program, Nasu produced a proposal for the US State Department, detailing political and economic reasons for "sending [farm youths] as transient, migratory farm workers to earn wages while cultivating a political outlook in consonance with the interests of the United States and Japan, and those of the Free World in general." Whereas "more than one million youths . . . ha[d] scarcely any prospect of getting farm land" or "urban employment" in Japan, Nasu argued, "there [was] a great shortage of farm labor in California." The economic difficulties Japanese farm youths faced would likely make many of them susceptible to "anti-American (communist) propaganda [that was] trying to penetrate into the rural districts." The opportunities for them to live and work in the United States would enable them to "have the right understanding of what America is and stands for," while enriching their home villages financially and contributing to the greater prosperity of California agriculture. Characterizing Japanese farm youths as "reliable, honest, diligent, and intelligent," Nasu emphasized that there would be "less danger of their going underground" than Mexican bracero workers.[8] After the US Ambassador forwarded the proposal to Washington with his endorsement, Nasu traveled to the United States and met with Japanese American farmers and white agribusiness leaders of California, who gave his guest-worker proposal enthusiastic support.[9] Encouraged, he submitted more detailed proposals to the Japanese foreign ministry and the State Department in 1955.[10]

Based on his earlier AICF work, Nasu had cultivated close partnerships with some of the most influential Japanese American farmers in the Golden State. They included Keisaburo Koda, Tameji Eto, and Yaemon Minami. In California, Koda and

Minami were known as the "rice king" and "lettuce king," respectively, and Eto was a leading pea grower.[11] These immigrant community leaders were eager to sponsor a large number of Japanese guest workers.[12] Coupled with his access to political heavyweights in Japan, Nasu's alliance with these Japanese-speaking California farm leaders gave his blueprint for labor importation considerable credibility and local backing—something that younger Nisei leaders and US and Japanese officials could not easily ignore.

Concurrently, inspired by the first contingent of AICF agricultural trainees in 1952, some Japanese American farmers and other ethnic leaders took it upon themselves to recruit a larger number of Japanese field hands. In particular, Frank Tsunekusu Kawasaki of Delano and Henry Seiichi Mikami of Fresno coordinated a group of interested employers stateside and a pool of prospective migrant workers in Japan in order to spearhead transpacific labor importation. A Japan-born foreman for a six-thousand-acre farm owned by the DiGiorgio Fruit Company, Kawasaki persuaded a white executive to support the recruitment of supplementary Japanese field hands, and, as president of the California Farm Production Association, the executive then got other white agribusiness groups involved in the scheme.[13] The Nisei proprietor of a travel and insurance agency and a local Japanese American Citizens League (JACL) leader, Mikami was supposed to manage the transportation of migratory workers from Japan.[14]

Lacking direct access to political insiders and policymakers in Washington or Tokyo, Kawasaki and Mikami used their personal connections in rural California and with specific regions of Japan to make arrangements. As early as 1952, Kawasaki already discussed with the governor of Wakayama—his prefectural origin—an ambitious plan to recruit several thousand Japanese for work on a two-year contract.[15] Even though this initial attempt had to be scrapped over objections from the American Federation of Labor (AFL), the Refugee Relief Act of 1953 led Kawasaki to revive the idea and visit Wakayama repeatedly hoping to bring over new immigrants under the law. After this scheme was reported in ethnic newspapers in California, local Japanese American farmers flocked to Mikami's Fresno office eager to employ young workers from their ancestral land.[16]

Based in southern Japan, another individual named Zen'ichiro Uchida joined Kawasaki and Mikami, aggressively recruiting prospective emigrants from Kagoshima Prefecture. A member of the first AICF contingent, Uchida embraced Nasu's idea of farming as a peaceful means of extending Japanese national influence, and upon his return to Kagoshima from California, he encouraged his neighbors and friends to cross the Pacific for farm work. Through his contacts in Fresno, Uchida got in touch with Kawasaki and learned about the possibility of Japanese immigrating to the United States as "refugees." During their trips to Japan, Kawasaki and Mikami visited Uchida's home region to recruit refugee applicants. Soon, letter-writing campaigns began in Kagoshima and Wakayama to convince the US embassy and the State Department to conduct interviews with self-proclaimed Japanese refugees.[17]

The 1953 law "defined 'refugee' as any person who was out of his usual place of abode and unable to return thereto because of persecution, fear of persecution, natural calamity, or military operations."[18] Uchida and Kawasaki advised recruits to exaggerate their stories of hardships when interviewed by US consular inspectors to appear eligible under the refugee act. Some were even encouraged to lie about their property and crop damages resulting from typhoon flooding and landslides. Uchida himself claimed that his house had been set on fire by communists who allegedly detested his positive discussions of America. Nasu offered to visit the US embassy with Uchida to warn diplomats that escalating communist intimidations and the unresponsiveness of the United States to refugee petitions had made Uchida's village neighbors quickly lose faith in America. In the context of the Korean War and perceived communist threats inside and outside the Japanese archipelago, this rhetorical spin worked well, prompting a formal interview process to commence.[19] Between May 1955 and May 1956, a total of 2,268 Japanese "refugees," many from Kagoshima and Wakayama, entered the United States, where they immediately started to work on Japanese-owned California farms, including Kawasaki's. Nasu's AICF processed their emigration paperwork.[20] The arrival of Japanese "refugees" not only served as another precedent for the formal agricultural guest worker program of 1956–1966, but it also constituted an integral part of the larger flow of postwar labor migration from Japan that had begun with agricultural "trainees" in 1952.

Mike Masaoka as Intergovernmental Political Broker

While architects of AICF and its participants collaborated to transform refugee migration into farm-labor importation, Mike Masaoka, the most influential JACL leader, was responsible for yet a third scheme. According to historian Go Oyagi, Masaoka's project, especially his close cooperation with Japanese diplomats, demonstrates the Nisei leader's "diasporic internationalism," which motivated him to act as a transpacific political broker from 1953.[21] Based in Washington, DC, Masaoka was well connected with US government insiders and the Japanese diplomatic corps—an advantage that the other brokers of Japanese labor importation lacked. During the trying years of wartime incarceration, Masaoka had sought to represent the entire Japanese American community through his leadership in JACL, the only surviving ethnic organization of the time. He was the first volunteer for the all-Nisei 442nd Regimental Combat Team, and as its public relations officer he collaborated with the War Relocation Authority and the US military to impose a skewed image of Japanese Americans as superpatriotic, assimilated Americans.[22] Serving as the JACL national legislative director after the war, Masaoka worked closely with immigrant leaders, like Koda and Eto, in the successful repeal of the alien land laws and the federal ban on Japanese naturalization.[23] Yet, regarding the question of labor importation, Masaoka and the immigrant leaders were not on the same page. When he approached Japanese diplomats with his own proposal for a guest-worker scheme, the JACL leader lacked influence over the alliance between Nasu/AICF and leading Japanese farmers of California and collided with their blueprint.

Because he wanted to avoid the appearance of race-based cooperation, if not conspiracy, between alien Japanese and Japanese Americans, Masaoka was initially unenthusiastic about the idea of bringing a large number of working-class immigrants from his ancestral land. In January 1952, Masaoka offered State Department officials his views of "Japanese Migratory Labor" in response to Kawasaki's failed first attempt at migrant recruitment. "Any large scale importation of Japanese labor would perhaps again raise all the last troubles connected with the 'yellow menace,'" the Nisei leader cautioned, "and [it would] revive persecution suffered by Japanese residents of California in periods in the past."[24] By 1953, however, Masaoka shifted his position in favor of a Japanese guest-worker program. One key development that led to this change was the ongoing political debate in Washington that appeared to be signaling the end of Public Law 78, the legal basis of the bracero Mexican-labor program. Although the law was eventually renewed, the prospect for the suspension of the Mexican program led Masaoka to view supplementary Japanese labor as beneficial to California agribusiness and Nisei farm interests.[25]

At the same time, his highly publicized, triumphant visit to Japan in late 1952 made him reconsider the benefits of working as a political broker in US-Japan bilateral relations—an opportunity that had been inconceivable a few years prior. His racial ancestry, albeit always secondary to his primary American identity, now looked like an asset for a career and the ethnic community he claimed to represent.[26] Believing that his "contacts" and "talents" in Washington would be deemed desirable, he tried his hand at working as a lobbyist for the Japanese government and corporate interests after returning to the United States. Masaoka soon learned "a very discouraging fact; the big Japanese business interests (and diplomats) just don't have confidence in the Nisei." As "bitter" as he was, he thought he should "hold off for a while and hope that something will come up to prove to these guys that we can also cut the mustard in business." That "something" arose with the project of Japanese labor importation. Indeed, by 1953, Masaoka had been contacted by "some California farmers" who "want[ed] us to work out a program to bring in several thousand Japanese farm laborers a year on work contracts."[27]

While Masaoka was briefly involved in Kawasaki's refugee-recruitment scheme, his gaze was primarily directed at a larger endeavor to establish a full-fledged guest-worker program between the United States and Japan, thus overlapping with other similar ideas and proposals, especially Nasu's. In February 1954 Masaoka approached not only US policymakers, like Rep. Walter Judd, but also the Japanese diplomatic corps in Washington, presenting an outline of his ideas about a contract-labor system.[28] In promoting the importance of Japanese labor, the JACL leader employed rhetoric that reinforced prevailing racist discourse that vilified Mexican workers as illegal and influenced by dangerous communist militancy, and he also stressed the "abuses that have plagued the Mexican labor project" because of the "wetbacks."[29] In contrast, Japanese would form "an effective and reliable labor force," for their "efficiency and loyalty . . . on the farms of California, as indeed throughout the Far West [we]re legendary." Masaoka called for a migrant labor agreement with Japan, which would be "of mutual advantage to both countries." He predicted that returning contract workers would be "champions of continued friendship with this country [and its democracy in Japan]."[30]

As Oyagi documents, Masaoka's ability as a lobbyist and access to US government officials had impressed the Japanese diplomatic corps, compelling an embassy member to advise Tokyo to "heed to Mike Masaoka's opinions."[31] Masaoka seized upon this increasing confidence in him. He told the Japanese ambassador that he would be an ideal "unofficial liaison between the governments of the United States and Japan" because he was a private citizen "with no special interests to serve."[32] As they correctly anticipated formidable opposition from various interest groups, including labor unions and the US Department of Labor, Japanese diplomats also regarded highly Masaoka's personal connections to Immigration and Naturalization Service (INS) Commissioner Joseph M. Swing, a close friend to President Eisenhower, who oversaw the existing guest-workers programs.[33] Swing's support was absolutely indispensable for the large-scale importation of Japanese field hands. Fortunately for Masaoka, Swing was already predisposed to support supplementary Japanese labor in the context of his leadership in Operation Wetback, which entailed the mass deportation of "illegal" Mexican farmworkers from California. Swing held more favorable views of Japanese and Japanese Americans, partially through his involvement in the military occupation of Japan as a US army commander. His interactions with "loyal" Nisei translators and cooperative natives in occupied Japan rendered Swing a strong supporter of postwar US-Japan "friendship" and a defender of Japanese Americans in domestic race politics.[34]

In March 1955, with Masaoka as a de facto lobbyist, the Japanese foreign ministry set the ball rolling for the establishment of a formal guest-worker program. At a March 2 meeting the JACL leader confided to top embassy staff that Swing had embraced the program idea, requesting formal submission of a concrete plan. Separately, Swing also notified the Japanese that the US attorney general had approved INS consideration of supplementary labor importation from Japan.

Moreover, having already assessed Nasu's proposal, as Masaoka observed, the State Department also appeared to be on their side. He told Japanese diplomats that the deputy undersecretary of state expressed a strong interest, asking the JACL leader to start working with INS. As the Japanese authorities wanted to keep a low profile, Masaoka was charged with the responsibility of "produc[ing] a concrete blueprint to make it happen."[35] The resulting "working draft" on supplementary Japanese labor importation fundamentally dovetailed with Nasu's proposals and emphasized similar economic and geopolitical benefits, albeit with some significant differences.[36] After the Japanese found Masaoka's recommendation "a way to go" and approved the working draft, an extended version was formally submitted to the INS and State Department in May 1955.[37]

Two elements of Masaoka's proposal particularly impressed Japanese diplomats, especially in comparison with Nasu's versions. First, the Nisei withdrew his previous support for the bracero model and instead explained the advantage of the British West Indies (BWI) precedent as a "more satisfactory" alternative for the Japanese. Whereas Nasu anticipated the predominant role of Japan's national government in negotiating guest-worker importation as in the Mexican program, Masaoka's suggested method rejected a formal intergovernmental agreement and the potential diplomatic complications that might arise by emulating the BWI program. Unlike its bracero counterpart, the BWI scheme required no consistent government overseers on either the sending or the receiving side. Instead, because it made US-based growers' organizations responsible for legally contracting and procuring workers through the agency of nonstate entities in the sending country, the BWI method would only involve initial scrutiny by the INS. This arrangement relieved Tokyo from formal involvement and minimized the meddling of the US Department of Labor—which would likely disrupt rather than facilitate labor importation due to its connections to organized-labor interests. Furthermore, while the Mexican bracero program only provided for six months of work, its BWI counterpart allowed low-skilled "supplementary workers" to remain for the maximum of three years under an H-2 provision of the 1952 Immigration and Nationality Act.[38]

Masaoka's proposal also differed from Nasu's with regard to the question of who would primarily employ Japanese workers. Nasu had not explicitly identified preferred/prospective employers; however, repeated mention of Japanese American farmers' support hinted that he hoped they would play a central role once the program materialized.[39] Masaoka's version was the polar opposite. Mindful of the need to secure white American backing, the JACL leader insisted that "only the large growers and employers of agricultural labor should be solicited" to serve as sponsors of Japanese guest workers, and that those newcomers should "constitute only a small portion of an employer's labor pool to avoid charges that Japanese workers are replacing American labor."[40] When he submitted this document to the Japanese embassy, Masaoka then verbally explained what he really meant—a sensitive but important point he refrained from putting in writing. He wanted only white agribusiness leaders to serve as employers, since "Japanese Americans in California were politically rather powerless so that they would not be able to manage this delicate matter that organized labor would surely criticize."[41]

Due to his longstanding struggle against racial discrimination, Masaoka's concerns were understandable, but they clashed with the wishes of many California Japanese farmers, especially those who had backed Nasu's AICF work and Kawasaki's refugee scheme. For their part, Japanese consuls in California also felt that a main source of employment for temporary workers should come from the landed white farming class, but they were keenly aware of the divide between Masaoka, a white-collar Nisei in the East Coast, and leading Japanese immigrant (Issei) farmers of the western state. These Issei retained enormous influence over younger Nisei growers. In cooperation with Nasu, this group of California Japanese might sabotage the joint lobbying effort by Japanese diplomats and Masaoka. While foreign ministry officials made every effort, although in vain, to restrain Nasu, they thus eventually decided to allow "qualified" Japanese American farmers to petition for temporary workers when a BWI-modeled program was implemented.[42] Once the recruitment of Japanese workers officially commenced in the summer of 1956, Nisei and Issei farmers participated in the bidding process "on equal terms" with white agribusiness employers.[43] During the first year of the program, Japanese American growers already constituted almost 60 percent of the ninety-eight employers in California.[44]

As Masaoka's influence in California was limited even within his own co-ethnic population, the JACL leader sought to put together a grassroots public-relations machine there after May 1955, which would not only check Nasu's activities among local Japanese American farmers but also counter a revival of racist Yellow Peril fear mongering. In his "working draft," Masaoka had indeed already warned: "Care must be exercised that these dormant prejudices are not fanned into a white heat of hysteria and jingoism, for . . . the public acceptance of the resident Japanese . . . which was dearly purchased in World War II."[45] The Nisei leader knew the importance of collaborating with sympathetic white Americans in anti-racist counter-propaganda through his wartime experience as the chief JACL spokesperson and a publicist for the all-Nisei 442nd RTC. Instead of issuing publicity for Japanese labor importation in his own name, Masaoka opted to work discreetly on—and through—white journalists, political officials, and social and business leaders in California.[46]

The Japanese American lobbyist relied on a small circle of well-connected JACL insiders for his grassroots public-relations activities. Henry Mikami, a leader of the

170 · EIICHIRO AZUMA

Fresno JACL chapter, was recruited to work with potential employers among local white and Japanese American farm interests. He was a recognized figure in local politics as a member of the Democratic Party Central Committee of Fresno County and a close friend to State Assemblyman Wallace Henderson, who not surprisingly emerged as a major voice of support for growers' demand for Japanese workers.[47] Joe Grant Masaoka, Mike's older brother, strove to curry favor with state government officials and union bosses, drawing on his role as chief legislative director of the northern California JACL office, a position that held strong connections to the state's political establishment. By November 1955, Mikami and Joe Grant Masaoka boasted of their successful public-relations effort on major state agribusiness interests and politicians associated with them, as well as "many other responsible and influential farmers and civil associations too numerous to list." The latter groups would be instrumental in producing a formal petition to INS for labor certificates for one thousand Japanese. Organized labor remained unsupportive, however, and California Governor Goodwin Knight did not issue the official statement of farm labor conditions in the state that was needed to accompany the petition.[48]

Negotiations and Compromises between Government Bureaucracies

At national levels, the varying labor recruitment schemes shuttled between competing departments and intergovernment negotiations between Washington and Tokyo from May 1955 through June 1956. On the one hand, a tight alliance between Masaoka and Swing, who maintained close contact with Japanese embassy staff, worked on the Departments of State and Labor.[49] Having been exposed to Nasu's plan, American diplomats had anticipated that the Japanese temporary worker program would benefit geopolitical priorities—a perspective shared by a number of government insiders, including California-elected Republican senators and Vice President Richard Nixon. Thus, it did not take much effort to persuade State Department officials to partner with the Japanese foreign ministry. It was actually the deputy undersecretary who urged "a next step," that is, "consultation with the Department of Labor should be undertaken."[50]

The Masaoka-Tokyo lobby nonetheless had little sway over the Department of Labor, which was closely linked to organized labor. Both the AFL and CIO strongly objected to the idea of a new guest-worker program, which they predicted would "bring in cheap oriental labor"—the very racial rhetoric that Masaoka feared.[51] Labor Secretary James P. Mitchell and his staff were generally on the same page. Yet, because Mitchell had to take into account increasing support for Masaoka's plan within high-level inner political circles, especially in his own Republican Party, he left room for negotiations with amendments to the program structure and procedural arrangements. In particular, the Labor Department sought greater authority to regulate standards and supervise worker-employee relations. These were provisions absent from the BWI model, in which wage and labor conditions were dictated by private agreements between foreign workers and American employers.[52] In order to ensure the inclusion of these provisions, the Labor Department "was anxious to have an intergovernmental agreement with Tokyo somewhat along the lines of that now in effect in relation to Mexico." This point put the Labor and State Departments in direct conflict, for American diplomats disliked the idea of an intergovernmental agreement.[53] With these points of contention unresolved, negotiations came to a standstill within the US government until June 1956.

In Tokyo, serious rifts formed between the Ministries of Foreign Affairs and Agriculture, which caused their part of political preparations to stagnate. After Japanese diplomats embraced Masaoka's blueprint and his lobbyist role, Nasu and Ishiguro fought back along with their powerful agri-bureaucracy allies in Japan. The Nasu constituency wanted the labor-recruitment enterprise placed under AICF management, with the support of the agricultural ministry, which was eager to maintain control of all farming matters through Nasu's leadership.[54] With this backing, Nasu traveled to Washington in late 1955 and again in May 1956 to meet with State Department officials despite the foreign ministry's disfavor. He advocated for his plan by characterizing its primary goal as "acquaint[ing] Japanese farmers with democracy through living and working in the United States." He downplayed its guest worker aspects and predicted "no opposition" from US organized labor as long as the newcomers were portrayed as "farm trainees."[55]

Nasu's resistance to the Japanese foreign ministry's blueprint suspended the formation of a recruitment agency in Tokyo. Such an organization was a precondition for the operation of this guest-worker scheme, since it would not only act as the sole signatory to a labor-supply contract with California growers' organizations but also coordinate the Japanese domestic effort to recruit and ship out emigrants. Not until June 1956 was a compromise finally brokered between diplomats and the Nasu group under the arbitration of the Japanese prime minister for the establishment of such a semi-governmental agency. With an equal share of authority by the foreign and agricultural ministries, the Council for Supplementary Agricultural Workers (CSAW: Nōgyō Rōmusha Habei Kyōgikai) was established in Tokyo on June 12, 1956.[56] Representing the AICF and agriculture ministry faction, Ishiguro and Nasu nonetheless managed to reign over the CSAW Tokyo headquarters as the president and vice president, respectively, positioned to project their old dream of imperial settler colonialism onto a Japanese farm-labor migration scheme to the United States. CSAW adopted an internal policy in the selection process to give preference to applicants with the intention of immigrating to South America as "agricultural settlers" after returning from California.[57]

172 • EIICHIRO AZUMA

In late June 1956, news reports about CSAW generated a political crisis across the Pacific in the United States. Labor Secretary Mitchell was compelled to issue a public statement, articulating his department's concerns about a Japanese temporary-worker program. Formal letters were dispatched to California agribusiness leaders and their congressional backers, insisting that the Labor Department be "given administration over . . . all labor programs" to enforce "adequate safeguards" against labor abuse and wage depreciation. Mitchell also explicitly sought an intergovernmental agreement with Japan.[58] Not only organized labor but also other interest groups lent their voices to opposing "a program of importing cheap labor," or "yellow dogs."[59]

Mitchell's public articulations of "domestic" labor perspectives clashed with the State Department's "foreign relations" concerns. At that juncture, Japan was engulfed in a national election, and sharp divides between pro-US and anti-US factions had emerged in the form of the recently formed Liberal Democratic Party and the reunified Japanese Socialist Party. In the aftermath of the Korean War, American diplomats were extremely wary that a US rejection of Japanese "immigrants" would engender "murmurs of 'oriental exclusion,' propelling many Japanese to accuse Americans of racism.[60] As diplomats knew Japanese immigration exclusion of the 1920s had contributed to Japan's race-based hostilities and its wartime propaganda against the United States, they anticipated "a great deal of adverse publicity against [the US] government in the papers of Japan."[61] In light of the US geopolitical need to keep Japan a faithful junior ally in Cold War East Asia, any material for criticism of US policies—already seen in plenty during the 1956 election campaign—was "what we needed to look out for and seek to avoid," according to the deputy undersecretary.[62] Thus, in response to Mitchell's statement, State Department officials swiftly undertook to resolve the matter once and for all with their Labor and INS (Justice) counterparts.

It took two interdepartmental meetings with high-level representatives of the three agencies, including Mitchell, before a compromise was made. At the July 6 meeting, officials reiterated the basic positions of their home departments. INS and Labor did not see eye to eye on the issue of jurisdiction relative to the supervision of work conditions and wage scale, therefore leading them to diverge on preferences for the BWI or bracero versions. Labor and State clashed about intergovernmental agreement and State's disapproval of the bracero model.[63]

The second meeting, held on July 13, paved the way to an ultimate compromise, which allowed for the fusion of significant elements from the bracero program into the BWI model. Specifically, Labor gained authority to set the "prevailing" wage of Japanese workers "on a basis similar to the US-Mexican agreement."[64] Other terms from the bracero program shaped the final version of Japanese employment contracts with growers. The maximum work shift was, for example, reduced from ten hours to eight hours a day. The definition of "agriculture" now conformed to the Fair Labor Standards Act, so that the employer or the worker would not be able to take the contractual relationship outside the farming sector.[65] Despite these changes, Mike Masaoka's contributions to the basic arrangement of the Japanese temporary worker program were apparent, for the BWI model remained *the* prototype. Its basic procedures preserved the functions of the INS as the chief US government authority to evaluate growers' petitions and pre-inspect Japanese workers before their departure. This arrangement rendered Japan's CSAW the sole contracting agency for California growers in Japanese worker recruitment and transportation, displacing any need for a formal agreement between the United States and Japanese governments.[66] Two months after this interdepartmental compromise was reached in Washington, the Japanese agricultural worker program officially commenced.

Guest Worker Immigration and Cold War Soft-Power Cultural Diplomacy

On the US foreign policy end, the State Department played an important but less pronounced role in the redefinition of the Japanese guest-worker program. Under the influence of Nasu's longstanding lobbying, American diplomats viewed the program differently than government officials—particularly Labor Department brass—who deemed it a simple attempt to import cheaper foreign labor.[67] The State Department focused more on its diplomatic and geopolitical benefits, having for some time desired to "use our influence to guide the program if one is to be developed, along lines which will provide for specific training and educational activities."[68] During the Cold War, international educational endeavors to disseminate advanced American technologies and scientific knowledge, its modern civilization, lifestyle, and capitalistic material wealth, and the political values of freedom and democracy constituted a significant aspect of ongoing US soft-power diplomacy. The State Department embraced the propaganda value of the Japanese labor program, as its efforts at cultural diplomacy relied heavily on foreign student education and immigration in the United States.[69] Japanese temporary workers, ages twenty to thirty-five, would comprise a captive audience for a parallel form of education that would produce pro-US advocates in the country to which they were required to return after the three-year contracts ended. Of course, State Department officials knew all too well that the Japanese worker program could not be presented as "a trainee program" domestically in the US since newcomers from Japan were legally nothing more than supplemental agricultural field hands under the H-2 temporary-work scheme. American diplomats nonetheless felt that the plan still could and did form a "farm worker program with special educational and training aspects included," that would "teach them English, democratic government, etc."[70]

Whereas the US side was tightly bound by the basic legal arrangement of this "temporary worker" program, it was Japan's CSAW and foreign ministry that governed and operated the effort in the manner of an agricultural trainee and educational program, albeit without naming it as such. According to an official CSAW announcement, the recruitment process from the beginning included an intensive pre-departure educational program, mandating successful applicants to go through a series of academic lectures and practical training in Tokyo before leaving.[71] The foreign ministry also made it a point to collaborate closely with ongoing US cultural propaganda carried out by the American embassy and the US Information Service (USIS), because the ministry believed doing so would entice Washington to continue to support Japanese labor immigration regardless of union accusations of "bound labor." For instance, a number of USIS films were shown during the one-week orientation in Tokyo, and American representatives offered additional lectures on the importance of democracy, freedom, and US global dominance in the Cold War context.[72] During orientation, Japanese authorities especially emphasized the role of emigrant farm workers as "future linchpins of US-Japan friendship," telling them "not to disgrace the name of Japanese people anywhere and anytime." Having been selected from politically moderate youths with farming backgrounds, the emigrants were supposed to play the role of "agents of public diplomacy" by fostering a real firsthand grasp of "American people, the American way of life, and the American spirit." Presented by Japanese officials, didactic lectures suggested that the young men were also entrusted with a special task to shape pro-American sentiments at a grassroots level as new leaders of rural Japan upon their mandatory return.[73] A large portion of the applicant pool, which turned out to be more than ten times the annual limit of one thousand, included sons of leading families in rural Japan.[74] Wishing to "study American democracy" and "American-style farming," many of the applicants shared a similar outlook on the agricultural labor program, mistaking it for a technical training or education abroad scheme.[75]

In California, educational activities of a far more limited scope were available due to the program's legal identity as an H-2 temporary-worker program. However, from the outset, a special provision allowed Japanese newcomers to attend night school three times a week as long as they finished the day's work. On the matter of English-language instruction, an inspector noted: "In almost all cases facilities or opportunities have been made available for the boys to study English either through organized adult education classes, special tutoring, or private lessons given by the employer himself."[76]

In 1957 the collaborative efforts by US and Japanese diplomats successfully convinced the Labor Department to begin distinguishing between the Japanese temporary worker program and its Mexican and BWI counterparts. In the summer of 1957, when a joint team of State, Labor, Justice (INS) Department officials was slated for an investigative field survey in California, the Deputy Undersecretary of State and Japanese Ambassador held a special conference to reaffirm the centrality of the "public relations" aspect of the ongoing program instead of treating it simply as an "immigration" or "economic" matter.[77] Perhaps, under the initiative of a State Department representative, the joint interdepartmental team then decided to measure the program's success primarily in terms of "whether or not [this program] would make them leading pro-American voices of rural villages in Japan." In the end, all members, including Labor Department representatives, came to the conclusion that the enterprise "clearly differ[ed] from the Mexican program."[78] Although this does not mean that the Labor Department dropped its insistence on protecting US domestic workers' interests, the agency did become more attentive to the educational and foreign-policy benefits of the Japanese program. Thus, four years later, the assistant secretary of labor even encouraged Japanese authorities to "put more weight on educational matters [of Japanese workers] because they were unlike Mexican workers."[79]

Tacitly endorsed by the Labor Department, this unofficial but widely accepted attribute of the Japanese agricultural worker program came into sharp conflict with the original expectations and self-interests of agribusiness leaders and growers in California. To them, newcomers from Japan were supposed to be nothing more than productive, profitable, and expendable farmhands. But if they were required to bear the burden of workers' educational needs or spare extra time for nonwork matters, employers would end up incurring a financial loss. For this reason, growers had categorically rejected the idea of setting up a special committee to promote workers' education and recreation when Japanese authorities had proposed it back in 1956.[80] After the State-Labor-INS joint investigation of 1957 recommended providing Japanese workers with four hours of educational opportunity each week at no cost to them, growers doggedly resisted again. Only when Washington officials agreed to drop objectionable binding terms like "at no cost to [workers]" and "four hours" of nonfarm activities did growers grudgingly accept the new draft employment contract endorsed by the Labor Department.[81]

Contentious Relations between Japanese American Farmers and Japanese Workers

Although both Washington and Tokyo managed to maintain an equilibrium between the labor and propaganda aspects of the Japanese temporary-worker program, the contradictions between those varying mandates and identities generated not only confusion among Japanese workers but also acrimonious relations between them and their employers, especially Japanese American farmers. The first groups of California-bound workers consisted primarily of youths of "well-off families" in Japan's rural village communities who viewed themselves as "students on scholarships." The kinds of menial "stoop" labor they were subjected to in California baffled these bright-eyed youths, turning them into habitual complainers and shirkers—"shiftless, arrogant, and lazy" as one Nisei farmer bitterly criticized.[82] To alleviate this problem, Japanese authorities decided after 1957 to "select only the young men willing to work harder than any American or Mexican."[83] Nonetheless, negative remarks about living and work conditions continued to appear in public discourse. Even if Japanese youths conceded to being simple farmhands, many were still discontent with the daily routine of ten- to fourteen-hour labor and lower wages than expected. The problem of exploitation—real or perceived—resulted in a widely publicized desertion of twenty-four workers in September 1957.[84] By December 1958, more than eighty workers were "deported" to Japan for allegedly defying their employers.[85]

Whereas Japanese workers were misled to imagine overly rosy images of working and learning in California, Japanese American growers and farm foremen, as well as white agribusiness leaders, appreciated the value of the workers primarily for their economic benefit, utility, and manageability. First, the Japanese agricultural worker program enabled growers to avoid the revolving door of inexperienced farmhands every six months as stipulated by Public Law 78 for Mexican braceros. Japanese temporary workers could stay as long as three years in California, which made them less costly to employ even though initial outlays for transpacific travel were higher. The need for less frequent training also meant greater efficiency and dependability, saving employers both money and time.[86] Because most Nisei-owned farms were small-sized enterprises, the economic advantage of Japanese temporary workers was not insignificant.[87] The absence of direct supervision and consistent scrutiny by the Labor Department also gave unscrupulous employers more leeway to take advantage of them as well.

Second, racist ideas about Mexicans had permeated the thinking of growers to give rise to common beliefs in Japanese labor superiority. Since before the official beginning of the program, Mike Masaoka had profusely depicted braceros as "troublemakers," juxtaposing them with "reliable" Japanese whose "efficiency and loyalty" were "legendary."[88] During his public-relations activities in California, Mikami had also propagated the idea that "Japanese workers we[re] superior to . . . Mexicans" because they were "not only diligent workers but workers who will cause the minimum of problems through runaways, etc."[89] Similar arguments appeared often in public discourse thereafter. At a congressional subcommittee hearing, representatives of employer groups and individual growers from California "unanimously expressed the opinion that the Japanese workers are intelligent, easily learn how to satisfactorily perform work assigned to them . . . with considerably more willingness and aptitude than other foreign workers employed in the area."[90] According to a Los Angeles Japanese newspaper, 70 percent of the Japanese American farmers preferred to employ "more responsible and efficient Japanese."[91]

Japanese American farmers measured the utility of Japanese guest workers on the basis of racial/cultural ties and citizenship status. It was usually unarticulated but taken for granted that Japanese Americans enjoyed a special bond with people of Japan through their shared racial and cultural heritage; and yet, Nisei always insisted on the critical difference between the two groups in terms of citizenship status and psychological dispositions. Despite the racial commonality, these legal and psychic divides made Issei and Nisei thoroughly American/Americanized vis-à -vis Japanese temporary workers who were rendered alien and foreign.[92] A Nisei grower/shipper of Fresno represented many other Japanese Americans when he voiced this concern about the potential co-ethnic others at the advent of Japanese labor migration in 1956:

> We talk of integration—the absorption of ourselves and our children into the stream of American life and culture. We wish to suggest that this process will not be aided by the presence of large numbers of non-American-acting, non-English-speaking Japanese nationals at a time when other Americans are just getting used to the idea that Americans with Japanese faces can think and talk like other Americans.[93]

This manner of differentiation characterized a central strategy of public representation that most Japanese Americans had embraced when they had desperately sought acceptance in American society during and after the trying years of their wartime incarceration.[94]

The economic utility of foreign Japanese nonetheless did generally take precedence over the perennial ethnic concern of Japanese Americans about national belonging. The basic orientation of the temporary worker program relieved Nisei from the possibility of admitting the kind of "non-American-acting" members into the ethnic community, since there was no path toward permanent residency under the H-2 system. As long as Nisei vigilantly took on the "extra burden" to "police" the situation, Japanese workers would leave California after three years without becoming a permanent part of Japanese America.[95] The legally predetermined expendability of alien Japanese labor served as a key safeguard against the tarnishing of Nisei's self-made reputation as the full-fledged assimilated Americans with birthright citizenship. Moreover, it afforded Japanese American farmers with a workforce that was easy to manipulate because of racial bonds and shared cultural heritage. Expendable and highly manageable, Japanese supplemental workers were, as a Nisei journalist quoted from growers, "the best thing that happened to California in a long time."[96]

Even though many Japanese American farmers felt as if they held special chaperoning duties for temporary workers and actually treated them as members of their own families, others were not so kind, sympathetic, or respectful in the eyes of Japanese workers.[97] Indeed, negative remarks about Nisei growers frequently filled newspaper headlines and popular magazine articles in Japan within one year of the program's inception. Published in a major Japanese weekly, a sensationalized story of virtual "enslavement" at a Japanese American farm shocked the authorities and Nisei alike.[98] An Associated Press (AP) dispatch from Yokohama featured testimonies of disgruntled returnees from California, who singled out Nisei employers as worse than anyone else when they recalled their experiences across the Pacific. They remembered that white Americans were "known for their discrimination," but they were "nicer to us." On the contrary, Nisei farmers treated them "like trash," offered "poor medical care," and bombarded them with "don't, don't, don't everywhere." This dispatch made it into mainstream US media reports, not only incensing Japanese Americans but also throwing them into a panic.[99] Their collective image as model citizens was at stake, thereby propelling Nisei farmers and a local JACL chapter to hold an emergency "protest meeting" and issue a formal refutation.[100]

As many Japanese Americans had feared, some Japanese workers seemed to have been spoiling "the absorption of ourselves and our children into the stream of American life and culture" through not only their unassimilated behaviors but also their anti-Nisei statements. As in other cases, the rhetoric of racial kinship and good will was invoked in Japanese Americans' refutation against "an insult to the [ethnic] community" by the ungrateful foreign(ized) Japanese. "We built them a little house and installed all modern facilities and treated them as members of the family," a wife of a Nisei farmer contended in another AP report.[101] Not only did the dialectics of economic benefit and racial family rhetoric dovetail with the duality of guest-worker importation and cultural diplomacy in official state discourses, but at the heart of this dialectical narrative also lay the intricacies of Nisei's thinking and practices vis-à-vis postwar newcomers from Japan. There was room in Japanese America for idiosyncratic racial brethren to be posed as pseudo family insofar as they could engender advantages without disturbing the hard-won image of Nisei as exemplary American citizens, or a "model minority." When this image was threatened, however, the newcomers had to be distanced or disowned as the co-ethnic others in public representations. Whereas this rejection reveals the fundamental nature of conditional minority inclusion in postwar America through the display of undivided allegiance to US citizenship and democracy, it offers a glimpse into the complex broader relations between Japanese Americans and postwar immigrants from their ancestral land that was also a former national enemy.[102]

Despite the challenge of maintaining a delicate equilibrium between benefits to the ethnic farm economy and threats to collective group identity, Nisei farmers and Japanese America at large continued to support the Japanese agricultural worker program. By its demise in 1966, independent Nisei growers composed the vast majority of employers, who appreciated Japanese workers even more when contrasted against unionized Mexicans. Periodic opposition persisted as the AFL-CIO strove to paint the program as just another scheme to import cheap labor. Yet the INS, State Department, and Japan's foreign ministry continued to emphasize its contributions to the goal of Cold War diplomacy and US-Japan friendship. Along with agribusiness interests, Mike Masaoka acted as a chief voice in that campaign, representing not only Japanese diplomats but also Nisei growers and the larger Japanese American community.[103] When the end of the bracero program sounded the death knell for supplementary Japanese labor immigration, Nisei growers and the JACL took the lead in a last-ditch effort to have the US government "reappraise the program for employing Japanese" and allow "the [existing] labor contract . . . to continue without harassment."[104] This extension was granted by the Labor Department as a result of intergovernmental negotiations with Tokyo, but the Japanese agricultural worker program formally came to an end with the return of eighty-three workers from California in October 1966.[105]

Conclusion

This chapter has unveiled the multifaceted identities of the Japanese agricultural worker program that operated between 1956 and 1966. Very few scholars of US labor and immigration history or Asian American history have taken this subject seriously, for it looks like a simple side note to the much larger Mexican bracero program. Despite its small size and official legal designation as a guest-worker program, the systematic migration of Japanese farmworkers during the Cold War period actually bears broad implications. The Japanese agricultural labor program constituted an important site for contestation, negotiation, and collusion among diverse groups of Americans and Japanese that cut across racial, class, and national boundaries. It also elucidated the inner workings of government bureaucracies, as well as the activities of interest groups that collaborated with them, in the United States and Japan over the intersections of migration and education with the realignment of inter-imperial relations between the two Pacific powers. In these complex processes, Japanese Americans, as political brokers and employers of farmworkers, played indispensable roles in facilitating transpacific mobility and intergovernmental and interdepartmental compromises. Through the process of intraracial differentiation from "Japanese nationals," these "Americans with Japanese faces" also pursued the further "absorption of [them]selves and [their] children into the

180 · EIICHIRO AZUMA

stream of American life and culture." Against the background of the complex politics of migration, labor, and cultural imperialism, that slanted manner of national inclusion paved the way to public celebrations of the Nisei "success story"—and the model minority myth based on it—in 1966, the same year when the last batch of "non-American-acting, non-English-speaking" Japanese field hands left California and Japanese America.[106]

Notes

1. A recent article in Japanese by Ōyagi Gō offers the most sophisticated transnational analysis of the subject. See Ōyagi Gō, "Maiku Masaoka to Nihonjin tanki nōgyōrōdōsha dōnyū puroguramu," *Amerikashi Kenkyū* 38 (2015): 73–93 (cited hereafter as Ōyagi, "Maiku Masaoka."); and Go Oyagi, "Over the Pacific: Post–World War II Asian American Internationalism," PhD diss., University of Southern California, 2013), 32–72 (cited hereafter as Oyagi, "Over the Pacific."). On the Mexican bracero and British West Indies guest-worker programs, consult Deborah Cohen, *Braceros: Migrant Citizens and Transnational Subjects in the Postwar United States and Mexico* (Chapel Hill: University of North Carolina Press, 2011), and Cindy Hahamovitch, *No Man's Land: Jamaican Guestworkers in America and the Global History of Deportable Labor* (Princeton, N.J.: Princeton University Press, 2011).

2. See Minami Kashū Kagoshima Kenjinshi Henshū Iinkai, ed., *Minami Kashū Kagoshima kenjinshi* (Los Angeles: Nanka Kagoshima Kenjinkai, 1976), 165–73 (hereafter Henshū Iinkai, *Minami Kashū Kagoshima*).

3. Kokusai Nōgyōsha Kōryū Kyōkai, ed., *Nōgyō seinen kaigai haken jigyō gojyūnenshi* (Tokyo: Kokusai Nōgyōsha Kōryū Kyōkai, 2002), 6–8 (cited hereafter as Kokusai, *Nōgyō seinen*); Nihon Nōgyō Kenkyūjo, ed., *Ishiguro Tadaatsu-den* (Tokyo: Iwanami Shoten, 1969), 442–46; Michael Conlon, "A Brief History of the Japan Agricultural Exchange Council," *GAIN Report Number JA0501*, February 1, 2010; and Itō Atsushi, "Nōgyō rōmusha habei jigyō no seiritsu katei," *Nōgyō keizai kenkyū* 83, no. 4 (2012), 224–25. On this program as a form of US cultural diplomacy, see also Mary Ting Yi Lui, "Nōson seinen no Kariforunia hōmon" (trans. Tsuchiya Yuka and Nakamura Nobuyuki) in *Senryō suru me, Senryō suru koe*, ed. Tsuchiya Yuka and Yoshimi Shunya (Tokyo: Tokyo Daigaku Shuppankai, 2012), 157–81.

4. Asada Kyōji, "Takumushō no Manshū nōgyō imin keikaku," *Komazawa Daigaku Keizai Gakubu kenkyū kiyō* 32 (1974): 90; Nasu Shiroshi, *Nasu Shiroshi-sensei: Ibun to tsuisō* (Tokyo: Nōson Kōsei Kyōkai, 1985), 90–96.

5. Yoshizaki Chiaki, *Kokusai Nōyūkai ni tsuite* (Tokyo: Kokusai Nōyūkai, 1987), 3–4.

6. Ibid., 8; Sugino Tadao, *Kaigai takushoku hishi* (Tokyo: Bunkyō Shoin, 1959), 124–25; and Yoshizaki Chiaki, "Kokusai Nōyūkai ga umareru made," *Kokusai nōson* 1 (September 1952): 6–7.

7. Nasu Shiroshi, "Kokusai Nōyūkai no risō," *Kokusai nōson* 1 (September 1952): 4; Nasu, *Nasu Shiroshi-sensei*, 99.

8. American Embassy, Tokyo, "Admission of Japanese Farm Workers to the United States," September 29, 1954, in folder 1, box 375, Central Office Subject Files, 1949–1958,

Records of Immigration and Naturalization Service, RG 85 (hereafter COSF-INS), National Archives and Records Administration (NARA) I, Washington, DC.

9. Takeuchi, "Taibei kisetsu nōgyō imin ni kansuru Nasu Hakase no dan," December 6, 1954, in Nōgyō rōmusha habei kankei: Habei jisshi made no keii, v. 1, Diplomatic Records Office, Tokyo, Japan (hereafter NRHK-HJK).

10. See Nasu Shiroshi, "Kisetsuteki idō nōgyō rōmusha o Beikoku e sōshutsu suru anken," (ca. March 5, 1955), in NRHK-HJK, v. 1 (cited hereafter as Nasu, "Kisetsuteki"); and "Training of Japanese Farmers in United States," December 21, 1955, in box 7, Japan Subject Files, 1947–1956, Records of the Office of Northwest Asian Affairs, RG 59 (hereafter JSF-RONAA), NARA II, College Park, Md.

11. Kokusai, *Nōgyō seinen*, 13; Sugino, *Kaigai takushoku hishi*, 102–13; and Maruyama Manabu and Uchida Mamoru, *Etō Tameji-ou den* (Kumamoto: Kumamoto Kokusai Nōyūkai, 1977), 31–32.

12. Nasu, "Kisetsuteki."

13. Alton R. Storslee to Assistant [INS] Commissioner, September 5, 1956; State Department, "Proposal to Bring in Philippine and Japanese Workers for Temporary Agricultural Employment in California," January 16, 1956; Robert L. Kinney, "Meeting with Mr. Bruce Sanborn, Jr.," May 23, 1956; Sanborn to Bruce Barber, June 29, 1956; Barber to [INS] Commissioner, July 5, 1956, all in folder 1, box 375, COSF-INS; and "Rinji rōdō imin no keii," March 1, 1955, in NRHK-HJK, v. 1.

14. Kanbara to Tanetani, March 25, 1955, and Mike M. Masaoka to Iguchi, May 9, 1955, in NRHK-HJK, v. 1; and American Embassy, Tokyo, to State Department, January 4, 1957, in folder 2, box 375, COSF-INS.

15. "Rinji rōdō imin no keii," in NRHK-HJK, v. 1.

16. Henshū Iinkai, *Minami Kashū Kagoshima*, 165–68.

17. Ibid., 165–67; and Uchida Zen'ichiro, *Kuwa de Tairiku o tori* (Gilroy, Calif.: Privately printed, 1991), 35–53.

18. Yukiko Koshiro, *Trans-Pacific Racisms and the US Occupation of Japan* (New York: Columbia University Press, 1999), 210.

19. Henshū Iinkai, *Minami Kashū Kagoshima*, 168–72; and Uchida, *Kuwa de Tairiku o tori*, 52–62.

20. Koshiro, *Trans-Pacific Racisms*, 210; Henshū Iinkai, *Minami Kashū Kagoshima*, 173–74; and Katsuno to Shigemitsu, "Tanki nōgyō rōdō imin keikaku ni kansuru ken," May 23, 1955, in NRHK-HJK, v. 1.

21. Oyagi, "Over the Pacific," 57.

22. See T. Fujitani, "*Go for Broke*, the Movie: Japanese American Soldiers in US National, Military, and Racial Discourses," in *Perilous Memories: The Asia-Pacific War(s)*, ed. T. Fujitani, et al. (Durham, N.C.: Duke University Press, 2001), 239–66.

23. Little has been documented on the Nisei's collaboration with Issei leaders in their fight against institutionalized discrimination. On the role of JACL, see Bill Hosokawa, *Nisei: The Quiet Americans* (New York: William Morrow, 1969), 443–55; and Ellen D. Wu, *The Color of Success: Asian Americans and the Origins of the Model Minority* (Princeton, N.J.: Princeton University Press, 2014), 97–100.

182 · EIICHIRO AZUMA

24. "Problems of Interest to Japanese-Americans," January 15, 1952, in box 15, General Records, 1950–1952, Office of the US Political Advisor for Japan, Tokyo, Department of State, RG 84, NARA II, College Park, Md.

25. Takeuchi to Okumura, February 18, 1954, and Mike M. Masaoka to Takeuchi, February 11, 1954, in NRHK-HJK, v. 1.

26. "Nikkei Beijin no chichi," *Mainichi Shinbun*, October 5, 1952.

27. All quotes from: Mike M. Masaoka to Ike Masaoka, October 20, 1953, in folder 9, box 6, Mike M. Masaoka Papers (hereafter Masaoka Papers), Marriott Library, University of Utah, Salt Lake City.

28. Takeuchi to Okumura, February 18, 1954; Masaoka to Takeuchi, February 11, 1954; and Mike M. Masaoka to Seichi [sic] Mikami, January 27, 1955, in folder 19, box 6, Masaoka Papers.

29. Mike M. Masaoka to Walter H. Judd, February 11, 1954, in NRHK-HJK, v. 1.

30. See Mike Masaoka, "Memorandum: Japanese Farm Laborers," in Masaoka to Takeuchi, February 11, 1954.

31. Ōyagi, "Maiku Masaoka," 75.

32. Masaoka to Iguchi, May 9, 1955.

33. Ōyagi, "Maiku Masaoka," 75–76.

34. Takeuchi Ryūji, "Kisetsu nōgyō imin no ken," ca. Nov. 1954, in NRHK-HJK, v. 1; and Mike Masaoka, *They Call Me Moses Masaoka: An American Saga* (New York: Morrow, 1987), 251, 271.

35. Nakajima, "Honpōjin nōgyō rōdōsha no taibei tanki imin keikaku no ken," March 4, 1955, in NRHK-HJK, v. 1.

36. See Ōyagi, "Maiku Masaoka," 76.

37. Katsuno to Shima, March 24, 1955; Mike M. Masaoka, "Working Draft: Temporary Japanese Agricultural Workers," 2, ca. March 1955, in NRHK-HJK, v. 1; and Mike M. Masaoka, "Confidential Memorandum: Use of temporary, supplemental farm labor from Japan," in folder 1, box 375, COSF-INS.

38. See Masaoka, "Working Draft"; and "Japanese Temporary Worker Program," March 19, 1957, in folder 2, box 375, COSF-INS.

39. See Nasu, "Kisetsuteki."

40. Masaoka, "Working Draft," 8.

41. Nakajima, "Honpōjin nōgyō rōdōsha no taibei tanki imin keikaku no ken"; and Masaoka, "Working Draft," 7.

42. Katsuno to Shigemitsu, "Tanki nōgyō rōdō imin keikaku ni kansuru ken," May 23, 1955; and "Tanki rōdō imin ni kansuru ken (3)," August 30, 1955, in NRHK-HJK, v. 1. On negative publicity on Nasu, see Itō, "Nōgyō rōmusha habei jigyō no seiritsu katei," 227.

43. Ban, "Shoken," August 22, 1956; Nakamura to Takasaki, "Tanki nōgyō rōmusha habei ni kansuru ken," August 23, 1956; and Takasaki to Nakamura, "Tanki nōgyō rōmusha habei ni kansuru ken," August 25, 1956, all in Nōgyō rōmusha habei kankei: Jisshi kankei (hereafter NRHK-JK), v. 1, Diplomatic Records Office, Tokyo.

44. See "Directory of Japanese Agricultural Workers," undated, in Pacific Citizen File, Japanese American National Museum, Los Angeles. Tally by the author.

45. Masaoka, "Working Draft," 7.

46. See Wu, *Color of Success*, 77–80, 83, 89–95.

47. Masaoka to Iguchi, May 9, 1955; and "Tanki rōdō imin ni kansuru ken (3)," August 30, 1955.

48. Masaoka to Iguchi, May 9, 1955; "Tanki rōdō imin ni kansuru ken (3)," August 30, 1955; Henry Mikami and Joe Grant Masaoka to Mike Masaoka, November 12, 1955; and Iguchi to Shigemitsu, December 5, 1955, in NRHK-HJK, v. 1. See also Ōyagi, "Maiku Masaoka," 78.

49. Ōyagi, "Maiku Masaoka," 77–79.

50. Robert Murphy to Joseph M. Swing, July 19, 1955; Albert Del Guercio, "Japanese Agricultural Laborers," October 24, 1955; and Department of State Instruction, "Proposed Japanese Farm Labor Program," June 1, 1956, all in folder 1, box 375, COSF-INS. The quote is from the first source.

51. Guercio, "Japanese Agricultural Laborers," October 24, 1955. See also "Memorandum of Conversation," 2, ca. February 1956; and "Memorandum of Conversation," 1, March 21, 1956, in box 7, JSF-RONAA.

52. Daniel Goott to Phillip B. Sullivan, "Temporary Importation of Japanese and Philippine Agricultural Workers," February 14, 1956, in box 7, JSF-RONAA.

53. A. C. Devaney, "Importation of Japanese and Philippine Agricultural Workers," July 6, 1956, in folder 1, box 375, COSF-INS (hereafter Devaney, "Importation.")

54. On the dispute between the two ministries in the context of policymaking process in Tokyo, see Itō, "Nōgyō rōmusha habei jigyō no seiritsu katei," 225–33; and Wakatsuki Yasuo, *Gaimushō ga keshita Nihonjin* (Tokyo: Mainichi Shinbunsha, 2001), 16–17, 63.

55. Department of State, "Training of Japanese Farmers in United States," December 21, 1955; and Department of State, "Plan for Bringing Young Japanese Farmers to the United States," ca. January 18, 1956, in box 7, JSF-RONAA. See also Ito, "Nōgyō rōmusha habei jigyō no seiritsu katei," 225–29.

56. Ōyagi, "Maiku Masaoka," 79; American Embassy, Tokyo, "Memorandum of Conversation," May 29, 1956, and "Proposed Japanese Farm Labor Program," June 6, 1956, in reel 37, Confidential US State Department Special Files: Japan, 1947–1956 (hereafter CUSSD-SFJ), RG 59, NARA II, College Park.

57. Kokusai, *Nōgyō seinen*, 68, 72.

58. "Memorandum: Japanese Agricultural Laborers," June 25, 1956, in folder 1, box 375, COSF-INS; Secretary of Labor to Secretary of State, undated, in box 183, Records of Secretary James P. Mitchell, Records of the Department of Labor (hereafter RSJPM-RDL), RG 174, NARAII, College Park, Md.; Robert Murphy, "United States Employer Proposals to Bring in Japanese and Philippine Workers for Temporary Agricultural Employment in California," July 10, 1956, and "Developments in Connection with US Employers' Proposal to Bring Japanese and Filipino Workers for Temporary Agricultural Employment in California," July 12, 1956 (hereafter "Developments"), in reel 37, CUSSD-SFJ; and Devaney, "Importation."

59. Joint United States-Mexico Trade Union Committee, "Press Release No. 8," July 15, 1956; Philip B. Sullivan to American Embassy, Tokyo, August 1, 1956; and Fay Bennett to

Joseph M. Swing, August 6, 1956, all in folder 1, box 375, COSF-INS. The quotes are from the second source.

60. Walter S. Robertson to Robert Murphy, "Importation of Foreign Agricultural Workers," July 6, 1956, in box 7, JSF-RONAA.

61. Devaney, "Importation."

62. "Developments."

63. Devaney, "Importation"; and Devaney, "Japanese and Philippine Labor," July 13, 1956, in folder 1, box 375, COSF-INS.

64. Alton R. Storslee to Assistant Commissioner, "Japanese Agricultural Workers," August 3 and 7, 1956, in folder 1, box 375, COSF-INS. The quote is from August 7.

65. Devaney, "Japanese and Philippine Labor"; and Devaney, "Japanese Agricultural Workers" (attachment), July 30, 1956, in folder 1, box 375, COSF-INS. See also Ōyagi, "Maiku Masaoka," 79–80.

66. Storslee to Assistant Commissioner, "Japanese Agricultural Workers" (esp. attachment), August 7, 1956. In this program, three sets of contracts were signed and executed: the first one between a worker and CSAW in Japan; the second between CSAW and California growers' organizations; and the third between a worker and a grower in California.

67. Devaney, "Importation."

68. Goott to Sullivan, "Temporary Importation."

69. Madeline Hsu, *The Good Immigrants: How the Yellow Peril Became the Model Minority* (Princeton, N.J.: Princeton University Press, 2015). On the place of education in US soft-power diplomacy and cultural imperialism, see Mire Koikari, *Cold War Encounters in US-Occupied Okinawa: Women, Militarized Domesticity, and Transnationalism in East Asia* (Cambridge: Cambridge University Press, 2015); and Paul A. Kramer, "Is the World Our Campus? International Students and US Global Power in the Long Twentieth Century," *Diplomatic History* 33 (November 2009), 775–806.

70. Sullivan to American Embassy, August 1, 1956; and "Memorandum of Conversation," 2, March 21, 1956.

71. See "Shōwa 31-nendo habei nōgyō rōmusha boshū yōryō," ca. July 1956, in Nōgyō rōmusha habei kankei: Nōgyō Rōmusha Habei Kyōgikai (hereafter NRHK-NRHK), Diplomatic Records Office, Tokyo; and Ishiguro, "Habei nōgyō rōmusha no kyōiku kōshū ni tsuite," August 17, 1956, in Nōgyō rōmusha habei kankei: Boshū, senkō, kōshū, kunren, sōshutsu (hereafter NRHK-BSKKS), Diplomatic Records Office, Tokyo.

72. Ban, "Tanki nōgyō rōmusha habei keikaku no suishin ni kansuru ken," August 12, 1956, in NRHK-JK, v. 1; Imin-kyoku, "Tanki nōgyō rōmusha kyōyō kunren keikaku," August 17, 1956, in NRHK-BSKKS; Takasaki to Katsuno, August 30, 1956, NRHK-JK, v. 1; "Shōwa sanju ichinendo habei nōgyō rōmusha boshū yōryō," ca. July 1956; Tani to Kishi, March 21, 1957, in NRHK-JK, v. 4; Tani to Kishi, March 25, 1957, in NRHK-JK, v. 4; Nishiyama to Fujiyama, September 3, 1957, in NRHK-JK, v. 4; and Kokusai, *Nōgyō seinen*, 71.

73. "Aisatsu," August 28, 1956, and "Daiichijin kaikōshiki aisatsu," September 7, 1956, in NRHK-JK, v. 1.

74. Kokusai, *Nōgyō seinen*, 71.

Japanese Agricultural Labor Program • 185

75. Nishiyama to Fujiyama, September 3, 1957, in NRHK-JK, v. 4; and Tani to Takasaki, August 7, 1956, in NRHK-JK, v. 1.

76. Tani to Takasaki, August 7, 1956; "Shōwa 31-nendo habei nōgyō rōmusha boshū yōryō," ca. July 1956; and Consul General of Japan, San Francisco, "Interim Report: The Supplementary Japanese Agricultural Workers' Program," 5, February 15, 1957, in folder 2, box 375, COSF-INS. The quote is from the last source.

77. Asami to Fujiyama, August 15, 1957, in NRHK-JK, v. 4.

78. Nishiyama to Fujiyama, September 3, 1957.

79. "Nōgyō rōmusha habei jigyō keizoku-kata hanashiai keii," October 29, 1956, in NRHK-NRHK. US Congress also publicly accepted the notion of "certain imponderable, incidental benefits derived from the program to broader aspects of international cooperation and the further improvement of American-Japanese relations." See US House Subcommittee No. 1 of the Committee on the Judiciary, *Japanese Agricultural Workers: Report* (85th Congress, 1st Session: House Report 780) (Washington DC: GPO, 1957), 16.

80. Nishiyama to Fujiyama, September 13, 1957, in NRHK-JK, v. 4.

81. Asami to Fujiyama, September 11, 1957; Nishiyama to Kishi, October 1, 1957; Nishiyama to Fujiyama, October 9, 1957; and Nishiyama to Fujiyama, December 5, 1957, all sources in NRHK-JK, v. 4; and "Future of Japanese Farm Labor Program Unsettled," *Nichi Bei Times*, October 16, 1957.

82. "Japan Government Officials Report Cal. Farm Findings," *Hokubei Mainichi*, November 7, 1959; Mike Masaoka, "Washington Newsletter," *Pacific Citizen*, December 18, 1959; Nakamura to Fujiyama, September 3, 1957, in NRHK-JK, v. 4; Nishiyama to Fujiyama, September 3, 1957, NRHK-JK, v. 4; Nishiyama to Shigemitsu, October 26, 1956, in NRHK-JK, v. 2.

83. "Japan Government Officials Report Cal. Farm Findings."

84. *Rafu Shimpo*, September 27, 1957, October 1, 1957, and December 21, 1957 (all in Japanese section).

85. Ibid., December 24, 1958 (Japanese section).

86. Nishiyama to Fujiyama, September 13, 1957; and *Rafu Shimpo*, December 21, 1957 (Japanese section).

87. See "Directory of Japanese Agricultural Workers." Tally by the author.

88. Masaoka, "Memorandum: Japanese Farm Laborers," in Masaoka to Takeuchi, February 11, 1954.

89. S. H. Mikami to Takashi Suzuki, October 3, 1956, in NRHK-JK, v. 2.

90. US House Subcommittee No. 1, *Japanese Agricultural Workers: Report*, 7.

91. *Rafu Shimpo*, August 3, 1957 (Japanese section).

92. On contentious relations between postwar Nisei and foreignized Japanese, see Eiichiro Azuma, "Brokering Race, Culture, and Citizenship: Japanese Americans in Occupied Japan and Postwar National Inclusion," *Journal of American-East Asian Relations* 16 (Fall 2009): 183–211; and Eiichiro Azuma, "Race, Citizenship, and the 'Science of Chick Sexing,'" *Pacific Historical Review* 78 (May 2009), esp. 259–75.

93. Oyagi, "Over the Pacific," 57.

94. See, for example, Masaoka's statement in US House Subcommittee No. 1, *Japanese Agricultural Workers: Report*, 13; and Ōyagi, "Maiku Masaoka," 81.

95. See Saburo Kido, "Observation," *Pacific Citizen*, October 20, 1956.

96. Henry Mori, "County Farmers Heartily Support Importation of Japanese Laborers," *Rafu Shimpo*, May 1, 1957.

97. See, for example, a statement on CSAW, "Impressions of the Three-Year Agricultural Worker," November 5, 1959, in *Pacific Citizen* File, JANM; *Rafu Shimpo*, November 22, 1957 (Japanese section); and Consul General of Japan, San Francisco, "Interim Report," 6.

98. "Kyōsei sōkan no shinsō," *Shūkan Shinchō* 3 (February 1, 1958), 74–80; and Tamotsu Murayama, "Deportation of Seasonal Workers," *Pacific Citizen*, February 2, 1958.

99. See "Japan Workers Bitter After Staying in State," *Los Angeles Times*, October 21, 1959; and "Issei-Nisei in Marysville Area Incensed over Recent Attacks," undated, in *Pacific Citizen* file, JANM.

100. See "Issei-Nisei in Marysville Area"; and "Employers Dispute Stories of Serfdom," *Los Angeles Times*, October 21, 1959.

101. "Employers Dispute Stories of Serfdom."

102. See Azuma, "Brokering Race," 194–208; and Azuma, "Race, Citizenship," 259–70.

103. See his statement in US House Subcommittee No. 1, *Japanese Agricultural Workers: Report*, 11–14; Takamura, "Tanki habei rōmusha mondai to ni kansuru Maiku Masaoka tono kondan ni kansuru ken," November 25, 1959, and Asami to Kosaka, February 9, 1961, in NRHK-JK, v. 6.

104. "Nisei Growers Ask Contracts with 'Tanno' Be Completed," *Pacific Citizen*, February 19, 1965.

105. Kokusai, *Nōgyō seinen*, 105.

106. Amid the radicalization of the black movement in 1966, University of California sociologist William Petersen published an article titled "Success Story: Japanese American Style" in the January 9 issue of the *New York Times Magazine*, leading off US public discourse on Asian Americans as the well-assimilated, trouble-free model minority.

PART III

"Who Is a Citizen? Who Belongs?"

The immigration legislation passed during the late nineteenth and early twentieth centuries altered the overall number and source countries of immigrants admitted to the United States and rendered immigrants from certain parts of the world ineligible for citizenship, preventing their full integration into American life. During this period the United States also grappled with the consequences of its military, commercial, and territorial expansion overseas, particularly in the Philippines and Puerto Rico, forcing Americans to define what rights and privileges—if any—the residents of the so-called "unincorporated" territories, migrating in ever-growing numbers to the United States, would have. The chapters in this third section of the anthology address American and immigrant understandings of citizenship and national belonging during the 1924–1965 period.

Those who secured admission to the United States—or entered the country without authorization—during the 1924–1965 period encountered a suspicious American population that needed their labor but viewed them as economic, cultural, and political threats to the nation, even if, as in the case of Puerto Rican workers, they were US citizens. The pressure to "Americanize"—to adapt one's language, dress, affect, and cultural and political values to a proverbial American norm—became especially intense after the 1924 Johnson-Reed Act. Policymakers viewed Americanization as essential to national cohesion. Across the nation, schools, churches, civic groups, and other institutions assisted in the cultural integration of those who migrated

188 · PART III

to the continental United States. "Americanization" was difficult to resist, and most immigrants understood it as a survival strategy that might facilitate their acceptance, adaptation, and upward mobility in US society. Americanization did not guarantee rights and protections, however, especially if immigrants were racial minorities or lacked permanent immigrant status.

The chapters in this section examine the experiences of those who struggled to understand, define, and assert their citizenship or human rights in US society. The section begins with "The Undertow of Reforming Immigration," by Ruth Ellen Wasem, which examines the political engagement of immigrants and their children, as revealed in public opinion surveys, naturalization rates, and organizational life. During the 1940s and 1950s the agents of immigration reform were kept in check, Wasem writes, by a strong political "undertow" that kept reformers just short of achieving their goals. The citizenry was changing, however. In the years leading up to the Immigration Act of 1965, naturalization among immigrant groups increased dramatically, reflecting a more expansive understanding of citizenship and creating possibilities for political engagement. This new generation of Americans successfully challenged the reactionary segments of US society who had advocated for exclusion and racial purity, and helped facilitate the passage of a new, more welcoming immigration policy.

Lorrin Thomas's chapter, "Foreign, Dark, Young, Citizen," examines the adaptive strategies of Puerto Ricans who began migrating to the continental United States in large numbers after the 1920s. Puerto Rico, a territory acquired as spoils of the Spanish-Cuban-American War of 1898, was a mystery to many Americans. Because their US citizenship exempted them from visas, passports, quotas, and other migratory controls imposed on immigrants, American businesses recruited Puerto Ricans in large numbers to make up for the loss of immigrant labor caused by the Johnson-Reed Act. By 1930, thirty thousand Puerto Ricans lived in New York City alone, but thousands more worked in factories and fields across the continental United States, and as far away as Hawai'i.

Despite their US citizenship, Puerto Ricans were vulnerable to the racist anxieties of the period and scapegoated like many immigrant groups and racial/ethnic minorities. By midcentury, Thomas writes, many Americans perceived and characterized Puerto Ricans as mentally deficient, prone to juvenile delinquency and criminal behavior, and a threat to postwar American safety and prosperity. Puerto Ricans bore the consequences of these characterizations: in racist educational policies, segregated neighborhoods, diminished opportunities for upward mobility, and as victims of police brutality. In the 1950s and 1960s, young Puerto Rican leaders became their own advocates, writes Thomas. Through their organizational life and institution building, and their emphasis on education, civic engagement, and community development, these young leaders countered the negative stereotypes and demonstrated their countrymen's ambition, work ethic, and pro-democratic values. Working with youth of all races, they also became important political actors in the era's mass movement for social change.

The challenges posed by family-focused immigration policies are the subject of Arissa Oh's chapter, "Japanese War Brides and the Normalization of Family Unification after World War II." During the early Cold War period, Congress eased the draconian anti-Asian immigration laws to facilitate what Oh calls the "conditional inclusion" of select populations. The Japanese war brides of white and African American servicemen were among the principal beneficiaries of these new policies. The War Brides Act and the 1952 Immigration and Nationality Act allowed Asian immigration specifically for the purposes of family unification: to reward American GIs who had served their country and now wished to sponsor their wives and children. But these policies also served to counter the criticism directed at the United States for its racist and discriminatory policies.

Oh examines American popular reactions to these mixed-race families during an era when segregation was legally and socially sanctioned, and anti-miscegenation laws were common. According to Oh, American politicians, journalists, and filmmakers challenged the perceived sexual and racial threat of these interracial families by portraying Japanese women—the single largest group of war brides—as demure, submissive, hyperfeminine suburban housewives, and characterizing their children as safe and acceptable models of racial mixing. Since Japanese women entered the United States as members of American families and did not concentrate in ethnic enclaves, their advocates argued that they were well positioned to assimilate and become model citizens. These tailored accommodations for American GIs contributed to making family unification a central tenet of post-1965 immigration policy.

Ana Elizabeth Rosas examines the impact of migration on the families of the Mexican agricultural laborers of 1940s and 1950s. The prolific scholarship on the Emergency Mexican Farm Labor Program (Bracero Program) generally focuses on three principal topics: its effects on regional economic development, on diplomatic relations, and on day-to-day lives of the workers themselves. Rosas's essay offers a novel examination of the emotional lives of workers and the loved ones they left behind in México. Drawing on oral histories, films, and songs of love, Rosas narrates a fascinating account of how the journeys of Mexican workers—both Braceros and undocumented workers—shaped understandings of gender roles, family, community, and belonging back home. These workers, whom Americans regarded as both vital and threatening, left family and loved ones with the hopes of securing a better financial future and improving the life chances of those left behind. They contributed to productivity and economic growth in the United States, but they also contributed to the upward mobility of those who loved them. It is easy to villainize them as the usurpers of American jobs, writes Rosas, and it is easy to lose sight of their humanity in the statistics of policy reports. Rosas reveals their fears, disappointments, and frustrations, as well as their hopes, joys, and aspirations.

Together, these four case studies remind readers that democracy and citizenship are works in progress. As Gary Okihiro has noted, the core values of the United States emanate from peoples on the margins of US society. It is in their struggles for inclusion that the ideals of the founders are continually reaffirmed and the United States becomes a more democratic nation.

CHAPTER 9

The Undertow of Reforming Immigration

RUTH ELLEN WASEM

Over the two decades between the end of World War II and the passage of the Immigration Act of 1965, the agents of immigration reform were checked by a strong undertow that kept them just short of achieving their objectives. The establishment of the national origins quota system in the 1920s was driven by an ideology of deserving (distinguishing people by class or selectivity), a belief in ethnic and racial superiority (eugenics and racism), and desire of the Southern and rural regions of the country to retain control over the Congress (power or apportionment politics). Demographic data and public-opinion surveys from this period illustrate a changing citizenry that challenged these three factors.[1]

In the years leading up to the Immigration Act of 1965, a growing sense of citizenship as well as an actual increase in naturalization among immigrant groups was shifting the balance. More precisely, the naturalization rate (in other words, percent of foreign-born residents who become US citizens) rose from just over half (52 percent) in 1920 to over three-quarters (80 percent) in 1950. Just as the accomplishments of immigrants and successes of their children were directly challenging old notions of selectivity and racial superiority, the electoral clout of naturalized immigrants and their children was beginning to alter the political landscape.

Coupled with the increasing civic engagement of immigrants was a broader societal push toward equality in mid-twentieth-century United States. There is considerable scholarship on how the war against fascism abroad turned the mirror on inequality in the United States and fueled campaigns for civil rights, workers' rights, women's rights, and other struggles for equality. At issue was how long the

Opportunities and Challenges of the Postwar Period

The immediate postwar period was a heady time for the nation. The United States and its allies had defeated the powers of fascism and, in the process, had risen out of the Great Depression. Sacrifice and austerity gave way to pent-up consumer demand, and the federal government committed to a full-employment economy. Immigrant workers were energizing the American labor movement, most notably with Congress of Industrial Organizations (CIO), and flexing political muscle that made labor unions one of the most powerful constituencies of postwar liberalism. By all indications, the timing seemed optimal for the United States to liberalize its immigration policies.

In 1945 the House Select Committee on Postwar Immigration considered the option to end racial discrimination in immigration during its deliberations. This move came at the same time when liberals fought for racial equality in a variety of areas, most notably in the arena of employment.[3] Committee counsel Thomas Cooley reported that support for ending racial discrimination was expressed consistently in hearings around the country. "Numerous recommendations to this effect were made by a wide selection of witnesses in all parts of the country. They were explicitly opposed by west coast organizations specializing in opposition to the immigration or naturalization of orientals." The recommendations that arose from the hearings included an end to racial discrimination in immigration and naturalization laws and a retention of quotas, provided the quotas were assigned on a nondiscriminatory basis. Despite the outpouring of support to end race-based admissions at the hearings, the committee did not endorse an end to the national-origins quota law.[4]

As Europe filled with millions of displaced persons after World War II, it became abundantly clear that most in Congress were wedded to retaining national origins as a basis of immigrant admissions. Even though the Displaced Persons Act of 1948 provided for the admission of four hundred thousand refugees, it did so within the framework of the national-origins quotas. More precisely, the admissions of displaced persons were "mortgaged" against 50 percent of their home countries' quotas. There was no groundswell for increased immigration, and opinion polls estimated that only 40 percent of the public supported admitting two hundred thousand refugees displaced after World War II.[5]

While there was a consensus among liberals that race- or national-origins-based admissions policies had to go, there was not a clear alternative to current law. No major case was being made for a return to immigrant admissions limited only by the grounds for exclusions. There was some support for increasing the total levels but few voices for removing numerical limits. Designing an alternative system for allocating visas fairly proved to be a challenge for the 1950s.

In 1947, Senate Resolution 137 authorized the funding for a "full and complete investigation" of immigration, which included field investigations in various locations across Europe and the Western Hemisphere.[6] Conservative senator Pat McCarran (D-NV), chair of the Senate Committee on the Judiciary, led the Senate immigration investigation. Although the Senate Special Subcommittee to Investigate Immigration and Naturalization did not publish any hearings, it did produce an official report in 1950 (Senate Report 1515) that numbered 985 pages. Senate Report 1515 concluded that the national-origins quotas served well as a method for the numerical restriction of immigration, but the report criticized the national-origins quotas for not admitting the proper mix of white people. More precisely, the report stated that "only about half of the anticipated proportion of immigrants have come from northern and western Europe, while twice the contemplated proportion have come from southern and eastern Europe." The report concluded, "As a method of preserving the relationship between the various elements in our white population, the national origins system has not been as effective." While Senate Report 1515 was an affront to the liberal movement for equality, fairness, and expansive citizenry, it is unclear if many people actually read it.[7]

When Congress did pass a reform measure in 1952, it retained this basic system for immigration restriction despite criticisms of the national origins system and its privileging of immigrants from northern and western Europe. The McCarran-Walter legislation based the annual number of immigrant visas issued each year on the 1920 census and set the level at 0.16 percent of the 1920 population of the United States. The computation resulted in just under 155,000 immigrants annually. The legislation formally removed the racial bars on immigrant admissions and gave the minimum quota to all countries outside of the Western Hemisphere. It also retained the policy of unlimited immigration from the Western Hemisphere, with inclusion of the Asia-Pacific Triangle language limiting those of Asian descent. Displaced persons continued to be counted under the national-origins quotas, as the effort to remove the mortgages failed again. The resulting national-origins quotas were quite similar to those in place before the passage of McCarran-Walter.

McCarran-Walter did, however, reform the way immigrant visas were distributed within each country's quota. The preference system to allocated visas that McCarran-Walter established was as follows:

- 50 percent (plus rollover from unused preferences below) to persons of high education, technical training, specialized experience, and exceptional ability;
- 30 percent to parents of US citizens at least twenty-one years old;

- 20 percent to spouses and children of LPRs; and,
- any remaining (up to 25 percent) for siblings, sons, and daughters of US citizens.

For the first time, US immigration policy was prioritizing the immigration of highly skilled individuals. The significance of this shift in policy grew in the coming years. From this point forward, business interests and organized labor had even larger stakes in the immigration debate. Given the importance of immigrant workers to both union mobilization and US employers, their power as a constituency had more potential.

Finally, the McCarran-Walter Act, by removing the racial bars to citizenship, opened the door for all foreign nationals with legal permanent-resident status to seek citizenship. Perhaps as many as thirty thousand Asians previously barred from naturalization became US citizens by 1955. More meaningful than the numbers of people naturalized in the immediate aftermath is the principle that all persons, regardless of race, were therefore eligible to become citizens under the law.[8]

Building Steam for Equal Treatment

The watershed moment in the drive to end national-origin admissions came when President Harry Truman vetoed the McCarran-Walter Act. Many had assumed Truman would sign the legislation. Neither Attorney General McGranery nor Secretary of State Dean Acheson had publically voiced opposition to the legislation, and both submitted memoranda to the president recommending that he sign it. McGranery acknowledged that the legislation contained objectionable provisions, but he also concluded that it was an improvement over existing law. The State Department characterized the bill as a "much-needed and long overdue codification" and referred to the provisions it would add as "improvements and liberalizations."[9]

The Bureau of the Budget, however, offered President Truman a biting analysis of the legislation heading for his desk. The analysis attached to the Budget Bureau director's memorandum pointed to the racially based restrictions placed on the immigration of Asians by addition of the Asia-Pacific Triangle provision. The analysis also cited the "racially discriminatory" treatment of colonial immigrants, particularly "Negroes from the West Indies."[10]

On June 25, 1952, the President sent Congress a veto message that was scathing and vigorous; moreover, it took aim directly at the national-origins quota laws. "The greatest vice of the present quota system, however, is that it discriminates, deliberately and intentionally, against many of the peoples of the world." The message went on to detail what the administration considered the discriminatory

The Undertow of Reforming Immigration • 195

aspects of the law, citing its treatment of Asians, Italians, Greeks, Poles, Rumanians, Yugoslavs, Ukrainians, and Hungarians. Truman continued to argue that "the basis of this quota system was false and unworthy in 1924. It is even worse now. At the present time, this quota system keeps out the very people we want to bring in. It is incredible to me that, in this year of 1952, we should again be enacting into law such a slur on the patriotism, the capacity, and the decency of a large part of our citizenry." As he drew to a conclusion, Truman observed:

> In no other realm of our national life are we so hampered and stultified by the dead hand of the past as we are in this field of immigration. We do not limit our cities to their 1920 boundaries; we do not hold corporations to their 1920 capitalizations; we welcome progress and change to meet changing condition in every sphere of life except in the field of immigration.[11]

Analysis of the roll-call vote on whether to override or sustain the president's veto reveals the importance of the immigrants as new or prospective citizens. More precisely, the proportion of the state or district's population that was foreign-born offers an explanation for the senators and representatives who deviated from their party's position. The Senate vote was quite close, and Senate Republicans who voted to sustain Truman's veto were from states that had foreign-born populations that were 5.6 percent or greater. They largely represented the East Coast or Mid-Atlantic regions of the country. Conversely, Senate Democrats who voted to override Truman's veto were overwhelmingly from the states with 1.7 percent or fewer foreign-born constituents. The patterns on the House roll-call vote on Truman's veto are quite similar to the Senate pattern. Those House Republicans who voted to sustain Truman's veto tended to be from states with higher percentages of foreign-born residents, and House Democrats who voted to override Truman's veto were more likely to be from the Southern states with very few foreign-born residents.

In his veto message, Truman had asked Congress to establish a commission to conduct a careful reexamination of immigration law. When Congress did not act, the president created a special Commission on Immigration and Naturalization on September 2, 1952, tasked with bringing immigration law "into line with our national ideals and our foreign policy."[12] The Truman Commission held a series of hearings across the country and sought the voices of local witnesses. More precisely, the commission met in eleven cities and heard more than four hundred testimonies. The commission further received more than 230 written statements after the hearings were concluded. As a result, the Truman Commission garnered a fair amount of local media coverage as well as national press. The visible role of the commission no doubt played a key part in raising public awareness of immigration issues.[13]

The Truman Commission recommended that the national-origins quota be abolished and that immigrants be admitted without regard to national origin, race, color, or creed. That meant the end of the exemption of the Western Hemisphere countries from numerical limits. It further recommended that the annual level of immigration be set at 250,000, which was comparable to current levels when the Western Hemisphere flows were added to the 155,000-quota limit. The Truman Commission further recommended that the 250,000 visas be distributed on the basis of "unified" flexible quotas according to the needs of the United States.

Competing Views of Public Opinion

Opponents of the McCarran-Walter Act expressed confidence that the majority of the public supported reforming the law. During hearings before the Senate Judiciary Subcommittee on Immigration and Naturalization in the summer of 1955, witnesses cited a recently released Gallup survey reporting that more than half of those interviewed who were familiar with the McCarran-Walter Act thought it should be changed. Of those who thought the law should be changed, Gallup reported that 68 percent favored making the law more liberal. Only 26 percent (of the 53 percent who supported changing the law) expressed the view that the law should be made stricter.[14]

Figure 1. Gallup Survey of Support for McCarran-Walter Act in 1955

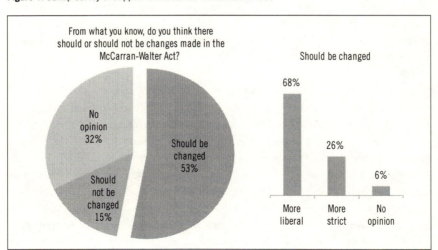

Source: "Prospects for Immigration Amendments," by Harry N. Rosenfield, *Law and Contemporary Problems*, Spring 1956.

In contrast to the Gallup survey cited by advocates for reform, the National Opinion Research Center (NORC) found in April 1955 that only 13 percent of those surveyed thought that immigration levels should be increased. The proportion who said immigration levels were "about right" (37 percent) was comparable to those who said the United States was admitting too many immigrants (39 percent). Figure 2 displays these data.[15]

How questions are worded is obviously critical to these differing results, as one survey asked about liberalizing the law and the other asked about immigration levels. No doubt there were individuals surveyed by either Gallup or NORC who opposed the national-origins system but did not want to increase immigration. Conversely, some might have approved of increased levels but not repealing the national origins system. Also, when the calculation of 68 percent of the 53 percent is completed, the result is that 36 percent of Gallup's respondents overall favor liberalizing the McCarran-Walter Act.

Although the surveys did not directly ask a question about national origins or diversity, NORC takes their survey a bit further by asking two follow-up questions of respondents who said they disapproved of admitting "so many." The majority of the 39 percent who supported reducing immigration gave economic reasons for their position, as figure 3 illustrates.[16] Of the economic reasons cited—competition

Figure 2. NORC Survey of Public Support for Increased Immigration in 1955

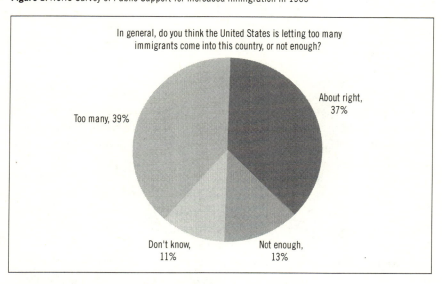

Source: National Opinion Research Center, April, 1955.

Figure 3. Top Reasons Given for Reducing Immigration in 1955

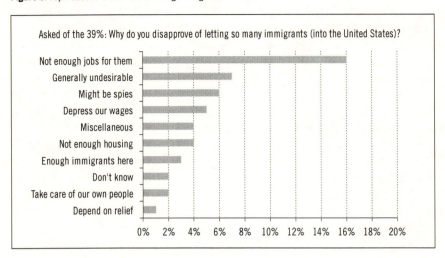

Data:

Depend on relief	1%
Take care of our own people	2%
Don't know	2%
Enough immigrants here	3%
Not enough housing	4%
Miscellaneous	4%
Depress our wages	5%
Might be spies	6%
Generally undesirable	7%
Not enough jobs for them	16%

Source: National Opinion Research Center, April 1955.

for jobs—led the opposition to immigration. Lack of housing and concern that wages would be depressed were other economic reasons given. Only about 7 percent overall said that immigrants were undesirable, and another 3 percent said that there were "enough immigrants here now."[17]

In response to NORC's asking those who disapproved of admitting "so many" immigrants what particular groups or nationalities they had in mind, it was apparent that memories of the war and fears of communism were the leading factors. As figure 4 shows, communist countries and the former Axis powers of Germany, Japan, and Italy led as the least-favored source countries for immigrants, reflecting a more political or ideological approach to restriction. Rather striking, however, was the comparably small percentage of respondents who otherwise identified groups or nationalities as prompting their disapproval. For example, only 3 percent

Figure 4. NORC: Nationalities Opposed by Those Who Would Reduce Immigration in 1955

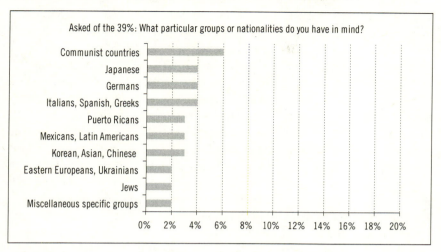

Data:

Miscellaneous specific groups	2%
Jews	2%
Eastern Europeans, Ukrainians	2%
Korean, Asian, Chinese	3%
Mexicans, Latin Americans	3%
Puerto Ricans	3%
Italians, Spanish, Greeks	4%
Germans	4%
Japanese	4%
Communist countries	6%

Source: National Opinion Research Center, April 1955.

mentioned Mexicans and Latin Americans, and only 2 percent listed Eastern Europeans, Jews, and Ukrainians. These data may have reflected the shifting social norms against expressions of bigotry and prejudice rather than an actual change in attitudes toward immigrants.[18]

1960 Opens

Critical to the growing civic participation of immigrants was the establishment of the nonpartisan American Citizenship and Immigration Conference (ACIC) in 1960. ACIC was a merger of the National Council on Naturalization and Citizenship and the American Immigration Conference. This umbrella group brought together the ethnic groups, religious entities, and civic organizations that sought immigration reform. The American Immigration Conference had been an association of thirty-one immigration-related organizations and agencies that advocated for a "nondiscriminatory alternative" to the existing national-origins quota system. The National Council on Naturalization and Citizenship had been an association of organizations and individuals who advocated for "humane, uniform, and simple" immigration laws. Ruth Z. Murphy, who had founded the American Immigration Conference earlier, led the new ACIC in its efforts to change immigration laws. A strong institutional structure for immigrants' civic engagement was fully in place.[19]

In terms of public opinion, however, foreign policy dominated the top concerns of the citizenry in 1960. When Gallup asked a sample of the American people what they considered to be the top problem facing the nation, the threat of war and keeping the peace led the list of concerns, averaging 20 percent. Relations with Russia and general foreign relations followed closely, each averaging 15 percent. Racial problems ranked first among the domestic policy issues at 7 percent, with unemployment and inflation rounding out the top ten.[20]

The 1960s also began with nonviolent civil rights protests in the South. In February, black students staged a sit-in at a whites-only Woolworth's lunch counter in downtown Greensboro, North Carolina. Six months later, that same lunch counter served its first meal to a black customer. National coverage of the civil rights movement was increasing, and an emerging leader of the movement, the Reverend Dr. Martin Luther King Jr. was arrested at an Atlanta sit-in that October.

The seeds of a Latino or Chicano rights movement were sprouting in the early 1960s as well. For example, Edward Roybal was the founding president of the Mexican American Political Association in 1960 and was elected to the US Congress from California in 1962. Henry Gonzalez co-chaired Viva Kennedy in 1960, won a special election to the US Congress from Texas in November 1961, and went on to expose the exploitation of the migrant workers under the Bracero Program. An emerging migrant-workers' rights movement led by agricultural workers of immigrant descent was gaining traction. Dolores Huerta, who would later co-found the United Farm Workers with César Chávez, established the Agricultural Workers Association in 1960.

There was not a national immigrant rights movement per se, as most of the immigrant groups were organized by nationality. The bulk of the ethnic organizations in the United States were focused on changing the immigrant admissions law (rather than on the rights of immigrants already in the United States). These ethnic and religious groups formed the core of the immigration reform movement. One of the most active was the American Committee on Italian Immigration, which had about 120 chapters across the country. Similarly, the American Jewish Committee and the B'nai B'rith played prominent roles and had offices around the country. The American Hellenic Educational Progressive Association, originally formed in

The 1920s to combat discrimination, had more than four hundred local chapters by the early 1960s. The ACIC worked to engage these disparate nationality groups as part of its broader efforts to expand citizenry.

Significance of the 1960 Presidential Election

Senator John Kennedy had championed immigration reform for many years. It was a key campaign issue when he defeated Henry Cabot Lodge Jr. for Senate in 1952. When Kennedy chaired the Immigration Subcommittee in the Senate, he managed to accomplish what other supporters of immigration reform had been unable to do—co-sponsor legislation (with Congressman Francis "Tad" Walter [D-PA]) that liberalized immigration law. For his running mate, Kennedy chose Senate Majority Leader Lyndon Johnson (D-TX) who had come in second to him for the Democratic nomination in the convention voting. Johnson's position on immigration had evolved from supporting the McCarran-Walter Act in 1952 to crafting the Senate-passed immigration reform bill in 1956. Kennedy chose his rival Johnson with the objective of gaining electoral votes in the South.

The 1960 presidential election was one of the closest in the twentieth century. Kennedy won with only 0.17 percent of the popular vote. Kennedy's Catholic religion was a major issue in the 1960 race, and much has since been written about whether the Catholic vote pushed Kennedy over the top.[21] The Kennedy-Johnson ticket exceeded expectations in Johnson's home state of Texas, particularly along the immigrant-rich Rio Grande Valley. The turnout in Chicago, coordinated by Mayor Richard Daley Sr., was similarly impressive in precincts with ethnic voters, enabling Kennedy to carry the state by a slim margin. Indeed, turnout in the major urban areas was decisive for the Democrats. At this point in history, the correlation between the Catholic faith and foreign-born or first-generation ethnic Americans was significant. Published research has shown that the Kennedy-Johnson ticket made much greater gains with the Catholic vote than the Nixon-Lodge ticket did with the Protestant vote. It is safe to assume that voters of foreign stock were instrumental in this election.[22]

Kennedy's victory was pivotal in the eyes of immigration reformers. They had worked with him on reform efforts while he served in the Senate when he opined, "Perhaps the most blatant piece of discrimination in our nation's history is the so-called National Origins formula." The relationship between Kennedy and the immigration reform movement was arguably symbiotic: Kennedy gained their electoral support, and the immigration reformers increased their political access.[23]

The post-election euphoria among immigration reformers was tempered by the situation in Congress. The bulwarks against immigration reform—Senate Judiciary Chairman James Eastland (D-MS) and House Judiciary Subcommittee on

Immigration Chairman Tad Walter (D-PA)—retained their positions of power over immigration legislation. The president continued to be respectful of Congressman Walter and also worked to maintain cordial relationship with Senator Eastland.[24]

As he had many times before, Judiciary Chairman Emanuel Celler introduced legislation abolishing the national-origins quota system. His bill in the 88th Congress (H.R. 3926) would have increased the ceiling on immigration to 250,000 annually and would have allocated these visas accordingly: 40 percent family reunification; 20 percent needed occupational skills; 20 percent refugee-asylee; and 20 percent other resettlement. By the 1960s, Celler no longer proposed to place immigrants from Western Hemisphere countries under the numerical limits.[25]

Across the US Capitol in the Senate, the architect of immigration reform became Philip Hart (D-MI). Hart came with a strong record on civil rights and labor issues and rather naturally took up the cause of immigration reform once in the Senate. In 1962, Hart had introduced legislation (S. 3043) with bipartisan support that would have abolished the national-origins quota system and increased the ceiling on immigration to 250,000. Up to fifty thousand visas were set aside for refugees. The Hart bill also would have added to the nonquota (in other words, unlimited) category those immigrants whom the Secretary of Labor deemed were urgently needed because of high education, specialized experience, and technical training. Immediate relatives of U. S. citizens and immigrants from Western Hemisphere countries were also unlimited under S. 3043, and the bill would have revised the law to include Jamaica, Trinidad, and Tobago among the Western Hemisphere nations.

It was not until July 1963 that the Kennedy administration sent a proposal to Congress that sought a total phase out of the national-origins quota system over five years. In contrast to Celler's and Hart's legislation, the administration proposed to only raise the ceiling to 165,000. The administration bill also picked up a provision from Hart's bill that became known as the per-country caps. The bills stated that not more than 10 percent of the total number of visas allocated by the preference system could go to any one country. Celler had a comparable provision, but he had set his per-country cap at 15 percent of the total. The administration bill shared a provision with Senator Hart's earlier legislation that redefined the Western Hemisphere exemption to include all countries and adjacent islands.[26]

In September 1963, more than half of the American public surveyed by Gallup stated that racial problems (including integration, segregation, and civil rights) were the top problems facing the nation. Racial problems stayed first on the list throughout 1964. Civil rights had been an urgent issue for the Democratic Party for several years, but it laid bare the wide schism between the Southern Democrats and the rest of the party on matters of race. As House Judiciary Chairman Emanuel Celler and Senator Phil Hart were the leading legislators on civil rights and voting rights legislation, their attention was squarely focused on moving these bills before taking up immigration.[27]

The assassination of President Kennedy devastated a nation that watched much of the tragedy unfold on television. The country in general grieved the loss of the charismatic commander in chief, and proponents of immigration reform in particular mourned the death of a president who had championed their cause. These proponents were very suspicious of the newly sworn-in President Lyndon Johnson because he had voted for the McCarran-Walter Act and because he was from Texas—a state infamous for being inhospitable to immigrants. Defenders of the immigration status quo were equally suspicious of Johnson because he had a reputation of squeezing votes out of members of Congress in order to achieve his objectives, including the immigration amendment he moved through the Senate in 1956.

As discussed at the outset, the establishment of the national-origins quota system was driven by selectivity, race, and power. Now, the justifications for abolishing it grew out of a basic sense of fairness (selectivity), equality of treatment (race), and representational politics (power). The legislative alternative was one based on the contributions and the potential of the prospective immigrant rather than the country of birth. In other words, merit would replace class and family reunification would replace race. The political incentives for Democrats were found in the foreign stock voters who disproportionately supported them, completing the third element—power.

The increasing civic participation of immigrants was working in the Democrats' favor. By 1964, a record proportion of the foreign-born population had become citizens. Naturalization data from the former Immigration and Naturalization Service indicated that almost 1.7 million immigrants had become citizens in the years 1951 to 1964. Presidential advisor Myer "Mike" Feldman prepared detailed maps of the United States by the percentage of foreign stock. Feldman used these census data to prepare an extensive list of members of Congress who represented districts with noteworthy percentages of foreign-stock residents. Feldman added the names of the member's administrative assistant (lead staffer) to create a very useful targeting tool for legislative support as well as get-out-the-vote drives.[28]

Republicans Divided in 1964

The chasm within the Democratic Party on immigration reform was apparent for decades, but the Republican Party of this period also had a deep divide over immigration policy. While the rift in the Democratic Party was largely regional, the Republican split was more nuanced. Most of the Republicans who supported immigration reform also advocated for civil rights legislation, broader funding of education, and an activist federal role to bolster the US economy. The conservative wing of the Republican Party painted a picture of pro-immigration Republicans as elites who were out of touch with average Americans.

In 1964, Arizona Senator Barry Goldwater won the Republican nomination for president, heralding a sharp turn to the right in the Republican Party. The platform called for reinstating the controversial Bracero Program for migrant agricultural workers from Mexico. As his running mate, Goldwater chose the chairman of the Republican National Committee, Congressman William Miller of New York, and it was Miller who made immigration an issue.

At an event on Labor Day in South Bend, Indiana, the Republican vice-presidential nominee warned that LBJ's immigration bill would "completely abolish our selective system of immigration and instead open the floodgates." He went on to suggest that immigrants would take jobs from the American workers. Rather than winning over the crowd of autoworkers who had suffered from major lay-offs earlier in the year, Miller's speech riled those in the audience of eastern and southern European backgrounds. Many Americans viewed the floodgates that Miller warned against opening as actual barriers keeping family members apart. The American Citizenship and Immigration Conference (ACIC) swung into action with letters to the Goldwater-Miller campaign and to the press. The AFL-CIO and its many affiliates responded that they supported the LBJ's immigration proposal and were confident that it would not cost American workers' their jobs. More than forty ethnic, religious, and civic organizations engaged in letter-writing campaigns against the speech. The outpouring of criticism of Miller's anti-immigrant remarks illustrates just how much notions of citizenship were broadening to encompass people born abroad.[29]

A public-opinion poll taken in the midst of the controversy over Miller's remarks found that the plurality (46 percent) of Americans surveyed in the fall of 1964 were content to keep the number of immigrants admitted each year at the existing level. More than one-third (38 percent) expressed the preference to decrease immigrant admissions, as figure 5 shows. Support for decreasing immigration levels held steady when compared to the 1955 NORC survey, in which 39 percent thought immigration levels were too high. Only 6 percent of those surveyed supported increased levels of immigration, a proportion down from 13 percent in 1955.[30]

Those people who were upset with Miller's speech might have heard his remarks as anti-immigrant rather than as a critique of the administration's bill. There was clearly no groundswell to increase immigration, but Miller's comments might have served as a "dog whistle" that was intended to motivate certain anti-immigrant voters. Foreign-stock voters heard the whistle too, energizing an important base in the Democratic party.

Lyndon Johnson won by a landslide, winning 61.1 percent of the votes cast and carrying forty-four states and the District of Columbia. Barry Goldwater won only Arizona (his home state) and the southern states of Alabama, Georgia, Louisiana, Mississippi, and South Carolina. Pro-immigration Republicans such as Keating

Figure 5. Public Attitudes toward Immigration Levels, September 1964

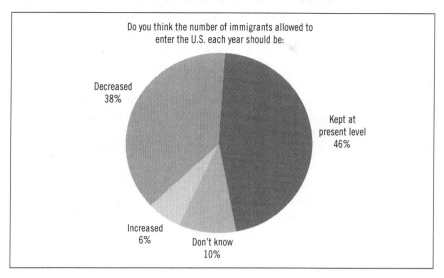

Source: Gallup, September 1964.

also lost in the Democratic sweep. The Johnson-Humphrey coattails brought in a net gain of thirty-six seats for the Democrats in the House, which provided them with a two-thirds majority. Similarly, the Democrats, by winning a net gain of two seats in the Senate also had a two-thirds majority. It appeared that there would be a sufficient number of Democratic Senators and Congressmen to place the "Great Society" agenda, including immigration reform, within reach.

Shaping Public Opinion

In his first State of the Union Address, President Johnson linked immigration reform to his civil rights agenda. While distinguishing it from civil rights legislation, he made clear that he considered the existing immigration system to be discriminatory. Johnson pitted the needed skills of the immigrants and the commitment to family reunification against the national-origins quotas. These principles were in the legislative package that Kennedy had sent to Congress in 1963, but Johnson had sharpened the framing of the issues to those of fairness, equality, and an expanding citizenry.

Within days of his State of the Union, President Johnson brought representatives of the leading organizations concerned with immigration and refugee issues to the White House. More than three dozen private citizens representing a range of faith-based, secular, and organized-labor groups gathered in the Cabinet Room with hand-picked senators, representatives and key administration officials. Civic engagement was at full throttle, as immigrant group leaders were literally "at the table" with the president, senators, and representatives who were tasked with rewriting immigration law.

Well aware of the significance of the moment, the president also staged a press conference at the meeting. Johnson opened by stating that existing immigration law had "overtones of discrimination," opting to be a bit less strident than other advocates for reform. He echoed the phrase from his State of the Union: "We should ask those who seek to immigrate now, what can you do for our country? But we ought never to ask, in what country were you born?" With television cameras running, the president made clear that he supported an expanded citizenry based upon equal treatment.[31]

The undertow of political forces thwarting immigration reform picked up the gauntlet the president had thrown down to them. During a hearing that the national press extensively covered, Senator Sam Ervin questioned Secretary of State Dean Rusk on immigration reform. As Ervin began his remarks, he was echoing the "mirror of America" theme that it was only fair to favor northern and western Europeans in the quota law. Ervin then said the reform legislation discriminated against northern Europeans because it would treat them the same as Ethiopians. Ervin went on to state, "I don't know of any contributions that Ethiopia has made to the making of America." Ervin's blatant racism was another affront to equality, fairness, and expansive citizenry and a clear message to the president and all proponents of reform.[32]

There was significant variation in media coverage of Ervin's comments, largely centered on whether the article included Ervin's comment about Ethiopia or merely his assertion that the bill would discriminate against northern Europeans. Some of the coverage also included Senator Jacob Javits's outburst that he could not "sit still for this proposition uttered by my colleague from North Carolina that ethnic groups that came from Northern Europe and England made America." The *Washington Post* featured the hearing as a clash between the "descendent of Anglo-Saxon slave owners" and the "son of New York Jewish immigrants." Whether the particular newspaper included Rusk's response to Ervin was especially telling. The Secretary of State had replied that "there's no question but that Negroes have contributed enormously to American life." Sadly, few in the media included Rusk's reply.[33]

Given the auspicious start of the legislative campaign for immigration legislation, supporters of immigration reform were very disheartened when Louis Harris published the results of his nationwide survey disclosing that LBJ's proposal to ease immigration laws was opposed by a 2 to 1 margin. The administration and congressional supporters knew that there was little public support for increasing immigration levels and had considered the increased levels in their proposal to be modest.

Equally troubling was Harris's analysis of what drove the anti-immigrant opinions. Harris observed that "part of the reason for the reluctance of Americans to lower the barriers to immigration obviously rests in the aversion many Americans express to people from countries covering over three-quarters of the world's population." Harris went on to list the countries and regions considered least desirable sources for immigrants, a list topped by Russia, with Asia and the Middle East as second and third, respectively.[34]

The Harris poll results garnered wide press coverage beyond the initial article in the *Washington Post*. The poll showed that even in the proverbial strongholds of immigration reform—the cities and the East—support for easing immigration law was less than 50 percent of those surveyed (figure 6). Defenders of the status quo were quite pleased by the results and were generous in referencing the survey in their speeches and commentary.[35]

Figure 6. Public Attitudes on Increased Immigration, May 1965

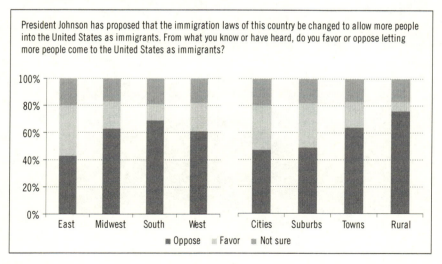

Data:

	East	Midwest	South	West	Cities	Suburbs	Towns	Rural
Oppose	43	63	69	61	47	49	64	76
Favor	37	20	12	21	33	33	19	7
Not sure	20	17	19	18	20	18	17	17

Source: Harris, May 1965.

The single bright spot in the Harris poll results from May 1965 was that only 29 percent of those interviewed supported the national-origins system, compared with 36 percent who favored basing immigrant admissions more on the skills of the individual (figure 7). Almost an equal portion expressed the view that it made no difference or that they were not sure. The task for immigration reformers was to shift as much as possible of the remaining one-third of the public to their side of the issue. Clearly, the target groups were the indifferent and the undecided.

Grassroots Campaign to Pass the Bill

No one knew better than Emanuel Celler that a major communication campaign was needed if immigration legislation was going to move forward. Celler acknowledged, "There is not a burning desire in the grassroots of this country to change our immigration policy." As he spoke to a gathering of the leaders and grassroots of the immigration reform movement at an ACIC conference, Celler emphasized the need for a public-education campaign. "It must be the task of groups like yours . . . by force of logic to overcome the unrealistic fear which possesses so many people at the thought of any change in our immigration law."[36]

Figure 7. Attitudes on Skills vs. Country of Origin, May 1965

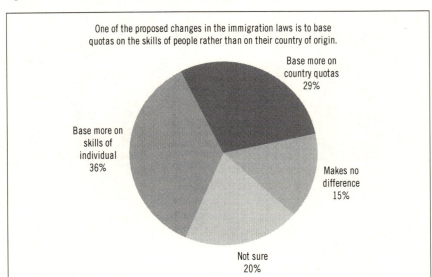

Source: Harris, May 1965.

By spring 1965, a grassroots campaign was underway to gin up support for the legislation. The ACIC had long published monthly newsletters, but in May 1965 they also disseminated an "action kit" aimed at whipping up support for the legislation. ACIC member organizations held public meetings to discuss the administration's bill across the country. Donald Anderson, director of Lutheran Immigration Service, reported to Chairman Celler that "these discussions have been with Jewish, Catholic, Protestant and labor groups." Anderson concluded, "In all these discussions we have found complete acceptance of the President's proposal—after it has been explained and studied."[37]

In response to the controversy brought on by the Harris poll, the White House had reached out to the Gallup public-opinion-research firm to ask questions that were more finely tuned to the legislative options on the table. In turn, Gallup conducted a nationwide survey in June 1965 that yielded somewhat different findings than the Harris poll from a month earlier (figure 8). Although a majority of those interviewed continued to oppose any increases in overall immigration levels, a slim majority (51 percent) now favored skills-based admissions over the national-origins quota system.[38]

This survey further found that respondents who supported the national-origins quota law were largely the same individuals who favored decreasing levels of immigration. Gallup had performed special breakdowns of their data for the Johnson

Figure 8. Attitudes on Skills vs. Country of Origin, June 1965

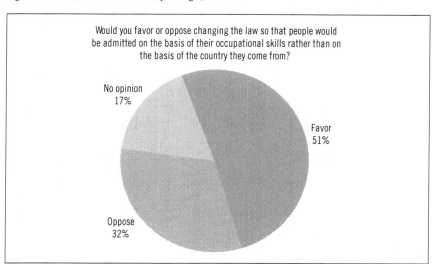

Source: Gallup, June 1965.

210 · RUTH ELLEN WASEM

Administration that revealed that the responses to the questions were correlated. According to the internal analysis, Gallup found "a hard core 1/3 of the population who desire very restrictive immigration policies."[39]

The administration was especially happy to learn that 71 percent of those surveyed by Gallup listed occupational skills as the most important criteria for admitting immigrants. Just over half (55 percent) of the respondents also included "relatives in the US" as one of the top criteria. Gallup analysts concluded that the results indicated "a clear mandate for a policy based upon occupational skills." The strategy of emphasizing merit over national origins appeared to be a wise one.[40]

Surprisingly, little of the language on merit survived the final throes of the legislative process. Despite their shrinking political base, the forces of the undertow forced proponents of reform to focus on what they considered most critical and feasible at that time. Repealing the national-origins quota system always remained front and center. The centrality of this theme led to a majority of legislators on both sides of the aisle to vote for the final bill. By replacing the national-origin quotas with a system of per-country ceilings, the Immigration Act of 1965 enabled a more racially diverse and culturally vibrant flow of future citizens.[41]

Notes

1. This chapter draws on the October 2015 Kluge Lecture titled "The Struggle for Fairness" that the author gave while she was a fellow at the John C. Kluge Center at the US Library of Congress and from her forthcoming book on the legislative drive to end race- and nationality-based immigration in twentieth-century United States.

2. Campbell Gibson and Emily Lennon, *Historical Census Statistics on the Foreign-Born Population of the United States: 1850–1990*, US Census Bureau, Population Division, table 11, 1999.

3. For example, President Truman joined liberals in pushing for an end to racial discrimination in hiring by arguing for a permanent authorization of the Fair Employment Practices Committee.

4. US House of Representatives, *Hearings Pursuant to H. Res. 52 Authorizing a Study of Immigration and Naturalization Laws and Problems*, part 3, July 3, 1945, 80–81.

5. In April 1948, the National Opinion Research Center (NORC) at the University of Chicago surveyed the public about the Displaced Persons legislation.

6. US Senate, Committee on the Judiciary, *The Immigration and Naturalizations Systems of the United States*, S. Rept. 81-1515, April 20, 1950.

7. Ibid., 430–32 and 445–46.

8. US Department of Justice, *Annual Report of the Immigration and Naturalization Service for 1955*, tables 38 and 39. See https://babel.hathitrust.org/cgi/pt?id=osu.32435028570315 ;view=1up;seq=3.

9. Memorandum, "Department of State Views H.R. 5678 Immigration and Nationality Bill," ca. May 1952, Presidential Papers of Harry S. Truman; Memorandum from Attorney

The Undertow of Reforming Immigration • 211

General James McGranery to Frederick J. Lawton with Attachment, June 17, 1952, Presidential Papers of Harry S. Truman. See https://www.trumanlibrary.org/publicpapers.

10. Executive Office of the President, Bureau of the Budget, "Memorandum for the President," by F. J. Lawton, May 9, 1952, Presidential Papers of Harry S. Truman.

11. Harry S. Truman, Veto of the McCarran-Walter Immigration Act, 82nd Congress, 2nd Session, House Document 520, June 25, 1952.

12. Memorandum from Julius C. C. Edelstein to Richard E. Neustadt with Attachments, June 28, 1952, Presidential Papers of Harry S. Truman; Stephen T. Wagner, "The Lingering Death of the National Origins Quota System: A Political History of United States Immigration Policy, 1952–1965," PhD diss., Harvard University, October 1986, 41–42.

13. Public Papers of Harry S. Truman, Special Message to the Congress Transmitting Report of the President's Commission on Immigration and Naturalization, January 13, 1953.

14. Harry N. Rosenfield, "Prospects for Immigration Amendments," *Law and Contemporary Problems*, Spring 1956, 411.

15. National Opinion Research Center, University of Chicago during April 1955, and based on personal interviews with a national adult sample of 1,226; data provided by the Roper Center for Public Opinion Research, Cornell University.

16. The United States had experiencing a recession in 1953 that was brought under control by the end of 1954. John W. Sloan, *Eisenhower and the Management of Prosperity* (Lawrence: University of Kansas Press, 1991); Saul Engelbourg, "The Council of Economic Advisors and the Recession of 1953–1954," *Business History Review* 54, no. 2 (Summer, 1980).

17. National Opinion Research Center, University of Chicago, during April 1955, and based on personal interviews with a national adult sample of 1,226; data provided by the Roper Center for Public Opinion Research, Cornell University.

18. Ibid.

19. The American Immigration Conference formed in 1930, and the National Council on Naturalization and Citizenship formed in 1954.

20. Gallup (AIPO) polls from February 1960 through October 1960; data provided by the Roper Center for Public Opinion Research, Cornell University.

21. Kennedy was only the second Catholic nominated to run for president and the first to win. New York Governor Al Smith, who lost in 1928, was the first Catholic nominated by a major party.

22. Philip Converse, "Religion and Politics: the 1960 Election," in Angus Campbell, Philip Converse, Warren Miller, and Donald Stokes, *Elections and the Political Order* (Hoboken, N.J.: Wiley, 1966), 96–124; and Christopher P. Gilbert, *The Impact of Churches on Political Behavior: An Empirical Study* (Santa Barbara, Calif.: Praeger, 1993).

23. Wagner, *Lingering Death*, 119–121, 310; Betty Koed, "The Politics of Reform: Policymakers and the Immigration Act of 1965," PhD diss., University of California, Santa Barbara, 1999, 75.

24. Meyer Feldman Personal Papers, box 96, JFK Presidential Library, Boston, Mass.

25. In terms of Western Hemisphere migration, Celler was more focused on efforts to end the Bracero Program with Mexico due to concerns of migrant worker exploitation.

26. Memorandum to the Acting Secretary of State from Abba Schwartz, June 25, 1963, copied to Gordon Chase at the White House June 25, 1963, Files of Gordon Chase, National Security files box 7, LBJ Presidential Library, Austin, Tex. S.2585/H.R. 6820 in 1953 had featured the per-country caps and had set the level at 10 percent of the total number of preference visas.

27. Gallup reported that 52 percent of those surveyed listed racial problems, integration, segregation and civil rights as the top issue. It was rare for any issue to be listed by more than half of those surveyed. Gallup (AIPO), September 1963; data provided by the Roper Center for Public Opinion Research, Cornell University.

28. US Department of Justice, *Annual Report of the Immigration and Naturalization Service for 1964*, tables 42 and 44, https://babel.hathitrust.org/cgi/pt?id=osu.32435066733346; Personal Papers of Myer Feldman, box 96, JFK Presidential Library.

29. Dom Bonefede, "GOP to Limit Immigration—Miller," *Boston Globe*, September 8, 1964, 8; Robert S. Boyd, "Miller Speech May Be Major Blunder," *Washington Post*, September 17, 1964; Copy of letter to William Miller from Ruth Murphy, Papers of Emanuel Celler Papers, US Library of Congress (hereafter, Celler Papers, LOC), and Koed, *Politics of Reform*, 196–201.

30. Gallup AIPO, September 1964.

31. Office of the White House Press Secretary, "Remarks of the President to Representatives of Organizations Interested in Immigration and Refugee Matters," January 13, 1964, Papers of President Lyndon B, Johnson, 1963–69, Immigration-Naturalization, box 1, LBJ Presidential Library.

32. John H. Averill, "Rusk Hit on Immigration Law Change," *Los Angeles Times*, February 25, 1965; Andrew J. Glass, "Senate Racial Clash," *Boston Globe*, February 25, 1965; "Who Built America," *Hartford Courant*, March 1, 1965; "Ervin and Javits Clash at Hearing on Easing Immigration Restrictions," *Washington Post*, February 25, 1965; Senate Judiciary Hearings, 61–63.

33. Senate Judiciary Hearings, 61–63.

34. Louis Harris, "US Public Is Opposed to Easing of Immigration Laws," *Washington Post,* May 31, 1965; Memorandum from Larry O'Brien to Mike Manatos, June 4, 1965, White House Central File Collection, Larry O'Brien files, LBJ Presidential Library; Wagner, *Lingering Death*, 422–23.

35. Wagner, *Lingering Death*, 422–23.

36. Celler speech to American Citizenship and Immigration Conference, 1963, Celler Papers, LOC.

37. Letter to Emanuel Celler from Donald E. Anderson, June 15, 1965, Celler Papers, LOC.

38. Memo to Bill Moyers based on telephone conversation with Irving Crespi, July 21, 1965, Office Files of Bill Moyers, box 8, LBJ Presidential Library.

39. Ibid.

40. Ibid.

41. The legislation to reform immigration had actually gotten shorter, from 211 pages in 1953 to the twelve-page Immigration Act of 1965.

CHAPTER 10

Foreign, Dark, Young, Citizen

Puerto Rican Youth and the Forging of an American Identity, 1930–70

LORRIN THOMAS

In the late 1950s two teenage Puerto Rican boys represented the darkest side of social change in New York City. One, Salvador Agrón, or the "Capeman," was a real person, a gang leader who was convicted and sentenced to death for the unprovoked murder of two boys in 1959. The other, Bernardo, was fictional, leader of the Puerto Rican street gang the Sharks and brother of the tragic heroine Maria in *West Side Story*, which opened on Broadway in 1957. Both characters reinforced the era's archetypal urban delinquent. In photographs, both boys appeared dark-skinned and menacing; less visibly, both embodied the politically incongruous combination of foreign birth and American citizenship.[1]

At this point in the New York's twentieth-century journey from immigrant metropolis to a city divided into "minority" and white (a category that by midcentury included the descendants of all those "swarthy" Europeans), Puerto Ricans stood at a crossroads—at least as far as many young migrants and second-generation youth were concerned. A growing cadre of young Puerto Rican leaders in the 1950s and 1960s, in an era of unprecedented prosperity, decided it was time to make good on the guarantees of inclusion and opportunity that their citizenship had promised but not yet delivered. Through their community leadership and political activism, they would try to ensure that the rights conferred by US citizenship were not limited by class status or racial or national identity. In the process, they would help redefine rights of American citizenship for Puerto Ricans in the United States.

Migrants from Puerto Rico had begun settling in New York City in increasingly large numbers between the end of World War I and the mid-1920s, for reasons both connected and unrelated to the impact of excluding most other immigrants from the United States in the same period. Puerto Rico had been taken by the United States as a prize of war in 1898; and after US lawmakers ratified the extension of citizenship to Puerto Ricans in 1917, migrants began arriving in the United States by the thousands. As the number of European immigrants entering the country dropped dramatically by the early 1920s, and as the prosperity of that decade increased demand for workers, the Puerto Rican migration increased annually. In just over a decade, Puerto Ricans had built a thriving community, and with great expectations they took steps in the climb toward the middle class—with the added benefit of their citizenship to help them gain a foothold.

The Great Depression dashed those hopes. Jobs evaporated, decent housing became both scarcer and more expensive, and migrants faced intensifying prejudice in the labor market and in the streets. The prejudice was generic to a degree—Puerto Ricans were still decidedly "foreign," and their island's connection to the United States was mysterious to many. But the specificity of American anti-black racism was also translated, with few intermediate steps, to apply to mixed-race Puerto Ricans. Over time, racial prejudice—with its peculiarly American, binary categorization—came to characterize much of Puerto Ricans' experience, supplanting traditional anti-immigrant prejudices.

Young Puerto Ricans experienced this shift in the 1930s perhaps even more viscerally than their parents did, through their close connections to the most interventionist of American institutions: schools. Children of immigrants, the "second generation," had been an object of reformers' and city officials' preoccupation dating back to the nineteenth century, but the rapidly growing numbers of Puerto Rican children living in New York by the 1930s inspired a particular mix of liberal reformist concern and racist assumptions about their dangerous influence on American society.[2] In these midcentury decades, Puerto Rican youth were at first accused of criminality and low intelligence, and then of delinquency—the targets of familiar, if increasingly racialized, expressions of anti-immigrant bias.

However, as the place of youth in American society changed, and as young Puerto Ricans' racial self-identification evolved with the nation's changing political and racial climate, they began to assert a new political consciousness. Accused by some of destructive political militancy in the late 1960s, Puerto Rican youth accomplished far more than simply increasing the visibility of Puerto Ricans and their disadvantages in US society in that era through their radical community organizing. As a result of their demands for more open access to education and their commitment to generating new networks of legal and civil rights activism, they also created a legacy of empowerment that continues to define Puerto Ricans' engagement as citizens in the United States.

"Delinquents and criminals"

Although there were probably thirty thousand Puerto Ricans in New York City by 1930, their residential concentration in East Harlem and near the Chelsea Piers and the Brooklyn Navy Yard meant that many New Yorkers outside of those neighborhoods were unaware of their presence: they blended with other "Spanish" immigrants, of which there were substantial numbers by the 1920s. Most members of these growing Spanish-speaking communities were Latin American migrants—from Cuba, Colombia, and a handful of other countries—whose entry into the United States from within the Western Hemisphere had not been limited by the passage of restrictive immigration laws that targeted Europeans (most of them from southern and eastern Europe) and Asians.

New York's Spanish-speaking world may have been invisible to many city residents, but the rapidly growing number of Puerto Ricans in the city began to make some observers nervous by the early years of the Depression. Puerto Ricans protested their poor treatment at Home Relief offices (where aid was distributed to the unemployed and single mothers before the advent of federal New Deal programs); they objected loudly to what they perceived as damaging statements about Puerto Ricans by First Lady Eleanor Roosevelt following her goodwill trip to the island in 1934 (where she noted high rates of tuberculosis); and they petitioned the Mayor's Office for stronger political representation following a major riot in Harlem in 1935 (although the rioting took place in the mostly African American part of Harlem, the riot was sparked by the arrest of a Puerto Rican boy).

Immediately after the riot, a member of the New York City's Chamber of Commerce wrote to inform Mayor LaGuardia that Puerto Ricans had been "flooding" into Harlem since the mid-1920s and to warn that "this class presents a problem . . . which nobody knows how to handle."

> We find that a tremendous number of [them] are on "relief" of some kind or other. They do not learn to speak English. Apparently, their morals are undesirable and they seem to be altogether a pretty nearly hopeless group.
>
> I bring this up because I understand that there is no bar to the immigration of these people. I do not think most people realize how many there are in the city and what a burden they are to the community . . . and in my opinion they are a source of danger from propaganda and from their inability to mix with other elements in the city.[3]

A few months later, the Chamber of Commerce's Special Committee on Immigration and Naturalization hired two psychologists to conduct a study on the intelligence of Puerto Rican children in New York City, using the standard tests of that era. According to the psychologists, the students' poor results proved that Puerto Rican migrations would "deteriorate standards already so seriously impaired by mass immigration of the lowest levels of populations of many nations."[4]

The lead investigator, Dr. Clairette Armstrong, was a staff psychologist for the city's Children's Court and an expert on juvenile delinquency—and a well-known voice in New York's anti-immigrant circles. A year before beginning the study, she had written to the editor of the *New York Times*: "Juvenile delinquency on the whole results from the clash of civilizations. Low-grade, intellectually dull immigrants thrust into our complicated, highly organized civilization are unable to adjust their likewise intellectually dull offspring to the exigencies of such environment."[5] Although Americans' obsession with eugenics and scientific racism had peaked in the 1920s, Armstrong could still count on the support of many likeminded colleagues (and a receptive white public) in the 1930s. Discourses about the racial basis of intelligence focused, of course, on African Americans and on immigrants, especially those not considered white. Mexicans and Mexican Americans in the western states also were subjected to IQ testing throughout the 1920s and 1930s, with pronouncements about their intellectual deficits and social undesirability nearly identical to Armstrong's summation of Puerto Ricans' IQ.[6]

The study's results were circulated widely enough that they triggered a reaction from a number of Harlem activists, including members of the Puerto Rican–dominated Spanish Welfare League as well as Leonard Covello, a prominent East Harlem educator who was the principal at the community's progressive Benjamin Franklin High School.[7] Covello, himself an Italian immigrant, pointed out that Italian immigrant children had also been "attacked" in the press after an intelligence study in 1921. "When the Binet tests were given to Italian children they had the same difficulty because of the foreign expressions and idioms. Only after the tests were revised was it possible to use them for American children," he said.[8] This incident—from the commissioning of the study to the contested interpretation of its results—showed the aggressiveness of a growing anti-Puerto Rican lobby in New York in the 1930s, and it punctuated the worst two years to date, in terms of hostile and discriminatory discourse, for the new Puerto Rican community in New York. Using a familiar rhetorical strategy of identifying children as the vector of the contagion, the IQ study presaged the extent to which young Puerto Ricans would stand on the front lines of bitter battles with white New Yorkers.

So it was that the most visible eruption out of the simmering conflicts between Puerto Ricans and Italian Americans in East Harlem in the late 1930s—when Puerto Ricans began to replace Italians as the largest group in the neighborhood—happened among youth. According to reports, there had been ongoing tensions between rival gangs across "the line" that separated the Italian and Puerto Rican sections of East Harlem. The "feud" was exacerbated when some of the Italian boys

Foreign, Dark, Young, Citizen • 217

referred to Congressman Vito Marcantonio as a "spic lover."[9] The physical conflict that ensued took place adjacent to Benjamin Franklin High School, and Covello received at least a dozen furious letters from Italian American parents who resented having to send their sons to one of the city's few racially integrated schools. One letter, signed only with a crudely drawn skull and crossbones, presented Covello with a "WARNING. No damn lousy Spics are allowed in Franklin . . . This is your last warning. The next time we will use more *drastic* measures." A few of the letters avoided explicitly racial language, but to the same effect, like the one from a father named Ralph De Donato: "I take pride in stating that my son has been reared in strict adherence to the traditions of well bred people, and has been trained to carry to school a pen and pencil, rather than an ice pick or a razor."[10]

In his responses, Covello was determined to convince other New Yorkers that the Puerto Rican "newcomers" were "just like other immigrants." While it was true that European immigrants, like Puerto Ricans, had been reviled in very similar terms for their allegedly weak morals and ill health, Covello's logic sidestepped the key aspects of Puerto Ricans' difference from their immigrant predecessors: their mixed-race heritage and their American citizenship. These differences, combined with a generational shift in American society—the emergence of a more independent youth culture, and attendant preoccupation by adults with delinquency— meant that young Puerto Ricans in New York were poised to be targeted as the city's most dangerous citizens. Indeed, this was what they faced in the decades to come.

"Juvenile gangsters. . . . in a world apart"

Nascent fears among white New Yorkers of a "Puerto Rican problem" receded briefly during World War II, then exploded as migration from Puerto Rico increased dramatically after the war. As the number of migrants in the city approached 150,000 by 1947 (the "influx" averaged about forty-five thousand migrants annually between 1946 and 1954), other New Yorkers read dozens of newspaper stories about Puerto Ricans living in crowded tenements, unable to speak English and unprepared for life in a cold city. These warnings did sound a lot like the invective applied to European immigrants half a century earlier. But, contrary to what Covello implied about their shared plight, those immigrants had not been so obviously different in racial terms—the most powerful terms of difference in American society—and those immigrants had not had the formal protections of citizenship, which would prove to offer little protection for Puerto Ricans buffeted by both anti-black and anti-immigrant sentiment.

Puerto Rican youth were doubly burdened by this discourse. Throughout the 1950s, Puerto Ricans under age twenty-five constituted New York's most rapidly expanding demographic group, and they became ready targets of the public's anxiety about a postwar world in flux. Punctuated by the "zoot suit" riots in Los Angeles in 1943, then a spike in gang activity and youth homicides later in the decade, the postwar years witnessed a national obsession with youth, especially those with dark skin.[11] The rate of juvenile court appearances by children ages ten to seventeen continued to rise, nearly doubling between 1948 and 1957. Delinquency rates, measured through juvenile arrest counts, had first peaked in the United States in 1943, declined in the first years after the war, and then began rising precipitously by 1949. By 1957, across the nation, more than twenty-three in one thousand children ages ten to seventeen appeared before juvenile court for alleged delinquency, nearly double the 1948 rate of about twelve per thousand.[12] In New York, black and Puerto Rican youth were scapegoated in the media as the most dangerous and irredeemable of these delinquents.

Liberal social scientists tried occasionally to counter such allegations with empirical evidence but got little traction.[13] Puerto Rican leaders argued repeatedly that juvenile delinquency was a temporary problem resulting from postwar social changes, one that was not unique to Puerto Ricans. Indeed, Joseph Montserrat, the head of the Migration Division (a social-service office in New York City sponsored by the Puerto Rican government), quipped in 1957 that juvenile delinquency was "just second-generationitis."[14] If what Montserrat meant by "second-generationitis" was a temporary failure on the part of youth to conform to their immigrant parents' expectations, "second generationitis" certainly did not explain the problem of teenage gang violence in the Puerto Rican and Italian areas of East Harlem (among other neighborhoods) throughout the 1950s. Police increasingly intervened in gang conflicts. In August 1956 in Hell's Kitchen, for example, a series of confrontations among the multiethnic "Sportsmen," "Dragons," and "Enchanters" resulted in several murders of rival gang members, which led to interventions by police, priests, social workers, and other community leaders. A temporary truce was reached, and at least one of the gangs "went social," meaning it transformed into a social club that collaborated with other community leaders in social events and community organizing.[15]

Most outcomes were not so positive, however. More often, law enforcement's approach to gang violence only exacerbated already tense relations between police and youth. Aggressive enforcement of seemingly arbitrary rules, including confining ethnic and racial groups to "their" neighborhoods, as well as the liberal use of racial slurs and frequent recourse to physical abuse of teens on stoops and street corners, were common through the 1950s. Puerto Rican community members organized a protest against police brutality in 1949, triggered when two detectives killed a Puerto Rican youth under questionable circumstances. Protests over incidents like this continued sporadically throughout the 1950s.[16]

Foreign, Dark, Young, Citizen • 219

This was the backdrop when *West Side Story* hit Broadway in September 1957. The play was a story of doomed love between a white boy (of indeterminate ethnicity, probably Italian), Tony, and a Puerto Rican girl, Maria; it followed the plotlines of *Romeo and Juliet*. While *West Side Story* offered a sympathetic portrayal of Puerto Ricans—striving immigrants who endured the indignities of their new life but expected the best, just like the European immigrants who came before them—it also powerfully reinforced a hardening stereotype of juvenile delinquency in New York in that era: the image of dark and menacing Puerto Rican gang members who would wield their switchblades without a second thought to defend the honor of one of their own.

Concerns about juvenile violence and gangs reached their apex in New York less than two years later. Six gang-related homicides happened during the summer of 1959; then, during the last week of August, there were four more. The final incident involved the murder of two non-gang (or "straight") youth, both white, by a group of teenagers from several Puerto Rican gangs.[17] The boy charged as the main perpetrator of the murders, who was wearing a black cape during the late-night attack on the victims in a West Side playground, quickly became known as the "Capeman," or "Drácula" in the Spanish-language press.

The "Capeman" murders confirmed white New Yorkers' worst fears about Puerto Rican youth, and they presented Puerto Rican leaders with the realization of their worst nightmare of anti-Puerto Rican publicity. *El Diario* regularly ran stories with headlines like "Victims of Juvenile Gangs Symbolize the Failure of Community" and "'Gang' Says: We Want to Be Good, but Nobody Helps Us."[18] About a week after the murders, thousands of individual Puerto Ricans gathered with representatives of more than 160 Puerto Rican organizations in meetings, press conferences, and community forums throughout East Harlem and across New York City. New York's tabloids and even the *Washington Post* noted the community's efforts in editorials that commented on the injustice of putting a Puerto Rican face on youth violence.[19]

Joseph Montserrat, in testifying a month later before the US Senate Subcommittee to Investigate Juvenile Delinquency, pointed to "poverty, insecurity, ignorance, prejudice and discrimination, living in slums, and substandard wages" as the "major causes" of juvenile crime. Montserrat argued that "juvenile delinquency is inextricably linked with broader problems such as nationwide population shifts, housing conditions, opportunities for education and employment, and economic development."[20] Meanwhile, a Brooklyn judge who regularly handled juvenile cases, Samuel Liebowitz, pushed Mayor Wagner to discourage further Puerto Rican migration to the city, arguing this would be the most effective step the city could take to turn back the tide of juvenile crime in the next decade.[21] For many New Yorkers, the links Montserrat identified were invisible; they only saw

220 • LORRIN THOMAS

that the Capeman was the embodiment of the stereotypical violent delinquent, the youthful symbol of the city's ongoing Puerto Rican problem.

"A positive image to counter 'pathology and fear'"

While readers of New York's tabloids followed this melodrama, a rising cadre of young Puerto Rican leaders was quietly constructing an entirely different image of youth in their communities. Puerto Rican college students had formed a group called the Hispanic Association Pro-Higher Education (HAPHE) earlier in 1959 to support Puerto Ricans attending or aspiring to attend college. When HAPHE hosted its second Puerto Rican Youth Conference in 1960, organizers addressed the Puerto Rican community's trauma following the Capeman incident. The goal of the conference, they said, was "to set a positive image to counter 'pathology and fear' to show the Puerto Rican as ambitious, with a desire and increasing ability to climb upwards, as have all past newcomers to the city. . . . The bad publicity of the summer of 1959 still affects [the Puerto Rican]."[22]

In terms of their focus on educational achievement, with its promise of middle-class status, young Puerto Ricans were indeed much like "all past newcomers to the city." The 1950s had been an important decade for the expansion of opportunities for them. Just as city officials half a century earlier had worried over the school-ing—and "Americanization"—of impoverished children of European immigrants who did not speak English, so were officials in the 1950s preoccupied with meeting the educational needs of the tens of thousands of young Puerto Ricans arriving each year. A 1951 report on Puerto Rican school children compiled by the new Mayor's Committee on Puerto Rican Affairs (MCPRA) had insisted, "The need for teachers who can speak Spanish is urgent."[23] That year, the school district employed only ten bilingual teachers; given the student population, the report asserted, the school district needed to hire approximately one thousand more.[24]

The Board of Education did not hire a thousand bilingual teachers—not even close—though it did begin recruiting trained teachers on the island for jobs in New York. In terms of educational advancement, the leadership energy of young Puerto Ricans themselves in the 1950s was far more important than the inconsistently executed strategies of city officials. In 1951 a young migrant named Antonia Pantoja, who had arrived in New York to take a job in a factory during the war and was finishing her bachelor's degree at Hunter College, helped found the first formally organized, youth-led Puerto Rican organization in New York, the Hispanic Young Adult Association (HYAA). Pantoja and her cohort wanted to inspire creative and hopeful energy in the community's young leaders. "We described this approach as one of community development instead of 'firefighting,'" recalled Pantoja.[25]

"Firefighting" was still necessary, however, as Puerto Rican children faced even more frequent prejudice and exclusion in their neighborhoods and at school than they had in the 1930s. The same year HYAA was founded, a group of Puerto Rican students from Benjamin Franklin High School wrote to the editors of the Spanish-language newspaper *El Diario*, asking that the paper publicize the intimidation and beatings they were experiencing at school, perpetrated by gang members from the adjacent Italian community. "We believe that we have the right to study without being harassed by anyone," the students wrote, "since we are American citizens and our parents pay taxes just like [the Italians] do."[26]

Firefighting and community development went hand in hand. Within a few years, Pantoja and a few of her colleagues created a new organization, the Puerto Rican Association for Community Affairs (PRACA), led by young Puerto Rican professionals and activists, although it was not officially organized to serve youth.[27] Shortly after the creation of PRACA, Pantoja, who by then had earned a master's degree in social work from New York University, helped found yet another leadership organization, the Puerto Rican Forum, designed to support both general institution building in the Puerto Rican community and the fostering of young leaders who would initiate Puerto Rican-run programs.[28] Many of the participants of these groups described them as modeled after "uplift" and "community defense" groups like the NAACP, but with a focus on the younger generation.[29] Pantoja described her goal for the Forum as "influencing policy using the language and values of democratic society": young citizens would create a new path using familiar tools.

Although this movement of youth activists was well underway before the Capeman murder in 1959, that incident, and the renewed flood of anti-Puerto Rican vitriol that followed, sparked a new wave of organizing by young leaders. Two years after the founding of the Hispanic Association Pro-Higher Education by Puerto Rican college students, members of the Puerto Rican Forum's board of directors created a youth organization that would become more influential (and long lasting) than they could have imagined. They named the organization Aspira, "to aspire." With its commitment to the teaching of Puerto Rican history and culture and to a youth-run leadership structure, Aspira stood out as a challenger of the status quo within New York's social service and education networks.[30] Though sometimes accused by more radical Puerto Rican activists of promoting an assimilationist agenda, Aspira served as an early model of cultural pride and community autonomy and an incubator of youth activism, all of which proved central to Puerto Rican community organizing in the 1960s and beyond.[31]

"Political mobilization of the discontented"

Building leadership was an essential starting point for community development, and access to basic educational opportunities had to be part of the equation. The struggle for an adequate education by Puerto Rican parents and children gained powerful momentum in the 1960s, when concerns over equality in education brought Puerto Ricans and African Americans together in civil rights collaborations that would define the experience of young Puerto Ricans in that decade. The most well-documented collaboration in this period emerged from a shared resentment among parents and community leaders about the board of education's failure to take adequate steps toward integration—nearly ten years after the Supreme Court's 1954 decision that "separate but equal" schools were unconstitutional. In 1963 Gilberto Gerena Valentín, an activist in labor and civil rights groups since the 1950s and head of the recently founded National Association of Puerto Rican Civil Rights (NAPRCR), worked with African American civil rights leaders Rev. Milton Galamison and Bayard Rustin to plan a citywide school boycott. Their goal was to force the New York City Board of Education to take seriously the problems of resource inequality and segregation of schools in black and Puerto Rican neighborhoods.

Puerto Rican and African American communities across the city embraced the plan. Migration Division officials organized meetings to encourage parents and other community members to support the boycott, and Gerena Valentín and Galamison mobilized their fellow New York activists. The boycott commanded national press coverage and was by all measures a success: 45 percent of students and 8 percent of teachers stayed out of school, and twenty-six hundred picketers marched in front of three hundred of the city's 860 schools in spite of twenty-degree temperatures. Counting the number of total participants—those who marched and those who stayed home—Rustin called it the largest civil rights protest in the nation's history.[32] Gerena Valentín staged a follow-up event a month later, a two-thousand-person silent march from City Hall in Manhattan to the board of education office in Brooklyn to demand improvement of facilities for Puerto Rican schoolchildren. At the rally that followed, Galamison joined Gerena Valentín in addressing the crowd, along with a dozen other speakers, including leaders of Jewish and labor organizations and Migration Division head Joseph Montserrat. According to the *New York Times* in its front-page coverage, some of the Puerto Rican speakers "shouted that the Puerto Rican civil rights movement had come of age."[33]

While parents, children, and other residents of black and Puerto Rican neighborhoods did see the 1964 school boycott as a success in terms of the publicity they generated for the issue of inequality in schools, that event was clearly just another battle in the ongoing struggle for civil rights in education. The de facto segregation in northern urban schools was intransigent and produced many layers of disadvantage for black and Puerto Rican students. In 1966 half the students in New York's schools were African American (30 percent) or Puerto Rican (20 percent), but both groups comprised only a tiny proportion (3.6 percent and 1.6 percent, respectively) of those graduating from academic high schools. The vast majority attended schools where there were a quarter the number of licensed teachers as

Foreign, Dark, Young, Citizen • 223

at "top" (white) schools, and where teachers earned substantially lower salaries.[34] Such statistics showed, said protesters, the impact of inequality: black and Puerto Rican students were being inadequately supported by the school system.

With these frustrations motivating them, activists redoubled their organizing efforts, asserting that what black and Puerto Rican children really needed was not integration but rather the radical restructuring of the city's schools. The push by community activists for greater participation in the leadership, decision making, and everyday operation of their communities' schools intensified in 1966. That fall, parents and activists protested the outcome of a newly created intermediate school (I.S. 201) in East Harlem, which the board of education had promised would attract an integrated student body. Many of the picketers pointed out that the school was only "integrated" if integration was taken to mean both black and Puerto Rican students; with the school sited in the heart of East Harlem, no white parents had applied to enroll their children.[35]

As with the 1964 school boycott, leaders of national organizations offered their visible support to this new chapter in the push for equality in the schools: Stokely Carmichael of the Student Nonviolent Coordinating Committee joined the demonstrators, as did members of the Black Panthers, along with representatives of community organizations like MEND (Massive Economic Neighborhood Development) and the East Harlem Tenants Council, founded by a Puerto Rican man in his mid-twenties. The activists' goals could only be accomplished, they said, through "community control"—a rallying cry that activists borrowed from a phrase popularized by Stokely Carmichael around the same time: "what we need . . . is community control of institutions." By December 1966, a group of activists expressed its frustration by staging a two-day takeover of a board of education building, calling for the "People's Board of Education."[36]

This action marked the beginning of a highly politicized movement to establish the community control of several school districts in New York City. Shortly before the board of education takeover in late 1966, Evelina Antonetty, a Puerto Rican parent and active participant in the demonstrations, founded United Bronx Parents (UBP) to organize and empower parents of schoolchildren and their families in the Puerto Rican South Bronx; UBP quickly became active in issues and communities well beyond its base.[37] Although the community control "experiment" would only last for three years before breaking down in the face of violent pushback from the powerful New York City teachers' union, those who took part in the movement had forged a model for participatory community empowerment.[38] In summarizing the early work of UBP a few years later, Evelina Antonetty stressed the importance of the "political mobilization of the discontented"—the participation by black and Puerto Rican youth and their parents—in driving forward this era of tremendous change in the city.[39]

"More meaningful dialogue"

Young Puerto Rican activists by the mid-1960s were no longer simply focused on "countering pathology and fear," as HAPHE leaders had exhorted their audience just a few years before. They were now making bigger claims for equality and were mobilizing across age groups and cultural divisions within their communities. Puerto Rican youth still carried the burden of presumptions that they were prone to delinquency and other dangerous behaviors. At least one thing had changed by the mid-1960s, though, as they stepped onto a new national stage alongside other youth, of all races, to engage in mass movements for social change: young Puerto Ricans for the first time were no longer cast as *foreign.* They had become, instead, a "national minority," not so much because the contrast with new waves of immigrants after 1965 (the social impact of that shift would not become obvious for at least a few years) but because young Puerto Ricans, making the most of their citizenship, became very visible as American political actors struggling for civil rights, often alongside African Americans, during the 1960s.

As the phenomenon of the mass social movement continued to gather strength by the mid-1960s, with ongoing civil rights campaigns plus Black Power demonstrations and early antiwar protests, so did expressions of discontent within New York's Puerto Rican communities—and in many other marginalized communities, with a majority of black and Latino residents, in other cities across the nation. In July 1967, El Barrio in East Harlem, still the city's largest Puerto Rican neighborhood, exploded in a massive riot. A young Puerto Rican man had been shot to death by an off-duty police officer who claimed the youth had been wielding a knife. Street protests developed into a full-blown riot that shook the Puerto Rican community for three days. Hundreds of community leaders organized dozens of community meetings to try to halt the violence. There were no fatalities during the riot, but there were scores of arrests and substantial property damage.

After the second day of rioting, Mayor Lindsay assembled a group of forty Puerto Rican leaders for a conference at Gracie Mansion, hoping to develop a strategy to stem the violence, both in the moment and for the future. Pressed for "answers," there was no singular cause to which the community leaders could attribute the riot. Among the most essential insights came from a twenty-four-year-old community organizer, Arnold Segarra, who emphasized the need for "more meaningful dialogue" between East Harlem youth and both police and antipoverty workers. "Tell a kid you're putting $1 million [into the community], and he says, 'That's got nothing to do with me.'" A similar perspective was expressed in a less conciliatory way by Aníbal Solivan, also twenty-four, who worked for an antipoverty organization in East Harlem. He had been invited by the Mayor to a smaller meeting of Puerto Rican community workers the day before but was not part of the Gracie

Mansion conference. Solivan criticized leaders who seemed removed from the struggles of the young people rioting in El Barrio: "That's the established power structure of the community. None of those cats was there during the weekend. They're not in the streets when they're needed. They don't relate."[40]

Throughout the following year, tensions remained high all over the city; rioting had resurfaced, though on a smaller scale, in Puerto Rican communities during the summer of 1968. (And not just in New York: riots shook Puerto Rican communities in a handful of smaller cities in New Jersey and Connecticut as well.) The New York police deployed a specialized riot unit, the Tactical Patrol Force, which caused growing resentment in the neighborhoods they descended upon at the first sign of unrest. In one leaflet distributed in the Lower East Side in July 1968, community activists proclaimed: "We are not animals . . . We do not need the Tactical Police Force in our neighborhoods to show our human dignity." A year later, the consecutive years of summer riots were a major topic of concern during New York's contentious mayoral primary race. In a meandering essay he wrote for the *New York Times* to broadcast his candidacy (alongside eight other contenders), writer Norman Mailer picked apart the city's growing sense of social breakdown, concluding that "our fix is to put the blame on the blacks and Puerto Ricans. But everybody knows that nobody can really know where the blame resides."[41]

Young African Americans and Puerto Ricans in New York and other cities rocked by riots took the measure of this "breakdown" long before white media commentators began wringing their hands about it. They confronted daily the ways that police, city officials, and other disgruntled whites blamed young blacks and Puerto Ricans for intensifying—if not causing—the era's urban social crises. In New York, young activists fought back, assembling in storefronts and back rooms and tenement apartments all around East Harlem and the Lower East Side. Organizations formed by young Puerto Ricans in the late 1960s tackled in radical ways the inequalities they perceived in housing, healthcare, and educational access.

These young activists took seriously the idea of "maximum feasible participation of the poor," as the new Community Action Programs described their collaborations with community members. Young Puerto Rican activists also worked toward the maximum feasible participation of the young. A radical social-work organization in the Lower East Side called the "Real Great Society" had gained prominence in 1967 when it started a program called the "University of the Streets." One admiring journalist noted that this program had managed to bring together "young Puerto Ricans and hippies from the Lower East Side." Within six months of its founding, Real Great Society's University of the Streets had won a large grant from the federal Office of Economic Opportunity (OEO), opened branches in several locations in the Lower East Side and two in East Harlem, and served thirty-six hundred people for classes ranging from karate to photography to Puerto Rican and

African American history. Within a couple of years, the Young Lords Organization emerged, engaging in similar projects of radical community building—including, famously, the occupation of an East Harlem church that the Young Lords converted into the "People's Church," as well a variety of community public-health campaigns and political protests.

Another dimension of this burgeoning Puerto Rican movement grew out of the activism on college campuses beginning in the mid-1960s. Following several years of meetings and small protests by groups at various campuses in New York, Puerto Rican and African American students at the City College of New York in 1969 organized a takeover to publicize their demands for more equal access of students of color to higher education. One of the key demands of the protesters was the creation of degree-granting programs in Black studies and Puerto Rican studies. Puerto Rican activists wanted to see greater acknowledgement of Puerto Rican issues on their campuses, more support for admissions of Puerto Rican and other poor students to CUNY colleges, and a commitment to teaching Puerto Rican history and culture at the university level. Protesters gained momentum in achieving these goals from a growing national trend: throughout the late 1960s and early 1970s, students on diverse campuses around the country made successful demands for programs in Black studies, Chicano studies, and Third World studies.[42]

In New York City, guided by savvy and determined student protesters and supportive faculty and community allies, CUNY administrators authorized the creation of Black studies and Puerto Rican studies programs or departments at seventeen of the nineteen senior college and community college campuses between 1969 and 1973 and founded several new community colleges in poor and underserved areas of the city. Hostos Community College, founded in 1970 in the Bronx, was the first of these schools geared primarily toward Puerto Ricans. The Center for Puerto Rican Studies, the nation's first research center dedicated to scholarship on Puerto Ricans, was founded at another CUNY school, Hunter College, in 1973.

The creation of these programs did not just change the opportunities for Puerto Rican students to "study themselves," as one critic complained during the takeover in 1969. Creating Puerto Rican studies programs involved the very political act of demanding that Puerto Rican history and culture (and, likewise, Black and Chicano histories and cultures) be acknowledged both within and beyond the academy. Supreme Court Justice Sonia Sotomayor recounted in her memoir, *My Beloved World*, how she had solicited the help of history professor Peter Winn to design an independent study course on Puerto Rican history for a group of undergraduates at Princeton in the early 1970s, since none then existed. This was "taking ownership of Puerto Rican history," as one of the founders of the Center for Puerto Rican Studies later put it, a process by which activists challenged the historical silence about their people and also made this history accessible to people outside the academy, both within and beyond Puerto Rican communities.[43] In so doing, these young activists proclaimed themselves full citizens with the right to a visible history.

Inside the academy these programs provided a remedy for many years of academic misinformation and distortion of Puerto Ricans' lived experience in the United States. All through the 1950s and 1960s, respected academics, many of them liberals sympathetic to the plight of "minorities," had published observations about Puerto Ricans that focused almost exclusively on their deficits. Even the more nuanced work tended to be based on thin data, causing many well-meaning liberal scholars to misrepresent their subjects. Historian Oscar Handlin, for example, explored Puerto Ricans' socioeconomic stagnation in his 1959 book *The Newcomers*, which cited Puerto Ricans' political apathy, their lack of "associational life," and the "tragically rare" instances of Puerto Ricans who were "willing and able to exercise creative leadership."[44]

Just over a decade later, as the movement of Puerto Rican youth was still exploding in 1970, sociologist Nathan Glazer and Senator Daniel Patrick Moynihan wrote a new introduction to their 1963 book *Beyond the Melting Pot*, in which they pilloried young Puerto Ricans for their "militant" actions at CUNY the year before—and at the same time wrote the students off as insignificant historical actors, incapable of developing their own political analysis. "The radical white college youth, who are now so influential in the mass media, will try to convince [Puerto Rican youth] that they are 'colonized.'" In fact, the political education of the nation's youth was often happening in the opposite direction: young Puerto Rican activists shared their persuasive critiques about American colonialism with leaders of Students for a Democratic Society and other mostly white campus organizations in countless forums and publications throughout this era.[45]

This moment marked the full flourishing of a Puerto Rican civil rights movement, and it was born out of the experience of the community's youth—many of whom grew up with stories of parents and grandparents who, as students and young adults themselves, had pushed back against marginalization in their own time. Young Puerto Ricans who came of age in the 1950s and 1960s inaugurated a new era of civil rights activism, built on a foundation of both radical and mainstream political dreams. Whether staging the takeover of an ailing Bronx hospital to demand better service for its largely Puerto Rican patients, as the Young Lords did in 1970, or working to fight for bilingual education and voting rights in state and federal courts, as the lawyers of the Puerto Rican Legal Defense and Education Fund began to do a couple of years later, young Puerto Ricans continually reinforced the decades-old lesson that they must serve as their own advocates. For those who could not count on fair and equal treatment, claiming their rights as US citizens and members of the American nation was part of the process of coming of age.

228 · LORRIN THOMAS

Notes

1. I use "foreign" here in a cultural rather than a legal sense. Puerto Rico is widely considered a country separate from the United States in that it possesses a distinct culture and history, yet it is at the same time part of the US—an "unincorporated territory" from 1898 to 1952, and thereafter a self-governing commonwealth.

2. The vast majority of Puerto Rican migrants settled in New York City until about 1950, when the diaspora began to spread rapidly to other cities and regions.

3. Charles S. Brown Jr. to William Jay Schieffelin, Esq., March 21, 1935, LaGuardia Papers, reel 76, New York City Municipal Reference and Research Center.

4. Vito Marcantonio, "Puerto Rican Children in New York Schools," *Congressional Record* vol. 80, part 10 (74th Congress, 2nd session) June 19, 1936, 10310; Pedro A. Cebollero, Assistant Commissioner of Education, San Juan, "Reactions of Puerto Rican Children in New York City to Psychological Tests" (San Juan: Bureau of Supplies, Printing, and Transportation, 1936).

5. Henry W. Thurston, *The Education of Youth as Citizens: Progressive Changes in our Aims and Methods* (New York: Richard R. Smith, 1946), 37–38.

6. See Elazar Barkan, *The Retreat of Scientific Racism: Changing Concepts of Race in Great Britain and the United States between the World Wars* (New York: Cambridge University Press, 1993); David K. Yoo, "Testing Assumptions: IQ, Japanese Americans, and the Model Minority Myth in the 1920s and 1930s" in Sucheng Chan, ed. *Remapping Asian American History* (Lanham, Md.: Altamira, 2003), and George Sánchez, *Becoming Mexican America: Ethnicity, Culture, and Identity in Chicano Los Angeles* (New York: Oxford University Press, 1995), 259.

7. See Gerald Meyer, *Vito Marcantonio, Radical Politician 1902–1954* (Albany: State University of New York Press, 1989), 11–13.

8. Minutes of the Racial Committee Conference, February 7, 1936, Covello Papers, series VI, box 51, folder 15, Balch Institute, Historical Society of Pennsylvania; "Results Based on the Henmon-Nelson Tests of Mental Ability," February 1936, Covello papers, series VI, box 48, folder 30; "A Report of the Special Committee on Immigration and Naturalization of the Chamber of Commerce of the State of New York . . .," December 31, 1935, Covello papers, series VIII, box 74, folder 3.

9. "New York's Sorest Spot," *New York Tribune*, November 21, 1938.

10. Rita Mellone to Leonard Covello, October 1, 1945; Ralph De Donato to Leonard Covello, October 1, 1945, series VI, box 54, folder 12; Leonard Covello, "We Hold These Truths," unpublished manuscript, n.d. [1938], box 5, folder 13; Leonard Covello to BFHS students, regarding reaction to "clashes," October 26, 1938, box 51, folder 13; Covello, "An Experiment in Building Concepts of Racial Democracy," 1941, box 56, folder 10, all Covello Papers.

11. See Mauricio Mazón, *The Zoot Suit Riots: The Psychology of Symbolic Annihilation* (Austin: University of Texas Press, 1984), and Schneider, *Vampires, Dragons, and Egyptian Kings: Youth Gangs in Postwar New York* (Princeton, N.J.: Princeton University Press, 2001), 55–77.

12. Richard Perlman, *Delinquency Prevention: The Size of the Problem* (Washington, DC: GPO, 1960), 3. Children's Bureau of the US Department of Health, Education, and Welfare, *The Children's Bureau and Juvenile Delinquency* (Washington, DC: GPO, 1960), 32.

Foreign, Dark, Young, Citizen · 229

13. Erwin Schepses, "Puerto Rican Delinquent Boys in New York City," *Social Science Review* 23 (March 1949): 51–61.

14. Board of Education of New York City, "The Puerto Rican Study, 1953–57" (1958), 120–21, New York City Municipal Reference and Research Center. Clarence Senior, "The Newcomer Speaks Out," National Conference on Social Welfare, June 1960, series X, box 103, folder 2, Covello Papers. "Puerto Rican Unit Reports Lag Here," February 7, 1954, *New York Times*; Spanish-American Youth Bureau Conference Program, "Topic: Youth of Hispanic Origin and Delinquency," February 26, 1955, and Spanish-American Youth Bureau Conference Program, "Topic: Community Efforts in Combating the Development of Juvenile Delinquency among Puerto Rican and Hispanic Youth," February 25, 1956, box 102, folder 13, Covello Papers. Presentation by Joseph Montserrat at Institute of the Welfare Council, Chicago, October 17, 1957, series X, box 109, folder 20, Covello Papers; "Muñoz Niega Juventud Boricua Sea Culpable de Crímenes y Violencia," October 8, 1957, *El Diario*, 2.

15. Christopher Rand, *The Puerto Ricans* (New York: Oxford University Press, 1958), 90–91.

16. "NAACP Meeting to Protest Increasing 'Police Brutality,'" *Amsterdam News*, August 5, 1950.

17. "1,400 City Police Shifted to Fight on Youth Crimes," *New York Times*, September 1, 1959.

18. "Víctimas De Pandillas Juveniles Simbolizan Fracaso De Comunidad," August 30, 1959, 3; "Juventud Sigue Bañando En Lágrimas Los Rostros y Corazones De Madres," and "Panilleros Juveniles Viven En Un Mundo Aparte Y Hasta Tienen Su Propio Lenguaje," September 1, 1959, 9; "'Ganga' dice: Queremos Ser Buenos, Pero Nadie Nos Ayuda y Todos Nos Persiguen," September 2, 1959, 5.

19. "Puerto Rican Community Takes Initiative to Combat Juvenile Delinquency in New York," press release, Council of Puerto Rican and Spanish-American Organizations of Greater New York, September 8, 1959, series X, box 106, folder 4, Covello Papers; "Civic Contribution by Puerto Ricans," *New York Herald-Tribune*, September 8, 1959; "Responsible Action," *New York World-Telegram and Sun*, September 11, 1959; and "Ethnology and Crime," *Washington Post* and *Times Herald*, September 11, 1959, series X, box 106, folder 4, Covello Papers. Senior, "The Newcomer Speaks Out," National Conference on Social Welfare, June 1960, p.14, series X, box 103, 2, Covello Papers.

20. The Senate subcommittee on juvenile delinquency was established in 1953. Joseph Montserrat, "Statement for the record of the US Senate Subcommittee to investigate Juvenile Delinquency," Septembr 25, 1959, series X, box 106, folder 4, Covello Papers.

21. "Liebowitz Sued on Jury's Inquiry," *New York Times*, November 6, 1959.

22. Puerto Rican Association for Community Affairs, Second Puerto Rican Youth Conference, "We the New Yorkers Contribute," 1960, series X, box 102, folder 10, Covello Papers.

23. MCPRA, "The Puerto Rican Pupils in the Public Schools of New York City," 18, and Committee of the Association of Assistant Superintendents, "A Program of Education for Puerto Ricans in New York City," 1947, 103, both reprinted in Francesco Cordasco, ed., *Bilingual Education in New York City: A Compendium of Reports* (New York: Arno, 1978).

24. Cordasco, *Bilingual Education*.

25. Antonia Pantoja, *Memoir of a Visionary*, (Houston, Tex.: Arte Público, 2002), 74, 98; José Morales, interview with the author, December 13, 2007.

26. "Pandillas italianas atropellan y roban a estudiantes hispanos," November 2, 1951, *El Diario*, 1; "5 Puerto Rican Students Attacked by Members of the Italian 'Red Wings'" *El Diario*, January 17 1952, 2.

27. Pantoja, *Memoir of a Visionary,* 76–77.

28. Ibid., 76–77. See also Virginia Sánchez-Korrol, "Building the New York Puerto Rican Community, 1945–65: A Historical Interpretation," 11–12, in Gabriel Haslip-Viera, Angelo Falcón, and Felix V. Matos Rodriguez, eds., *Boricuas in Gotham* (Princeton, N.J.: Markus Wiener, 2005).

29. History Task Force, Centro de Estudios Puertorriqueños, *Labor Migration under Capitalism* (New York: Monthly Review Press, 1980), 152; José Morales interview, December 13, 2007.

30. Pantoja, *Memoir of a Visionary*, 103.

31. Ibid., 99; History Task Force, *Labor Migration under Capitalism,* 52.

32. "Boycott Cripples City Schools; Absences 360,000 Above Normal; Negroes and Puerto Ricans Unite," *New York Times*, February 4, 1964.

33. "1,800 Join March for Better Schools for Puerto Ricans," *New York Times*, March 2, 1964.

34. Hector Vázquez, "Puerto Rican Americans," *Journal of Negro Education* 38 (Summer 1969): 247–56.

35. "Harlem Factions United on School," *New York Times*, September 23, 1966.

36. Anthony De Jesus and Madeline Pérez, "From Community Control to Consent Decree: Puerto Ricans Organizing for Education and Language Rights in 1960s and '70s New York City," *Centro Journal* 21 (2009): 17–31.

37. In 1970, Evelina López Antonetty was a Delegate of the White House Conference on Children and Youth.

38. "The Setting of United Bronx Parents' Work: Summary Description of the South Bronx," box 2, folder 14, United Bronx Parents papers, Centro de Estudios Puertorriqueños.

39. Ibid., 323.

40. Peter Kihss, "Puerto Rican Story: A Sensitive People Erupt," *New York Times*, July 26, 1967, and Pete Hamell, "Coming of Age in Nueva York," *New York* (November 1969): 33–47.

41. "Why Are We in New York?" *New York Times*, May 18, 1969.

42. Lillian Jiménez, "Puerto Ricans and Educational Civil Rights: A History of the 1969 City College Takeover," *Centro Journal* 21 (Fall 2009): 159–75; "Black Studies Programs," *Chicago Daily Defender*, July 26, 1969.

43. Sonia Sotomayor, *My Beloved World* (New York: Knopf, 2013), 149–51; Nélida Pérez, "Two Reading Rooms and the Librarian's Office: The Evolution of the Centro Library and Archives," *Centro Journal* 21 (Fall 2009): 199–220.

44. Oscar Handlin, *The Newcomers: Negroes and Puerto Ricans in a Changing Metropolis* (Cambridge, Mass.: Harvard University Press, 1959), 111.

45. See Lorrin Thomas, *Puerto Rican Citizen: History and Political Identity in Twentieth Century New York City* (Chicago: University of Chicago Press), 225–27.

CHAPTER 11

Japanese War Brides and the Normalization of Family Unification after World War II

ARISSA H. OH

For years, conventional American immigration history traced a rise and fall in anti-Asian laws that went something like this: Congress first restricted Asian immigration by passing the 1882 Chinese Exclusion Act, then established an Asiatic Barred Zone in 1917 from which it refused migrants. Finally, at the high-water mark of immigration restriction, the 1924 Johnson-Reed Act implemented a notoriously discriminatory national-origins quota system and prohibited the migration of Asians as "aliens ineligible to citizenship."[1] After World War II, two overhauls of immigration law slowly lowered the walls against Asians: in 1952, Congress lifted the racial requirements for immigration and naturalization, which allowed Asians to migrate (albeit in very small numbers); and by removing the national-origins quota system altogether in 1965, it ushered in an unprecedented wave of immigration from Asia.

This narrative has implied a kind of fallow period between 1924 and 1965, but in fact two important and intertwined trends, usually thought of as post-1965 phenomena, actually emerged during these years: the slow dismantling of Asian exclusion, and the rise of family unification as a central principle of immigration policy. Although America's gates were indeed shut against Asians in 1924, Asian exclusion, while strict, was never absolute.[2] Cracks in the barriers against Asian immigration appeared after 1924 in the form of exceptions that recognized family ties, particularly marital relationships. The steady accretion of these small-scale exemptions admitted increasingly larger numbers of Asian immigrants and contributed to the reforms of 1952 and 1965.[3] The not-so-absolute ban on Asian immigration after 1924 suggests that we might reperiodize and recharacterize anti-Asian immigration restriction. Rather than describing 1924 as a moment when Asians were summarily excluded, it may be more illuminating to focus on how state selection allowed for "conditional inclusion."[4] In this light we can see that laws against Asian immigration were "not about erecting impenetrable borders" but calibrating them "so that they were porous to some things while remaining barriers to others." This was a case, then, of a gatekeeping nation carving out "privileged exemptions" for certain Asian immigrants based on class, education, gender—and family ties.[5]

At the same time anti-Asian immigration laws eroded between 1924 and 1965, the principle of family unification emerged as a central pillar of immigration policy. This is an aspect of immigration reform that is much remarked on but not well studied. Although many scholars cite the 1965 Immigration and Nationality Act (INA, also known as the Hart-Celler Act) as the law that made family unification a cornerstone of the US immigration regime, Congress first codified a commitment to family unification almost fifty years earlier, in the Immigration Act of 1917. The acknowledgment of family unification as a goal of US immigration policy was not new. Family unification had been available to racially eligible immigrants, by custom and by law, for decades before 1917; and after 1917 Congress reinforced the US commitment to family unification in the immigration laws of 1921 and 1924. What *was* new about the 1952 INA (also known as the McCarran-Walter Act) is that it enshrined the principle of family unification *regardless of race*.[6] This is especially notable given that the same law also preserved quotas based on nationality and race despite significant opposition, including a presidential veto.

This chapter explores the question of how family unification *regardless of race* became normalized in American immigration policy by examining the case of Japanese war brides after World War II.[7] By tracing the legislative reforms that made Japanese war bride migration possible, as well as how journalists, filmmakers, and novelists sought acceptance for these women by positioning them as ideal mothers, wives, immigrants, and citizens, we can see how the notion of family unification expanded to include formerly racially inadmissible spouses, and how war brides, their husbands, and their supporters redrew the racial boundary around what constituted a legitimate, acceptable American family. A convergence of factors and considerations persuaded Congress to pass race-blind family unification laws: moral arguments about keeping families together and rewarding citizen-soldiers for their service; lobbying by Asian American groups; and the geopolitical imperatives of the Cold War, which required the United States to prove itself as a global leader of democracy and win friends in Asia. Against the political and social backdrop produced by these forces, Japanese war bride migration helped to drive the legal and cultural normalization of family unification—including interracial family unification—in American law and culture.

Family Ties versus Racial Exclusion

Congress changed immigration laws after World War II to admit racially undesirable Japanese war brides for two main reasons. First, supporters of war bride laws positioned them as rewards for deserving citizen soldiers.[8] It seemed obvious that men who had selflessly and heroically served their country should have the right to bring their wives and children to the United States.[9] Servicemen saw themselves as "deserving war heroes" whose rewards should include the right to have their wives with them, like the corporal in Japan who wrote, "The way I look at it my citizen's rights are to let me marry who I want to."[10] Second, servicemen's demands to bring their Japanese wives home forced Congress to resolve a fundamental tension in American immigration law and policy, between family unification and racial exclusion. The US immigration service and federal courts had historically demonstrated a tendency to facilitate family unification even before the principle was codified as law in 1921.[11] But family unification was not consistently available to Asians.[12] Laws allowing Japanese war bride migration represent the first time in US history that immigration laws explicitly and systematically prioritized family unification over racial exclusion.

Japanese war bride laws have to be understood in the larger political context of immigration reform during and after World War II. A coalition of Asian and US state officials, Asian American community leaders, and their white American allies campaigned to end Asian exclusion.[13] They had some powerful forces on their side: Congress members' attitudes toward immigration were swayed by Cold War considerations—especially the need to win friends overseas by demonstrating the racial liberalism of the United States, the leader of the free world.[14] Yet those imperatives were not enough to convince Congress to eliminate the national-origins quota system or completely end Asian exclusion. At a time when a comprehensive overhaul of immigration laws seemed out of reach, reformers had to be satisfied with more piecemeal achievements such as the 1943 Magnuson Act, which ended Chinese exclusion, and the 1946 law that gave Indians and Filipinos the right to immigrate and naturalize. The Japanese American Citizens League (JACL) wanted Congress to give the Japanese the right to immigrate and naturalize. They had to settle for Japanese war bride laws instead.

Chinese wives were the first Asian women to benefit from the erosion of anti-Asian immigration laws in the face of family ties. The Act of 1930 allowed Chinese women who had married Chinese men with US citizenship before 1924 to enter the United States; under this law, 607 Chinese wives were admitted between 1931 and 1940.[15] Chinese women were also the first Asian wives to enter the United States after World War II, under the War Brides Act of 1945. This law, passed in response to the demands of thousands of servicemen, allowed US citizens to bring foreign spouses and children to the United States on a nonquota basis, meaning they would not be charged against the annual quota set for their country of birth. Chinese were the only Asian spouses who could migrate under the War Brides Act thanks to the 1943 repeal of Chinese exclusion; other Asians were still inadmissible.[16] Finally, the Act of August 9, 1946, allowed all Chinese wives to immigrate on a nonquota basis.[17] Backers of the law pitched it as something that would benefit Chinese American men, and they emphasized that Chinese were "good citizens" and "good soldiers" who deserved to have the same right to bring their wives as other Americans did.[18] They also reassured Congress that only a small number of Chinese women would take advantage of the new law.[19]

Although they are part of the same movement toward the end of Asian exclusion, Chinese wife migration differed significantly from the later migration of Asian military brides. Only 7,449 Chinese wives came to the United States between 1945 and 1950, a relatively small number. Given how many more wives came from other Asian countries in the decades to come, Japanese, Korean, Vietnamese, or Filipino women came to represent the war bride in a way that Chinese women did not. Chinese wives were also mostly in intraracial marriages with Chinese American men. This set them apart from later war bride migrations, which involved mainly interracial couples. Additionally, laws permitting Chinese wife migration reunified already-married couples—some had been married for several years—whereas laws facilitating the migration of other Asian war brides prevented separation of relatively newer couples.[20]

Japan hosted hundreds of thousands of American military and government personnel during the 1945–1952 US occupation, and despite official nonfraternization policies (later lifted), American men and Japanese women embarked on romantic relationships.[21] However, Americans who hoped to bring their Japanese girlfriends or wives home to the United States faced formidable obstacles. Servicemen who wanted to marry Japanese women had to receive approval from their commanding officers and the US occupation government, known as the Supreme Commander for the Allied Powers (SCAP). Commanding officers and chaplains alike strongly counseled against such marriages and denied permission outright, justifying their denials in two ways: US immigration law deemed Japanese racially ineligible for US citizenship, meaning Japanese wives would not be able to accompany their husbands to the United States; and many states in the United States—thirty at the time—prohibited miscegenation.[22]

Despite these discouragements, servicemen pressed Congress for the right to bring their Japanese wives to the United States. Through their legislators, they filed hundreds, perhaps thousands, of private immigration bills, each of which significantly increased the Immigration and Naturalization Service's workload and slowed down the legislative process. This strategy, historically used by Americans unable to find help under existing laws, often compels Congress to make changes to public law.[23] In this case, Congress responded with the Act of July 22, 1947 (PL 213), which provided the first, albeit extremely temporary, opportunity for Japanese war brides to enter the United States. It amended the 1945 War Brides Act by adding a section that stated, "The alien spouse of an American citizen by a marriage occurring before thirty days after the enactment of this Act, *shall not be considered as inadmissible because of race*, if otherwise admissible under this act."[24] The JACL, with support from the ACLU and the American Jewish Congress, actively lobbied for the law. As it had with the 1945 War Brides Act, Congress passed the 1947 law quickly and with no debate—significant, given Congress's general hostility to immigration reform during this time. The law indicated Congress's recognition of the rights of citizen soldiers—especially white men—to choose their wives, as well as an admission that the 1945 War Brides Act was racially discriminatory.[25]

The 1947 law was not a sign of Congress's acceptance of or support for these marriages but a grudging provision. The opening it provided was unprecedented, but not generous: if a couple was not already married, they had only thirty days from the law's enactment to get married (that is, they had to marry by August 22, 1947). Given that it took a good ninety days for a serviceman to get a request to marry a white American woman through proper channels, the possibility of marrying a Japanese woman within thirty days was slim. And permission to marry did not mean permission to migrate, since wives could be denied visas on a range of grounds. Nevertheless, by the thirty-day deadline 823 couples were married, and 750 Japanese wives and five children entered the United States by December 28, 1948. In comparison, 85,896 European wives and children of American servicemen had entered the United States by that time. The JACL's Masaoka had opposed the "ridiculous" thirty-day clause, arguing it was too short, and condemned as "preposterously racist" the notion that "for one month Japanese women would be acceptable as immigrants, but after that they would revert to unwanted and unacceptable status." But even that small window was itself a compromise.[26]

In response to servicemen's continuing demands, Congress provided a second opening for Japanese war brides in 1950 (PL 717, Act of August 19, 1950).[27] Couples who had not married within the thirty days provided by the 1947 law had been separated because husbands were rotated back to the United States while their racially inadmissible Japanese wives were unable to follow them; as of 1950, a reported 760 wives and children of US servicemen had been left behind in Japan.[28] Like the 1947 law, the 1950 law provided only a temporary window, but it was a more generous one that gave couples six months, rather than thirty days, from the enactment of the law to marry. And like the 1947 law, and the 1945 War Brides Act that preceded it, the 1950 law was passed with no debate.[29]

Servicemen's requests for marriage applications "overwhelmed" SCAP officials. By the time the 1950 law expired in February 1951, "officials at American consulates throughout Japan performed 2,230 marriage ceremonies." Congress extended the 1950 law for another year, giving couples until March 1952 to marry. It did this at SCAP's request and in recognition of the servicemen who had left their girlfriends in Japan to fight in Korea and had not had the time to complete the requirements for marriage under the 1950 law. The extension also helped a new group of military wives—from Korea.[30] By early 1951 members of Congress had seemingly accepted that men stationed abroad would want to bring back foreign wives, including those deemed racially inadmissible, and were willing—if not eager—to facilitate this migration.

Congress assumed that laws permitting Chinese and Japanese bride migration would allow Americans of Chinese and Japanese descent to bring to the United States "girls of their own race."[31] The drafters of the 1947 law had explicitly expressed a desire "not to encourage marriages between United States citizen service people and racially admissible aliens," a goal shared by SCAP's legal section, which asserted that any extension of the 1947 law should be for Nisei (US-born Japanese) servicemen only because they and the Japanese shared a common "bloodline."[32] Supporters of the 1950 bill acknowledged those fearful of race mixing, assuring them that "a considerable number of the citizen servicemen involved are themselves of Japanese descent." They also made clear that the larger issue of removing the racial bar to immigration and naturalization was separate, and that the law they proposed would only apply "in this type of limited case."[33]

In the case of Japanese war bride laws, the numbers confirmed Congress's assumption that war bride laws would facilitate intraracial marriage—at least initially. Of the 823 couples married under the 1947 law, 597 (72.5 percent) included a Nisei groom, 211 (25.6 percent) a white groom, and 15 (1.8 percent) a black groom.[34] While the JACL emphasized helping Nisei men to marry Japanese women, it soon found itself defending interracial marriages, since up to three-quarters of the married couples in Japan comprised a Japanese woman and a white or black American man.[35] Under the 1950 law the racial makeup of the couples changed significantly: now 73 percent of the couples included a white groom, 12 percent a black groom, and 15 percent a Nisei.[36] Thus, laws intended to facilitate intraracial marriages between Japanese Americans and Japanese nationals paved the way for decades of interracial marriages between women from Asia and American servicemen.

Three strands of logic lay behind the post–World War II laws that admitted Japanese war brides: recognition of men's rights to have their wives and children with them, reward for military service, and the principle of family unification. In fact, the belief that soldiers deserved to be rewarded for their service was so unquestioned that there was significant support among government officials—including the secretary of state, attorney general, and some INS officials—for an early version of the 1945 War Brides Law, never enacted, which would have made war brides citizens immediately upon their marriage to American GIs. Although arguments that emphasized the rights and rewards due to citizen-soldiers in return for their service were originally more prominent, at some point between the 1947 law and the 1952 McCarran-Walter Act, family unification came to the fore. During this time, lawmakers shifted from referring to war bride laws as "temporary" to seeing them as "interim"; in other words, situating them "within an arc of policymaking" that pointed, inexorably, toward a permanent, elevated place for family unification in immigration policy.[37]

Whether they were originally rewards for citizen-soldiers or representative of an American commitment to family unification (or both), laws that admitted racially inadmissible spouses set an important precedent for immigration law. War bride laws, and the assumption that keeping families together should be a goal of immigration policy, became folded into permanent immigration law in 1952 with little discussion or opposition.[38] They legitimized, however grudgingly or inadvertently, the notion that spouses should be together regardless of racial difference, years before the Supreme Court decided in 1967 that antimiscegenation laws were unconstitutional. And they also legitimized the view of family embodied by the majority of the war bride couples: one that was not monoracial. In essence, the 1952 INA signaled that Congress had resolved the longstanding tension between family unification and racial exclusion in favor of family ties.

Although the 1952 INA eliminated race as a barrier to naturalization, thereby making both entry and citizenship possible for Japanese war brides and all Asian immigrants, it was not a complete reform. Most notably, and controversially, it maintained the national-origins quota system. With regard to Asians, the law contained features that critics considered racist: it created an Asia-Pacific triangle within which individual countries received only token quotas, and it applied a global race quota that admitted only two thousand Asian immigrants per year regardless of nationality.[39] Japan received the "embarrassingly small" annual quota of 185, but thanks to the provision for family members, spouses and children of US citizens could migrate on a nonquota basis.[40] In 1952 alone, the United States admitted 4,220 Japanese war brides. Between 1952 and 1965 thousands of Japanese war brides entered the country each year (see table 1).

238 • ARISSA H. OH

Table 1. Yearbook of Immigration Statistics 1947–65: Japanese Nationals Classified as "Wives of Citizens" Who Immigrated to the United States

Year	Number
1952	4,220
1953	2,042
1954	2,802
1955	2,843
1956	3,661
1957	5,003
1958	5,027
1959	4,568
1960	3,990
1961	3,285
1962	2,749
1963	2,771
1964	2,665
1965	2,372

"Numbers from US Commissioner of Immigration and Naturalization, Annual Reports, 1947–75, Table 6" (Washington, DC). Cited widely in sources, for example, Caroline Chung Simpson, *An Absent Presence: Japanese Americans in Postwar American Culture, 1945–1960*. (Durham, N.C.: Duke University Press, 2002). Simpson notes that these figures are considered conservative (at 213n22).

Postwar Madame Butterfly Tales

Although laws to allow the migration of Japanese war brides were intended to facilitate intraracial unions between Japanese Americans and "girls of their own race," and although a quarter of the grooms were nonwhite, it was the white groom and Japanese bride who quickly became the public face of these marriages. American filmmakers, novelists, and journalists sought to culturally and socially normalize the Japanese war bride and her interracial marriage by presenting her as a "symbol of domesticity," depicting her as a perfect wife and mother, and thus an ideal female immigrant and future citizen. Her firm adherence to American middle-class values and her cultural disappearance into the white mainstream made palatable the expansion of the "racial boundary" of the American nuclear family that was necessary to allow her inclusion in the American national family.[41]

This reframing of the Japanese war bride reflected the geopolitical repositioning of Japan after World War II. After a viciously racist war, the United States sought to rapidly transform Japan from enemy to friend in American culture. This was because the United States needed Japan as its bulwark of democracy in Asia, especially as the Cold War intensified.[42] This reversal was a highly gendered one. Americans' dominant understandings of Japan had long been impressionistic and Orientalist; by World War II, Madame Butterfly was entrenched as the emblematic representation of Japan. In this extremely influential story, an affair between a white American naval officer, Lieutenant Benjamin Franklin Pinkerton, and a Japanese geisha, Cio-Cio-San, produces a child but ends tragically, with Cio-Cio-San's suicide. Pinkerton and his white wife adopt the child and return to the United States. In line with this narrative, American cultural producers typically represented the postwar US-Japan relationship as one between a white male conqueror and subjugated Asian woman. Interracial Japanese war bride marriages made this geopolitical relationship concrete at an intimate level: at the same time the American military government figuratively husbanded Japan's entrance into the democratic, modern world, American servicemen became the actual husbands of Japanese women.

Films, novels, and media coverage depicted Japanese women in ambivalent, Orientalist ways: submissive and obedient, but also exotic, hypersexual, and sometimes diabolical.[43] The Japanese war bride posed a sexual threat to American men and women alike: she stole American men from American women, who could not compete with her special brand of Japanese hyperfemininity, and she ensnared American men to gain access to the United States. The predominant American stereotype of Japanese womanhood before World War II had been the geisha, but the surge in sex work that accompanied the arrival of thousands of occupation personnel produced a new kind of Japanese woman: the common prostitute. Most Americans had never truly comprehended the difference between a geisha and a prostitute; now they simply conflated and merged them with the Japanese war bride. The press contributed to the widely held view that many of the war brides were "barmaids, entertainers, dance-hall girls and some outright prostitutes"[44] who had preyed on lonely American men and had been devious enough to slip through US military and consular screening.[45] The assumption that foreign war brides were actually prostitutes was not specific to Japan, having emerged in connection with French war brides after World War I, but Orientalist ideas about Asian female sexuality reinforced these stereotypes.[46] They would also attach to other Asian war brides as they began to arrive. These stereotypes circulated on both sides of the Pacific. Some servicemen who had been stationed in Japan used their limited knowledge of Japan and Japanese to harass war brides they encountered in the United States.[47] Japanese and Japanese Americans also tended to see the war brides as "just street girls." For them, one war bride said, "the war bride is a synonym for prostitute."[48]

Defenders of Japanese war brides used various strategies to counter these stereotypes. Novelists and filmmakers foregrounded the purity and aristocratic origins of their war bride characters, and journalists, academics, and war brides themselves emphasized their respectable family backgrounds.[49] At a minimum, supporters of these women consistently depicted them as dainty and exceptionally well groomed.

240 • ARISSA H. OH

Cultural producers also tried to neutralize the Japanese war bride's sexual threat was by refiguring her as inherently domestic. In doing so, they paradoxically erased the war bride's perceived hypersexual, racial otherness by emphasizing that very racial otherness. The American press helped to racialize femininity and domesticity as innately Japanese traits with accounts of war brides who polished their husbands' shoes, greeted their husbands on bended knees, and bathed, massaged, and otherwise "worshipped" them.[50] Race and culture seemed to be one and the same when it came to Japanese war brides, and their subservience and servility became another thing Americans "knew" about them.[51]

Some war brides and their husbands took to print to publicly insist that they had married for love. One war bride told *Reader's Digest*: "'Because I love the man' does not seem to satisfy people. They think there must be more to it than that." A husband declared, "As to why 'our boys' marry Japanese girls, my answer is: For the very same reasons that people anywhere get married!"[52] In private, war brides spoke candidly about various other reasons for marrying: material and practical considerations, pregnancy, dreams of a better life in America, and a desire for escape or rebellion. One woman admitted that she married for the sake of her family's well-being: "Marrying an American was the only way I knew to get the support they needed." Many brides mentioned impressions of the United States as a land of abundance and comfort and of American men as being much more gallant and gentlemanly than their Japanese counterparts.[53] For others, marriage to an American was the best available option. After being raped by an American soldier, one woman resorted to prostitution, which shamed her family and ruined her chances for a proper Japanese marriage.[54] She confessed that although she did not love her husband, she accepted his proposal when she became pregnant. "I figured the sooner I could get away from my family, the better for everyone including myself." Another woman was even blunter: "My marriage . . . didn't have anything to do with loving or liking; it was more a matter of survival and escape . . . I was a social outcast and thus I no longer desired to live in Japan."[55]

Almost as soon as Japanese war brides began to arrive in the United States, scholars sought to assess their marriages; in fact, the marriages were a major driver behind academic studies of the general phenomenon of interracial marriage after World War II.[56] Researchers came to a wide range of conclusions: some found that the women were adapting well and the marriages were healthy, while others determined that Japanese war brides and their husbands had married because they were psychologically damaged.[57] But by the mid-1950s the media broadcast a largely optimistic narrative in which suburban America absorbed the Japanese war bride, defusing her racial threat and transforming her into a symbol of the attainability of American racial democracy. American novelist James Michener created the emblematic version of this story in a 1955 *Life* article featuring Frank and Sachiko Pfeiffer, a Chicago-area couple. Arriving in the United States in 1948, they had overcome racism and economic struggle to enjoy a peaceful house in the suburbs, close friendships with their white neighbors, and a restored relationship with Frank's formerly intolerant mother. The title of the article—"Pursuit of Happiness by a GI and a Japanese"—broadcast its essential purpose: to celebrate the Pfeiffers' attainment of the American dream.[58]

While the Pfeiffers had achieved success by postwar American standards of highly gendered domesticity and consumption—modern appliances, a mink coat for Sachiko—more important than economic success was their triumph over racial discrimination. At their first apartment, Sachiko had been threatened and called a "dirty Jap," so the couple was apprehensive about whether they would be accepted by their new neighbors: veterans of the Pacific war who told Michener that they had hated people of various racialized groups, especially blacks and Mexicans. Sachiko instantly won over the neighbors with her doll-like appearance and timidity. As a neighbor recalled, "She seemed so clean, so needing a friend that I started to cry." Sachiko's strict conformity to gender norms helped to compensate for her racial difference and won her the admiration of everyone around her. Indeed, like most Japanese war brides in the public eye, she was a superlative wife and mother. She encouraged her husband to return to school and supported their family in the meantime by working as a seamstress; thanks to her frugality, the Pfeiffers quickly paid down their debt and built a house of their own. She and the neighbor women bonded through feminine rituals of childcare and housecleaning while the men shared their tools and labor as they built their homes side by side.[59]

While opponents of Asian immigration had long argued that Asians' inability or unwillingness to assimilate justified and even necessitated their exclusion, Japanese war brides like Sachiko demonstrated that some Asians, at least, were actually highly assimilable. One sign of this was the marriages themselves: by marrying white American men, these women were seen as willing to become totally American. It also helped that war brides migrated in a pattern different from earlier Japanese immigrants: rather than settling in ethnic enclaves, which many non-Japanese saw as a sign of unwillingness to assimilate, war brides entered as members of American families and lived scattered across the country.

Feature articles in mainstream news outlets presented brides schools in Japan as proof of war brides' commitment to becoming ideal American wives and mothers. These schools, which were run by the Red Cross and staffed by volunteers— mainly the wives of American military or businessmen—were designed to equip Japanese war brides to smoothly and rapidly assimilate into American society. The schools offered a varied program that included lessons in American history and government; child care and feeding; clothing, good grooming, and etiquette; shopping; and cooking. In short, Japanese war brides received an intensive course in American domesticity and respectability, and were modernized and civilized in the process. Media coverage emphasized how their skills as wives and mothers radically transformed Japanese war brides from unassimilable due to their race to supremely assimilable, ideal future citizens.[60]

It is important not to overstate the importance of the brides' schools. Although they were an important ideological site and valuable source of propaganda, most Japanese war brides did not attend them.[61] Japanese war brides were lauded for displaying many of the characteristics prized by midcentury American domestic ideology: thrift, skillful household management, and industriousness. However, most Japanese brides probably did not gain these skills via American tutelage. Instead, many who came of age in the 1940s and 1950s had grown up in the straitened circumstances created by Japan's wars in Asia. Their ability to save money or to make do with available resources was more likely born of necessity, not brides' schools.

Two kinds of postwar Madame Butterfly tales emerged about Japanese war brides in the 1950s. The first, gloomy version was simply an update of Madame Butterfly except that the Japanese wife did not die like the original Madame Butterfly, but returned to Japan.[62] This was the story illustrated by real-life tragedies like the war bride in Chicago who killed her child, attempted suicide, and ultimately went back home.[63] These early narratives aligned with negative scholarly assessments of these marriages. Portrayals of unwholesome war bride marriages mitigated war brides' racial and sexual threat, assuring skeptics that unhealthy marriages were bound to fall apart and that the women would not remain in the United States. On the other hand, Sachiko Pfeiffer and others like her represented a second, progressive version of the Madame Butterfly tale, in which a desexualized, hyperdomestic war bride overcame racism to find acceptance in her new extended family, community, and nation. Likewise, the community overcame its justifiable but misinformed hostility toward her and made her one of their own. Her story assured her adopted country that it was correct to envision itself as a democracy that allowed all people equal access to the American dream, and that it could make the changes necessary to live up to its creed. The Pfeiffers' typical American suburb—with its Irish, Italians, Lutherans, Catholics, war veterans, and housewives—had proved its racial tolerance by embracing the "little Japanese girl," and America could do the same. Indeed, the neighborhood itself perfectly illustrated the colorblindness that was such a crucial component of postwar American liberalism, for it accepted Sachiko's racial and cultural difference by denying its existence. Everyone on the block showered Sachiko when her son was born, but a neighbor was quick to emphasize, "not a person . . . gave anything because Sachiko was a Japanese. We all gave because she was such a good human being."[64]

The uplifting Madame Butterfly stories that became dominant beginning in the middle of the 1950s confronted America's reputation for racism either by denying racism's existence outright or by showing that it could be defeated. While Sachiko Pfeiffer had endured epithets and threats, many war bride couples reported that they had never encountered racism or anti-Japanese sentiment. A war bride declared in *Reader's Digest* that American prejudice was "really a phantom." One man wrote in *The American Mercury* that he had had a chip on his shoulder when he had brought his wife home to the United States, but that "the only sideways looks that have been cast at her have been looks of admiration." He confessed to feeling ashamed for having doubted his country.[65] A former Japan missionary interpreted the good treatment of the war brides as proof of America's growing racial egalitarianism. "Apparently, we Americans are losing our race prejudice," he exulted. America's embrace of these women also served the country's Cold War agenda by strengthening relations with Japan, the United States' most important Asian ally.[66] In fact, white men and their Japanese wives "came to be seen as brave challengers of lamentable, and increasingly outdated, structures of American racism."[67]

In two important ways, the positive postwar Madame Butterfly tale reassured Americans that the racial situation was really not so bad. It provided a way for Americans to think about racial and cultural pluralism, but without having to confront the implications of impending black-white racial integration. Melrose Park, the suburb that so embraced Sachiko Pfeiffer, was near Oak Park, which had been the site of violence in 1950 when a black man moved in. One of Sachiko's neighbors had been raised to hate blacks but had learned to accept a Chinese family she had met a few years prior to meeting Sachiko, whom she instantly embraced. These comparisons suggest that the Japanese woman represented a racial midpoint between white and black; by accepting her, white Americans could claim some progress on racial problems. They also reflect how Japanese war brides both benefited from and contributed to the transformation of Asian Americans from not-white to not-black that was such an important part of the refiguring of Asianness that occurred after World War II.[68]

At the same time, the Japanese war bride offered an alternative symbol of Japan to Americans who did not want to think of Japanese Americans they had incarcerated.[69] This reluctance to confront Japanese internment might also explain why cultural producers focused so much on Japanese-white intermarriage rather than Japanese-Nisei marriages, which were, after all, the original impetus for the Japanese war bride laws. It was also true that in the intraracial Japanese war bride marriages, nationality differences were invisible, so there was nothing to celebrate. More important, they could not embody and underscore the new US-Japan friendship in same way a racially different husband and wife could. An African American man and his Japanese wife could not symbolize this alliance either because the

244 · ARISSA H. OH

black soldier was not as unmistakably American, as perfect a symbol of America, as the white soldier. In fact, in searching for the perfect test case to challenge miscegenation laws before the Supreme Court, civil rights groups had in mind as their ideal couple a white combat veteran and his Japanese or Korean wife. This pairing (as opposed to a black-white couple) would allow them to sidestep more controversial issues such as school desegregation.[70] Positioned in this way among whites, blacks, and Japanese Americans, the Japanese war bride was a sort of neutral thought zone, where white Americans could celebrate their racial liberalism without the discomfort of considering the more difficult challenges of integrating blacks or re-integrating Japanese Americans.[71]

Japanese women married to African American men hardly appeared in the postwar studies conducted by academics and social service agencies, and only the black press paid them much attention. The available evidence suggests that they experienced rejection from other war brides, Japanese Americans, and African Americans. Their absence from war bride networks no doubt resulted from racism: some women with Nisei or white husbands would not socialize with women married to black men, and some nonblack husbands forbade their wives from interacting with the wives of black men. The mainstream media likely did not focus on them because their struggles were uncomfortable reminders of the racism that remained prevalent in American society. Their numbers were small and their presence little remarked upon, these women seem to have vanished from the historical record most of all.[72]

In both the negative and positive versions of the postwar Madame Butterfly tale the Japanese war bride disappeared, either through repatriation or assimilation. But she did not disappear without a trace, since she, like the original Madame Butterfly, left her mixed-race child behind. Although sociological understandings of race mixture had emerged in the 1920s and 1930s to challenge the biological views of the nineteenth century, and eugenics had been largely discredited by the end of World War II, scientific views of race and race mixing lingered.[73] In the self-consciously racially liberal climate of postwar America some scholars, cultural producers, and ordinary citizens endorsed racial mixing with scientific theories of "hybrid vigor," the idea that "a crossing of strains—in dogs, cattle, horses or people" would produce superior offspring.[74] Some predicted that interbreeding would eventually erase racial difference and end race problems altogether.[75] Cold War politics also encouraged antiracist Americans to recast the mixed-race child, from maladjusted and "marginal" to a symbol of diversity, globalization, multiculturalism, and the promise of interracial harmony.[76] For them, these children were figures of hope.

Mainstream magazine and newspaper articles about war brides featured photographs of mixed-race children but included little commentary about them, suggesting the relative public acceptance of these children. There are several reasons

Americans might have found mixed-race Japanese children bearable. First, postwar Americans were developing a certain familiarity with mixed-race Asian babies. As US troops poured into Asia and had sexual encounters with local women, Americans at home became accustomed to images of mixed-race "GI babies" or "occupation babies."[77] Mainstream US media treated these children sympathetically, and many Americans identified with them and expressed a sense of responsibility for them because of their American paternity.[78] Second, a paradoxical understanding of race and racial mixture helped to whiten Japanese-white children. On the one hand, the principle of hypodescent dictated that the race of a mixed-race child followed that of the parent of the "lesser" race, meaning that children with white American fathers and Japanese mothers were Japanese. But this biological understanding of race coexisted with a contradictory cultural understanding of race, which asserted that the right environment could make Japanese-white children more American—that is to say, whiter.[79] A hint that Japanese-white children were perceived through this second, cultural lens, could be seen in the US Army's approach to mixed-race children during World War II. Under the mixed-marriage policy, so-called "mixed-blood" Japanese children who were at least 50 percent white and had white fathers could be released from internment camps if their home environments were found to be sufficiently "American" or "Caucasian" (with these terms used as synonyms).[80] Third, the couples who produced most of these children—Japanese women and white men—aligned with the gendered geopolitics of the time, and with racial and gender hierarchies that reserved sexual access to women (of all races) for white men only. Given that American opposition to Asian-white miscegenation stemmed partly from historic fears of Oriental males seducing or raping white women, children with Japanese fathers and white mothers would no doubt have been more problematic.[81] Fourth, in the quickly shifting postwar racial landscape of the United States, Asians were moving from not-white to not-black;[82] this, plus their white paternity, put Japanese-white children affirmatively on the not-black side of the color line. Finally, the one-drop rule removed ambiguity about Japanese-black children, making it simple to classify them as black. Thus, neither Asian-white nor Asian-black children undermined the racial order and were therefore tolerable.

When American journalists did discuss war brides' children, it was to provide examples of acceptance. The American Consul at Tokyo had "read thousands of letters concerning mixed marriages" but none "objected to the entry of an Oriental daughter-in-law or Eurasian grandchildren." A war bride in South Dakota received neighbors who had come for miles around for their first glimpse of a Japanese baby. Another reported that her twin daughters were a bridge between her and her neighbors: "They all loved the babies and it seemed to help us all get acquainted."[83] The majority of Japanese war brides and their non-Japanese husbands pursued strategies to help their children to blend in as much as possible: they gave their children English names, spoke to them exclusively in English, ate only American food, and maintained culturally Anglo-American homes. Perhaps because of these decisions, they anticipated that their sons and daughters would face little, if any, racial discrimination. Researchers echoed this confidence, even predicting in some cases that the children who were not overly Asian looking would face few problems.[84] Notably, these households contradicted old and prevailing ideas of mothers as the primary transmitters of culture. They also happened to fit the definition of what the wartime mixed-marriage policy had idealized: American/Caucasian family environments that erased Japanese ethnicity by erasing Japanese culture.[85]

The message of all these stories about Japanese war brides and their children was that what made these women excellent immigrants was they had "no discernible impact on the US," which is exactly what reformers had promised even as they worked to end Asian exclusion.[86] Sachiko Pfeiffer embodied this ideal in her eagerness to melt into her new American home. On the topic of marriage prospects for her two young children, Sachiko reflected, "Maybe my children want marry pure Japanese. Same by me. Maybe they more happy they marry pure Caucasian. I like same-same. I content to lose my Japanese blood stream in America. I gonna die in America. This is my home forever."[87] Sachiko assured readers that Japanese-white racial mixing would result not in a disrupting, destabilizing hybridity but in the gradual merging and dissolving of her threatening racial difference into the larger American body. This Japanese war bride thus promised America that it had the capacity to assimilate women like her, not just culturally but by literally incorporating her blood. On a symbolic level, this image suggested how easily foreigners might assimilate into American society and naturalized it as an organic process. It also reaffirmed the strength and durability of whiteness, its ability to absorb Asian blood without degenerating. Both the racially different Japanese war bride and her mixed-race children were firmly enclosed within the traditional, patriarchal, middle-class Cold War nuclear family, in which the white father and surrounding (white) American society was powerful enough to ensure the management and ultimately the absorption and disappearance of their racial difference.[88]

Conclusion

At a time when mixed-status families, deportation, unaccompanied child migrants, and border walls are daily conversation topics, and lawmakers wrestle with the enormous problem of immigration reform, the notion that US immigration law should prioritize keeping families together nonetheless endures as a bedrock assumption of both American politicians and the American public. While Congress made family unification part of formal immigration policy just one hundred years ago, and family unification regardless of race even more recently, politicians and policymakers treat it as if it were a time-honored practice that has existed since the nation's founding. Advocates argue that family members of US citizens bring important economic benefits to the country through their labor and entrepreneurship, and that allowing citizens to have their families with them creates a more stable, happy, and productive citizenry. They also argue, as they did with war brides, that immigrants who come to join US citizen family members assimilate and integrate better into American society. Finally, supporters of family-based immigration policies also argue that this kind of immigration is a reflection of true American values, that family preferences embody America's unique respect for family values.

Family unification has, however, become increasingly controversial. The crafters of the 1965 INA had not anticipated that the law, and its family preferences, would admit unprecedented numbers of migrants from Asia and Latin America. Critics concerned about the changing racial makeup of the country began attacking family preferences in the 1980s while fears about undocumented immigration, national security, and the United States' ability to compete internationally have prompted others to call for Congress to drastically narrow family unification provisions and increase skill-based immigration instead.[89] Proposals include eliminating preferences for all but nuclear family members, meaning that parents, siblings, and adult children of US citizens and permanent residents would no longer receive preferential treatment.

In this sense, we see a move away from the expansions of the postwar period in which Japanese war brides, their husbands, their children, and their supporters played an important role. They challenged and won the arguments about who could be married, who could form families, and who could be part of the American family. In this way, they redefined the family in American immigration policy and in American society and culture, and pushed the principle of family unification to the center of immigration policy. These are enlargements and progressions in notions of family and nation that even the most ardent restrictionists in Congress will not be able to reverse.

Notes

1. The Immigration Act of 1924, PL 139.

2. Elliot Young, *Alien Nation: Chinese Migration in the Americas from the Coolie Era through World War II* (Chapel Hill: University of North Carolina Press, 2014); Erika Lee, *At America's Gates: Chinese Immigration During the Exclusion Era, 1882–1943* (Chapel Hill: University of North Carolina Press, 2003).

3. Madeline Hsu, *The Good Immigrants: How the Yellow Peril Became the Model Minority* (Princeton, N.J.: Princeton University Press, 2016), 103; Philip Wolgin, "Beyond National

Origins: The Development of Modern Immigration Policymaking, 1948–1968," PhD diss., University of California, Berkeley, 2011, 57.

4. Madeline Hsu and Ellen D. Wu, "'Smoke and Mirrors': Conditional Inclusion, Model Minorities, and the Pre-1965 Dismantling of Asian Exclusion" *Journal of American Ethnic History* 34, no. 4 (Summer 2015): 43–65; Hsu, *Good Immigrants*, 4.

5. Kornel S. Chang, "Reconsidering Asian Exclusion in the United States" in *Oxford Handbook of Asian American History*, ed. David Yoo and Eiichiro Azuma (New York: Oxford University Press, 2016), 161.

6. The Immigration Act of 1917, PL 301. On family unification in the 1921 Emergency Quota Act, see Yuki Oda, "Family Unity in US Immigration Policy, 1921–1978," PhD diss., Columbia University, 2014, ch. 1. For more on how family unification became "a driving force" of immigration law between 1952 and 1965, see Wolgin, "Beyond National Origins," ch. 3.

7. Although some find the term "war bride" to be objectionable, I use it in this essay to reflect the terminology of the period I am discussing.

8. Martha Gardner, *The Qualities of a Citizen: Women, Immigration, and Citizenship, 1870–1965* (Princeton, N.J.: Princeton University Press, 2005); Angela Lynn Tudico, "'They're Bringing Home Japanese Wives': Japanese War Brides in the Postwar Era," PhD diss., University of Maryland, 2009); Nancy K. Ota, "Private Matters: Family and Race and the Post–World War II Translation of 'American'" *IRSH* 46 (2001): 209–34.

9. Interestingly, the 1945 War Brides Act was gender neutral, allowing both men and women in the armed forces to take advantage of it to bring alien spouses into the country.

10. Ota, "Private Matters," 230.

11. Act of May 19, 1921 (PL 5).

12. Oda, "Family Unity," 94.

13. Jane Hong, "Reorienting America in the World: Race, Geopolitics, and the Repeal of Asian Exclusion, 1940–1952," PhD diss., Harvard University, 2013; Charlotte Brooks, *Between Mao and McCarthy: Chinese American Politics in the Cold War Years* (Chicago: University of Chicago Press, 2015). For broader foreign policy context, see Meredith Oyen, *The Diplomacy of Migration: Transnational Lives and the Making of US-Chinese Relations in the Cold War* (Ithaca, N.Y.: Cornell University Press, 2015).

14. Mary Dudziak, *Cold War Civil Rights: Race and the Image of American Democracy* (Princeton, N.J.: Princeton University Press, 1994/2011); Charlotte Brooks, *Alien Neighbors, Foreign Friends: Asian Americans, Housing, and the Transformation of Urban California* (Chicago: University of Chicago Press, 2009); Cindy I-Fen Chen, *Citizens of Asian America: Democracy and Race during the Cold War* (New York: NYU Press, 2014); Ellen D. Wu, *The Color of Success: Asian Americans and the Origins of the Model Minority* (Princeton, N.J.: Princeton University Press, 2013).

15. Todd Stevens, "Tender Ties: Husbands' Rights and Racial Exclusion in Chinese Marriage Cases, 1882–1924," *Law and Social Inquiry* (2002): 271–305; Unpublished Hearing re HR 3976, HR 4109, HR 4179, House of Rep. Committee on Immigration and Naturalization, November 14, 1945, 16; Brooks, *Between Mao and McCarthy*.

16. The end of Chinese exclusion in 1943 meant that Chinese American veterans, unlike other Asian veterans, were also able to bring their fiancés or fiancées to the United States under the 1946 act that provided temporary admission for aliens intending to marry US citizens who had served in the armed forces.

17. Act of August 9, 1946 (60 Stat. 975); Xiaojian Zhao, *Remaking Chinese America: Immigration, Family, and Community, 1940–1965* (New Brunswick, N.J.: Rutgers University Press, 2002), 25.

18. Catherine Lee, *Fictive Kinship: Family Reunification and the Meaning of Race and Nation in American Migration* (New York: Russell Sage Foundation, 2013), 84; Unpublished Hearing re HR 3976, HR 4109, HR 4179, 15, 16; Brooks, *Between Mao and McCarthy*.

19. Senate, Committee on Immigration, "Placing Chinese Wives of American Citizens on a Nonquota Basis," Report 1927, 79th Congress, 2nd session, Aug 1 (legislative day July 29), 1946. Besides the Chinese, the other Asian spouses admissible were from the Philippines and India because of the Act of July 2, 1946 (60 Stat. 416), which allowed the admission and naturalization of people from those countries. See Roland L. Guyotte and Barbara M. Posadas, "Interracial Marriages and Transnational Families: Chicago's Filipinos in the Aftermath of World War II," *Journal of American Ethnic History* 25, no. 2/3 (Winter-Spring, 2006): 134–55; Karen Leonard, *Making Ethnic Choices: California's Punjabi Mexican Americans* (Philadelphia, Pa.: Temple University Press, 1994); and Nayan Shah, *Stranger Intimacy: Contesting Race, Sexuality and the Law in the North American West* (Berkeley: University of California Press, 2012).

20. Zhao, *Remaking Chinese America*, 81–84; Philip Wolgin and Irene Bloemraad, "'Our Gratitude to Our Soldiers': Military Spouses, Family Re-Unification, and Postwar Immigration Reform," *Journal of Interdisciplinary History* 41, no. 2 (Summer 2010): 39.

21. US occupation personnel numbers fluctuated according to the year, from 125,000 to 465,000. Michiko Takeuchi "'Pan-Pan Girls' Performing and Resisting Neocolonialism(s) in the Pacific Theater," in *Over There: Living with the US Military Empire from World War Two to the Present*, ed. Maria Hohn and Seungsook Moon (Durham, N.C.: Duke University Press, 2010), 78, 105n2. For more on the US Occupation of Japan, see John Dower, *Embracing Defeat: Japan in the Wake of World War II* (New York: Norton, 1999); Naoko Shibusawa, *America's Geisha Ally: Reimagining the Japanese Enemy* (Cambridge, Mass.: Harvard University Press, 2006); and Yukiko Koshiro, *Trans-Pacific Racisms and the US Occupation of Japan* (New York: Columbia University Press, 1999).

22. Shibusawa, *America's Geisha Ally*, 41; Koshiro, *Trans-Pacific Racisms*, 156; Masako Nakamura, "Families Precede Nation and Race? Marriage, Migration, and Integration of Japanese War Brides after World War II," PhD diss., University of Minnesota, 2010, 38. Not all miscegenation laws were enforced, and not all of them prohibited marriage between whites and the category that we today refer to as "Asian." Peter Wallenstein, *Tell the Court I Love My Wife: Race, Marriage, and Law—An American History* (New York: Palgrave Macmillan, 2002), 199; Wolgin and Bloemraad, "Our Gratitude to Our Soldiers," 42; Hrishi Karthikeyan and Gabriel J. Chin, "Preserving Racial Identity: Population Patterns and the Application of Anti-Miscegenation Statutes to Asian Americans, 1910–1950," *Asian Law Journal* 9, no. 1 (2002): 1–40.

250 · ARISSA H. OH

23. See Bernadette Maguire, *Immigration: Public Legislation and Private Bills* (Lanham, Md.: University Press of America, 1997), and Ota, "Private Matters."

24. Act of July 22, 1947 (61 Stat. 401). Emphasis added.

25. Mike Masaoka and Bill Hosokawa, *They Call Me Moses Masaoka: An American Saga* (New York: Morrow, 1987), 204; Wolgin and Bloemraad, "Our Gratitude to Our Soldiers," 36; Maddalena Marinari, "Divided and Conquered: Immigration Reform Advocates and the Passage of the 1952 Immigration and Nationality Act," *Journal of American Ethnic History* 35, no. 3 (Spring 2016): 19; Peggy Pascoe, *What Comes Naturally: Miscegenation Law and the Making of Race in America* (New York: Oxford University Press, 2010), 234; Eunhye Kwon, "Interracial Marriages among Asian Americans in the US West, 1880–1954," PhD diss., University of Florida, 2011, 239; Rose Cuison Villazor, "The Other *Loving*: Uncovering the Federal Government's Racial Regulation of Marriage," *New York University Law Review* 86, 1420.

26. Nakamura, "Families Precede," 62n124, 63; Tomoko Tsuchiya, "Cold War Love: Producing American Liberalism in Interracial Marriages between American Soldiers and Japanese Women," PhD diss., University of California, San Diego, 2011, 111; Masaoka, *They Call Me Moses Masaoka*, 204.

27. Notably, the 1950 law also allowed US servicemen to petition for their Japanese fiancées as well as their wives. This put Japanese fiancées on equal footing with European and Chinese fiancées, who had been provided for by the 1947 Alien Fiancés and Fiancées Act (PL 471).

28. House of Representatives, Committee on the Judiciary, "Permitting of Alien Spouses and Minor Children of Citizen Members of the United States Armed Forces," House Report 2768, 81st Congress, 2nd session, 2.

29. The Senate's Committee on Immigration had originally proposed a ninety-day window, which the House Committee expanded to the six months denoted in the law.

30. Regina Lark, "They Challenged Two Nations: Marriages between Japanese Women and American GIs, 1945 to the Present," PhD diss., University of Southern California, 1999), 206–7; Villazor, "The Other *Loving*," 1419; "Admission of Alien Spouses and Minor Children of Citizen Members of Armed Forces," *Congressional Record* 82nd Cg, 1st session, vol. 97 (January 18, 1951), 441; "Admission of Alien Spouses and Minor Children of Citizen Members of the United States Armed Forces," Senate Report 56, 82nd Congress, 1st session, January 29, 1951.

31. "Amending the Act to Expedite the Admission to the United States of Alien Spouses and Minor Children of Citizen Members of the United States Armed Forces," House Report 478, 80th Congress, 1st session, May 28, 1947, 2. The corresponding Senate report includes the same phrase.

32. "Amending the Act to Expedite the Admission to the United States of Alien Spouses and Alien Minor Children of Citizen Members of the United States Armed Forces," H. Rept. 478, 80th Congress, 1st session, May 27, 1947, 1; Lark, "They Challenged Two Nations," 205.

33. "Permitting the Admission of Alien Spouses and Minor Children of Citizen Members of the United States Armed Forces," House Report 2768, 81st Cg, 2d session, 1, 2; "Removal of Racial Restrictions Now Prohibiting Admissions to United States of Wives

of World War II Veterans Asked to Meet Problem Arising in Japan and Other Pacific Countries," *Congressional Record* Vol. 96, January 31, 1950, A691–A692.

34. Tsuchiya, "Cold War Love"; Nakamura, "Families Precede." It is unclear how grooms of Mexican descent, for example, would have been categorized.

35. Pascoe, *What Comes Naturally*, 199. Of the total 10,517 US citizens who married Japanese women between June 22, 1947, and December 31, 1952, more than 75 percent were white. Villazor, "The Other *Loving*," 1419n380. There were an estimated three thousand to five thousand Japanese-black marriages during the fifteen years after World War II. Michael Cullen Green, *Black Yanks in the Pacific: Race in the Making of American Military Empire after World War II* (Ithaca, N.Y.: Cornell University Press, 2010), 80.

36. Villazor, "The Other *Loving*," 1418–19.

37. Tudico, "They're Bringing Home," 216, 33; Wolgin and Bloemraad, "Our Gratitude to Our Soldiers," 43.

38. Wolgin, "Beyond National Origins," 63.

39. While other immigrants arrived via the national quotas of the countries of their birth, Asians were counted according to their ancestry. This meant, for example, that a Chinese person born in France was counted against the Chinese quota, whereas a French immigrant of non-Asian descent was counted against the more generous French quota.

40. Koshiro, *Trans-Pacific Racisms*, 148.

41. Robert Lee, *Orientals: Asian Americans in Popular Culture* (Philadelphia: Temple University Press, 1999), 162; Oda, "Family Unity," 78.

42. Shibusawa, *America's Geisha Ally*, ch. 1.

43. Two representative novels include Pearl S. Buck's *The Hidden Flower* (1952) and James Michener's bestselling *Sayonara* (1953), both of which appeared as serials in *Women's Home Companion* and *McCall's*, respectively, before being published as books. Michener's book was later made into an Oscar-winning movie starring Marlon Brando (1957). Another less popular film was King Vidor's *Japanese War Bride* (1952).

44. William Worden, "Where Are Those Japanese War Brides?" *Saturday Evening Post*, November 20, 1954, 134.

45. Before a man could marry, he had to have his marriage approved through military and consular channels, and show proof of citizenship, his single status, and his ability to support his wife. His wife and her entire family were screened and checked by the Japanese police and American military counterintelligence.

46. Susan Zeiger, *Entangling Alliances: Foreign War Brides and American Soldiers in the Twentieth Century* (New York: NYU Press, 2010).

47. Paul Spickard, *Mixed Blood: Intermarriage and Ethnic Identity in Twentieth Century America* (Madison: University of Wisconsin Press, 1991), 139–40; Worden, "Where Are Those Japanese War Brides?" 133; Leon K. Walters, "A Study of Social and Marital Adjustment of Thirty-Five American-Japanese Couples," master's thesis, Ohio State University, 1953, 83.

48. "The Winsome Geisha—Of an Old and Honored Calling," *Newsweek*, January 25. 1954, 93; Spickard, *Mixed Blood*, 140; Worden, "Where are Those Japanese War Brides?" 133–34; Nakamura, "Families Precede," 166–67, 263.

49. See, for example, Buck's *The Hidden Flower* and Vidor's *Japanese War Bride.*

50. "The Loneliest Brides in America," *Ebony*, January 1953; "The Truth about Japanese War Brides," *Ebony*, March 1952; Ray Falk, "GI Brides Go to School in Japan," *New York Times Magazine*, November 7, 1954.

51. Walters, "Study of the Social and Marital Adjustments . . ." 127, 147–49; "Letters to the Editor," *Ebony*, May 1952, 6–7; O'Reilly, "Our East-West Marriage Is Working," *American Mercury*, December 1955; James Michener, "Pursuit of Happiness by a GI and a Japanese," *Life*, February 21, 1955. Husbands protested that, contrary to popular opinion, their wives were not subservient, and they joked about the consequences of crossing them. But wives' supposed lack of subservience was only in areas that advanced their image as good wives and mothers. For example, a husband might jokingly complain about how strict his wife was about his spending habits but would also admit that he had a healthy savings account as a result.

52. J. P. McEvoy, "America through the Eyes of a Japanese War-Bride," *Reader's Digest*, April 1955, 97; O'Reilly, "Our East-West Marriage," 18; Janet Wentworth Smith and William L. Worden, "They're Bringing Home Japanese Wives," *Saturday Evening Post*, January 19, 1952, 81.

53. Patricia Anderson Kataoka, "Why Japanese War Brides Married: Four Case Studies," master's thesis, University of Oregon, 1988, 46, 48; Kyoko Kondo, "Experiences of Japanese War Brides and Assimilation into Appalachia: Understanding the Intersection of Ethnicity and Gender," master's thesis, Marshall University, 2000, 26; Yoshiko Gloria Yamaji, "The Impact of Communication Difficulties in Family Relations Observed in Eight Japanese War-Bride Marriages," master's thesis, University of Southern California, 1961, 93.

54. Robert Fish, "The Heiress and the Love Children: Sawada Miki and the Elizabeth Saunders Home for Mixed-Blood Orphans in Postwar Japan," PhD diss., University of Hawaii, 2002, ch. 2.

55. Kataoka, "Why Japanese War Brides Married," 25, 52

56. Nakamura, "Families Precede," 175; Allison Varzally, *Making a Non-White America: Californians Coloring Outside Ethnic Lines, 1925–1955*, Berkeley: University of California Press, 2008, 215.

57. Two of the most-cited of these studies are Anselm L. Strauss, "Strain and Harmony in American-Japanese War-Bride Marriages," *Marriage and Family Living* 16, no. 2 (May 1954): 99–106, and George A. DeVos, *Personality Patterns and Problems of Adjustment in American-Japanese Intercultural Marriages* (Taipei: Orient Cultural Service, 1973). See Nakamura, "Families Precede," appendix B, for a list of studies of Japanese war brides and their marriages from the 1950s to the early 1960s.

58. Michener, "Pursuit of Happiness," 124.

59. Ibid., 135, 138, 141.

60. For more on war brides' schools, see Tudico, "They're Bringing Home Japanese Wives," ch. 3; Nakamura, "Families Precede," ch. 2; Lark, "They Challenged Two Nations," ch. 4.

61. Nakamura, "Families Precede," 123.

Japanese War Brides and the Normalization of Family Unification • 253

62. Pearl Buck told this kind of story in her novel *The Hidden Flower* (1952), only her heroine returned quietly to Japan, leaving her mixed-race child in the United States with an adoptive mother, a German-Jewish Holocaust survivor.

63. Ruth Moss, "Mother Slays Baby; Relates Tale of Abuse," *Chicago Tribune*, November 15, 1953; "Jap War Bride Who Killed Son Tries Suicide," *Chicago Tribune*, February 20, 1954; "Jap Wife Who Slew Baby Set to Fly Home," *Chicago Tribune*, May 16, 1954.

64. Michener, "Pursuit of Happiness," 136.

65. Walters, "Study of the Social and Marital Adjustment . . ."; John W. Connor, *A Study of the Marital Stability of Japanese War Brides* (San Francisco: R&E Research, 1976); Strauss, "Strain and Harmony"; McEvoy, "American through the Eyes," 98; Worden, "Where Are Those Japanese War Brides?" 39; O'Reilly, "Our East-West Marriage," 19.

66. Worden, "Where Are Those Japanese War Brides?" 133, 134.

67. Pascoe, *What Comes Naturally*, 233.

68. Wu, *The Color of Success*; Arissa Oh, *To Save the Children of Korea: The Cold War Origins of International Adoption* (Stanford, Calif.: Stanford University Press, 2015).

69. The 1952 film *Japanese War Bride* portrayed a Japanese American family, resettling in California after having been interned. The inclusion of this uncomfortable fact surely contributed to the movie's unpopularity and criticism that the film overstated the "distasteful theme of race prejudice." Zeiger, *Entangling Alliances*, 196.

70. Pascoe, *What Comes Naturally*, 232; Shibusawa, *America's Geisha Ally*, 49–50.

71. Simpson, *An Absent Presence*, 151–52, 183; Michener, "Pursuit of Happiness," 132.

72. Green, *Black Yanks*; "Loneliest Brides"; "Truth about Japanese War Brides." For more, see Alex Lubin, *Romance and Rights: The Politics of Interracial Intimacy, 1945–1954* (Jackson: University of Mississippi Press, 2005); Yasuhiro Okada, "'Cold War Black Orientalism': Race, Gender, and African American Representations of Japanese Women during the Early 1950s," *Journal of American and Canadian Studies* 29 (2009): 45–79.

73. Emma Teng, *Eurasian: Mixed Identities in the United States, China, and Hong Kong, 1842–1943* (Berkeley: University of California Press, 2013), ch. 5.

74. "Hawaiian Medley," *Collier's*, December 11, 1943, 16; Cynthia Nakashima, "An Invisible Monster: The Creation and Denial of Mixed-Race People in America," in *Racially Mixed People in America*, ed. Maria P.P. Root (Newbury Park, Calif.: Sage, 1992).

75. Ralph Linton, "The Vanishing American Negro," *American Mercury*, February 1947, 133–9; Henry Yu, "Mixing Bodies and Cultures" in *Sex, Love, Race: Crossing Boundaries in North America*, ed. Martha Hodes (New York: NYU Press, 1999), 455–56.

76. Robert E. Park, "Human Migration and the Marginal Man," *American Journal of Sociology* 33, no. 6 (May 1928): 881–93; Teng, *Eurasian*, 143–44.

77. Pearl S. Buck used the term "Amerasian" to refer to the mixed-race Chinese children produced in World War II, but the term only became widely popular with the Vietnam War and continues to be identified with mixed-race people from Southeast Asia. Although she is credited with the term, it was actually suggested by someone in the State Department. Emily Cheng, "Pearl S. Buck's 'American Children': US Democracy, Adoption of the Amerasian Child, and the Occupation of Japan in *The Hidden Flower*," *Frontiers: A Journal of Women Studies* 35, no. 1 (2014): 188.

254 · ARISSA H. OH

78. Oh, *To Save the Children of Korea*. For more on how the Japanese saw these children see Koshiro, *Transpacific Racisms*.

79. Jennifer Ann Ho, *Racial Ambiguity in Asian American Culture* (New Brunswick, N.J.: Rutgers University Press, 2015), 39. This idea that the right cultural influences could overcome racial inferiority was not unique to the United States. European imperial powers had also applied these beliefs in their colonies. See, for example, Christina Firpo, *The Uprooted: Race, Children, and Imperialism in French Indochina, 1890–1980* (Honolulu: University of Hawaii Press, 2016), and Ann Laura Stoler, *Carnal Knowledge and Imperial Power: Race and the Intimate in Colonial Rule* (Berkeley: University of California Press, 2002).

80. Ho, *Racial Ambiguity*, 22, 30. The mixed-marriage policy allowed "568 people of Japanese ancestry (predominantly women and children) . . . to escape incarceration." Ho, *Racial Ambiguity*, 22.

81. See for example, Mary Lui, *The Chinatown Trunk Mystery: Murder, Miscegenation, and Other Dangerous Encounters in Turn-of-the-Century New York City* (Princeton, N.J.: Princeton University Press, 2007).

82. Wu, *Color of Success*.

83. Smith and Worden, "They're Bringing Home Japanese Wives," 81; McEvoy, "America through the Eyes," 95; Worden "Where Are Those Japanese War Brides?" 133.

84. Walters, "A Study of the Social and Marital Adjustments . . ." ch. 7.

85. Ho, *Racial Ambiguity*, 30–31.

86. Hsu and Wu, "Smoke and Mirrors," 49.

87. Michener, "Pursuit of Happiness," 139.

88. Arissa H. Oh, "From War Waif to Ideal Immigrant: The Cold War Transformation of the Korean Orphan," *Journal of American Ethnic History* 31, no. 4 (Summer 2012): 34–55; Simpson, *Absent Presence*, 183.

89. US Congress, House of Representatives, Subcommittee on Immigration, Citizenship, Refugees, Border Security, and International Law, *Role of Family-Based Immigration in the US Immigration System*, 110th Cong., 1st Sess. (Washington, DC, 2007), 25–26.

CHAPTER 12

Love as Mirror and Pathway

The Undocumented Emotive Configuration
of Mexican Immigration

ANA ELIZABETH ROSAS

In April 2012, fifty-two-year-old Virginia Martínez was deported from Los Angeles, California, to Río Tijuana, México, and separated from her ten children. Upon hearing that US authorities had placed five of her children into adoption, she tried to ease her desperation with drugs and quickly became addicted. Her story is not atypical. The tents and shacks of the Rio Tijuana encampment, just across the river from San Diego, have provided shelter to countless other deported—and now homeless—Mexican immigrant parents. Feeling angry, abandoned, and hopeless, they, like Martínez, have often succumbed to illicit behaviors as a way of coping. They are victims of inhumane binational policies that have separated them from their spouses and children. Their stories—and their humanity—are all too easy to ignore.

On September 16, 2013, *La Opinion*, the Spanish-language and Los Angeles–based newspaper published a story that examined cases such as Virginia Martínez's, to try to raise awareness about the plight of Mexican immigrant women and men in the drug-ridden Rio Tijuana encampment.[1] *La Opinion* told its readers that it was extremely difficult to investigate and write this news story because of the shame that these recently deported women and men felt about their descent into drug addiction, prostitution, and other crimes just to survive. They did not want their families—and anonymous readers—to know the depths of their despair and deprivation. Despite their reticence to share too many details, their love for their children and spouses, left behind in places like South Central Los Angeles, is evident in the newspaper account. Their stories are essential to understanding

256 · ANA ELIZABETH ROSAS

the culture of absence born out of the day-to-day emotional lives of Mexican immigrants who have risked—or experienced—separation from their loved ones, either because of restrictive immigration policies that limit family reunification or because of coerced deportation.

This chapter investigates the emotional lives of one group of Mexican immigrants: those who migrated to the United States in the mid-twentieth century (1940–1960), often on temporary labor contracts and without their families, in the hope of improving their financial futures. Some of these immigrants later remained in the United States undocumented, working and sending money to loved ones back home. The chapter also explores the emotional lives of the spouses and children they left behind. Throughout the mid-twentieth century, Mexican women and men of varying legal statuses tried to maintain long-distance romantic and familial relationships across the US-México border. However, records of these interactions are absent from policy reports, newspapers, and the legal and social histories of immigration.[2] I seek to recover this culture of absence, thereby contributing to a more *humane* history of immigration. Drawing on oral interviews, I try to capture the emotional weight and toll of separation from loved ones as immigrants traveled across the US-México border in search of better economic opportunities.

Interviews offer valuable tools for recapturing lost or erased histories. For this chapter I drew on interviews with twenty elderly Mexican immigrant women and men who gave me a sense of their emotional investments, courage, and resourcefulness over time and across borders. In my interviews over the years, I have learned that discussing films and songs of love with my interviewees allows my subjects to discuss difficult emotional lives marked by absence and love more easily with *desconocidos* (strangers). Films and songs of love become pathways for exploring personal issues that, in some cases, my interviewees had never acknowledged or discussed before. Some of my interviewees were/continue to be undocumented. Their humanity becomes fully evident in their life stories, allowing me (and the reader) to resist calling their experience "living in the shadows," a familiar but dehumanizing trope common among scholars and journalists who write about immigration.[3] Hence, the history of Mexican immigration, and as Virginia Martinez's absence reveals, is steeped in emotional lives marked by love, longing, and the US-México border.

The Bracero Program and Operation Wetback

Many of my interviewees were separated from their loved ones as a result of the temporary labor programs (Bracero Programs) of 1942–1946 and 1951–1964, and the deportation program called Operation Wetback (1954). During World War II the United States needed workers to plant and harvest the crops that fed its soldiers, wartime allies, and domestic population. The federal government turned to its

Love as Mirror and Pathway · 257

southern neighbor, México, for this labor. Mexican President Manuel Ávila Camacho supported the idea on the grounds that temporary contract labor in the United States rehabilitated rural Mexican men and turned them into modern citizens. Confident that after earning US wages and learning US methods and skills, these men would return adequately prepared to invest and labor in México and move the nation forward on the path toward technological sophistication and modernity, Ávila Camacho overlooked the Bracero Program's toll on braceros (Mexican men participating in this program) and the families they left behind. The Mexican government did not provide these families with information or funds to help them weather the absence of their bracero family relatives. Instead, these men and their families were expected to derive comfort from varying notions of México's close geographic proximity to the United States.[4]

Preventing families from migrating together, the Bracero Program especially strained romantic and family relationships and made it difficult for men and women to express and nurture their love for each other. After their contracts ended, Mexican workers were required to return home. Indeed, part of their wages were withheld by authorities and returned to them only after they arrived in México, to guarantee repatriation. (In many cases, these funds were never returned.)[5] It was not unusual for braceros to skip out on their contracts, hoping to find better-paying and more humane employment elsewhere. Many remained in the United States undocumented for a time, sending part of their wages back home to support their spouses and children.

In the midst of such emotional turmoil, braceros undertook rigorous and poorly compensated labor in the United States. American growers who were beneficiaries of bracero contracts were required to provide their workers with reliable housing, hearty meals, and healthy working conditions. These growers were also entrusted to transport workers to and from their employment destinations, pay them the prevailing wage for hours worked, and provide them adequate medical services when physically injured or sick. Many growers did not meet these contractual obligations. Living conditions in the agricultural fields were often dire, with poor and unsanitary housing, inferior food, long hours, and dangerous transportation and work conditions. Despite these problems, Americans generally considered the wartime bracero program a success. Another bracero program was established in 1951 and lasted thirteen years until its termination on December 31, 1964. Over its lifetime, the program paved the way for temporary (and permanent) migration of an estimated five million Mexican immigrants (mostly men), which had long-term consequences for their lives and livelihoods, as well as for the lives of their loved ones back home.[6]

During the 1950s the Mexican undocumented population grew. Some of the undocumented were former braceros who continued working in the United States. Others were workers who were enticed by American growers to migrate across

258 • ANA ELIZABETH ROSAS

the porous US-México border, often with the full cooperation of the US Border Patrol.[7] The federal government was forced to crack down, however, in response to a growing concern that Mexican workers were displacing US-born workers. During the summer of 1954 the US government, with Mexican government cooperation, invested in the widely publicized Operation Wetback: the deployment of border enforcement agents operating airplanes, buses, helicopters, and jeeps to detect, interrogate, and deport undocumented Mexican immigrants to the interior of México.[8] Deportation became a US government priority because of the perceived "invasion" of Mexican undesirable aliens.

Operation Wetback had an unintended consequence, however: it redirected many undocumented Mexican immigrant men away from agriculture and into employment where they would not be easily detected by law enforcement agents and would perhaps even earn higher wages. This, in turn, meant longer periods of separation from their relatives, girlfriends, fiancés, and/or spouses. This continued separation exacerbated all types of fears among those left at home in México: that their loved ones would be ill-treated in the United States; that they would fail to realize their financial goals; that they would begin new lives in the States and forget them.

The families of those who migrated expected their loved ones to remain faithful and in relationship across the distances, even when there was little or no written communication. Such expectations—and the failure to meet them—were a source of untold emotional pain for the women and men caught up in these long-distance romantic relationships. The films and songs of love they consumed offered solace and gave them an acceptable outlet for expressing their anxieties and their concerns about the safety and whereabouts of their loved ones. For young people, in particular, hoping to marry once their loved ones returned home, these films and songs of love offered cautionary tales about what might happen if they did not exercise patience and behave with proper decorum. The absence and emotions born out of Mexican immigration reveals the intense expansiveness of the emotional grip of mid-twentieth-century immigration restrictions on the imaginaries and hearts of Mexican women and men separated across the US-México border.

Cartas a Eufemia (Letters to Eufemia)

The 1952 film *Cartas a Eufemia* (Letters to Eufemia) exemplifies the social and emotional challenges of waiting for the return of one's boyfriend.[9] According to several of my interviewees, the film urged Mexican women not to lose hope, to "wait with the utmost patience" for letters from their loved one, and to count on an eventual reunification.[10] Failure to exercise such patience would undermine their reputations and perhaps lead to their public ostracism.

The film's principal characters are Eufemia, a nineteen-year-old Mexican woman, and her boyfriend, Luterio. Because Eufemia's elderly father has been wrongfully accused of arson, Luterio travels to México City to attend her father's court case and to earn money for their future life together. Luterio's departure sends Eufemia into an emotional tailspin. Townspeople begin complaining about her volatility and her many *desencuentros* (failure to live up to expectations). She goes to the post office daily to mail pleading letters to her beloved and pines publicly when she does not receive a response, much to the amusement or disgust of the townspeople. The lack of written communication leaves Eufemia utterly devastated. She eventually gives up on Luterio and begins to spend time with another young man, Ignacio, thus exposing herself to public ridicule and censure. One of the town's patriarchs, a wealthy landowner rejected by Eufemia, commissions a special song to criticize her lack of commitment, which raises suspicions about her virtue and moral character. The song is played by the town band, and sung in mocking tone by the town's women.[11]

"CARTA A EUFEMIA" (LETTER TO EUFEMIA)

Cuando recibas esta carta sin razón, Eufemia
Ya sabrás que entre nosotros todo terminó
When you receive this letter without reason, Eufemia
You will know that everything between us has ended

Si no la hubieses recibido por traición, Eufemia
If you did not receive it as an act of betrayal, Eufemia

Te devuelvo tu palabra
Te la vuelvo sin usarla,
Y que conste en esta carta que acabamos de un jalón

I return your word
I return it without using it
And let it be known in this letter that we are all at once through

No me escribistes
You did not write me

Y mis cartas anteriores no sé si las recibistes
And my previous letters I don't know if you received them

Tu me olvidastes
You forgot me

Y mataron mis amores el silencio que les distes
And your silence killed my love

A ver sí a esta si le das contestación Eufemia
Let's see if you actually answer this one, Eufemia

260 • ANA ELIZABETH ROSAS

Though shocked and in deep emotional despair over the public attack, Eufemia does not respond to such slandering of her public reputation. In this, she adheres to gendered expectations that women must refrain from publicly confronting men. Nonetheless, Ignacio, out of his love for her, enlists the same band to perform, "Contestación de Eufemia" (Eufemia's Response), a song which explains her actions, and defends her honor and sexual virtue:[12]

"CONTESTACIÓN DE EUFEMIA" (EUFEMIA'S RESPONSE)

Tengo en mis manos la última carta
que me escribistes
Luterio

I hold in my hands the last letter
You wrote me
Luterio

Y hablando de ella y su contenido
debo expresarte lo que en renglon te digo

And talking about it and its content
I have to express what in each line I tell you

Pides motivo de rompimiento
y del silencio que piensas que te di
debo decirte Luterio de mi vida que de tus anteriores
ninguna recibí

You ask for reasons for our break up
And of the silence you thought that I gave you
I must tell you Luterio of my life that of your previous letters
I did not receive

Mira Luterio
Te acuerdas de aquel Roque con quien tu te emborrachastes
Ahora es cartero
Y dice que me quiere desde que nos presentastes
Ya ves como andan en el correo
Mejor tus cartas debia certificar

Look Luterio
You remember that Roque that you got drunk with
Now he is a mail carrier
And he says he loves me since you introduced us
You know how they are at the post office
It would have been better if you had certified your letters

Love as Mirror and Pathway • 261

Y aquí termino
Devuelveme mis cosas
Perdoname la letra y el papel
Eufemia

And here is where I end
Return my things
Forgive my handwriting and paper
Eufemia

At the conclusion of *Letters to Eufemia*, Luterio eventually returns to formally end his courtship with Eufemia, her father is released from jail, and Ignacio and Eufemia profess their eternal love. But despite the apparent happy ending, Mexican viewers were offered one final public humiliation. The local priest, the town's moral authority, also publicly humiliates Eufemia, calling her "the town's laughingstock [and] reason for scandal."[13] Although Eufemia insists that she "has not done anything to anyone," the town's priest has the last word.[14] Having found true love in Ignacio may make for a satisfactory ending, but it does not overshadow this film's emphasis on the dangers of impatience, faithlessness, and lack of decorum. Such emphasis resonated with Mexican audiences, as it welcomed a film that discouraged young Mexican women from expressing their feelings of love and longing for their absent Mexican immigrant boyfriends when in the company of extended family relatives, neighbors, and friends.

For Mexican film audiences, the message came loud and clear: women must remain constant in their affections to their absent immigrant boyfriends and husbands, no matter what the circumstances, or risk public humiliation and perhaps social ostracism. As I learned from the oral interviews, the women who saw *Cartas a Eufemia* found the film deeply meaningful. It helped them process their feelings of love for their absent boyfriends and husbands—as well as acknowledge their fears of abandonment—and offered them a cautionary tale of what might happen if their virtue and moral character were called into question. Catalina Ruiz remembers viewing the film with her friends in her rural hometown of San Martín de Hidalgo, Jalisco. She remarked that she and her friends all "feared the humiliation showcased in this film" and "did not dare express" their "anxiety and concern when not hearing from their boyfriends in the United States for months."[15] This film made the "dangers to their public reputation" "all too real for them to ignore the film."[16]

As I collected oral life histories with women raised to consider the importance of this film's message, and who navigated long-distance romantic relationships with Mexican immigrant men in adulthood, I came to appreciate the difficulties of waiting patiently for a loved one to return. *Cartas a Eufemia* discouraged them from questioning the irregularity of written communication with their absent boyfriends or husbands. If they feared being forgotten, or their love unrequited, they were warned to keep those fears to themselves. María Elena Medina, one of my interviewees, revealed that, like Eufemia, she "was not encouraged to ask questions" or to feel entitled to "receive a letter that detailed her boyfriend's plans for return."[17] Her parents "insisted" that it was in her best interest to wait until "her boyfriend [could account for] his actions upon his return."[18] *Letters to Eufemia* illuminated for Mexican women the consequences of making too many demands and having too many expectations.

Beginning in 1952 and until 1980, *Letters to Eufemia* was screened in local movie theaters and regularly aired on television channels throughout the Mexican countryside. The majority of the women and men who have been formative to my investigation of the emotional lives of mid-twentieth-century undocumented Mexican immigration in México and the United States singled out the power of this film to me. They consistently identified this film as "*the* film" that instilled a deep-seated fear of making too many demands of their boyfriends or husbands working in the United States. María Teresa Garza remembered that "the film inspired us to fear the distance, the border, the expectations that divided us from our boyfriends."[19] It made clear "that not keeping our love, our relationships to ourselves would make an already painful reality worse."[20] The public humiliation Eufemia endured was all too real for them to discount as just a fictional plotline. They, too, experienced the longing, sadness, and worry that had driven Eufemia to need—and expect—continual correspondence with Luterio. Almost all of these women explained that the film taught them to be extremely patient, and as discreet as possible when in public. Carmen explained, "We were Eufemia, waiting was hard work in private and public."[21] The danger of their being publicly chastised as Eufemia had been was very real for these women. Mexican women's recollections of *Letters to Eufemia* magnifies the emotional incentives for these women to wait patiently for the return of their absent Mexican immigrant boyfriends.

I must admit that I first learned of *Letters to Eufemia* in 1987, at age nine, while living in South Central Los Angeles. Throughout my upbringing, my mother, Dolores Graciela Rosas Medina, had entrusted María Teresa with picking me up from school and caring for me until the end of my mother's workday. This allowed me to enjoy countless afternoons with María Teresa listening to her impressive musical record collection, which included Pedro Infante's musical performance of "Letter to Eufemia" and "Eufemia's Response" (1952).[22] María Teresa loved Pedro Infante. In her estimation, he was the most talented Mexican musical artist to ever sing or record a song, so despite my visceral aversion to the mocking language in these songs, she insisted that I endure our listening to these songs together. Without fail or my paying close attention to the lyrics of this song, I would automatically cringe whenever these songs were a part of our musical rotation. The mean-spiritedness of these lyrics was very palpable and too severe for me to enjoy.

Eventually, María Teresa would use our listening to "Letters to Eufemia" and "Eufemia's Response" to caution me against publicly asserting my affection, most especially in writing, toward any boyfriend. She shared with me in the strictest of confidence that in 1961 she had been in a long-distance romantic relationship with a young man who was working undocumented in the United States, and that her mother had used these songs and the film *Letters to Eufemia* to scare her. She was urged to be discreet when corresponding with this boyfriend or else risk public ridicule. Although María Teresa did not have a copy of the film to share with me, she insisted that *Letters to Eufemia* and these songs were to be taken seriously, as they illustrated the range of feelings that made corresponding with one's boyfriend, and expressing love for him in public, a dangerous proposition for women navigating mid-twentieth-century expectations. The lessons of this film outlived the Bracero Program and Operation Wetback and marked what these women and men remembered most intimately about their coming of age.

The binational policies that prevented women and men from enjoying their romantic relationships and family lives forced alternative pathways for nurturing their long-distance romantic relationships, as well as for shouldering their heartache when these relationships did not survive. They had to reconceptualize how to remain emotionally connected to each other across the US-México border and be hardworking despite the weight of a broken heart in the face of governmental obstruction of their personal and even written communication and restrictive gender expectations. Moreover, laboring as undocumented Mexican immigrant workers for indefinite periods, separated from each other, and under the constant fear of deportation and public humiliation inspired women and men in these long-distance romantic relationships to be most resourceful as they strived to remain emotionally connected to each other. Catalina explained, "Keeping silent required us to listen to songs of love with all of our heart, our imagination."[23]

Listening to Love

Mid-twentieth-century films and songs of love allowed elderly Mexican immigrant women and men to acknowledge the emotional toll that long-distance romantic relationships exerted on their lives. They also made mourning the absence or loss of romantic relationships that did not survive the emotional strain of separation viable for them. Lorenzo Macías and Pablo Martínez were among the Mexican immigrant men I interviewed who listened to and reflected on the lyrics of songs, especially more recent musical recordings such as Banda la Costeña's "Una Aventura" ("An Adventure," 1995) and Vicente Fernandez's "Aca Entre Nos" ("Between

Us," 1998), which they feel perfectly articulate their experiences so many decades ago. These songs of love, all performed and recorded by highly celebrated Mexican musical artists, have inspired them to recognize without fear or shame the emotional heartache they suffered when they were betrayed or rejected by the women they loved. Ironically, it was their love for these women that had led them to migrate to the United States in the first place, hoping to earn enough money to one day offer them financial security. More than seventy years later, the men continue to grieve the loss of these relationships, and the music and lyrics offer them a safe and acceptable outlet for expressing their emotions.

Having lost the love of women who "had either been their first love or the love of their lives" was "emotionally devastating" for Mexican immigrant men coming of age as braceros and undocumented Mexican immigrant men, said Pablo Martínez.[24] Men were expected to recover easily from such emotional pain, but it was difficult to do so working long hours and living among strangers. Asked to reflect on their experience many decades later, they finally acknowledged the "emotional wounds that had been too shameful to recognize at the time of their occurrence."[25]

During my interview with Lorenzo Macías, we listened to Banda la Costeña's "An Adventure," and Macías was drawn immediately to the storyline in the ballad: a story of love and betrayal.[26] Macías wept as he heard the lyrics, reminded of the first woman he truly loved, Judith Méndez, who rejected him in 1955 after a year's separation. Judith's betrayal had not been easy for Lorenzo to overcome when laboring in Los Angeles as an undocumented Mexican immigrant. His blind confidence in Judith's love for him had rendered him vulnerable. He had ignored the unevenness in their expressed feelings and their correspondence. "Separated from each other, from the woman you loved across borders made being in love that much more challenging," he said. "You fell in love harder and pined for this woman wholeheartedly."[27] He had spent three years of savings to finance his undocumented entry into the United States, with the hopes of returning a year later with enough money to purchase an apartment, and to marry and raise a family. Instead, he learned that days after his departure, Judith began dating, and eventually married, one of his closest friends. The double betrayal was a powerful blow to his heart. It took two-and-a-half years for him to overcome his broken heart and commit to another romantic relationship.

Now, many decades later, he was an elderly married man with adult children of his own, but it wasn't until the telling his life history that he finally acknowledged and mourned his suppressed heartache. Listening to "An Adventure" as part of his oral life history interview allowed Macías to revisit his failed romantic relationship and to recognize it as formative to his gender identity. It afforded him the emotional courage to mourn his first love, to admit that such loss had made it harder to return to his family and hometown, and to eventually fall in love with someone else.

"UNA AVENTURA" (AN ADVENTURE)

Que te quise mucho no podrás negarlo
Y que mi cariño no supiste amar
Que te di mi vida sin pedirte nada
Solo me engañabas me hiciste llorar
Solo sufrimiento diste a mi vida
Este cruel despecho no lo he de borrar
Aun después de todo yo te sigo amando
Y quien sabe cuando te podré olvidar

That I loved you very much, you cannot deny
And that my love you did not know how to cherish
That I gave you my life without asking you for anything
Only suffering you brought to my life
This cruel heartbreak I cannot erase
Despite everything I continue loving you
And who knows when I will be able to forget you

Muy ilusionado estaba yo contigo
Como fui tan ciego para no entender
Que era una aventura lo que tu buscabas

Very illusioned I was with you
How was I so blind to not understand
That it was an adventure that you were looking for

Y yo por confiado donde fui a caer
Solo sufrimiento diste a mi vida
Este cruel despecho no lo he de borrar

And because I trusted you I ended very badly
Only suffering you brought to my life
This cruel heartbreak I cannot erase

Heartbreak was very difficult for the former braceros and the undocumented Mexican immigrant men to admit and discuss. In 1953 Pablo Martínez learned that his girlfriend of one-and-a-half years, María de la Cruz Álvarez, had broken her promise to wait for him during his sojourn in the United States.[28] After tirelessly picking cotton for a year in La Mesa, Texas, he returned to find María de la Cruz engaged to a family friend, and he felt spurned and humiliated. He believed so much in her love that he had endured labor exploitation for the sake of a more financially secure future with her. Days and even years after María de la Cruz's rejection, Pablo refused to discuss or mourn his loss.

266 · ANA ELIZABETH ROSAS

In my 2007 interview with Pablo Martínez, he discussed the first time he heard the lyrics of "Between Us," in the company of fellow sojourners from México. The lyrics, he said, helped him realize that he had suffered in silence for years. "This song made it easier to recognize [my] love for her, the pain of being separated, in love, and without hope of a future together."[29] Listening and reflecting on this song's lyrics in the company of immigrant men who had also had their hearts broken made it possible to mourn her loss. Despite his fears of being publicly perceived as an emotionally broken and desperate man, the song's lyrics gave him the "nerve to recognize and mourn how truly heartbroken [he] had been for years."[30] He was finally able to admit that María de la Cruz's rejection had informed his 1956 decision to delay his return to his hometown of Ameca, Jalisco, until 1962 simply because he could not fathom running into her as a happily married woman. The song became an essential part of his immigration story:

"ACA ENTRE NOS" (BETWEEN US)

Por presumir, a mis amigos les conte
Que en el amor ninguna pena me aniquila
Que pa' probarles
de tus besos me olvide
Y me bastaron unos tragos de tequila

To brag, to my friends I told them
That in love there was no pain that had gotten the best me
That to prove I had forgotten your kisses
Some shots of tequila had been enough

Les platiqué que me encontré con otro amor
Y que en sus brazos fui dejando de quererte
Que te aborrezco desde el dia de tu traición
Y que hay momentos que he deseado hasta tu muerte

I told them that I found another love
And that in her arms I stopped loving you
That I hate you since the day of your betrayal
And there are moments that I had wished even your death

Aca entre Nos
Quiero que sepas la verdad
No te he dejado de adorar
Alla en mi triste soledad
Me han dado ganas de gritar
Salir corriendo
Y preguntar que es lo que ha sido de tu vida

Between us
I want you to know the truth
I have not stopped adoring you
There in my sad loneliness
I've wanted to scream
Go out running
And ask what has become of your life

Aca entre nos
Siempre te voy a recordar
Y hoy que a mi lado ya no estás
No queda mas confesar
Que ya no puedo soportar
Que estoy odiando sin odiar
Porque respiro por la herida

Between us
I will always remember you
And today that you are not by my side
There is nothing left but to confess
That I cannot endure
That I am hating without hating
Because I breathe through the wound

Listening to songs of love also became an important outlet for Mexican women when separated from their Mexican immigrant boyfriends by the US-México border. Eighty-four-year-old Carmen Quezada is among the women who finds solace in "Ya lo Sé" ("I Already Know"), the famous *ranchera* popularized by Mexican artists such as Vicente Fernández, Juan Gabriel, and the late Mexican American singer Jenni Rivera. This song reminds her of a period of her youth when she longed for her absent Mexican-immigrant boyfriend, Ricardo, as he labored in the United States.[31] She recollects that when listening to this song, she did not resent her absent boyfriend or his decision to labor in the United States. Instead, this song emboldened her to acknowledge and feel "the heartache and loneliness of his absence and waiting for him" in the privacy of her parents' household as integral to his being able to labor in the United States.[32] Carmen understood his laboring in the United States to earn funds for them to marry and begin their life together, but she found it emotionally painful to accept that his immigration and labor required his absence and their separation across the US-México border. Songs of love render the emotional underpinnings of Mexican women's responses to mid-twentieth-century Mexican immigration and US employment conditions, as well as their impact on their emotional welfare.

Carmen listened to songs of love when alone, and like many women in long-distance romantic relationships, she wore a white shawl over her head and shoulders when out in public to signal to others that she was in a committed relationship and did not want to answer any sensitive questions about the state of this long-distance romantic relationship. Wearing the white shawl came at a high price, however. It required women like Carmen to be discreet: to remain silent about their fears of abandonment, unrequited love, and infidelity. My interviewees explained that shouldering such "emotional anxiety honorably, in silence, earning and keeping the right to wear the white shawl" made for "many a sleepless night, tears shed alone," and made it difficult to derive much joy from day-to-day social interactions in Mexican society.[33]

Beginning in 1950, when she first entered into her relationship, until 1955, Carmen pretended that she was not in emotional pain in order to prove herself worthy of the white shawl, but the performance of fidelity meant hardly ever talking, losing a considerable amount of weight, and crying herself to sleep for weeks at a time as she listened to songs of love. Her boyfriend, Ricardo, failed to return quickly, as he had promised, and this led her to question the seriousness of his emotional commitment to their love and to their future marriage.

Carmen was exhausted from keeping her fears and doubts to herself. She found it easier to spend her time cleaning the family home, because it shielded her from conversation with anyone beyond her family relatives. Carmen feared breaking into tears in public, which would call into question her fidelity, and thus her right to wear the white shawl. Revealing the intensity of her emotional anxiety in public would have cast indelible doubt on her moral character, honor, and confidence, as well as her emotional commitment, jeopardizing her (and her family's) public reputation as well as her prospects of marrying Ricardo or any other suitor. With so much at stake, Carmen suffered alone and in silence throughout the years of separation. Songs of love like "Ya lo sé" (I Already Know) offered a safe and acceptable outlet for expressing the feelings she kept bottled up inside.

In 2009, decades after wearing the white shawl, and after fifty years of marriage to the man she waited for in an arduous silence, Carmen rediscovered "Ya lo sé" and noted that she still found comfort and healing in the song. Although now an elderly woman with children and grandchildren of her own, Carmen listens and often sings along to "Ya lo sé" in the comforts of her family home in Los Angeles. She reflects on the song's qualities that made it possible for her to express her feelings in a socially acceptable way. "Being in love, in a romantic relationship with a Mexican immigrant man was very difficult," said Carmen. "It was a complicated and difficult emotional world."[34]

Carmen confided that it would have been impossible for "her heart to let [Ricardo] go." The lyrics of "Ya lo sé" captured the depths of her love for him and her fears of losing him—feelings that convention prohibited her from expressing:

"YA LO SÉ" (I ALREADY KNOW)

Vuelveme a decir que no me quieres
para que me quede bien clarito
para ver si en todas las paredes
dejo de escribir te necesito

Tell me again that you don't love me
So that it is very clear to me
To see if on all the walls
I stop writing that I need you

Ya lo sé
Que aunque llore y te pida
Y te implore
No vas a volver
Ya lo se pero
A mi corazon como diablos se lo hago entender

I already know
That even if I cry and ask you
And implore you
You will not return
I already know
How in hell do I make my heart understand

. . .

Draconian immigration policies and rigid gender expectations imposed untold restrictions on the lives and relationships of Mexican women and men in the mid-twentieth century. These stories are largely untold. Recapturing the emotional lives of immigrants and the loved ones they left behind provides an important lens for understanding the immigrant experience.

Now well into their eighties, the women and men I interviewed can more willingly reflect on the long-distance relationships that defined much of their lives. The inability to maintain regular communication with their loved ones, sometimes for months at a time, was agonizing. Films and songs of love were often the only acceptable outlets for expressing anxiety, fears, and other emotions when facing the absence of their Mexican immigrant loved ones. These films and songs of love, together with oral histories, now allow us to appreciate and understand the emotional lives of immigrants: stories that have been largely ignored in the historical narratives on immigration.

As the case of Virginia Martínez and her co-nationals in the Río Tijuana encampment demonstrates, recovering the life stories of immigrants is not easy, but it is a task worth undertaking. Silence and ignorance leads to erasure. To understand the full impact of immigration policies on workers and their families, the stories of ordinary women and men must be told. Only then can historians claim to have written a humane history of immigration.

Notes

1. Isaias Alvarado, "Angeles del Purgatorio," *La Opinion*, September 16, 2013.

2. Alicia Schmidt Camacho, *Migrant Imaginaries: Latino Cultural Politics in the US-Mexico Borderlands* (New York: New York University Press, 2008).

3. Matthew Frye Jacobson, *Special Sorrows* (Boston: Harvard University Press, 1995); Roger Rouse, "A Making Sense of Settlement: Class Transformation, Cultural Struggle and Transnationalism among Mexican Migrants to the Unites States," *Annals of the New York Academy of Science* (1992): 25–52; Roger Rouse, "A Thinking Through Transnationalism: Notes on the Cultural Politics in the Contemporary United States," *Public Culture* 7, no. 2 (Winter 1995): 353–402; Douglas Massey, Rafael Alarcon, Jorge Durand, and Humberto González, *Return to Aztlan: The Social Process of International Migration from Western Mexico* (Berkeley: University of California Press, 1990); Deborah Cohen, *Braceros: Migrant Citizens and Transnational Subjects in the Postwar United States and Mexico* (Chapel Hill: University of North Carolina Press, 2011); Jose Alamillo, *Making Lemonade out of Lemons* (University of Illinois Press, 2007); Matt García, *A World of Its Own* (Chapel Hill: University of North Carolina Press, 2003); David G. Gutiérrez, *Walls and Mirrors* (Berkeley: University of California Press, 1995); Kelly Lytle Hernández, *Migra! The History of the US Border Patrol* (Berkeley: University of California Press, 2010); Stephen Pitti, *The Devil in Silicon Valley* (Princeton, N.J.: Princeton University Press, 2003); Zaragosa Vargas, *Labor Rights and Civil Rights* (Princeton, N.J.: Princeton University Press, 2004); Yen Le Espiritu, *Homebound* (Berkeley: University of California Press, 2004); George J. Sánchez, *Becoming Mexican American* (New York: Oxford University Press, 1993); and Vicki L. Ruiz, *From Out of the Shadows* (New York: Oxford University Press, 1998).

4. Manuel Ávila Camacho to Eduardo Zepeda, August 4, 1942, series 19, folder 60, Archivo San Martin de Hidalgo, Jalisco, Mexico.

5. US House of Representatives Committee on the Judiciary Subcommittee on Immigration, "Citizenship, Refugees, Border Security, and International Law," Testimony by Stephen Pitti, open-file report, 2–4, April 19, 2007, https://judiciary.house.gov/_files/hearings/April2007/Pitti070419.pdf.

6. Ibid.

7. Ana Elizabeth Rosas, *Abrazando El Espiritu: Bracero Families Confront the US-Mexico Border* (Berkeley: University of California Press, 2014), 66–69.

Love as Mirror and Pathway • 271

8. Juan Ramón Garcia, *Operation Wetback: The Mass Deportation of Mexican Undocumented Workers in 1954* (Westport, Conn.: Greenwood, 1980); and Kelly Lytle Hernández, "The Crimes and Consequences of Illegal Immigration: A Cross-Border Examination of Operation Wetback, 1943 to 1954," *Western Historical Quarterly* (Winter 2006): 421–44.

9. "Cartas a Eufemia" (Letters to Eufemia), Argel Films S.L., 1952.

10. María Teresa Garza, oral history interview by author, Los Angeles, California, 2009.

11. "Carta a Eufemia" (Letter to Eufemia), 1952, Pedro Infante.

12. "Contestación de Eufemia" (Eufemia's Response), 1952, Pedro Infante.

13. "Cartas a Eufemia" (Letters to Eufemia), Argel Films S.L., 1952.

14. Ibid.

15. Catalina Ruiz, oral history interview by author, Los Angeles, California, 2010.

16. Ibid.

17. María Elena Medina, oral history interview by author, Los Angeles, California, 2010.

18. Ibid.

19. María Teresa Garza interview.

20. Ibid.

21. Carmen Quezada, oral history interview by author, Los Angeles, California, 2009.

22. María Teresa Garza interview.

23. Catalina Ruiz interview.

24. Pablo Martinez, oral history interview by author, Guadalajara, Jalisco, 2007.

25. Ibid.

26. Lorenzo Macías, oral history interview by author, Los Angeles, California, 2007; Banda la Costeña, *Una Aventura* from *Una Aventura*, Musart—Balboa B000S5730I, 1995, compact disc; Vicente Fernandez, *Aca Entre Nos* from *La Historia de un Idolo*, Sony Special Products B00138J3YM, 2000, compact disc.

27. Ibid.

28. Pablo Martínez interview.

29. Ibid.

30. Ibid.

31. Carmen Quezada inteview; Jenni Rivera, *La Gran Señora*, Fonovisa B002TV20K6, 2009, compact disc.

32. Ibid.

33. Ibid.

34. Ibid.

Afterword

The Black Presence in US Immigration History

VIOLET SHOWERS JOHNSON

The foreign-born of African descent have always been at the periphery of American immigration historiography. General histories of race, ethnicity, and immigration clearly demonstrate this shortcoming. Gradually increasing attention to Asian and Latino immigrants, they focus heavily on European immigrants, while immigrants of African descent are omitted or mentioned briefly. Even studies that set out to rescue "forgotten" immigrants from obscurity give relatively scant attention to communities established by African-descended immigrants.[1] By the second decade of the twenty-first century, there seemed to have emerged a plethora of studies focusing specifically on the Black immigrant experience in America. However, the monographs, articles, edited volumes, and life histories belie the shortcomings of an uneven scholarship. Very little of the burgeoning literature is in the discipline of history, as most of the studies have been undertaken by sociologists, anthropologists, and scholars of literary and cultural studies.[2]

The scarcity of research and experts in the historical study of the Black immigrant experience in the United States thus poses a challenge for an anthology like *A Nation of Immigrants Reconsidered: The US in an Age of Restriction, 1924–1965*, which seeks to pursue a wide breadth of topics and racial and ethnic groups. Compounding the problem for such a volume, which focuses on the pre-1965 era, is the fact that Black immigrant scholarship, vastly more robust for the post-1965 period, is skewed. With only a few works that study mostly Afro-Caribbean or West Indian immigrants of the early twentieth century,[3] US immigration history, as a field, is inarguably deficient in the coverage of the experiences of foreign-born Blacks

274 · AFTERWORD BY VIOLET SHOWERS JOHNSON

in the period covered by the anthology. Consequently, where and how could an anthology like this have located the research on Black immigration before 1965 in order to balance its focus and content? This afterword addresses this challenge by offering an overview of African and West Indian immigration.[4] Why the paucity in scholarship on pre-1965 Black immigrants from Africa and the West Indies? Are there research materials for that period? Where are they? What would pique interest in this era and prompt students and scholars to study it through historical methodologies, even if also grounded in interdisciplinary approaches?

Devaluation of the Black immigrant presence before 1965 is a casualty of the premium placed on numbers. Immigration statistics and census records consistently revealed that immigrants of African descent arrived in trickles and established very small communities. In fact, because they mostly settled in communities already established as "Black neighborhoods" by American-born Blacks, they disappeared into generalized American Black/African American communities. The enormity of their invisibility is aptly captured by renowned historian of African American history Ira Berlin, who observed that "their [Black immigrants'] percentage of the population was to the right of the decimal point."[5]

While the statistics about their representation in the American population were accurate, their experiences as immigrants, erroneously, were seen as so negligible as to be undeserving of scholarly attention. For example, in 1934 the British Ambassador in Washington, DC, sent a circular to all consular officers instructing them to gather information on West Indian communities in their respective jurisdictions. In response, the consul general in Boston reported that there was no need to gather information about the Black British subjects of that city, as they had "not formed a cohesive group worth researching."[6] In reality, by that time, West Indians of Boston had established a church, a newspaper, a mutual benefit association, and sports clubs. There was, indeed, a West Indian community worth researching but which, demographically, was subsumed in a larger Black Bostonian community. New York City had a more established, more visible West Indian community at the same time. Similar, even if smaller, Afro-Caribbean communities had taken root in other parts of the eastern seaboard, in cities like Hartford, Connecticut, and Miami, Florida. Cape Verdeans in New England, especially in New Bedford, confirmed the permanent presence of voluntary immigrants from the African continent.

West African students, mostly from Nigeria and Ghana, were also among the arrivals of foreign Blacks in the first decades of the twentieth century. As early as the 1920s and 1930s, they had started enrolling in historically Black colleges and universities (HBCUs) like Howard University in Washington, DC, Fisk University in Nashville, Lincoln University in Pennsylvania, Hampton University in Virginia, and Tuskegee University in Alabama. Given this affiliation, it is not surprising that they interacted closely with African Americans, especially African American activists of the Harlem Renaissance. Two famous Lincoln alumni from this cohort are Kwame Nkrumah, first prime minister of Ghana, the first sub-Saharan country to attain independence, and Nnamdi Azikiwe, first president of Nigeria. These iconic figures recounted in their memoirs their experiences in America as students and temporary residents. But while this phase of their lives and its importance in their political maturity is often emphasized in African history, they are hard to find in American immigration history. Like Nkrumah and Azikiwe, during this period the students overwhelmingly returned home to join in nation-building. Still, some remained and formed the nucleus of West African immigrant communities that emerged in the 1960s and 1970s, especially in the Maryland–Washington, DC–Virginia area, where most of them had studied.

These experiences point to an American immigration story that has not been fully explored. The existence of Black immigrant ethnic institutions, created and sustained in subcultures within a larger Black American milieu, underscores that there is no denying the viable presence of foreign-born Blacks from Africa and the Caribbean in pre-1965 American society. The Boston British consul's response, when asked to research Black foreigners in his jurisdiction, is the epitome of a trend that, considering that Black foreigners were to the "right of the decimal point," completely dismissed their relevance to immigration scholarship.

In the period covered by this anthology, because the already small numbers of Blacks entering the United States were curtailed further, their scholarly insignificance would seem to warrant more justification. However, paradoxically, Black foreigners featured in the discourse on immigration reform, including official debates in the legislature, even before 1924. In 1914, US Representative Percy E. Quinn from Mississippi, arguing for the exclusion of all people of African descent, boldly lamented, "Of all the misfortunes that the civilization of this Republic has fastened to the body politic it is the African race which stands as the worst."[7] Some within and outside Congress did not think that Black immigration was worth addressing. The November 9, 1914, editorial of the *Boston Post* observed: "The exclusion is all the more offensive because it is in no way needed, even if one agrees that the dark peoples ought to be excluded. Only a few Negroes enter the United States each year. They come from the West Indies and they are generally useful types of laborers."

The perception of "foreign Negroes" of the first half of the twentieth century as small in number and marginalized as simply "useful types of laborers" discounted them as insignificant. This perception has contributed directly to the enduring lacuna in American immigration historiography. Studies like *A Nation of Immigrants Reconsidered* provide the opportunity to revisit a significant period in US immigration and begin to fill this gap. The chapters in this volume offer comparative and gendered perspectives for understanding the history of immigration from Europe, Asia, and Mexico. These are perspectives that can be used to study African and

Afro-Caribbean immigration in the same period. As the anthology affirms for other groups, the age of restriction, far from being a lull, saw a lot happen in the history of non-native-born Blacks in America, in spite of their small numbers and inconspicuous immigrant enclaves. The themes, questions, and emphases of the collection can serve as pointers of what to pursue in ferreting out and discussing developments in US Black immigration history in the four decades preceding Hart-Celler, especially as they related to evolving US immigration policies and their repercussions.

Like European, Asian, and Latin American migration flows of the first half of the twentieth century, the arrival and settlement of Black migrants from Africa and the Caribbean were vitally influenced by larger international developments. Therefore, in revisiting the pre-1965 era to illuminate the Black immigrant experience, researchers must address questions like: How did political and social movements of the era influence Black immigration and attitudes toward Black foreigners? What did the decolonization campaigns in Africa and the Caribbean, especially during and after the two world wars, do to shape US debates and discourses on immigrants and immigration? How did political and economic developments in Europe and its former colonies affect migration of Blacks from the Caribbean and other parts of the British and French empires? How did the Cold War shape, subtly and overtly, the evolving history of African immigrants in America?

In the early stages of the Cold War, for example, as the United States and the Soviet Union vied for "clients" in Africa, both stepped up their outreach to African students. Through such initiatives as the Africa-America Institute (AAI), founded in 1953, the Africa Scholarship Program of America Universities (ASPAU), founded in 1960, and the African Graduate Fellowship Program (AFGRAD), founded in 1963, the United States began an aggressive policy of providing opportunities for Africans to pursue advanced studies at US institutions with the objective of preparing them to serve as a vanguard for the development of their newly independent nations. These programs introduced Africans to the many opportunities in America, not just for the scholarship recipients but also for their family and friends. It was thus not a coincidence that during the Cold War and the dawn of the postcolonial era, more Africans looked to the United States than Europe for opportunities. In fact, some of the first beneficiaries of the new US international educational policy did not return to their countries of origin, and many others who returned eventually came back to settle in the United States, thus laying the foundation for the first visible and permanent African immigrant communities. Therefore, studying these "student-to-immigrant" communities within the framework of Cold War and postcolonial politics certainly enriches our understanding of the ways domestic and global developments shaped US immigration policies and immigrant communities.

The Black Presence in US Immigration History • 277

More work about the Black immigrant experience would further complicate the useful glimpses into the labor experiences of Europeans, Asians, and Latin Americans that the chapters in this volume provide. The experience of Cape Verdeans from West Africa, who have been coming to America since the nineteenth century, and Jamaican migrants represent two examples of the type of contribution more studies in this area would add to migration studies. Though they first worked in the whaling industry, by the 1920s and 1930s, Cape Verdeans had become a reliable labor force in the cranberry bogs of New England, especially in New Bedford, where they established a visible enclave.[8] Similarly, tobacco farmers brought Jamaican men to the Connecticut River Valley for seasonal work on their farms under an agreement between the United States and Britain, the colonial power. Jamaicans and other West Indians were among the first beneficiaries of temporary-worker visas.

Studying African migration would also add to the history of migrant-labor agreements beyond the bracero program and Latin America. In 1943, for example, the United States and the colonial government of the Bahamas negotiated a migrant-farm-labor agreement that lasted until 1966. Known in the Bahamas variously as "The Contract" or "The Project," the program enabled thousands of Bahamian men and women to work on farms in several states across the United States: the workers harvested tobacco in Tennessee, peaches in Georgia, corn in Minnesota, citrus in Florida, and peanuts in North Carolina. During the program's existence, many of the workers carried on transnational lives that involved their going back and forth between the United States and their Bahamian homes. Some chose to settle permanently in the United States, particularly in Florida. This program, involving numerous families, left indelible marks in Bahamian society. While "The Contract" stands as an exemplar of the prominent place of Black immigrants in labor migration to the United States, especially between 1940 and 1965,[9] this and other contemporaneous "Black" labor-migration arrangements have yet to be studied fully.[10] More research would reveal crucial dimensions of this history: the debates for and against the program; reception of the Black migrants by the White and Black native-born in the states where they worked temporarily or settled permanently; the Bahamians' interactions with other migrants, especially other farm workers; and the facilitators of and impediments to the formation of Black Bahamian communities born out of temporary-farm-labor migration.

Like many for the immigrants discussed in this anthology, community building was a significant part of the evolving pre-1965 immigration history for African migrants as well. Future researchers should pay closer attention to how non-White communities of US-born and foreign-born Blacks changed during this critical period in US immigration history. Especially in urban areas of the Eastern seaboard, the confluences of migration streams from the American South, Puerto Rico,

278 · AFTERWORD BY VIOLET SHOWERS JOHNSON

Cuba, and other parts of the Caribbean profoundly transformed the demography of Black America. As the various "Black" groups settled in the same neighborhoods, the relationships that emerged were simultaneously collaborative, contentious, and ambivalent. Caribbean immigrants, more commonly known as West Indians, strived to develop and project a distinct successful and exemplary community, even as they, particularly their leaders, fought for civil rights alongside American-born Blacks.[11] The complex relationships forged within these non-White communities illuminate crucial aspects of immigration history of the period: how immigrants of African descent were racialized; how they straddled foreign and imposed racial identities; how native-born Blacks perceived these foreigners as occupiers of the same space in the margins of the United States.

Indeed, in explaining the United States as a nation of immigrants, a salient topic has to be the unique positioning of African Americans in immigration policy debates. Since the nineteenth century, Black intellectuals have addressed the impact of immigration on the country's "major" minority. From Booker T. Washington to Anna Julia Cooper, Robert Lee Vann, Carter G. Woodson, and Kelly Miller, African American leaders have discussed their relationship to immigrant communities. Many journalists and scholars have argued that African Americans oppose immigration because immigrants displace Black workers and adopt, as part of their Americanization, the racist views of White society. This interpretation is simplistic and does not do justice to the role of African Americans in US immigration history. Consideration of African Americans and the immigration question should go beyond a mere examination of Black and immigrant labor competition. Historians Arnold Shankman and Lawrence Fuchs were among the first scholars to point to the complexities of assessing African Americans, race, and immigration.[12] And, as sociologist Stephen Steinberg has noted, African Americans and their views and reactions must be central to any discussion of immigration. Historian Paul Spickard makes a similar point. In his book, *Almost All Aliens*, Spickard denounces the traditional Ellis Island paradigm of US immigration history, urging scholars and students to incorporate the stories from other points of entry and articulate the necessity of grasping African American history to understand the immigrant experience.[13]

Comparative analyses that establish the links and reveal the nuances between epochs, geographic regions, immigrant groups, and immigration flows would also be very useful. This comparative approach would be eye opening in numerous ways. Imagine comparing the experiences of Chinese sailors on British ships who "deserted" to the New York Chinese American community and that of West Indians, on the vessels of American fruit companies, who "stowed away" to the same American cities during the same period. How would debates over the admission of refugees in the 1940s, 1950s, and 1960s, when World War II and Cold War refugees predominated, compare with postcolonial debates over African civil war refugees and post-9/11 refugees, heavily Middle Eastern and Muslim? These are just two of a host of potentially exciting perspectives that could inform and shape a comparative approach.

Immigration archives are important repositories for reconstructing these histories. Some of these archives are waiting to be fully utilized. The National Archives and Records Administration houses important government records, but there are also smaller, more localized repositories, mostly affiliated with institutions of higher learning, like the Immigration History Research Center of the University of Minnesota and the Balch Institute for Ethnic Studies at the Historical Society of Pennsylvania. They house the letters, photographs, and records of individuals and organizations important to ethnic communities. Local and state historical societies and libraries are also custodians of this history. However, to recover the experiences of Black immigrants and other ethnic/immigrant communities absent in the scholarship, scholars must work directly with the individuals and institutions in said communities: religious and secular organizations, community centers, and professional and labor associations. An ethnic newspaper, minutes of association meetings, sermons, life histories or memoirs, and recreational publicity materials reveal important, missed facts about a community and its history within the American polity. Working with these communities often requires bi- or multilingualism, a skill that many researchers interested in studying African immigrants may not have. This handicap should not deter them. Instead, they should strive to acquire some practical understanding of the pertinent African languages and/or work with volunteers and paid research assistants, who may be members of the immigrant community being studied.

What happens when the written records are insufficient or nonexistent? Oral history is a vital resource in writing immigration history, especially for underrepresented groups whose voices may not be reflected in conventional sources like newspapers, diaries, journals, and official correspondences. Oral history has been useful for reconstructing the Black immigrant experience. Many national, local, and international repositories now carry audio, video, and digital recordings of interviews with immigrants and their children across different eras. I benefited from such collections when I studied the major waves of English-speaking Afro-Caribbean immigrants who arrived in Boston in the first half of the twentieth century. Although a legitimate method of collecting information, historians often look dubiously on oral history because of the unreliability of memory. Therefore, in using materials either from structured, institutional oral history collections, or from one's own ethnographic field work, scholars must seek productive ways to combine oral history/ethnography and written records to produce academically rigorous scholarship.

280 • AFTERWORD BY VIOLET SHOWERS JOHNSON

To write about immigration, scholars must also examine multiple national histories. For example, to fully understand the Bahamian Black immigrant experience in Florida in the 1940s and 1950s, one must understand both US labor and political history and Bahamian colonial history; and one must be able to navigate resources in the United States, the Bahamas, and the United Kingdom. In my own work, documents in the Jamaican National Archives in Spanish Town, Jamaica, and the British Public Records Office in England proved indispensable in reconstructing the British West Indian community of the early twentieth century that was hidden from scholarly view. Historian Donna Gabaccia is one of the foremost proponents of a multinational methodology: US immigration history can only be understood in global contexts.[14] As Gabaccia and her students have demonstrated, researchers should cast wide nets beyond the United States for data that help bring a vibrant past to life. Therefore, a meaningful address of pre-1965 Black immigrant history must involve a practical familiarity with the indigenous, colonial, nationalist and early postcolonial histories of the African and the Caribbean (im)migrants.

As the few existing historical studies on Afro-Caribbean immigrants and the untapped sources on African migration demonstrate, there is no question about the viability of pre-1965 Black immigration. The question is how to get historians to go back to this period and conduct much-needed studies on the experiences of Black immigrants and the impact of their presence on the American polity, beyond Black America. The biggest obstacle seems to lie in the comparison of two epochs. Black immigration to the United States since the last quarter of the twentieth century has been substantial. Not only has this development attracted researchers, it has also rendered the preceding era uninteresting. The trends of the "new Black immigration," as the post-1970s immigration has been labeled, are attention grabbing. The numbers alone pique the interest of the media, policymakers, and scholars. The foreign-born Black population increased nearly seven times between 1960 and 1980, and more than tripled between 1980 and 2005.[15] It moved to the left of the decimal point. While in the pre–Hart-Celler era, Black immigrants, especially Africans, were concentrated in only a few states, especially in the Northeast, the post-1965 immigration, which now comprises of former students, economic migrants, and refugees, saw them dispersed widely across the United States.

More important, this time they did not dissipate into native-born Black America. Instead, in conspicuous ethnic businesses, religious and other cultural institutions, they rapidly developed clearly recognizable enclaves. In fact, in Minneapolis, the number of Somali refugees and their American-born children became so big, outpacing the number of African Americans, that Black foreigners have become the face of Black America in that city. Such an outcome goes to the heart of how foreign Blacks, by 2000, were redefining Black America. This and other spectacular

The Black Presence in US Immigration History • 281

outcomes of the post–Hart-Celler Black immigration continue to attract researchers, eager to explain the many fascinating developments of the new immigration. Ira Berlin's description of how Black immigrants since the passing of Hart-Celler are changing America captures the vitality and allure of this history:

> In New York, the Roman Catholic diocese has added masses in Ashanti and Fante, while black men and women from various Caribbean islands march in the West Indian-American Carnival and the Dominican Day Parade. In Chicago, Cameroonians celebrate their nation's independence day, while the DuSable Museum of African American History hosts a Nigerian Festival. Black immigrants have joined groups such as the Egbe Omo Yoruba (National Association of Yoruba Descendants in North America), the Association des Sénégalais d'Amérique and the Fédération des Associations Régionales Haïtiennes à l'Étranger rather than the NAACP or the Urban League.[16]

This kind of unprecedented African and Afro-Caribbean cultural production put the spotlight on foreign-born Blacks more than ever.

The impact of a historical development is always a compelling reason to study that history. Undoubtedly, the impact of post-1965 Black immigration to America is glaring. However, this must not subsume the relevance of an earlier, less overtly dynamic period. Perhaps, the first step to a meaningful revision is a conscious reorientation of how the relevance of the Black immigrant presence in the first half of the twentieth century is perceived. What does the raising of the issue of Black immigration in debates on immigration restriction tell us about the imagined and real impact of Black foreigners in the United States during that period? How did diverse groups of foreign-born African-descended people navigate racial and racist challenges in a pre-civil-rights-movement America? How did they change Black America, however subtly, during that period? Answering these and other such questions, perhaps with the assistance of untapped sources, would demonstrate that far from being irrelevant, the history of Black immigration in the period covered by this anthology can serve as a useful context for understanding the phenomenal "new immigration" that came after 1970. While, as this afterword points out in the opening, Black immigration has been at the periphery of US immigration historiography, it does have something in common with other immigration histories: like the histories of other groups covered in this collection, consequences of the 1965 immigration reform, commonly described as unintended revolutionary outcomes, further blurred the history of pre-1965 Black immigration. With a reorientation in interpretation, a productive search for existing, even if obscure, sources, a stimulation of the interest of students and scholars, who must tackle the antecedents of a new Black immigration, that history can be recovered, researched, and disseminated.

282 · AFTERWORD BY VIOLET SHOWERS JOHNSON

Notes

1. See, for example, renowned historian Roger Daniels's well-received book, *Coming to America: A History of Immigration and Ethnicity in America* (New York: HarperCollins, 1990), where he only glosses over a few aspects of immigration of Blacks from the Caribbean. Another renowned historian of immigration history, David Reimers, did an outstanding job shedding light on "the other immigrants," as he called them, when he discussed non-Europeans—Mexicans, Central and South Americans, South and East Asians and Middle Easterners. While he made a decent attempt to unearth the Black immigrant experience, he lumped all Black immigrants—from the Caribbean and the vast continent of Africa—into one chapter, "The New Black Immigration." See David M. Reimers, *Other Immigrants: The Global Origins of the American People* (New York: New York University Press, 2005).

2. The following are a few notable examples: John Arthur, *Invisible Sojourners: African Immigrant Diaspora in the United States* (Westport, Conn.: Praeger, 2000); Kofi Apraku, *African Emigres in the United States: A Missing Link in Africa's Social and Economic Development* (Westport, Conn.: Praeger, 1991); Festus Obiakor and Patrick Grant, eds., *Foreign-Born African Americans: Silenced Voices in the Discourse on Race* (New York: Nova, 2002); and Mary C. Waters, *Black Identities: West Indian Immigrant Dreams and American Realities* (Cambridge, Mass.: Harvard University Press, 1999).

3. Notable works by historians in this field are: Winston James, *Holding Aloft the Banner of Ethiopia: Caribbean Radicalism in Early Twentieth-Century America* (London: Verso, 1998); Irma Watkins-Owens, *Blood Relations: Caribbean Immigrants and the Harlem Community, 1900–1930* (Bloomington: Indiana University Press, 1996); Violet Showers Johnson, *The Other Black Bostonians: West Indians in Boston, 1900–1950* (Bloomington: Indiana University Press, 2006). The only historical book-length study of African immigrants before 1965, for a long time, was Marilyn Halter's work, *Between Race and Ethnicity: Cape Verdean American Immigrants, 1860–1965* (Urbana: University of Illinois Press, 1993).

4. A rich literature exists on Black immigrants from Spanish- and Portuguese-speaking countries. Two of the largest sources of Black migration during the 1924–1965 period are Puerto Rico and Cuba. These Black Latino (im)migrants straddled different worlds: *Latinidad*, Blackness, and foreignness. In the case of Puerto Ricans, they were also US citizens.

5. Ira Berlin, "The Changing Definition of African-American: How the Great Influx of People from Africa and the Caribbean since 1965 is Changing What It Means to be African-American," *Smithsonian Magazine*, February, 2010, http://www.smithsonianmag.com/history/the-changing-definition-of-african-american-4905887.

6. Report of the British Embassy, Washington, DC, to the Foreign Secretary, March 1934, Public Record Office, Kew (PRO) FO 598/15.

7. US Congress, *Congressional Record*, 63rd Cong., 3rd Sess., vol. 52, pt.1, December 31, 1914, S 1134.

8. For more on Cape Verdean migration, see Halter, *Between Race and Ethnicity*.

9. Recruiting beyond the Bahamas, Jamaica, and Barbados, eager to offset labor shortage, especially during the war years, the United States formulated a West Indian

temporary-labor plan that lasted decades. See J. C. Vialet, "The West Indies (BWI) Temporary Alien Labor Program, 1943–1977: A Study Prepared for the Subcommittee on Immigration of the Committee on the Judiciary, United States Senate," (Washington, DC: GPO, 1978), http://www.dloc.com//UF00087215/0001.

10. In 1993, Bahamas affirmed the significance of The Contract in its history, when the Oral History Department of the College of the Bahamas kicked off a multiyear oral history project to capture the experiences of surviving contract workers. Bahamian scholars especially have begun to benefit from the outcomes of this project. See, for example, T. L. Thompson, "Remembering 'The Contract': Recollections of Bahamians," *International Journal of Bahamian Studies* 18 (2012): 6–12, http://journals.sfu.ca/cob/index.php/files/article/view/169/217. Examining gender and sexuality in Miami from its founding in 1896 to 1940, historian Julio Capó offers useful glimpses into immigration from the Bahamas, Cuba, and Haiti. See, Julio Capó, *Welcome to Fairyland: Queer Miami before 1940* (Chapel Hill: University of North Carolina Press, 2017).

11. See Watkins-Owens, *Blood Relations*; and Showers Johnson, *Other Black Bostonians*.

12. Arnold Shankman, *Ambivalent Friends: Afro-Americans View the Immigrant* (Westport, Conn.: Greenwood, 1992); Lawrence H. Fuchs, "The Reactions of Black America to Immigration," in *Immigration Reconsidered: History, Sociology, and Politics*, ed. Virginia Yans-McLaughlin (Oxford University Press, 1990), 293–314.

13. See for example, Stephen Steinberg, "Immigration, African Americans, and Race Discourse," *New Politics* (Summer 2005), http://newpol.org/content/immigration-african-americans-and-race-discourse. Steinberg succeeded in generating further interest and a discussion on African Americans and immigration, as evidenced in the responses to this piece. See, for example, Adolph Reed, "A Response to 'Immigration, African Americans, and Race Discourse,'" *New Labor Forum* 15 (2006): 59–61; Gary Gerstle, "A Response to 'Immigration, African Americans, and Race Discourse,'" *New Labor Forum* 15 (2006): 65–68; Paul Spickard, *Almost All Aliens: Immigration, Race, and Colonialism in American History and Identity* (New York: Routledge, 2007).

14. Donna R. Gabaccia, *Foreign Relations: American Immigration in Global Perspectives* (Princeton, N.J.: Princeton University Press, 2012).

15. Mary Mederios Kent, "Immigration and America's Black Population," *Population Bulletin* 62 (December 2007), www.prb.org.

16. Berlin, "Changing Definition of African-American."

Contributors

EIICHIRO AZUMA is Alan Charles Kors Term Chair associate professor of History and interim director of Asian American Studies at University of Pennsylvania. He is author of *Between Two Empires: Race, History, and Transnationalism in Japanese America*, and co-editor, with Gordon H. Chang, of Yuji Ichioka, *Before Internment: Essays in Prewar Japanese American History*. In 2016 Azuma also co-edited the *Oxford Handbook of Asian American History* with David K. Yoo. He has served on the editorial boards of the *Pacific Historical Review, Journal of Asian American Studies*, and *Journal of American Ethnic History*. Since 2009 he has served as a co-editor of the Asian American Experience series published by the University of Illinois Press.

DAVID COOK-MARTÍN (NYU Abu Dhabi) is a political sociologist whose work focuses on understanding migration, race, ethnicity, law, and citizenship in an international field of power. He is author of *The Scramble for Citizens: Dual Nationality and State Competition for Immigrants* (ASA's Thomas and Znaniecki Best Book on International Migration Award 2014) and co-author with David FitzGerald of *Culling the Masses: The Democratic Origins of Racist Immigration Policy in the Americas* (ASA's 2017 Distinguished Scholarly Publication Award, MSS Distinguished Book Award, APSA's Best Book on Migration and Citizenship 2015, ASA's Thomas and Znaniecki Best Book on International Migration 2015, ASA's Best Scholarly Contribution to Political Sociology). David has published articles and chapters on migration-control regimes, gendered citizenship and migration policy, Latin American migrations to Europe, ethnic return migration, integration, diffusion, and transnational reli-

286 · Contributors

gious networks. He is currently working on a new project that examines temporary migration regimes in global and historical perspective.

DAVID SCOTT FITZGERALD is Theodore E. Gildred Chair in US-Mexican Relations, professor of Sociology, and co-director of the Center for Comparative Immigration Studies at the University of California, San Diego. His research analyzes policies regulating migration in countries of origin, transit, and destination. FitzGerald's books include *Culling the Masses: The Democratic Origins of Racist Immigration Policy in the Americas*, which won the American Sociological Association's Distinguished Scholarly Book Award, and *A Nation of Emigrants: How Mexico Manages its Migration*. His current projects include directing the California Immigration Research Initiative and writing a book, tentatively titled *Refuge beyond Reach: How Reach Democracies Repel Asylum Seekers*, on efforts to deter asylum seekers from reaching North America, Europe, and Australia.

MARÍA CRISTINA GARCÍA, a 2016 Andrew Carnegie Fellow, is the Howard A. Newman Professor of American Studies in the Department of History at Cornell University. She also holds a joint appointment in the Latino Studies Program. García specializes in refugee and immigration history and policy. She is the author of *The Refugee Challenge in Post-Cold War America*; *Seeking Refuge: Central American Migration to Mexico, the United States, and Canada*; and *Havana USA: Cuban Exiles and Cuban Americans in South Florida*. She is currently completing a book on the environmental origins of refugee migrations.

MADELINE Y. HSU is professor of history and Asian American Studies at UT Austin. She is author of the multiple-award-winning monograph, *The Good Immigrants: How the Yellow Peril Became the Model Minority*, and *Asian American History: A Very Short Introduction*. Her current research explores circular migrations and exchanges across the Pacific as key strategies for international relations emerging from the Cold War era.

MONIQUE LANEY is assistant professor in the History Department at Auburn University, where she teaches courses in the history of technology. She earned her M.A. in Amerikanistik at the Johann Wolfgang Goethe-Universität in Frankfurt, Germany, and her PhD in American Studies at the University of Kansas in 2009. Her book *German Rocketeers in the Heart of Dixie: Making Sense of the Nazi Past during the Civil Rights Era* received best-book awards from the American Astronautical Society and the American Institute of Aeronautics and Astronautics, as well as honorable mention for the Deep South Book Prize of the Summersell Center for the Study of the South at the University of Alabama. Her current research focuses on the history of immigrants with "special skills."

Contributors · 287

HEATHER LEE is assistant professor of history at NYU Shanghai. She is completing a book on the history of Chinese restaurants in New York City and developing a database of historical Chinese restaurants in the United States. Her research has been featured in NPR, *Atlantic* magazine, and Gastropod, a podcast on food science and history. She has advised and curated exhibitions at the New York Historical Society, the National Museum of American History, and the Museum of Chinese in America.

KATHLEEN LÓPEZ is associate professor with a joint appointment in the Department of Latino and Caribbean Studies (LCS) and the Department of History at Rutgers University. She is author of *Chinese Cubans: A Transnational History*, which received the 2014 Gordon K. and Sybil Lewis Prize of the Caribbean Studies Association. She is also a contributor to the recently published volumes *Immigration and National Identities in Latin America*, *Critical Terms in Caribbean and Latin American Thought*, and *Imagining Asia in the Americas*. Her research and teaching focus on the historical intersections between Asia and Latin America and the Caribbean, postemancipation Caribbean societies, race and ethnicity in the Americas, and international migration.

LAURA MADOKORO is a historian and assistant professor in the Department of History and Classical Studies at McGill University. She is author of *Elusive Refuge: Chinese Migrants in the Cold War* and co-editor of the collection *Dominion of Race: Rethinking Canada's International History* in addition to numerous articles that have appeared in publications such as *Photography and Culture*, *Social History / Histoire Sociale*, *Modern Asian Studies*, *International Journal*, and the *Journal of Refugee Studies*. She is interested in questions of race, humanitarianism, migration, and settler colonialism. Her current research explores the history of sanctuary in North America from the 1800s to the present.

MADDALENA MARINARI is assistant professor of history at Gustavus Adolphus College. She has written extensively on immigration restriction, US immigration policy, and immigrant mobilization, including articles published in the *Journal of Policy History* and the *Journal of American Ethnic History*. Her book *From Unwanted to Restricted* on Italian and Jewish mobilization against restrictive immigration laws from 1882 to 1965 will appear in 2019 with the University of North Carolina Press. She is currently working on a project on undocumented Italians to the United States prior to 1965.

RONALD L. MIZE is associate professor in the School of Language, Culture, and Society at Oregon State University. He was trained as a journalist at the University of Colorado-Boulder and went on to study Sociology at Colorado State University

288 · Contributors

(MA) and University of Wisconsin-Madison (PhD). In 2016 he was the Fulbright-Garcia Robles Chair in US Studies at el Instituto Tecnológico Autónomo de México. His scholarly research focuses on the historical origins of racial, class, and gender oppression in the lives of Mexicano/as residing in the United States. Professor Mize is author of more than fifty scholarly publications, including four books: *Latina/o Studies*, *The Invisible Workers of the US-Mexico Bracero Program: Obreros Olvidados*, *Consuming Mexican Labor: From the Bracero Program to NAFTA* with Alicia Swords, and *Latino Immigrants in the United States* with Grace Peña Delgado.

ARISSA H. OH is associate professor in the History Department at Boston College, where she teaches and researches migration in US history, particularly in relation to race, gender, and kinship. Her book on the history of international adoption, *To Save the Children of Korea: The Cold War Origins of International Adoption*, was published by Stanford University Press in 2015. She is currently working on a history of marriage migration and immigration fraud since the nineteenth century.

ANA ELIZABETH ROSAS is associate professor of history and Chicana/o-Latina/o Studies at the University of California, Irvine. She is the author of *Abrazando El Espíritu: Bracero Families Confront the US-Mexico Border* and is currently researching the emotive configuration and impact of continuous displacement on Mexican immigrant family life in Mexico and the United States.

VIOLET SHOWERS JOHNSON is professor of History and associate dean in the College of Liberal Arts, Texas A&M University, where she also teaches courses on the African diaspora and Africana studies. Her scholarship examines the experiences of immigrants of African descent in twentieth-century America. Her publications include *The Other Black Bostonians: West Indians in Boston, 1900–1950* and *African and American: West Africans in Post–Civil Rights America* (co-authored with Marilyn Halter). Her next monograph, *Black While Foreign*, uses three high-profile cases in the last quarter of the twentieth century to illustrate how Caribbean and African immigrants experienced and reacted to race and racism in America.

LORRIN THOMAS is associate professor and chair of the history department at Rutgers University-Camden. She is author of *Puerto Rican Citizen: History and Political Identity in Twentieth Century New York City* and, with Aldo Lauria Santiago, of the forthcoming book *Rethinking the Struggle for Puerto Rican Rights*.

RUTH ELLEN WASEM is professor of Public Policy Practice at the Lyndon B. Johnson School of Public Affairs at the University of Texas, where she teaches courses on immigration policy and policy development. For more than twenty-five years, Wasem was a domestic-policy specialist at the US Library of Congress's Congressional Research Service. Wasem earned master's and doctoral degrees in history at the University of Michigan, largely funded by the Institute for Social Research. Wasem is writing a book about the legislative drive to end race- and nationality-based immigration, receiving the John Kluge Staff Fellowship and the Abba P. Schwartz Research Fellowship in support of this research. She is currently engaged with a group of international scholars who are researching asylum and the rise of the political right. Other recent publications include "The US Visa Waiver Program: Facilitating Travel and Enhancing Security" and "Welfare and Public Benefits" in *American Immigration: An Encyclopedia of Political, Social, and Cultural Change*, and *Tackling Unemployment: The Legislative Dynamics of the Employment Act of 1946*.

ELLIOTT YOUNG is professor in the History Department at Lewis and Clark College, where he teaches Latin American and borderlands history. In 2003 he co-founded the Tepoztlán Institute for Transnational History of the Americas. Professor Young published three books on borderlands, migration, and transnational history, *Alien Nation: Chinese Migration in the Americas from the Coolie Era through WWII*, *Catarino Garza's Revolution on the Texas-Mexico Border*, and *Continental Crossroads*, a volume of essays by new scholars in the field. His columns have appeared in the *Huffington Post*, *Utne Reader*, *North American Congress on Latin America* (NACLA), *Oregonian*, *Portland Tribune*, *Oregon Humanities*, and the *History News Network*.

Index

Page numbers in italic indicate figures or tables.

Acheson, Dean, 90, 194
ACIC (American Citizenship and Immigration Conference), 199–200, 201, 204, 208, 209
ACLU (American Civil Liberties Union), 108, 111, 235
Act of August 9, 1946 (60 Stat. 975), 234, 249n16
Act of August 19, 1950 (PL 717), 235–236, 250n27
Act of July 2, 1946 (60 Stat. 416), 233, 249n19
Act of July 22, 1947 (PL 213), 235
adoption, 9
AFL (American Federation of Labor), 164, 170
AFL-CIO (American Federation of Labor and Congress of Industrial Organizations), 92–93, 179, 204
Africa-America Institute (AAI), 276
African Americans: Black immigrants and, 274, 275, 277–278, 280–281; collaborating with Puerto Ricans on civil rights issues, 222–223, 224–227; contribution to American life, 206; immigration policy debates and, 278; Jamaican workers and, 128; Japanese war brides and, 236, 243–244, 251n35. *See also* civil rights; race

African Graduate Fellowship Program (AFGRAD), 276
African immigrants: increase in, post-WWII, 11; research deficit on, 14, 273–274; as students, 274–275, 276. *See also* Black immigrants; specific countries
Africa Scholarship Program of America Universities (ASPAU), 276
AFSC (American Friends Service Committee), 66, 71–72, 74
agricultural workers: Black immigrants as, 277; British West Indies (BWI) guest-worker program, 168, 171, 172–173; compulsory savings system for, 137–138; Cuban sugar industry, 49; employers bear transportation costs, 132, 133–134, 137; recruitment, 136; West Indies recruitment, 123, 125, 128–130. *See also* Bracero Program; temporary workers; visas, H-2
agricultural workers, Japanese, 105, 161–180; AICF and, 162–165; Cold War diplomacy and, 161–162, 173–175; employers of, 168–169; government departments and, 170–173; immigrating as "refugees," 164–165; Japanese Americans' relations with, 175–179; Mike Masaoka and, 165–170
Agricultural Workers Association, 200

292 · Index

Agrón, Salvador "the Capeman," 213, 219
AICF (Association for International Collaboration of Farmers; Kokusai Nōyūkai), 162–165, 171
Aid Refugee Chinese Intellectuals Inc. (ARCI), 66, 71, 72–73, 76, 81nn42, 51
Alarcón, Rafael, 138
Albania, 6
alien passenger law (1837 revision), 32
Alien Seamen Program, 108, 115, 117–118
"aliens ineligible for citizenship" category, 4, 26, 84, 231. *See also* Asian exclusion
American Century, 3, 16n5
American Citizenship and Immigration Conference (ACIC), 199–200, 201, 204, 208, 209
American Civil Liberties Union (ACLU), 108, 111, 235
American Committee on Italian Immigration, 200
American Federation of Labor (AFL), 164, 170
American Federation of Labor and Congress of Industrial Organizations (AFL-CIO), 92–93, 179, 204
American Friends Service Committee (AFSC), 66, 71–72, 74
American Hellenic Educational Progressive Association, 200–201
American Immigration Conference, 199–200, 211n19
Americanization, 14, 187–188. *See also* assimilation
American Jewish Committee (AJC), 66, 67, 68–69, 75, 80n26, 200
American Jewish Congress, 235
The American Mercury, 243
Anderson, Donald, 209
Angel Island, 5, 28, 32, 38
Anglo-American Caribbean Commission, 129
anti-racism, 88–90, 166, 169
anti-racist resolutions, 87
anti-Semitism, 58
Antonetty, Evelina, 223
apportionment politics, 191
ARCI (Aid Refugee Chinese Intellectuals Inc.), 66, 71, 72–73, 76, 81nn42, 51
Armenia, 6

arms development, 1, 146, 153
Armstrong, Clairette, 216
Asia, 3, 4; eugenics and, 5; Johnson-Reed Act and, 5–6; race and, 8; visa waitlists in, 40. *See also specific countries*
Asian Americans, 94; race of, 243, 245. *See also* Japanese Americans
Asian exclusion: Asia-Pacific Triangle provision, 91, 193, 194, 237; Asians tracked by race as opposed to nationality, 8, 51, 251n39; historical narrative of, 231–232; Japanese exclusion, 5, 84, 92, 162, 172, 237; vs family unification, 189, 233–237. *See also* Chinese exclusion; racial exclusion through national-origins quotas
Asian immigrants: back door entry, 37, 45, 52–53, 59; demographics in US, 12, 83; Hart-Celler Act and, 95; increase in, post WWII, 11; Johnson-Reed Act and, 85; national-origins quotas and, 251n39; opposition to, *199*; PHS rejection rates, 30–32; restrictions on in McCarran-Walter Act, 162, 193, 194. *See also* Chinese exclusion; *specific countries*
Asia-Pacific Triangle, 91, 193, 194, 237
Asiatic Barred Zone, 5, 30, 85, 231
ASPAU (Africa Scholarship Program of America Universities), 276
Aspira, 221
assimilation: of Japanese Americans, 162, 165–166, 177, 178, 179–180, 186n106; of Japanese war brides, 189, 238, 240–242, 246. *See also* Americanization
Association for International Collaboration of Farmers (AICF; Kokusai Nōyūkai), 162–165, 171
Australia, 90
Austria, 40, 148
Austrian specialists. *See* German and Austrian specialists
Ávila Camacho, Manuel, 257
Axster, Herbert Felix, 144, 146, 154
Axster, Ilse, 154
Azikiwe, Nnamdi, 275

the Bahamas, 280; agricultural laborers recruited from, 123, 125, *126–127*; migrant-labor agreement with, 277, 283n10
Bailey, David, 29

Index • 293

Banda la Costeña, 263, 264
Barbados, 125, 128, 129
Batista, Fulgencio, 59
Bejarano, Margalit, 55
Benjamin Franklin High School, East Harlem, New York, 216, 217, 221
Benton, William, 91
Berlin, Ira, 274, 281
Bethe, Hans, 7
Black Americans. *See* African Americans
Black immigrants, 273–281; community building by, 14, 277–278, 280–281; comparative approach to history and, 278–279; Cuba and, 282n4; marginalization of, 275; as migrant labor, 277; national-origins quotas and, 9, 91; new wave of (increase in), 280–281; racial exclusion laws, worldwide, 84; research deficit on, 14, 273–274; research questions about, 276, 281; resources for understanding history of, 278–280; settlement/"disappearance" into African American communities, 274, 275. *See also specific countries*
Black studies programs, 226
B'nai B'rith, 200
Board of Immigration Appeals, 117
Bond, Niles W., 58
border crossing, illegal, 12
border patrolling, 6, 17n11, 46, 258
Borjas, George, 95
Boston Post, 275
Box, John, 85
Bracero Program, 7, 10, 123–124, 130–140; braceros killed by employers, 131; Chávez and, 94; discrimination and, 132, 133; employers bear braceros' transportation costs, 132, 133–134; end of, 104, 123, 135; First Bracero Program (WWI), 132, 142n21; H-2A visas and, 138; inception and provisions, 131–135, 142n21; reauthorization of, 135; recruitment center locations, 134; scale of, 141n4; separation from loved ones and, 189–190, 256–258; US states employing braceros, 130–131, 132–133; wages and, 134. *See also* agricultural workers; Mexican immigrants; temporary workers
bracero workers, Mexican: contracts of,

257; families of, 189–190; Japanese farm workers characterized in opposition to, 163, 167, 175, 176–177; Japanese immigrant labor and, 166, 176; treatment of German specialists in contrast with, 145
Braun, Marcus, 37
Brazil, 89
Britain, 29, 89–90, 147
British Shipping Mission, 111
British wartime shipping, 107–111, 113–120; cheap labor needed for, 107–108, 114, 117; conditions of, 108, 109–110, 114–116, 119; desertion by non-Chinese seamen, 114–115, 116; punishment for desertion, 116–119; shore leave, 108, 109, 111, 113, 114, 117; US government involvement, 104, 107, 108–109, 115–119. *See also* Chinese sailors, desertion of British ships by; World War II
British West Indies: guest-worker program, 168, 171, 172–173; national-origins quotas for, 47, 91
British West Indies Central Labor Organization (BWICLO), 129, 136, 137–138
Brown, Richard, 72
Burton, Antoinette, 119

Calavita, Kitty, 135
California Farm Production Association, 164
Cameroonian immigrants, 281
Canada, 36–37, 45–46, 90
Canadian immigrants, 28, 126–127, 129
Canary Islands, 48
Cape Verde, immigration from, 274, 277
Caribbean. *See* West Indies
Caribbean immigrants. *See* West Indian immigrants
Carmichael, Stokely, 223
Cartas a Eufemia (Letters to Eufemia) (1952), 258–263
Catholic church groups, 67
Catholicism, Kennedy election and, 201, 211n21
Celler, Emanuel, 75–76, 94, 202, 208
Center for Puerto Rican Studies, 226
Central Intelligence Agency (CIA), 39
Channel, William, 74
Chávez, César, 94
Chiang Kai-shek, 88

294 · Index

children, 7, 68, 255; exempt from quotas, 9, 11, 54, 94; mixed-race children of Japanese war brides, 189, 244–246; reformist concern and, 214. *See also* family reunification; Puerto Rican youth

Chin, Gabriel, 83, 95

China: AFSC in, 71; Dumbarton Oaks meetings and, 89; Jewish refugees move to, 69; remote control in, 26; wartime relations with Britain, 110. *See also* Hong Kong

China Daily News, 88, 114

Chinese exclusion: Chinese Exclusion Act, 4, 29, 36, 48, 70, 88, 231; Cuba and, 36–37, 46, 48–49, 52–53, 55, 57, 59–60; enforcement of, 5, 26, 29–32, 34–37, 48–49; laws, worldwide, 84, 88; Magnuson Act repeals, 7, 70, 88, 233, 234, 249n16; Mexico and, 36–37, 61n3; tracked by race as opposed to nationality, 8, 251n39; US entry through neighboring countries, 45, 52–53, 59, 61n3. *See also* Chinese refugees

Chinese Exclusion Act (1882), 4, 29, 48, 70, 88, 231

Chinese immigrants: family unification and, 233–234, 236, 249n16; opposition to, *199*

Chinese Nationalist Daily, 114

Chinese refugees, 69–74; ARCI and, 66, 71, 72–73, 76, 81nn42, 51. *See also* refugee policy

Chinese sailors, desertion of British ships by: after agitating for improved conditions, 108, 109–111, 114, 118, 119; Alien Seamen Program and, 108, 117; British tactics to prevent, 109, 111, 117; compared to other nationalities, 114–*115, 116*; impact on shipping, 111; punishment for, 118–119; racism influences, 104, 114–119; raids to find, 107, 118–119; restaurant employment and, 104, 108, 112–113; shore leave and, 108, 109, 111, 113; social networks assist, 104, 108, 112–113, 119; US government involvement, 104, 107, 108–109, 116–119; wage gap influences, 104, 109–110, 111, 114, 117. *See also* British wartime shipping

Christensen, Thomas, 111, 114–115

Chung Wing Kee, 113

citizenship, 34; in Cuba, 57–58; eligibility criteria, 3, 4, 6; experiences of, 14,

187–190; path to, for German/Austrian specialists, 148–154; status of Filipino immigrants, 6, 36, 187; status of Puerto Rican immigrants, 187, 213, 214. *See also* Americanization; assimilation

citizenship restrictions, 3, 14, 103, 105

civil rights: collaboration between African Americans and Puerto Ricans, 222–223, 224–227; emergence of movement, 200; linked to immigration reform, 205–206; as top problem for US, 202, 212n27

Civil Rights Act (1964), 10, 83, 92

civil rights movement, 83, 90, 94

class-based exclusion, 28; LPC clause, 4, 17n11, 29, 36

Clay, Lucius D., 150

Cold War, 4; African students and, 276; Asian exclusion and, 233; fear of communism, 149–150, 165, 198–*199*; immigration of German specialists and, 149–151, 156; Japanese agricultural worker program and, 161–162, 172, 173–175; national-origins quotas and, 3, 7–8, 60, 86; politics of, refugee policy debates and, 68–70, 73, 75, 76, 77n1, 78n4

colonialism, 17n6, 119, 141n15, 227; decolonization, 4, 8, 70, 88–89, 276; Japanese agricultural labor program and, 171; national-origins quotas and, 9, 47, 85; US-Japan relations and, 162–163

Colorado, 132–133; labor relief program in, *126*

colorblindness, 242

Commission on Immigration and Naturalization (Truman Commission), 92, 195–196

communism, fear of, 149–150, 165, 198–*199*

communism, policy on refugees fleeing, 9, 11, 18n18, 69–70, 72–73, 75, 78n4. *See also* Cold War

community building, by Black immigrants, 14, 277–278

Congress, 3, 6, 68, 84; Asian exclusion and, 231, 233, 234; Japanese war brides legislation and, 234–236; national-origins quotas and, 192–193, 201–202; restrictionists in, 7–8, 10, 12, 13, 22, 86; Truman's veto on McCarran-Walter Act and, 195

Congress, refugee policy and. *See* refugee policy

Congress of Industrial Organizations (CIO), 88, 170, 192

Cooley, Thomas, 192

"coolies" (Chinese indentured laborers), 29, 48, 114. *See also* Chinese immigrants

Council for Supplementary Agricultural Workers (CSAW; Nōgyō Rōmusha Habei Kyōgikai), 171, 173, 174

Covello, Leonard, 216, 217

criminality, 4; German war criminals, 148, 149, 155; Puerto Rican youth accused of, 188, 214, 215–217. *See also* immigration law enforcement

Crowder, Enoch, 55, 56

Cuba, 7, 45–61, 89; Chinese exclusion and, 36–37, 46, 48–49, 52–53, 55, 57, 59–60; demographics of immigrants in US, 12; Jewish refugees and, 46, 50–52, 58; national-origins quotas by, 47, 57; nativist movements and, 57–59; smuggling in, 56, 63n39, 64n41; as source of Black migration, 282n4; upholds its own policy, 55; US entry through, 22, 45–46, 55–56; US-imposed legislation in, 22, 48–49, 55, 56, 59; "wet foot, dry foot" policy, 60–61, 64n54; whiteness and, 48–49; WWII and, 57–59

Cuban Adjustment Act (1966), 18n24, 60

Cuban Revolution (1959), 9, 49

Curran, Joseph, 111

Davis, J. J., 53

debarment, 28. *See also* deportation and repatriation

Debus, Kurt Heinrich, 144, 146, 154–155

decolonization, 4, 8, 70, 88–89, 276. *See also* colonialism

Delany, J. F., 109

de la Torriente, Cosme, 47

democracy, promotion of in Asia, 162, 163, 167, 171, 173, 174, 238. *See also* communism, fear of

Democratic Party: civil rights and, 202; divide over immigration reform, 203; Japanese American public relations and, 170; Johnson election and, 204–205; Kennedy election and, 201; support

by foreign-stock voters, 201, 203, 204; Truman's veto on McCarran-Walter Act and, 195

denazification, 149–151, 154

deportation and repatriation, 28; of agricultural workers, 123, 136; from Cuba, 57; demographics, 63n26; of H-2 workers, 136–137; of insubordinate seamen, 108, 116, 117–118; of Mexican immigrants, 6, 17n13, 255; Operation Wetback, 136, 167, 256, 258; racial exclusion and, 40–41; shipping companies held liable for, 33; of sick immigrants, 37

desertion. *See* British wartime shipping; Chinese sailors, desertion of British ships by

deserving, ideology of, 191, 233, 234, 237

detention conditions, 114–115

DeWind, Josh, 136

El Diario, 219, 221

Dimock, Marshall, 118

diplomacy, Japanese agricultural worker program and, 161–162, 173–175, 178

discrimination. *See* racial exclusion through national-origins quotas; racial stereotypes

discrimination types, 96–97

displaced person quotas, 67–68. *See also* refugee policy

Displaced Persons Act (1948), 9, 18n23, 145, 148, 156, 210n5; amendments to (1950), 68; Celler on, 75; discrimination against Jewish migrants and, 67–68; national-origins quotas and, 8, 68, 192, 193. *See also* refugee policy

Diversity Program, 96

domesticity, Japanese war bride as symbol of, 238, 240, 241–242

Dominican Republic, 12, 46, 47, 64n47, 89

drug addiction, 255

Du Bois, W. E. B., 87

Dulles, John Foster, 89

Dumbarton Oaks meetings, 89

Durand, Jorge, 94

Eastern European immigrants, 6, 50–51, 57, 84; Cuba and, 50, 59; enter US through neighboring countries, 22, 37, 45, 55, 59; number of, 4, 92, 193, *199*; opposition to, *199*. *See also* Jewish refugees

296 · Index

Eastern hemispheric caps, 5–6, 10, 94–95. *See also* hemispheric caps

East Harlem Tenants Council, 223

Eastland, James, 201–202

education: activism in higher education, 226–227; Japanese agricultural worker program as, 162–163, 173–174, 175; Puerto Rican youth and, 214, 220–223. *See also* students

Einstein, Albert, 7, 103

Eisenhower, Dwight D., 72

Eisenhower administration, 68

Ellis Island, 5, 28, 32, 36

El Salvador, 12, 41

Emergency Quota Act (1921), 5, 38, 50, 52, 63n25, 84, 85

emotional lives of Mexican immigrants, 189–190, 255–270; Bracero Program and, 256–258; *Cartas a Eufemia (Letters to Eufemia)* (1952) and, 258–263; films and songs of love offer solace, 258, 269–270; men listen to songs of love, 263–267; women listen to songs of love, 267–269

employment. *See* agricultural workers; temporary workers

employment assistance for Chinese insubordinate sailors, 112–113

Empress of Scotland (British vessel), 107, 112, 118

Ennis, Edward J., 117

equality, societal push toward, 191–194

Ervin, Sam, 206

Escapee Program, 72

ethnic-based exclusion, 28

Eto, Tameji, 163–164, 166

eugenics, 5, 85, 191, 216, 244

Europe, 4, 6; decrease in immigration from, post WWII, 11; Displaced Persons acts favor, 8; medical inspections favor white European immigrants, 30–32; national-origins quotas and, 11. *See also specific countries*

European Command, 154

European immigrants: to Cuba, 49; Emergency Quota Act and, 5, 38, 50, 52, 63n25, 84, 85; favoring of Northern Europeans, 8, 145, 193, 206; national-origins quotas and, 5–6, 47, 193; politically undesirable, 52. *See also* Eastern European immigrants

Executive Order 8802 (1941), 132

Executive Order 9604 (1945), 147

extraterritorial migration control. *See* remote control system

Fairchild, Amy, 27, 28

family reunification, 2; Asian migration and, 95; as central principle of immigration policy, 231–232, 246–247; Chinese immigrants and, 233–234, 236, 249n16; Hart-Celler Act and, 83, 92; Jewish refugees and, 7; Johnson-Reed Act and, 6; as loophole to national-origins quotas, 9, 11, 54, 94; prioritization of, 9; public opinion on, 210; refugee policy and, 66, 68; war brides and, 189, 233–237. *See also* long-distance romantic relationships

Far East Refugee Program (FERP), 72, 73. *See also* communism

farm work. *See* agricultural workers; Bracero Program; temporary workers

Federal Bureau of Investigation (FBI), 150, 152

Feighan, Michael, 11

Feldman, Myer "Mike," 203

Fernandez, Vicente, 263–264

Fiancées and Fiancés Act (1946), 8

Field Information Agency, Technical (FIAT), 149

Filipino immigrants, 8, 233, 249n19; citizenship status of, 6, 36, 187; demographics in US, 12; war brides, 234

films and songs of love, 189, 256; "Aca Entre Nos" ("Between Us"), 263–264, 266–267; "Carta A Eufemia" (Letter to Eufemia), 259, 262; *Cartas a Eufemia (Letters to Eufemia)* (1952), 258–263; "Contestación de Eufemia" (Eufemia's Response), 260–261, 262; "Una Aventura" ("An Adventure"), 263, 264, 265; "Ya lo Se" ("I Already Know"), 267, 268, 269

First Inter-American Demographic Congress, 87

Florida Rural Legal Aid, 137

Fong Wing Kee, 112

foreign policy, 3, 13; Chinese immigrants as allies, 7; Cuban nativism and, 57–59; Latin America and, 46, 86–87; as top concern of Americans, 200; US-imposed legislation in Cuba, 48–50. *See also* Chinese exclusion;

Cold War; international relations; national-origins quotas, removal

Foreign Service, 35

France, 40, 146

Fuchs, Lawrence, 278

Gabaccia, Donna, 36, 280

Galamison, Milton, 222

Galarza, Ernesto, 135

Gallup surveys: on concerns of Americans, 200, 202, 212n27; on immigration levels, *205*; on McCarran-Walter Act, *196–197*; on skills-based admissions, *209–210*

gang conflicts, and Puerto Rican youth, 216–217, 218, 219

gatekeeping strategies, 36, 45–47, 51–57, 59, 61n3

geishas, 239

Gentlemen's Agreement (1907–1908), 5

Gerena Valentín, Gilberto, 222

German and Austrian specialists, 105–106, 144–156; Debus and Axter, 144, 146, 154–155; evaluation of, 150–152; exploitation of, 146–148; number of, 148, 153; on path to citizenship, 148–154; viewed as apolitical, 149–150; visas for, 152–153; von Braun, 1, 2, 8, 153

Germany, 1; denazification process in, 150–151; Jews emigrating from (to Cuba), 58; national-origins quotas and, 6; opposition to immigration from, *198–199*; Visa Waiver Program and, 40

Ghanaian immigrants, 274–275

Glazer, Nathan, 227

Golden Venture (ship), 45, 61

Goldwater, Barry, 204

Gonzalez, Henry, 200

Good Neighbor policy, 86

Great Depression, 4

Greek immigrants, 195, *199*

Green, John C., 147

green cards (permanent residency cards), 12, 156

Griswold, Elizabeth, 65

Guam, 46, 85

Guantanamo Bay prison camp, 39

Guatemala, 12, 14

guest-worker programs: British West Indies (BWI) guest-worker program, 168, 171, 172–173. *See also* agricultural workers; Japanese agricultural worker program

Gutierrez, David, 135

H-2 visas. *See* visas, H-2

Haggard, Godfrey, 111

Haiti, 46, 47, 64n47

Hall, Prescott, 5

Handlin, Oscar, 227

Harris, Louis, 206–*207*

Harris, William, 86

Hart, Philip, 94, 202. *See also* Hart-Celler Act

Hart-Celler Act (1965), 2–3, 10–11, 15n1, 39, 46, 59–60; Black immigration after, 280–281; "Communist or Communist-dominated lands" category added, 75–76; criteria in, 92; effects of, 95, 96; family reunification and, 136, 232, 247; hemispheric quotas introduced, 27–28; H-2 programs in, 104–105, 123, 136–140; immigrant status differentiated in, 104; impact of, scholarship on, 66, 78n4; intellectuals and, 103; length of, 212n41; preferred status in, 54; provisions, 94, 136, 140; public opinion and, 208–210; refugee policy debates and, 22, 65–66, 75–77, 77n1. *See also* refugee policy

Harvest of Shame (farmworker expose), 135

Hebrew Sheltering and Immigrant Aid Society (HIAS), 69

hemispheric caps, 27–28; Eastern Hemisphere, 5–6, 10, 94–95; Western Hemisphere, 10–11, 12, 94–95, 193, 202

hemispheric caps, exemptions, 47, 84, 91, 94–95, 193, 196, 202; criticism of, 54, 59–60, 85–86; Emergency Quota Act, 52, 85; Latin American migrants and, 6, 12, 60, 85–87, 215

hemispheric gatekeeping, 36, 45–47, 52–57. *See also* immigration law enforcement

Henderson, Wallace, 170

highly-skilled labor. *See* labor, highly skilled

Hispanic Association Pro-Higher Education (HAPHE), 220

Hispanic Young Adult Association (HYAA), 220

historically Black colleges and universities (HBCUs), 274

Ho, Jimmie, 113

298 · *Index*

Ho C. Lui, 113

Honduras, 41

Hong Kong: AFSC and, 71–72, 74; ARCI and, 72–73, 76; Chinese refugees in, 70, 80n29; US consuls in, 28, 29, 34. *See also* China

Hoover, Herbert, 86

Hoover, J. Edgar, 152

Ho Ping, 112–113

Hostos Community College, 226

hotel industry, 138, 139. *See also* temporary workers

House Select Committee on Postwar Immigration, 192

Huerta, Dolores, 200

Hughes, Charles, 55

humanitarianism, 77; in conflict with indigenous repression, 66–67; Hart-Celler Act and, 92; US projects image of, 65–67, 70, 71–76

human rights movement, 4, 89

Hungarian immigrants, 195

Hungarian Revolution, 9

Husband, W. W., 36, 54

immigrant groups, racialization of, 156

immigrant rights groups, 200–201

immigrants, political engagement of, 188, 191, 203

immigrants, undocumented, 2, 189–190; Bracero Program and, 257–258; deportation of, 136, 258; emotional lives of, 256, 257–258, 262–265, 263, 264; employer accountability, 138; Hart-Celler Act and, 12; IRCA and, 140; US entry through neighboring countries, 27

immigration, illegal, 156; Bracero Program and, 135; deportation and, 10, 167; detention of, during WWII, 38–39; Hart-Celler Act and, 11, 12; Jewish immigrants, 64n49; national-origins quotas and, 12; racism toward, 167; US entry through neighboring countries, 22, 37, 45, 46, 50, 51, 55–56, 59; waitlist for legal entry, 40. *See also* smuggling

Immigration Act (1882), 32

Immigration Act (1891), 32

Immigration Act (1903), 30

Immigration Act (1907), 5, 32, 97n14

Immigration Act (1917), 5, 116, 117, 232

Immigration Act (1924). *See* Johnson-Reed Act

Immigration and Nationality Act (1952). *See* McCarran-Walter Act

Immigration and Nationality Act (1965). *See* Hart-Celler Act

Immigration and Naturalization Service (INS), 108, 109; admissibility of scientists with Nazi affiliation and, 144, 154; Alien Seamen Program and, 117–118; Japanese agricultural labor and, 167, 168, 172; raids to detain Chinese seamen, 118–119; remote control system in 1930s, 6–7

Immigration Bureau, 5, 29, 35, 104, 109. *See also* Immigration and Naturalization Service (INS)

immigration history: comparative approach to, 278–279; periodization of, 2–3, 21; resources for understanding Black immigrant history, 278–280

immigration law, enforcement challenges in, 7, 9, 50; entry through neighboring countries, 27, 37, 45, 55–56, 59; temporary workers remain permanently, 12, 106, 139

immigration law enforcement, 4–5; Alien Seaman Program and, 108, 115, 117–118; Border Patrol, 6, 17n11, 258; Chinese exclusion and, 5, 26, 29–32, 34–37, 48–49; contemporary discrimination in, 40–41; in Cuba, 57–59; fines and repercussions for smuggling aliens, 32; hemispheric gatekeeping, 36, 45–47, 52–57; Immigration Bureau and, 5; inspections at Ellis Island, 5, 28, 32, 36; by private transit companies, 27, 29, 35, 38; in sending and transit countries, 13, 21–22, 26–27, 36–37, 60–61; state *vs.* private, 26, 27; at US consuls, 29; of US policy by Latin America and Cuba, 46, 48, 61n3. *See also* immigrants, undocumented; immigration, illegal; remote control systems

immigration levels, public opinion on, *196–199, 204, 205*

immigration periodization scholarship, 2, 21

immigration quotas, 5–7; Emergency Quota Act, 5, 38, 50, 52, 63n25, 84, 85; for highly skilled labor, 145, 156. *See also* hemispheric caps; Johnson-Reed Act (1924); racial exclusion through national-origins quotas immigration reform, 191–210; Asian exclusion and, 233–234; changes in the early 1960s, 199–201; Goldwater campaign and, 204–205; under Johnson administration, 205–208, 209–210; under Kennedy administration, 201–202; linked to civil rights, 205–206; movement for, 200–201; national-origins quotas and, 192–193; passage of McCarran-Walter Act, 193–194; political engagement of immigrants and, 188; presidential election of 1960 and, 201–203; veto of McCarran-Walter Act, 194–196

Immigration Reform and Control Act (IRCA, 1986), 104, 124, 138

immigration restrictions. *See* Chinese exclusion; immigration law enforcement; racial exclusion through national-origins quotas; remote control systems; temporary workers

indentured labor, 48, 116–117, 136

India, 8, 9, 88, 118

Indian immigrants, 8, 12, 233, 249n19

indigenous peoples, 66–67

Infante, Pedro, 262

inspections: at Ellis Island, 5, 28, 32, 36. *See also* medical inspections; remote control systems; US consuls

intellectuals, recruitment of, 66, 71, 72–73, 76, 81nn42, 51; H-1 visas and, 130. *See also* labor, highly skilled

intelligence studies, 215–216

Inter-American Conference on Problems of War and Peace, 89

International Convention on the Elimination of All Forms of Racial Discrimination (ICERD), 93

International Refugee Organization, 68

international relations, 3, 13; Cuba, US-imposed legislation in, 22, 48–49, 55, 56, 59; Japan-US relations, 105, 162–163, 172, 174, 238; Latin American response to national-origins quotas, 47; US influence and cooperation, 36; US neighbor country relations, 85–86. *See also* immigration reform

interracial couples: as embodiment of US-Japan relations, 239, 243–244; normalization of, 238; numbers of, 251n35;

reactions to, 189; studies of, 240; war bride laws and, 234, 236, 237

IRCA (Immigration Reform and Control Act), 104, 124, 138

Ishiguro, Tadaatsu, 162–163, 171

isolationism, 13

Issei (Japanese immigrants), 169. *See also* Japanese Americans

Italian Americans, 216–217, 221

Italian immigrants, 195, 216

Italy, 30, 198–*199*

Jackson, Ashley, 129

Jamaica, 202, 277, 280

Jamaican workers, 125, *126–127*, 136, 137; race and, 128, 141nn12, 13

Japan: Alien Seamen Program and, 117; brides' schools in, 241–242; colonial expansionism of, 161–162, 162–163; education-abroad program from, 162–163; national quota for, 162, 237; occupation of, 234; opposition to immigration from, 198–*199*; relations with US, 105, 162–163, 172, 174, 238; US agricultural labor program and, 166–168, 171, 174

Japanese agricultural worker program, 105, 123, 161–180; AICF and, 162–165; bracero vs BWI model for, 168, 171, 172–173; Cold War diplomacy and, 161–162, 172, 173–175; end of, 179; government departments and, 170–173; immigration as "refugees" and, 164–165; Japanese Americans' relations with Japanese agricultural workers and, 175–179; Mike Masaoka and, 165–170

Japanese American Citizens League (JACL), 91; end of Japanese agricultural worker program and, 179; image of Japanese Americans and, 178; Masaoka's leadership in, 165, 166, 169–170; Mikami as leader in, 164; war bride laws and, 233, 235, 236

Japanese Americans: assimilation of, 162, 165–166, 177, 178, 179–180; internment of, 243, 245, 253n69; Issei influence over Nisei farmers, 169; relations with Japanese agricultural workers, 105, 175–179. *See also* Nisei (second-generation Japanese-Americans); war brides

300 · Index

Japanese exclusion, 5, 84, 85, 92, 162, 172, 237. *See also* Asian exclusion; Chinese exclusion; racial exclusion through national-origins quotas

Javits, Jacob, 206

Jewish immigrants, 7, 62n12; opposition to, *199*; WWII and, 58–59, 64nn46, 47, 49

Jewish refugees, 7; AJC and, 66, 67, 80n26; Cuba and, 46, 50–52, 58; Refugee Relief Act and, 68–69

Jewish Relief Committee (Cuba), 58

Jim Crow law, 128, 132

Johnson, Lyndon Baines, 11, 66, 94; election of, 204–205; immigration reform and, 10, 203, 205–206; as Kennedy running mate, 201

Johnson-Reed Act (1924), 2, 5, 21, 35, 47, 60; birthplace differentiated from residence in, 51; Caribbean, diplomacy and policy effects in, 52–57; European immigrant preference in, 84; Japanese immigration and, 162; pressure to Americanize and, 187; Puerto Rican immigration and, 188; remote control solidified through, 38; restrictions on Asian immigration in, 85, 231, 233–234. *See also* immigration quotas; national-origins quotas

Joint Intelligence Objectives Agency (JIOA), 149, 151, 152

Joppke, Christian, 95

Judd, Walter, 73

juvenile delinquency, 216–217, 218, 219

Katzenbach, Nicholas, 93

Kawasaki, Frank Tsunekusu, 164, 165

Kellogg, Frank, 86

Kennedy, Edward, 11

Kennedy, John F., 10, 74, 94, 135, 201, 203

Kerry v. Din (2015), 40

King, Martin Luther, Jr., 200

Knight, Goodwin, 170

Koda, Keisaburo, 163–164, 166

Kong Bo, 112

Koo, Wellington, 89

Korean immigrants, 12; brain drain effect and, 9; military brides, 234, 236, 244; opposition to, *199*

Korean War, 9, 91, 165, 236

labor, 3; indentured, 48, 116–117; nativist legislation in Cuba, 57

labor, highly skilled, 13–14; brain drain effect, 9; Hart-Celler Act and, 92; H-1B visas and, 138–139; Johnson-Reed Act and, 6; occupational needs *vs.* first-come, first-served, 54; prioritization of, 9; recruitment of intellectuals, 66, 71, 72–73, 76, 81nn42, 51. *See also* German and Austrian specialists; skills-based admissions

labor, unskilled, 1–2, 13–14, 15n1, 93, 103. *See also* agricultural workers; Bracero Program; temporary workers; visas, H-2

labor agitation: Bracero Program and, 135–136; for improved conditions on British ships, 108, 109–111, 114, 115, 118, 119; Jamaican agricultural workers and, 125, 128; UFW, 135–136; US Sugar protests, 128; by West Indian agricultural workers, 136

labor demand, 7, 13–14; medical inspection standards and, 35; restrictions lifted because of, 97n14; for shipping needs during WWII, 107–108; smuggling and, 53; for sugar industry, 48, 49. *See also* agricultural workers; Bracero Program; temporary workers

labor migration, 123, 130. *See also* Bracero Program; intellectuals, recruitment of

labor organizing, 92–93, 111, 192, 200

labor relief programs, *126–127*

labor shortages, 132, 142n23

La Follette Seamen's Act (1915), 117

La Guardia, Fiorello, 33, 108, 116

Lansing, Robert, 25, 35

Lasby, Clarence, 153

Latin America: arrests of aliens in, during WWII, 38–39; Dumbarton Oaks meetings, exclusion from, 89; hemispheric caps exemptions and, 6, 12, 60, 85–87, 215; race-based exclusion laws changed in, 23, 60, 84, 87; US-imposed legislation in, 46, 61n3; visa waitlists in, 40

Latin American immigrants: demographics in US, 12; in NYC communities, 215; opposition to, *199*. *See also* Mexican immigrants

Latino/Chicano rights movement, 200

Laughlin, Harry H., 5, 85

Law for Liberation from National Socialism and Militarism (1946, Germany), 150
Lee Choy, 113
Lee Joe, 113
legal status of immigrants. *See* immigrants, undocumented; immigration, illegal
Liebowitz, Samuel, 219
Life magazine, 1, 240–241
"likely to become a public charge" clause (LPC), 4, 17n11, 29, 36
Lindsay, John, 76, 93
Lin Young Tsai, 110
Liskofksy, Sidney, 69, 80n26
literacy tests, 5, 58, 97n14
long-distance romantic relationships: *Cartas a Eufemia* and, 258–263; emotional pain and, 258; ending of due to separation, 263–266. *See also* family reunification
Louisiana Purchase (1803), 46
Lutheran World Federation, 72

Machado, Gerardo, 55, 56, 57
Macías, Lorenzo, 1–2
Madame Butterfly stories: original story, 238–239; postwar versions, 242–243
Magnuson Act (1943), 7, 70, 88, 233, 234, 249n16
Mailer, Norman, 225
Malone, Nolan J., 94
Maloney, Deidre, 28
marriage. *See* war brides
Martí, José, 56
Martin, Philip, 135
Masaoka, Joe Grant, 170
Masaoka, Mike, 165–170, 176, 179, 235
Massey, Douglas S., 94
Mayor's Committee on Puerto Rican Affairs (MCPRA), 220
McCarran, Patrick, 91, 193
McCarran-Walter Act (1952), 1, 8–9; Asian exclusion and, 189, 237; Cold War foreign policy and, 60; effects of, 18n20; family unification and, 189, 232; German specialists and, 144, 145, 155, 156; H-2 visas and, 129–130, 136; Japanese agricultural workers and, 168; Japanese immigration and, 162, 189, 237; national-origins quotas and, 162, 193–194, 237; parole authority granted in, 9, 18n24; provisions,

136; public opinion on, *196–197*; racial exclusion and, 4, 7–9, 91, 93, 193–194, 232, 237; Refugee Relief Act and, 69; Truman vetoes, 194–196
McGranery, James, 194
McKeown, Adam, 26, 27
McLeod, Evan Ward, 124
Meany, George, 92–93
media attention: on Japanese American farmers, 178; on Japanese war brides, 238, 239–241; on juvenile delinquency, 218–219; on mixed-race children, 244–245; on smuggling, 45. *See also* public opinion; racial stereotypes
medical inspections, 26, 27, 30–38; from Canada, 37; data interpretation of, 37–38; racism and, 30–32; rates of rejection from, 37–38, 43n46; by shipping companies, 32–35; standardization of, 32
MEND (Massive Economic Neighborhood Development), 223
Menocal, F. E., 49
Mexican American Political Association, 200
Mexican immigrants: demographics in US, 12; deportation and repatriation of, 6, 17n13, 41; Hart-Celler Act and, 28; migrant labor, 1–2; national-origins quota and, 17n11; Operation Wetback and, 10, 136; opposition to, *199*; visa designations, 138–139; visa waitlists for, 40. *See also* Bracero Program
Mexican immigrants, emotional lives of, 189–190, 255–270; Bracero Program and, 256–258; *Cartas a Eufemia* and, 258–263; films and songs of love offering solace and expressions of concerns, 258, 269–270; men listen to songs of love, 263–267; women listen to songs of love, 267–269
Mexico, 4, 89; as alternate entry route, 45–46; Chinese exclusion and, 36–37, 61n3; US intervention in, 46
Michener, James, 1, 240, 251n43
Middle Eastern immigrants, 11, 19n28, 84
migrant labor. *See* agricultural workers; Bracero Program; visas, H-1; visas, H-2
Migration Division, 218, 222
Mikami, Henry Seiichi, 164, 169–170, 176
military, US: Air Force, 153; Army, 128, 153; Navy, 151, 153. *See also* Project Paperclip
military brides. *See* war brides

302 · Index

military interventions, 36, 48, 86
Miller, William, 204
Minami, Yaemon, 163–164
Ministry of Labor (Canada), 137
Ministry of War Transportation (Canada), 108, 110
miscegenation laws, 189, 234, 237, 244, 245, 249n38. *See also* interracial couples
Mitchell, James P., 170, 172
mixed-race children, 9, 189, 244–246
Monroe Doctrine (1823), 46
Montserrat, Joseph, 218, 219
Moy, Ernest, 72–73
Moynihan, Daniel Patrick, 227
Murphy, Ruth Z., 200
Murrow, Edward R., 135
Muslim-majority countries immigration ban, 41
Myrdal, Gunnar, 87

NASA (National Aeronautics and Space Administration), 1, 144, 155
Nasu, Shiroshi, 162–164, 165, 168, 169, 171
National Association of Puerto Rican Civil Rights (NAPRCR), 222
National Council of Jewish Women, 69
National Council on Naturalization and Citizenship, 199–200, 211n19
Nationality Act (1790), 4
National Lutheran Council, 66, 75
National Maritime Union, 111
National Opinion Research Center (NORC), 210n5; surveys on immigration levels, *197–199*
national-origins quotas. *See* immigration quotas; racial exclusion through national-origins quotas
national-origins quotas, exemptions, 9–10; adoption, 9; entry through other countries, 22, 50, 54, 55–56; family reunification, 9, 11, 54, 94; parole authority, 9, 18n24, 74, 77. *See also* hemispheric caps, exemptions; immigration quotas; refugee policy
national-origins quotas, removal, 66, 84–86, 231; bill introduced, 202; civil rights movement and, 83, 84, 92; global race-based restriction removal and, 60, 83–85, 87, 90–91, 92–93; hemispheric caps system replaces, 10–11, 12, 27–28, 94–95;

justification, 203; labor movement and, 92–93; reintroduced in 1976, 28; skills-based quotas replace, 145, 146, 156; visa quotas replace, 39–40, 44n62, 136. *See also* refugee policy
national security and defense, 150
naturalization: Chinese exclusion and, 88; data on, 203; racial exclusion, 70; rates of, 188, 191. *See also* McCarran-Walter Act
Naturalization Act (1790), 70
Nazi Party, 1, 58, 144, 148–150, 151, 154
New York City Chamber of Commerce, 215
New York Times, 51–52, 53, 57, 60, 154, 216, 222, 225
New York Times Magazine, 65
New Zealand, 90
Ngai, Mae, 3, 15n1, 156
Nicaragua, 46
Nigerian immigrants, 274–275
Nisei (second-generation Japanese-Americans), 105; ethnic/class politics of, 161; influence of Japanese immigrants over, 169; Japanese war brides and, 236, 243, 244; Mike Masaoka and, 165–166, 169; relations with Japanese agricultural workers, 175–179
Nkrumah, Kwame, 275
nongovernmental organizations (NGOs), 66, 67, 75, 77n1

Obama, Barack, 61, 65
Office of Military Government, United States (OMGUS) in Germany, 150–151
Okihiro, Gary, 190
"Operation Wetback" (1954), 10, 136, 167, 256, 258
La Opinion, 255
oral histories: Black immigrant experience and, 279, 283n10; of Mexican immigrant men, 263–264, 265–266; of Mexican women in long-distance relationships with immigrant men, 261–262, 267–269; Mexican workers' emotional lives and, 189–190, 256
organized labor, Japanese guest-worker program and, 167, 168, 169, 170, 172
Orientalism, 238, 239–240
Oyagi, Go, 165, 167
Oyen, Meredith, 111

Page Act (1875), 29, 70
Panama, 46, 89
Pantoja, Antonia, 220
parole authority, 9, 18n24, 74, 77. *See also* refugees
Passport Control Act (1918), 35
passports, 26, 34, 41n3, 109
peonage, 124–125
People's Republic of China. *See* China
Peru, 48
Pfeiffer, Sachiko, 1, 2, 241, 242, 246
the Philippines: annexation of, 36, 46; Asiatic barred zone and, 5; Chinese labor and, 35; national-origins quotas and, 8, 36, 85, 88; Tydings-McDuffie Act and, 6, 36, 85. *See also* Filipino immigrants
Platt Amendment (1901), 48, 49
police, 218, 225
Polish immigrants, 195
ports of entry/exit, 26, 28, 30, 32
Powderly, Terence, 25
Presbyterian groups, 67
Presidential Committee on Civil Rights (1947), 90
presidential election of 1960, 201–203
prison, insubordinate seamen in, 114–115, 116
Project Overcast. *See* Project Paperclip
Project Paperclip, 105–106, 144–156; Debus and Axter brought to US by, 144, 154–155; denying other countries access to specialists, 146–148; path to citizenship and, 148–154; setting precedent for labor preferences in immigration policy, 145, 155–156; as war reparations, 146
prostitution, 29, 239, 240
Public Law 78, 130, 166, 176. *See also* Bracero Program
public opinion: on American problems, 200; on immigration levels, *196–199*, 204, *205*; on immigration restrictions, 206–*208*, 209–210
Puerto Rican Association for Community Affairs (PRACA), 221
Puerto Rican Forum, 221
Puerto Ricans, 7; adaptive strategies of, 188–189; citizenship status of, 187, 213, 214; conflicts with Italian Americans, 216–217, 221; increase in numbers of,

213–214, 217; negative characterizations of, 188, 215–216; number of in NYC, 215; opposition to, *199*; protest their poor treatment, 215
Puerto Rican studies programs, 226–227
Puerto Rican youth, 213–227; criminality accusations, 188, 214, 215–217; intelligence study on, 215–216; leadership/ activism of, 188–189, 213, 214, 220–223, 224–227; scapegoating of, 217–218; shift from "foreign" to "national minority," 224
Puerto Rico: annexation of, 46, 188, 214; separate culture of, 228n1; as source of Black migration, 282n4
"Pursuit of Happiness by a GI and a Japanese" (Michener), 240–241
Pyndarius (British steamship), 113

Quakers, 71. *See also* AFSC (American Friends Service Committee)
Quarantine Law (1893), 30
Quinn, Percy E., 275
quotas. *See* immigration quotas; national-origins quotas

Rabkin, Sol, 69
race: of Asian Americans, 243, 245; Cuba and, 48–49, 55; employers of Japanese agricultural workers and, 105, 168–169; intelligence and, 215–216; Jamaican workers and, 128, 141nn12, 13; mixed-race children, 189, 244–246; national-origins quotas and, 192; racialization of immigrant groups, 156; as top problem for US, 202, 212n27; white settler societies and, 66–67. *See also* African Americans; Asian exclusion; Black immigrants; interracial couples
racial exclusion through national-origins quotas, 2, 4–12, 83–85; Asians tracked by race as opposed to nationality, 8, 51, 251n39; Asia-Pacific Triangle provision, 91, 193, 194, 237; Cold War and, 3, 7–8, 60, 86; colonialism and, 9, 47, 85; by Cuba, 47, 57; deportation and, 40–41; Displaced Persons and, 8, 68, 192, 193; Emergency Quota Act, 5, 38, 50, 52, 63n25, 84, 85; European immigration and, 5–6, 47, 193; *vs.* family unification, 189, 233–237;

304 · *Index*

racial exclusion through national-origins quotas (*cont.*) ideology driving, 191; indigenous displacement and, 66; from Japan, 162; Japanese exclusion, 5, 84, 92, 162, 172, 237; Latin American laws removed, 23, 60, 84, 87; Latin Americans and, 85–87; laws, worldwide, 17n8, 36–37, 83–84, 87; Magnuson Act and, 7, 70, 88, 233, 234, 249n16; McCarran-Walter Act and, 4, 7–9, 91, 93, 193–194, 232, 237; public opinion on, 93, *208*, *209*–210; quotas created, 5–6, 27, 28, 84; restrictionists, 7–8, 10; Truman opposes, 8, 18n19, 91, 194–196; Tydings-McDuffie Act exemptions, 6, 36, 85. *See also* Asian exclusion; Chinese exclusion; Hart-Celler Act (1965); hemispheric caps; immigration law enforcement; Johnson-Reed Act (1924); national-origins quotas, exemptions; national-origins quotas, removal; refugee policy; remote control systems

racial integration: Japanese war brides and, 243–244; Puerto Rican youth and, 217, 222–223; as top problem facing US, 202, 212n27

racial stereotypes: about Mexican vs Japanese workers, 163, 167, 176–177; of Japanese women, 189, 238, 239–240; of Puerto Ricans, 188–189, 214, 219

racism: Bracero Program and, 132, 133; British treatment toward Chinese sailors, 104, 114–119; Chinese Exclusion Act and, 48–50; denial of, 242–243; Japanese war brides and, 241, 244; Masaoka's anti-racist efforts, 165–166, 169; medical inspections and, 30–32; national-origins quotas and, 87; Puerto Ricans and, 214, 215–218

Reed, David, 85–86

Refugee Act (1980), 11, 19n29, 77

refugee policy, 65–77; AFSC, 66, 71–72, 74; AJC, 66, 67–68, 69, 75, 79n16, 80m26; ARCI, 66, 71, 72–73, 76, 81nn42, 51; Chinese refugees and, 69–74; Cold War politics shape, 68–70, 73, 75, 76, 77n1, 78n4; communism, defection from, 9, 11, 18n18, 69–70, 72–73, 75, 78n4; Displaced Persons Act, 67–68, 75, 79n16; Hart-Celler Act and, 11, 19n28, 65–66, 75–77, 77n1, 94;

Hong Kong and, 70–74, 76, 80n29; Jewish refugees and, 7, 67, 68, 69–70, 76, 80n26; race-based discrimination and, 66–67, 68, 70, 73, 74, 75, 78n4; Refugee Act, 11, 19n29; Refugee Relief Act and, 8, 68–69, 70–71, 75–76; resettlement assistance, 71, 73, 76, 79n16, 81n42, 82n59; US's humanitarian image and, 22, 65–67, 70, 71–76

Refugee Relief Act (1953), 8, 68–69, 70–71, 75–76, 162, 164, 165

refugees: Japanese agricultural workers as, 164–165; in Kennedy administration bills, 202; national-origins quotas and, 192, 193; population numbers, 80n29; Somalian, 280; Syrian, 65; UN definition of, 11, 19n29. *See also* Chinese refugees; Jewish refugees

Reimers, David, 95, 282n1

relationships, long-distance: *Cartas a Eufemia* and, 258–263; emotional pain and, 258; ending of due to separation, 263–266. *See also* family reunification

religious organizations and agencies: AFSC, 66, 71–72, 74; humanitarian efforts for refugees by, 67, 75; lobby for immigration law reform, 75; political handling of support from, 80n26

remote control systems, 6–7, 21, 25–41; bureaucracy of, 29, 32; definition, 26; Johnson-Reed Act and, 38; medical inspections, 26, 27, 30–38; private companies' reliance, 25–26, 27, 32; racism and, 30–32; state *vs.* private, 26, 27; strengthening of, 39, 54; US immigration officers posted internationally for preclearance, 39; US influence and international cooperation and, 25–26; during WWI, 35–39. *See also* immigration law enforcement; national-origins quotas

Republican Party: civil rights and, 203; divide over immigration reform, 203–204; Japanese American public relations and, 170; Johnson election and, 204–205; Truman's veto of McCarran-Walter Act and, 195

resettlement assistance: AFSC and, 71; ARCI and, 73, 81n42; Displaced Persons Act emphasizes, 79n16; Hart-Celler Act falls short, 66, 76, 82n59; for intellectuals, 73

residency certification, 26, 30, *31*
resident alien status: of German specialists, 145, 153. *See also* visas, H-2
restaurants, Chinese and, 104, 108, 112–113
restrictionists, 7–8, 10, 12, 13, 22, 86. *See also* racial exclusion through national-origins quotas
Rio Tijuana encampment, 255
Rogers Act (1924), 35
Roosevelt, Eleanor, 215
Roosevelt, Franklin Delano, 86, 88, 118, 132
Ross, Edward, 111
routes of entry via neighboring countries, 45–46; Chinese immigrants and, 48
Rowe, Captain (*SS Silver Ash*), 110
Roybal, Edward, 200
Rudolph, Arthur, 153
Rumanian immigrants, 195
Rusk, Dean, 93, 94, 206
Russia. *See* Soviet Union
Rustin, Bayard, 222

Scalia, Antonin, 40
scientists, German and Austrian. *See* German and Austrian specialists; intellectuals, recruitment of
Scott, T. T., 111, 117, 118
seasonal workers. *See* agricultural workers; Bracero Program; temporary workers; visas, H-2A; visas, H-2B
Segarra, Arnold, 224
Seidl, Tom, 136
Senate Immigration Subcommittee, 201
Senate Judiciary Subcommittee on Immigration and Naturalization, 196
Senate Report 1515 (Senate Special Subcommittee to Investigate Immigration and Naturalization, 1950), 193
Senate Resolution 137 (1947), 193
Senate Special Subcommittee to Investigate Immigration and Naturalization, 193
Shankman, Arnold, 278
Shanks, Cheryl, 78n4, 92
Shapiro, Nathan, 110, 114
Shaughnessy, Edward J., 117
Shenk, Janet, 136
Sheppard, Oliver H., 124
shipping companies: agriculture workers' transport, 125, 128; liability of, 32; medical

inspections by, 32–35; national-origins quotas and, 38; smuggling on, 22, 53–54. *See also* British wartime shipping; Chinese sailors, desertion of British ships by
Sinn, Elizabeth, 27, 29
skilled labor. *See* labor, highly skilled
skills-based admissions, 104, 105–106; in Celler bill, 202; in Hart bill, 202; H-1 visas and, 130; McCarran-Walter Act and, 145, 155, 156, 193–194; public opinion on, *208*, *209*–210. *See also* intellectuals, recruitment of; labor, highly skilled
slavery, 47, 124
smuggling: cost of, 53; Cuba and, 50–51, 52–53; *Golden Venture* incident, 45, 61; *New York Times* report, 53, 54; treaties banning, 56, 63n39, 64n41
Solivan, Aníbal, 224–225
Somalian refugees, 280
songs of love. *See* films and songs of love
Sotomayor, Sonia, 226
Southern regions of United States: braceros contracted in, 130–*131*; establishment of national origins quota system and, 191; Truman's veto on McCarran-Walter Act and, 195
Soviet Union, 7–8; defectors from, 72; exploitation of German specialists by, 146; opposition to immigrants from, 207; relations with, 200; UN charter and, 89–90
Spain, 48
Spanish immigrants, 55, *199*
Spanish Welfare League, 216
Spickard, Paul, 278
SS California Standard (British vessel), 114
SS Shanks (vessel transporting temporary workers), 125
SS Silver Ash (British vessel), 110
Steinberg, Stephen, 278, 283n13
Strughold, Hubertus, 153–154
Student Nonviolent Coordinating Committee, 223
students: African, 274–275, 276; Asian, 9, 12; Chinese intellectual refugees, 72–73; exemptions for, 9, 29, 48, 145; Japanese agricultural workers as, 162–163, 173–174, 175. *See also* intellectuals, recruitment of; Puerto Rican youth

306 · *Index*

Students for a Democratic Society, 227
Suez crisis, 9
sugar industry: in Cuba, 48, 49; temporary workers in, 124–129, 133, 136, 137; worker conditions, 124, 137
Supreme Commander for the Allied Powers (SCAP), 234, 236
Supreme Court, US, 40
Swing, Joseph M., 167, 170
Switzerland, 40
Syrian refugees, 65

Tai Pun (Dapeng) Association, 112
Taiwan, 9, 70, 73, 80n29
Technical Industrial Intelligence Committee, 147
Teller, Edward, 7
temporary workers, 15n1, 104–105; citizenship restrictions, 3, 14, 103, 105; deportation of, 123; distinguishing between permanent migrants and, 55, 56; IRCA and, 138; recruitment of, 134, 136, 138, 142n21; remain permanently, 12, 106, 139; restrictions lifted during WWI, 97n14; in sugar industry, 124–129, 133, 136, 137; visa classifications, 123–124, 130, 138–139, 140; West Indians as, 277. *See also* agricultural workers, Japanese; Bracero Program; labor, highly skilled; McCarran-Walter Act (1952); skills-based admissions; visas
Ting, Jan, 95
tobacco industry, 138
trachoma, 37, 43n46
transit countries, 13
travel documentation. *See* passports; visas
treaties, 55, 56, 63n36
Trinidad and Tobago, 202
Truman, Harry, 67, 90, 147, 151, 210n3; Commission on Immigration and Naturalization, 92, 195–196; vetoes McCarran-Walter Act, 8, 18n19, 91, 194–196
Truman Commission (Commission on Immigration and Naturalization), 92, 195–196
"Truman Directive" (1945 executive order), 67
Trump, Donald J., 40, 41, 64n54
Tydings-McDuffie Act (1934), 6, 36, 85

Uchida, Zen'ichiro, 164–165
Ukrainian immigrants, 195, *199*
undocumented immigrants. *See* immigrants, undocumented
unemployment, 57, 130, 200
United Bronx Parents (UBP), 223
United Farm Workers (UFW), 135–136
United Fruit Company (UFC), 125
United Nations, 19n29; charter of, 89–90; Conference on International Organization, 89; refugee definition of, 11, 19n29; Relief and Rehabilitation Administration, 71
United Presbyterians, 66, 75
United Service for New Americans, 69
United States: entry through neighboring countries, 45, 52–53, 59, 61n3; government assists Britain in recovering deserting seamen, 104, 107, 108–109, 116–119; humanitarian image of, 22, 65–67, 69, 70, 71–76; immigrant demographics in, 12, 83; labor relief programs, during WWII, *126–127*; neighbor country relations, 85–86; overseas expansion of, 187; political role after WWII, 13; racist image of, 90–91; relations with Japan, 105, 162–163, 172, 174, 238; smuggling treaties and, 56; UN charter and, 89–90
United States Escapee Program, 72. *See also* refugees
Universal Declaration of Human Rights (1948), 90
University of the Streets, 225
US Air Force, 153
US Army, 128, 153
US Border Patrol, 6, 17n11, 258
US Bureau of the Budget, 194
US-Canada border, 27
US consuls, 28–29; in Cuba, 51, 57, 58; in Hong Kong, 28, 29, 34; in Japan, 236; as labor recruiters, 29; visa denial at, 28, 40; visas for German specialists issued at, 152–153. *See also* remote control systems
US Department of Agriculture, 130
US Department of Commerce, 147–148
US Department of Justice, 124, 148–149, 152
US Department of Labor, 53; Bracero Program and, 134; H-2 program and, 136, 138, 139; Immigration Bureau and,

5, 17n11; Japanese guest-worker program and, 167, 168, 170–171, 172, 174–175, 179

US Department of State: German specialists and, 148–149, 151, 154; Japanese agricultural workers and, 163, 166, 168, 170, 171, 172, 173, 174–175; on McCarran-Walter Act, 194

US Department of Treasury, 5

US Department of War, 146, 147–148, 148–149, 150, 151, 152, 154

US Information Service (USIS), 174

US Marshall plan, 11

US merchant marines, 115

US-Mexico border, 5, 6, 10, 17n11, 27

US Navy, 151, 153

US Public Health Service (PHS), 30

US Sugar Corporation, 124, 128, 137

Vail Corporation, 139

Valenti, Jack, 94

Venezuela, 89

Vietnamese immigrants, 12, 93, 234

visas: discriminatory issuing of, 39–40; eligibility criteria, 3, 32; inspections of, 36; limits on, 10–11, 12, 40, 58–59, 193–194; procedures for obtaining by German specialists, 152–153; standardization of, 26, 35

visas, denial of: McCarran-Walter Act and, 18n20; rejection rates, 39–40, 44nn55, 57; remote control and, 28–29; at US consuls, 28–29, 40; during World War II, 6–7

visas, H-1, 130

visas, H-1B, 104, 124, 138, 156

visas, H-2, 104–105, 123–124, 129–130, 136–140; demographics and statistics of recipients, 138–139; Japanese agricultural labor and, 168, 173; long-term effects of program, 137–139; replaces Bracero Program, 123; sugar industry precedes issuing of, 124–125, 128–129, 133, 136. *See also* agricultural workers; Bracero Program; temporary workers

visas, H-2A, 124, 137, 138

visas, H-2B, 124, 138, 139

visas, H-3, 130

Visa Waiver Program, 40

Viteles, Harry, 51

Viva Kennedy, 200

von Braun, Wernher, 1, 2, 8, 153

Von Mach, M. E., 124

Voting Rights Act (1965), 10, 83, 92

V-2 rockets, 1, 146, 153

wages: for agricultural workers, 137; Bracero Program and, 133, 134; paid by US merchant marines, 115; for sugar workers, 124–125, 137; wage gap for Chinese sailors, 104, 109–110, 111, 114, 117

Wagner-Rogers bill, 7

Waldir, Amos, 34, 37

Wallace, Henry A., 147

Walter, Francis "Tad," 201, 202

war brides, 88, 162, 189, 231–247; brides' schools for, 241–242; as embodiment of US-Japan relations, 239, 243–244; legislation for, 234–237; Madame Butterfly tales and, 238–246; married to black men, 236, 243–244, 251n35; media depictions of, 238, 239–241; mixed-race children of, 189, 244–246; numbers of, 235, 236, 237–238; Pfeiffer, 1, 2, 241, 242, 246; reasons for change in immigration laws, 233; reasons for marriage, 240; as rewards for deserving soldiers, 233, 237; uplifting stories about, 240–241, 242–243

War Brides Act (1945), 8, 189, 234, 235, 248n9

war criminals, 148, 149, 155

War Food Administration, 128

War Labor Board, 128

War Relocation Authority, 165

Warren, Earl, 162

War Shipping Administration (WSA), 108, 109, 117–118

Washington Post, 206, 219

Wasserman, Jack, 117

Watkins, W. F., 112

Western Hemisphere nations: Eastern Hemisphere caps, 5–6, 10, 94–95; hemispheric gatekeeping by US, 36, 45–47, 51–52; immigration caps for, 10–11, 12, 94–95, 193, 202

Western Hemisphere nations, quota exemptions. *See* hemispheric caps, exemptions

West Indian immigrants: community building by, 274, 278, 281; demographics in US, 12; discriminatory treatment

308 · *Index*

of, 194; intra-Caribbean migration of, 47; Jamaican workers, 125, 128, 136, 137, 141nn12, 13; research on, 280; temporary-worker visas and, 277. *See also* Puerto Ricans

West Indies, 6; alternate routes to US through, 45; the Bahamas, 123, 125, 277, 280, 283n10; Dominican Republic, 12, 46, 47, 64n47, 89; guest-worker program, 168, 171, 172–173; Haiti, 46, 47, 64n47; Jamaica, 202, 277, 280; Johnson-Reed Act, effects on diplomacy and policy in, 52–57; national-origins quotas and, 9, 47, 91; Puerto Rico, 46, 188, 214, 228n1, 282n4; racial exclusion and, 91; research deficit on immigration from, 14, 273–274; upholds US immigration policy, 46, 61n3. *See also* Cuba

West Side Story, 213, 219

whiteness: assimilation of Asians and, 246; Cuban immigration and, 48–49; employers of Japanese agricultural workers and, 168–169; McCarran-Walter Act and, 156. *See also* interracial couples

white settler societies, 66–67, 70

Whom We Shall Welcome (Commission on Immigration and Naturalization report), 92

Wildman, Rounsevelle, 29

Williams, Rob, 137

Williamson, Neal, 124

Wilson, Woodrow, 25, 34, 35

Wise, Stephen S., 154

women: Chinese women immigrating as wives of citizens, 233–234, 249n16; Mexican women in long-distance relationships with migrants, 258–263. *See also* war brides

Wong Hand, 30, *31*

Wood, Leonard, 48

World War I, 35–39, 50

World War II, 4; China and, 70; Cuba and, 57–59; detention of illegal aliens in, 38–39; intellectual reparations after, 146; Jewish refugees denied US entry, 6–7; labor relief programs, by US state, *126–127*; national-origins quotas and, 86, 87–88; social change after, 192–194; US political role after, 13. *See also* British wartime shipping; German and Austrian specialists

You Gee, 113

Young Lords Organization, 226

Yugoslavian immigrants, 195

Yu Tsune-chi, 111

Zolberg, Aristide, 6, 26, 27, 77n1

STUDIES OF WORLD MIGRATIONS

The Immigrant Threat: The Integration of Old and New Migrants
   in Western Europe since 1850   *Leo Lucassen*
Citizenship and Those Who Leave: The Politics of Emigration and Expatriation
   Edited by Nancy L. Green and François Weil
Migration, Class, and Transnational Identities: Croatians in Australia and America
   Val Colic-Peisker
The Yankee Yorkshireman: Migration Lived and Imagined   *Mary H. Blewett*
Africans in Europe: The Culture of Exile and Emigration from Equatorial Guinea to Spain
   Michael Ugarte
Hong Kong Movers and Stayers: Narratives of Family Migration
   Janet W. Salaff, Siulun Wong, and Arent Greve
Russia in Motion: Cultures of Human Mobility since 1850
   Edited by John Randolph and Eugene M. Avrutin
A Century of Transnationalism: Immigrants and Their Homeland Connections
   Edited by Nancy L. Green and Roger Waldinger
Syrian and Lebanese Patrícios in São Paulo: From the Levant to Brazil
   Oswaldo Truzzi, translated by Ramon J. Stern
A Nation of Immigrants Reconsidered: US Society in an Age of Restriction, 1924–1965
   Edited by Maddalena Marinari, Madeline Y. Hsu, and María Cristina García

The University of Illinois Press
is a founding member of the
Association of American University Presses.

Composed in 10.25/13 Marat Pro
with Trade Gothic display
by Kirsten Dennison
at the University of Illinois Press
Cover designed by Megan McCausland
Cover illustration: Yee Shee visa application, 1929, Chinese
Exclusion Act case files, RG 85, National Archives-Seattle,
Yee Shee case file, Seattle Box 1155, 11627/3-3.

University of Illinois Press
1325 South Oak Street
Champaign, IL 61820-6903
www.press.uillinois.edu